Critical Management Perspectives on Information Systems

Critical Management Perspectives on Information Systems

Carole Brooke
Lincoln Business School
University of Lincoln, UK.

Routledge
Taylor & Francis Group

LONDON AND NEW YORK

First published by Butterworth-Heinemann

This edition published 2012 by Routledge
2 Park Square, Milton Park, Abingdon, Oxon OX14 4RN
711 Third Avenue, New York, NY 10017, USA

Routledge is an imprint of the Taylor & Francis Group, an Informa business

British Library Cataloguing in Publication Data
A catalogue record for this book is available from the British Library

Library of Congress Cataloging-in-Publication Data
A catalog record for this book is available from the Library of Congress

ISBN–978-0-7506-8197-1

Luminous days –
Do not weep that they are
over but rather smile that they have been.
Confucius

This book is dedicated to

Dr. Heinz Karl Klein

With love and sadness, we say our farewells to Heinz who died in Vienna,
Austria on Wednesday, the 18th of June 2008 at the age of 68 after an active and
fulfilling life. His zest for life and steadfastness of purpose filled all aspects of
his being as seen in his personal life and the success of his career. It is difficult
for us to imagine how we can close the gap which he has left.

Contents

9. Information Systems and Power: A Foucauldian perspective

Part III Review and Critique

10. Enamouring, Provoking and Imagining: Three Lenses of Critical Information Systems Research?

11. Critical Social IS Research Today: A Reflection of Past Accomplishments and Current Challenges

Acknowledgements

In addition to the chapter authors, thanks are due to the many individuals who contributed in different ways to the completion of this project, including:

Simon Parker, my student and editorial assistant. He joined the project in its final stages and has done so much to help it achieve closure.

The authors of the chapters that could not be, in the end, included here; especially to Kala Saravanamuthu for her very interesting work on Ghandi and Vedic philosophy and its contribution to our understanding of IS.

The various publishing house professional staff who saw the value of this project and supported us through the process.

The reviewers, for their time, valuable comments and advice.

David Raines for excellent I.T. and for being so helpful. Yufan, David and Scott for their support early in the project, and Jackie, Lydia, and Pete for being such a great team in the run up to submitting the completed manuscript.

Finally, and most poignantly, appreciation and respect are due to Heinz and Linda Klein. Heinz was a much-loved and well-respected friend and colleague to many in the field of IS research. He died before finishing changes to the final version of the last chapter of this book. It seemed eminently fitting that we dedicate the book to him. We are indebted to Linda for agreeing that the chapter be completed on his behalf and included in this volume.

Foreword

As I write this foreword, the news reaches us of the death of Heinz Klein, a founding father of the critical approach to information systems and contributor to this volume. The number of projects his death leaves us to complete is testimony not only to the generous way he worked with so many colleagues throughout the world, but also to his belief in extending and challenging the critical approach. This book is a further step in the process of extending, challenging and developing the critical approach to information systems. It takes seriously the need to acknowledge the historical roots of the subject in the socio-technical and critical management approaches and the contribution of work on Habermas and Foucault. However, it also takes seriously the call of Heinz Klein to diversify the approach, to bring in new voices and new ideas, and to revisit and extend older ideas.

This book addresses these points in a number of important ways. Stahl's attention to the ethical dimension of critical IS reminds us that ethics is at the heart of Habermas's work, yet it is often overlooked as a subject of enquiry, both in mainstream IS and in critical IS. Semiotics and ethnography are two areas hitherto minimally addressed in critical IS. They receive welcome attention in this book, adding to the push for the exploration of new approaches.

Critical IS research has, at times, been criticised for its lack of engagement with empirical issues. Thus, the chapters by Oliver and Romm on ERP systems and Doolin on healthcare systems are all the more welcome, especially as these are empirical areas subject to much discussion within mainstream IS. Two final chapters provide useful reflection. It is fitting that Heinz's chapter closes the book. However, this does not mean that he has the last word and that his work is over. Rather, it serves as a reminder that his legacy is to leave us with questions to answer and work to do in the critical tradition which he did so much to form and shape.

Professor Alison Adam
Director of the Information Systems,
Organisations and Society Research Centre
University of Salford, U.K.

Carole Brooke is currently Professor of Organisational Analysis in the Lincoln Business School at the University of Lincoln, UK. Her research focuses on social issues of organisation and IS and, most recently, she has begun to explore issues of 'faith' in the workplace. She has made particular contributions to the area of critical research approaches in IS, developing various international research networks. This has led, for example, to the editing of several special issues of premier IS journals, as well as this book. Current teaching interests include critical approaches to sustainable business practice, exploring notions such as social enterprise, fair-trade and co-operatives.

Bernd Carsten Stahl is Reader in Critical Research in Technology at the Centre for Computing and Social Responsibility, De Montfort University, Leicester, UK. His interests encompass philosophical issues arising from the intersections of business, technology, and information. This includes the ethics of computing and critical approaches to information systems. He is the Editor-in-Chief of the International Journal of Technology and Human Interaction. More information can be found under: http://www.cse.dmu.ac.uk/~bstahl/

Andrew Basden is Professor of Human Factors and Philosophy in Information Systems at the University of Salford, U.K. Currently he is exploring the use of critical theory and philosophy, especially that of Dooyeweerd, to provide frameworks for understanding major issues facing information systems today.

Dubravka Cecez-Kecmanovic is Professor and Head of School of Information Systems, Technology and Management at the Australian School of Business, University of New South Wales (UNSW), Sydney, Australia. Her research has spanned a wide domain from technological design and applications of formal logic in information systems (IS), studies of social systems of information, through to ethnographies of electronically-mediated work and communication. More recently she has focused on the sense-making approach to information, knowledge and IS in organizations, and the socio-technical ANT view of IS entanglement in organisational contexts. She has published in IS journals such as the Journal of Information Systems, Information Technology and People, Decision Support Systems, Journal of Information Technology, and the Journal of Knowledge Management Theory and Practice. She has made a particular contribution to the advancement of a critical social theory of IS.

Marius Janson is Professor of Management Information Systems in the College of Business Administration at the University of Missouri-St. Louis, St. Louis, Missouri, USA. His research focuses on social issues concerning the application of information systems in organisations, web-based individual and organizational learning, and electronic commerce. Janson's articles have appeared in Behaviour and Information Technology, Decision Sciences, Information & Management, Information Systems Journal, Journal of Management Information Systems, and Omega. He has held visiting faculty positions at the University of British Columbia, Vancouver, Canada, the University of Gdansk, Sopot, Poland, and Oulu University, Oulu, Finland.

Dave Oliver's most recent academic appointment has been as Senior Lecturer in Computing in the Faculty of Business and Informatics at Central Queensland University, Australia. Dave was awarded his PhD in 2005 for his thesis on how organisations rationalise the introduction of ERP systems. He also has a Masters of Technology degree in Computer Science from Brunel University, UK and an honours degree in Economics from Warwick University, UK. Dave's publications are in the areas of ERP adoption, computer science education, internet-based self-service and virtual teamworking. Dave has also worked as a computer programmer and lectured in the UK.

Celia Romm Livermore is Full Professor at Wayne State University, Detroit, U.S.A. She has written several books, including Electronic Commerce: A Global Perspective (1998) and Virtual Politicking (1999), and has published numerous articles in top academic journals. Before joining Wayne State, she was chair of information technology at Central Queensland University, Australia. She received her PhD in psychology from the University of Toronto, Canada. One of her most innovative teaching developments is an online teaching concept called "The Radical Model" which she used to help reach students at 13 international campuses and in places as remote as Antarctica, submarines and prisons.

Wendy Cukier is the Associate Dean, Ted Rogers School of Management, Ryerson University, Canada's largest undergraduate business school. She is also the Founder of The Diversity Institute which researches barriers to under-represented groups and ways of increasing their participation in the workplace. Her research interests are wide ranging, centering around critical perspectives on technology and public policy. She is also a recipient of the Meritorious Service Cross, one of Canada's highest civilian honours. In 2000, the University of Toronto named her among the "100 alumni who had shaped the century".

Sara Rodrigues is the Research Support Co-ordinator for the Ted Rogers School of Management at Ryerson University in Toronto, Canada. A recent graduate of the Arts & Contemporary Studies programme, Rodrigues established Arteries, the university's first undergraduate research conference at Ryerson, providing students with the opportunity to present their scholarly work to peers and faculty. Rodrigues' research interests are broad, ranging from psychoanalysis to cyborg theory. However, her main area of focus is at the inter-section of critical theory and popular culture where she writes primarily on television. She has presented work at both national and international conferences and intends to pursue graduate studies in critical theory and cultural studies.

Michael Chumer is a Special Lecturer and researcher in IT/IS at the New Jersey Institute of Technology (NJIT), U.S.A. He is researching strategic, tactical, and operational collaborations enabled by Information Systems and Information Technology "mash ups" during all dimensions of emergency and crises management (preparation, prevention, response, recovery). Critical research approaches explored to date include activity theory, action research, articulation and the continuing use of self ethnographies.

Laurie McAulay currently lectures on management and accountancy and is based in the Business School at Loughborough University, UK. Laurie's research interests cover a variety of topics, including: information technology evaluation, outsourcing, computer-mediated communications, financial expertise and agenda setting. Laurie has published many articles, books and chapters, and his research has been funded by the Economic and Social Research Council and the Chartered Institute of Management Accountants. Laurie is a past editor of the journal Management Learning. He is currently pursuing two lines of inquiry: control systems, leadership and short-termism; and discursive foundations for sustainability.

Bill Doolin is Professor of Technology and Organisation at Auckland University of Technology, New Zealand. His research focuses on the implications of information technology in organisations. Past research has included the role of management and information technologies in public sector health reform, and power and resistance in the implementation and use of information systems. His work is widely published in high-ranking journals.

Dr José-Rodrigo Córdoba-Pachón is a lecturer at the Business School of the University of Hull in the United Kingdom. As a native of Colombia, José studied for his first degree in computer science systems engineering and worked for several years as an information technology (IT) project manager. He developed an interest in exploring why information systems get developed and for whom. His Masters and PhD degrees focused on using systems thinking to promote more inclusive IT planning practices. Since 2003 he has been working with ideas of critical theory in information systems evaluation and systems methodology use. He has written articles in information systems and organisational theory journals, and collaborated in several international forums on critical perspectives in these areas. He currently researches on electronic government systems, systems thinking for education and project management.

Heinz K. Klein earned his Dipl.Kfm. (equivalent of MBA) and Ph.D. in the Faculty of Business Administration at the University of Munich, Germany. In 1998, he received an honorary doctorate from the University of Oulu, Finland, and in the following year his MISQ publication resulted in a Best Paper Award. From 2001 to 2004 he was doctoral program director at Temple University in Philadelphia. Most recently he was Invited Chair at Salford University in Greater Manchester, United Kingdom, and Adjunct Professor at the School of Management of the State University of New York at Binghamton, U.S.A. During his career he held a variety of research and teaching appointments at major research Universities in Germany, Canada, Finland, Denmark, New Zealand, and South Africa. Well known for his contributions to the philosophy of IS Research, foundations of IS theory and methodologies of information systems development, he wrote journal articles on rationality and the emancipatory ideal in information systems development, epistemological principles of interpretive field research, critical realism and the intellectual foundations of alternative approaches to information systems development. His work has been published in the best journals of the field. He authored and co-authored a wide variety of publications and held key positions on editorial boards. His mentoring of doctoral students and junior faculty has produced several nationally and internationally-renowned university professors.

In Search of Critical IS Research

In Search of Critical IS
Research

Chapter 1

The Punch and Judy of Critical IS Research

Carole Brooke

1.1 THAT IS THE WAY TO DO IT! OR IS IT?

Can we judge a book by its cover? Were you attracted by the cover? Intrigued? Shocked? Perhaps one of your first thoughts when you looked at this book was 'what is the relevance of Punch and Judy to research in IS?!' Perhaps you just saw a familiar form of entertainment with old-fashioned or historical roots.

Here we have an excellent example for critical analysis.

As you know, the Punch and Judy show is a harmless form of children's entertainment from a long and well-established tradition – a set of familiar characters and some repetitive routines that demonstrate appropriate morality and social behaviour. The 'moral of the story' is that 'good' wins over 'bad', the weak are protected and justice is delivered by those in authority over us. Or is it? What if I suggest that the imagery is disturbing, with a thinly-veiled theme of aggression and domestic violence? The Punch and Judy show is a story of gendered social roles, of sexual stereotypes and dysfunctional families? Or is it? The moral of the story is that equality does not exist, unequal power relations are a feature of daily life, and without intervention, less powerful 'voices' will tend to be marginalized, even silenced. Or is it? How about this reading: the Punch and Judy show is a fiction, a web of deception, a subliminal instrument of normativity, patriarchy, a form of social regulation, a grotesque depiction of human nature. Or is it?

The Punch and Judy show may not be what it seems. Somewhere, underneath it all, there are values and assumptions at work: 'theirs' and ours. Now, take a look at the back cover. Who is in control: Punch, Judy or the puppet master? Does this alter the way you view and interpret what is going on? These kinds of issues are at the heart of critical research or 'critical inquiry' within IS.

In 2003 I was invited to give a keynote address at a research methods conference.[1] I chose to talk about what I then saw as the newly-burgeoning field of 'critical research' approaches in IS. During my preparations I was reminded of Punch and Judy. Why? Too often in academic debates different approaches to research are seen as competitors 'slugging it out' until one emerges victorious. Rarely have I seen academic debates where there is a deep appreciation for diversity as opposed to similarity of theoretical analysis and interpretation. This apparent undercurrent of desire for intellectual convergence has been tangible even in contexts where rejection of grand narratives was espoused. Often the search seems to be for 'more' or 'less' suitable modes of IS evaluation with the implication that this will result in improved research findings and recommendations for change and 'improvement'.

Back in 2003, there seemed to be two fairly popular theoretical strands to IS research: work based on ideas developed by Habermas and work based on concepts drawn from Foucault. However, even within this limited frame of reference, it felt as if the two approaches as applied within the IS field were in competition with each other. This is not entirely surprising given that the progenitors (Habermas and Foucault) were themselves engaged in a fascinating discourse during their lifetimes. (Incidentally, I recommend you read a chapter by Conway (1999) that presents this dialogue in a very readable fashion.)

My reading of contemporary IS literature led me to conclude that researchers were applying the ideas of Habermas with much the same attitude. His 'followers' appeared to be privileging their discourse above others. That is, they were presenting their frameworks at one and the same time as 'critical' and yet somehow more productive than alternative approaches without actually investigating their own claims to knowledge. This is not to deny that there is a delicate tension between holding a 'critical' position whilst seeking to produce effective theories and methods of research, and this is a point to which we will return. However, I spotted a substantial influence of Habermas within 'critical' IS research, more or less to the exclusion of other approaches, or so it seemed. At the same time, I found very little in the literature that employed the ideas of Foucault or others from the 'critical' tradition. The one seemed to be growing at the expense of the other. At the risk of employing another metaphor, I have referred to this as a case of Habermasian critique becoming a 'cuckoo in the nest'.[2] Habermasian research was nudging the 'competition' out of the nest. In short, I sensed the danger of IS research lapsing into a form of paradigmatic hegemony. This seemed particularly ironic given that Habermas himself emphasized emancipation from domination.

1. European Conference on Research Methods in Business and Management, Reading University, 20–21st March 2003 (see www.academic-conferences.org).
2. European Conference on Research Methods in Business and Management, Reading University, 20–21st March 2003 (see www.academic-conferences.org).

So, how do we deal with the 'problem' of the Punch-like competitive element (aka the hegemonic relations) of IS research? Before I elaborate on my concerns for the IS discipline which began in 2003, we need to establish a starting point for considering the ideas of Habermas. So, here follows a very brief overview of some key ideas from his seminal works.

Habermas recognized that communications between individuals or groups tended to produce inequality at various levels. The overall context in which communication is played out he referred to as the 'Lifeworld'. He developed a framework that could be operated within the Lifeworld and he called it 'communicative rationality'. The purpose of communicative rationality was to provide a conceptual arena within which Lifeworld communications could take part, without inequality or, at least, where such inequalities were significantly reduced. Underpinning this logic is the assumption that it is possible to facilitate a 'more equal' process of communication. He referred to this condition as 'ideal speech'. The benefits of such an approach are clear to see within the field of IS, especially in systems design and implementation, where the importance of the involvement and engagement in dialogue of a wide variety of stakeholders has been attested (Sauer, 1993).

It seemed to me back then, however, that Habermas was more strident in his views, and less accommodating than Foucault who always tended to see more similarity between their philosophical aspirations than difference. As I read their respective writings and the work of others who applied their ideas, I gained the overall impression that there was an intrinsic contradiction in the claims of Habermas.

Stop! I now experienced a contradiction at two levels. In proposing the notion of 'ideal speech', I felt that Habermas was presenting us with a picture of an external reality, one which left little room for alternative constructions and interpretations to be identified and valued. This felt like a closing down of intellectual inquiry rather than an opening up. Within the context of scientific inquiry, where the overall aim is to produce a reproducible and generalizable set of 'norms' and behaviours, this tendency may be more acceptable, but even within the broad church of 'critical' research (Brooke, 2002a) this felt uncomfortable. In summary, there appeared to be a contradiction and tension between holding a 'critical' position whilst seeking to produce effective theories and methods of research.

For further explication, let us return to Punch and Judy.

The Punch and Judy show is our Lifeworld. Punch represents a devotee of Habermas. He believes that there is an external reality and that his views are more valid. Judy represents the Foucauldian (or any other 'critical' for that matter) researcher. Her power is more subtle. One of her concerns is to protect the baby. The baby is more obviously vulnerable in terms of power relations, although very vocal. I propose that the baby represents diversity of intellectual tradition and interpretation.

Punch is strong and aggressive, Judy is not so. Punch will try to dominate Judy and assert his voice over hers through physical acts. It will require the

Police Officer (communicative rationality) to use his truncheon (ideal speech) to ensure that justice prevails and, especially, that the baby is not harmed.

1.1.1 Or Is It?

Do you see the dilemma I encountered at that time? How can the very thing that purports to ensure the richness and diversity of communication prevails, also claim the status of 'authority'. It does not make sense. Rather than a Punch-and-Judy style confrontation, could we not choose to shift our frame of reference? For instance, we could choose to engage in an on-going dialectical dance. That would seem somehow more fluid and to allow for more mutuality of dialogue.

I must stress here that as researchers we do not need to mirror the same pattern of intellectual 'behaviour' as the thinkers who influence our ideas. I am not rejecting the possible contribution of Habermasian (or any other) theory to a richer understanding of IS. Indeed, I hope that you will find the chapters in this book provide some suitably convincing and diverse examples of the application of his ideas. No, the point I am making here is one of attitude and intention.

I think we had better abandon our Punch and Judy metaphor now because, as Morgan (1993) said, after a while it breaks down, but I hope that I have succeeded in opening up for you some challenging questions with regard to the state of critical research as it is within the field of IS. These questions are what motivated me to produce this edited collection.

Before we move on, though, you might take *another* look at the back cover. The artist (Roy Ealden) intended this to represent the gentleman who is operating the Punch and Judy show. For me, this is nicely emblematic of critical inquiry. A key aim of critical research is to discover/uncover underlying values and beliefs, quite often by exposing hidden or marginalized aspects. Frequently, there is an overall intention (though no guarantee) of some level of emancipation, a deeper understanding of power relations and an attempt at reflexivity. Once we have 'seen' the person behind the show, a whole new set of issues may emerge for us. Who is it? What is their motivation and intent? What drives their actions? And so on. We need to remain alert to these issues in organizational research.

Now that we have introduced the idea that critical inquiry is somehow useful and requires a level of intellectual diversity and an attitude of openness, we will take a closer look at what this might mean within the context of IS research and indicate how the chapters in this book can make a fruitful contribution.

1.2 BEING FRUITFUL: THE NEED FOR CRITICAL INQUIRY IN IS

Taking the somewhat political stance of the puppet master as our starting point, we might reasonably begin by asking who or what is 'behind' the academic development of critical thinking in IS? If we are to understand its recent past, its current state and its future potential for development, we probably need to know something about its historical roots.

How far back to go is a difficult decision to make when considering the genesis of an emerging approach. A relatively early protagonist is a contributor to this book – Heinz Klein. Yet we need to go back further, to the early 1960s at least, and note the essential contributions made by researchers like Joan Woodward, Enid Mumford and others to the field of technology and organizations. Such work, it was noted in 2007 (at an event to commemorate the work of Enid Mumford who had recently died[3]), is still relevant in today's 'post-modern' world. [The term post-modern is used here in the form that Hassard and Parker (1993) described as an 'epoch'.] The approach taken in this early research is often referred to as 'socio-technical' in nature, with its desire to recognize the role and contribution of people and its attempt to redress the imbalance towards an emphasis on purely technical matters.

More recently, and certainly since the 1990s, there have been many attempts to describe the nature of 'critical research', mainly within the field of general management (Alvesson & Willmott, 1992; Hassard & Parker, 1993). Still more recently, a critical research tradition has been developing from within IS, for which there is some evidence in the published literature. For instance, there have been special issues of journals (Database for Advances in Information Systems, 2002), and dedicated conference tracks at international conferences (e.g. Critical Management Studies; European Conference on Research Methods; American Academy of Management; European Conference on Information Systems).

Alvesson and Deetz (2000) have argued that critical research has at least three overlapping fundamental areas to address. These are gaining insight into lived experience (e.g. through more frequently conducting in-depth empirical work), undertaking a critique of the values and assumptions that underpin organizational and managerial practices, and transformative redefinition. By the latter they refer to the extent to which research can lead to the relevant knowledge and practice needed in order to effect change in approach and ways of working (Alvesson & Deetz, 2000).

The third area of work – transformative redefinition – is a particularly interesting one. It continues to provide a significant challenge to all researchers but, arguably, especially to those working from a critical viewpoint. As I suggested earlier in this introduction, there is a delicate tension between holding a 'critical' position whilst seeking to produce transformation that claims to be 'better' than that which previously existed. A critical voice seeks to shed light on something or bring a new perspective with the intention for generally 'good' outcomes. Thus, there is always some implied reference point in relation to which the 'good' is deemed to be an improvement, being contrasted to a notion of 'bad', of course. So we could argue that there is a role for an implied or necessary normativity here. Simultaneously, though, a critical approach needs to leave room for other voices to express different viewpoints on relative 'goodness', not to mention the researcher having to leave space for self-critique

---

3. Enid Mumford Celebration Event, Manchester Business School, 28th March 2007.

as well. This need to keep reflexing backwards and forwards between process and content whilst leaving room for other interpretations poses enough of a challenge but, where there is a normative element to the research, the task would seem even greater. Yet the problem does not end there. Much critical research has been taken to task, either for its lack of self-awareness and/or for its lack of transparency in the recruitment of normative concepts. A number of authors in this book recognize this situation, but the chapters by Stahl, Cecez-Kecmanovic and Janson, and Klein pay particular attention to it.

Various issues have been highlighted since Alvesson and Deetz' paper as needing treatment within the sphere of critical research, and the chapters in this volume seek to identify and address them. In so far as this book, then, brings together the philosophical and the practical, and re-visits the foundational values of critical IS, it addresses some of the significant gaps that were identified in the literature (Alvesson & Deetz, 2000).[4]

Historically, writings on 'critical' approaches to information systems have been fairly fragmented. In addition, what there is tends to give the impression that the study of information systems is dominated by a particular theoretical preference (especially critical systems thinking). Overall, authors of IS papers have tended to be less confident in adopting a critical approach, and in certain areas there have been few published accounts. This book calls upon those working in the field to broaden their approach, but at the same time it warns against the dangers of adopting too narrow a view of information systems research and practice (paradigmatic hegemony).

Before moving on to the next section, I want to re-emphasize my point of drawing upon the Punch and Judy metaphor. In doing this, I am inviting you, the reader, to consider the extent to which critical research in IS has historically become focused upon a relatively narrow spectrum of approaches, and the extent to which this situation is in danger of growing, with the concomitant risk that it could stifle other existing or potentially new approaches. As I indicated earlier, I see this situation as analogous to a cuckoo in the nest. It is interesting to note, for instance, that in the concluding chapter to this book, Heinz Klein is able to identify more than two strands of critical IS in contemporary research and yet reports a relative paucity of diversity in the published literature. Could it be that although critical IS is alive and kicking, it is still under-represented in mainstream consciousness? If so, is this simply a consequence of hegemonic peer review systems or could there actually be elements of a critical research approach that tend to mitigate against its own proliferation?

The 'critical' movement has become more evident in IS research in the last 10 years or so, and the time has now come for its practical application to be more

---

4. Other issues that are worth a special mention here, but which are not featured in this book, include resistance to the commodification of humanity, notably instrumental treatments of spirituality (Brooke, 2002b) and the need for representational, meaning-creation spaces within organizations (Brooke, 2001).

vociferously illustrated and debated. This book aims to provide a coherent set of reference points for students and researchers to see the issues at levels of theory, method and practice as well as to present a fuller picture of the different approaches that come under the 'critical' umbrella.

Indeed, it is important to recognize that definitions of critical research have considerably broadened over time. One of the consequences of this is that researchers from apparently disparate paradigms now claim to identify themselves with the 'critical' label. Notwithstanding significant concerns that have been raised elsewhere about paradigm and 'reality incommensurability' (Brooke, 2002b; Thompson & McHugh, 2002), this collection of works avoids being overly prescriptive about the variety of approaches it represents and which are harnessed in the service of criticality. On the contrary, it attempts to demonstrate that a rich diversity of approaches can contribute to our collective understanding of IS and organizations and encourage us to be more creative in our explorations.

1.3 IN SEARCH OF THE NATURE OF CRITICAL INQUIRY IN IS: AN OVERVIEW OF THE CHAPTERS

The book is divided into three main parts. Part one: 'In Search of Critical IS Research', includes this introductory chapter, along with two further chapters. The intention behind Part one is to introduce the reader to new theories and new perspectives on IS research. Here you will find issues about the underpinnings of critical IS research discussed from theoretical perspectives that are unlikely to be represented in other texts on your reading lists.

Part Two is called 'Critical IS Empirical Studies'. It is hoped that this section will prove to be particularly valuable since there are not many published accounts of how to actually operationalize a broad range of critical inquiries in IS. For this reason, the empirical section includes some quite detailed studies, and its length extends beyond the other two parts of the book. It is also intended that the six chapters which form this part of the book will be accessible and valuable as a resource for both teachers and researchers alike.

Part Three is a 'Review and Critique' and consists of two chapters. In providing an overview and summary of each chapter of this book, no attempt is made either to 'classify' them or critique them against a notional set of criteria or characteristics of critical research. Whilst each chapter of the volume in Parts one and two does this to a greater or lesser extent in relation to its own individual contribution, the two chapters of Part three are intended to provide a more holistic and reflective critique of the book itself. A generally accepted feature of critical research is the need to be self-reflective and open to the critique of one's own ideas. By including in this book the 'Review and Critique', the intention is to assist in discharging the critical 'duty' to be self-reflective; at least, the hope is that this is sufficiently done.

We now return to Part one in order to begin our summary of the remaining chapters, starting with chapter two by Bernd Stahl.

Stahl's chapter is placed early in the book because it provides a useful overview of critical research and IS. Stahl's main field of interest is ethics, and in this chapter he explores the rarely recognized overlap between ethics and critical IS. In particular, he gives us an historical introduction to critical research and its characteristic concern for 'emancipation'. In addition, he provides a valuable introduction to the development of the critical approach itself. In contrast to many existing published accounts, Stahl is careful to highlight the inter-relationships and similarities between positivist, interpretivist and critical accounts of the research debate. Thus, in at least two respects, it constitutes an original contribution to the field.

Stahl's chapter contains a helpful synthesis of theoretical explanation and insight into the nature of 'critical intent' with an argument for the importance of ethics. To this extent, it could be viewed as a 'call to arms' for critical researchers to recognize and address the ethical dimension of their work. Indeed, he begins with a bold statement: critical research is both based on and inspired by ethics. He goes on to support this perspective through a thorough review of the literature. Early in the chapter, Stahl makes a cogent and insightful observation of the orientation and motivation of critical approaches over time in IS such that we are encouraged to be more self-reflective in our own work. Particularly useful is the reminder that things are rarely as clear-cut as they are sometimes presented. Typically, research approaches become classified along over-simplified paradigmatic boundaries. Stahl suggests a potentially more fruitful system based on clarifying intentions, topics, theories and methods. Perhaps his most contentious statement is that critical research can be done through the use of quantitative methods or a positivist ontology. The key, he argues, is the critical intention behind them, that is, the desire to 'improve' circumstances and address 'justice' in capitalist systems.

Stahl refers to several links that can be said to exist between ethics and the critical intentions of a critical research approach. One key point here is that the critical intention implies some kind of normative state that it is desirable to achieve. After all, the changes that this approach seeks to bring about are presented in terms of improvement and, thus, must be seen as relating to some sort of notion of 'better' or 'worse' in that context. Stahl goes on to illustrate a similar point with reference to critical topics, critical theory and critical methodology. In each case, he seeks to illustrate the ways in which these can be viewed as involving some kind of stance on 'moral' issues. In closing, the author poses a challenge to all critical researchers in IS. The challenge is to render more apparent the normative basis for critical research in this area, thereby opening it up for scrutiny.

If these arguments are accepted, then it seems to me that not only would this facilitate the self-reflectivity that critical research promotes, but it would also potentially have more integrity as an expression of the ethical stance that the research itself would seem to espouse.

Andrew Basden's chapter follows on with a penetrating analysis of existing approaches to critical research that has relevance and explanatory power extending well beyond the domain of IS. He evaluates the philosophical ground motives of the research traditions that have come to dominate down the ages along with their underlying assumptions. In so doing, Basden is able to explain why research conducted from a critical perspective has often come to be seen as weak or even contradictory in its theory and application. He then goes on to demonstrate that philosophy, rather than being too abstract for our use, can direct us towards practical tools to address these criticisms. Basden takes us on a journey that includes (amongst others) Marx, Foucault, Checkland, Ulrich, Habermas and Dooyeweerd. An important milestone on this intellectual journey is Habermas' Theory of Communicative Action (TCA) and 'Lifeworld'

Whilst acknowledging the value of Habermas' ideas, Basden points out its weaknesses. Specifically, he argues that TCA has a tendency to reduce the diversity of the contexts of Lifeworld and, thereby, results in distortion, contradicting the very notion of 'ideal speech' to which it aspires. Rather than reject the concepts, though, Basden enlists the work of Dooyeweerd as a way to enrich the critical research approach.

We are introduced to Dooyeweerd's 15 aspects which (in contrast to 'mere categories') constitute spheres of meaning and law. These aspects cannot be reduced to each other, and this characteristic becomes key to avoiding the reductionist tendencies of other theories and frameworks of thought. As spheres of law, Dooyeweerd's aspects provide a set of basic types of 'Good' and 'Evil' that are irreducibly distinct. The aspects are intertwined in human activity, such that action in any aspect depends on action in other aspects.

Habermas' instrumental and communicative rationalities can be associated with Dooyeweerd's formative and lingual aspects. Hence, Dooyeweerd recognizes multiple rationalities and that these need to be incorporated into dialogue. Dialogue amongst the multiple aspects is needed, and this involves decision-making.

Dooyeweerd argues that such decisions have 'religious' roots (i.e. ultimate commitments). These roots need to be exposed since, for example, commitment to one aspect might be at the expense of another. Aspectual analysis of a situation can, thus, bring insight into taken-for-granted assumptions, reveal hidden agendas, disentangle basic kinds of meaning, and more fully recognize the virtues of an open dialogue. In summarizing, Basden presents in tabular form the ways in which Dooyeweerd's contribution can enrich a critical research approach. He then goes further to demonstrate the aspectual nature of research approaches and to situate the critical approach within this. Taking in turn each of the three categories of IS research approach (hard systems, soft systems and critical IS) he identifies their aspectual focus.

In his incorporation of Dooyeweerd's ideas, Basden not only addresses the potential weaknesses in Habermas' frameworks but also presents us with a direction for future work which takes account of criticisms levelled at critical IS research more generally; notably the paradoxes inherent in an emancipatory approach. Specifically, Basden demonstrates how the critical IS approach can address the different normative types of 'Good' and 'Evil' and treat them in a more rigorous way. In concluding the chapter, Basden is keen to remind us that Dooyeweerd recognized the necessity for reflexivity. Criticality must not be regarded as an absolute but rather an invitation to further critical evaluation. There is plenty of scope here for the reader to access new perspectives on IS research and to critically reflect on their relevance and usefulness, and their implications for thought and action.

Dubravka Cecez-Kecmanovic and Marius Janson provide us with a review and critique of emancipatory and participatory information systems development (ISD). They identify a need for such a review because on the one hand, such approaches have been condemned as naive and unrealistic and yet, on the other hand, they have been seen as vehicles of managerial instrumentalism, harnessing workers in the service of economic agendas. In order to conduct their evaluation, the authors present us with a longitudinal study of a Belgian retail company. Their search is for practical meaning of emancipatory and participatory ISD rather than its political or economic justifications. By so doing, they are able to propose ideas concerning the conditions under which such ISD may be carried out. They take the work of Hirchheim and Klein (1994) as their reference point for such conditions, highlighting systematic and meaningful user involvement, open and non-distorted communication and reasoned argumentation, based on cooperation and mutual understanding between developers, managers and employees.

In the course of presenting the Colruyt case study, the authors provide insight into subtle differences between approaches to ISD that liberate and empower and those that 'colonize and disempower'. In this, and other ways they attempt to present a critical and careful analysis of theory and practice rather than just a 'totalizing meta-narrative'. The chapter includes a useful historical context for the development of emancipatory ISD and its socio-technical studies of the 1960s and 1970s. There are similarities, it seems, between the Tavistock Institute's emphasis on employee training and involvement, and Colruyt's own approaches to worker development. Nevertheless, the case study surfaces interesting tensions in the participative practices at Colruyt that generate some new and stimulating problems. One example of this was the way in which conflict resolution was addressed. The lack of hierarchical control structures led to regular disagreements arising between colleagues rooted in differing personal interests and viewpoints. Colruyt's response to this situation was to provide focused training in communication skills.

The company's founder Jo Colruyt (and CEO until 1993) was pivotal in the development of an open and participative culture and practice. It was the vision of this apparently charismatic leader to establish his own high ethical standards within the business. He inculcated the participative rights of employees, a democratic work environment and open access to information.

One apparent side effect of this was the changing role of the trade union. We note that there was tension between the espoused views of the union about

Colruyt and their responses at an individual level during interviews. It is possible to interpret this ambiguity in terms of a reaction to a perceived or felt loss of union power and status in the workplace. Indeed, it seems clear that the act of democratizing information access and use resulted in significant shifts in political roles and power structures. However, the authors are careful to note that increased democratization led to an increased need for individuals to take responsibility for their actions. Here, there was also a role for information systems information dissemination (ISID), where technology could support and enhance the self-managed and autonomous nature of the work groups that formed; for instance, in relation to problem-solving activities.

Cecez-Kecmanovic and Janson evaluate their case study using Alvesson and Willmott's emancipatory framework. One important aspect of the framework that is assessed against the case study is the 'utopian element'. This is defined, not as an unrealistic striving for perfection but, rather, as a desire for improvement upon the status quo. One key conclusion was that the 'utopian element' in ISID actually generated critical thinking and surfaced novel practices, as was identified by Alvesson and Willmott in their framework.

This distinction between 'utopia' and 'perfection' is a fundamental one and resonates at another theoretical level too. In particular, we are told that some critics of Habermas have been too quick to discard his ideas because they fail to distinguish between these two states. The authors propose that Habermas' ideal speech situation holds far more analytical promise and explanatory power when viewed more in relation to 'utopia' than 'perfection'. Thus, we are encouraged to view the repertoire of practices at Colruyt as an expression of a rational discourse and as an example of the role of ISID in supporting and encouraging emancipatory outcomes.

In closing the chapter, Cecez-Kecmanovic and Janson suggest that their research has demonstrated instances of micro-emancipation within a context of a market leader seeking to attain excellence and efficiency whilst promoting and supporting open, democratic communications and an inclusive, cooperative culture. They argue that not only does their research show that emancipatory and participatory practice is 'realistic' but also that it confirms Hirschheim and Klein's (1994) arguments. The authors argue that participatory and emancipatory ISD can be a valuable foundation for the workforce creativity and self-managed autonomy demanded of a competitive and uncertain organizational environment. The case study indicates that, contrary to some claims, the emancipatory project can support critical self-reflection at all levels within a company, and contribute simultaneously to economic success and the equalizing of power relations. Whereas the socio-technical research approach tends to be limited to working conditions and individual worker satisfaction levels, participatory and emancipatory ISD addresses the wider concern of workplace democracy, devolved decision-making and self-transformation. The authors, thus, open up a space for further examination by academics and practitioners in the spirit of critical research through dialogue and self-reflective critique.

Oliver and Romm's chapter is a study of Enterprise Resource Planning (ERP) systems and the ways in which their adoption becomes justified by organizations. Using grounded theory, they conduct a multiple case study which analyses and evaluates the adoption of ERP across a range of universities.

Using data from electronically mediated sources, the authors develop a model of ERP adoption and then they critique it. Taking their lead from March (1988) the authors distinguish between research that involves analysing and predicting substantive outcomes and that which focuses on how organizational activities are perceived, interpreted and legitimated. It is the latter which distinguishes this chapter as taking a critical approach. Drawing on ideas from Weber and Habermas, the critical nature of the work presented resides primarily in its focus on issues of domination and emancipation, communication, rationality and legitimacy. Specifically, the study seeks to identify and understand the extent to which people occupy a subservient role vis-à-vis technology, and also in relation to organization and process.

The purpose of the research is to identify common themes across the case studies and develop from them a conceptual model of how ERP adoption is justified. Grounded theory enables them to construct these new conceptual categories. We are shown that what is considered of value and importance to an organization can be revealed using these techniques. They discover that there are a combination of drivers and influences on ERP adoption, including technical, value-driven and strategic, all of which enables the authors to interpret the underlying rationality types with reference to their rationality framework.

One of the most significant findings from the study was that the more money was invested in the technology systems and the greater their strategic importance, the less likely was the organization to apply a formal evaluation procedure. This echoes findings reported in the study by Oliver and Romm, this volume. It seemed the more complex the job of evaluating, the less persuasive its outcomes. Thus, from a critical perspective, there was little evidence of applied, instrumentally rational forms of organizational behaviour. Rather, behaviour appeared to show trend-following and imitative tendencies. Interestingly, the authors point out that, at a strategic level, this 'herding instinct' could produce some benefits, and they identify elements of image and status acquisition.

In concluding, Oliver and Romm consider that instrumental rationality is an inadequate explanation for the adoption of new technology. Rather, technology has become part of the social value system. Indeed, they echo Habermas in finding evidence for colonization of the life-world by technology and its privileging over and above people. They finish by observing that scant consideration was given by the universities to their core activities of teaching and research, and they urge researchers to continue exploring the impact of ERPs on the cultural missions of organizations.

Oliver and Romm's chapter makes a valuable contribution to an understanding of critical IS in several ways. ERP systems are of major concern in contemporary organizations, and this study demonstrates how grounded theory can be applied to a case such as this and yet be used in a critical way. Additionally, it illustrates that the ideas of Habermas can be applied within a more limited social context than is often done.

The subsequent chapter by Cuckier and Rodrigues is a longitudinal study (1992–2005) that combines critical discourse analysis and Habermasian critical theory in a critique of public discourse on technology. The authors also attempt to respond to criticisms that other researchers have directed specifically at IS research that draws upon critical theory. This contribution was inspired by widespread debates about the apparent gulf between the hyped rhetoric of what technology can achieve and deliver, and the 'reality' of actual reported experiences. A key motivation for exploring these issues is the belief that a better understanding of them will lead to improved organizational decision-making.

The authors propose critical discourse analysis as a way to understand institutional discourses, as well as a route to a better understanding of the environments in which they operate. Specifically, a discourse analysis of the limits to rationality that are imposed by an organization as part of a decision-making process can, for instance, expose underlying assumptions and biases, and social 'norms'. Using a Habermasian framework of analysis, based on the notion of communicative rationality, the authors explore cases of media discourse concerning e-learning. Habermas' four validity claims of truth, sincerity, legitimacy and clarity are used to analyse the texts in the research.

The analysis pulls out some interesting findings. For example, one of these is that the benefits technology-based learning are often asserted but rarely, if ever, evidenced. Another is that the level of investment in technology equipment is generally emphasized whilst the costs of providing development, support and infrastructure are either hidden or down-played.

Whilst the existing literature includes examples of communicative rationality applied to organizational ISD, this chapter demonstrates the value of applying it to media discourses on technology at the level of society. The case illustrates the 'absurd' situation that the costs of learning technology are rarely articulated in a holistic or coherent way, whereas benefits are taken for granted. The questions implied by communicative rationality (truth, sincerity, legitimacy, clarity) are proposed as ways to reduce the inherent uncertainties and to improve the decision-making process. Ultimately, this can help to differentiate between societal hype around technology and developments that are of genuine interest and benefit.

Given the discourse analysis focus of this chapter, it is unsurprising that it is one of the longest in this book. It is important to note that in presenting their research, Cuckier and Rodrigues provide us with a fairly detailed practical insight into 'data' and its analysis and this, of itself, is a valuable opportunity for the reader to see how critical theories and concepts can be applied in practice.

In outlining for use the current state of the field of discourse analysis, the authors make two very useful contributions. They present a brief overview and critique of the literature, and they present (in two tables) a synthesis of the different approaches and interests that can be derived from that literature base.

Laurie McAulay's chapter is primarily a general introduction to the use of semiotics (the study of signs) as an evaluative tool, but it also illustrates how this can be applied specifically within IS. In particular, we see how a critical approach can reveal interpretations that seem to challenge the 'authoritative voice', simultaneously revealing a complex web of stakeholders with their varied interests. In taking us on our journey through semiotics, we visit a range of theoretical influences including structuralism, post-structuralism and post-modernism, noting along the way how they have contributed to the development of semiotics and its application. The chapter gives focus to the importance of communication within the field of IS but also notes its tendency to become 'distorted'. It could be argued, then, that McAulay is raising a similar issue to that which motivated the development of Habermas' communicative rationality, but the response is a very different one.

Signs can be either a written text (such as books, annual reports, plays) or visual text (e.g. works of art, films, shop displays, road signs). The basic premise is that all these signs have been constructed by people with their own ethical and political ideals. Thus, these values become potentially 'inscribed' into the sign. In order to form an opinion and have an appropriate response, a critical reading must attempt to deconstruct the sign so as to explore the values that underpin it.

McAulay uses the financial reports of two very different organizations (Sainsbury and Cisco) as his material for deconstruction. In both cases it is information technology strategy that is the subject of discussion. These two examples were chosen for their contrasting styles of expression and not because they are the best examples of particular strategic choices. Nevertheless, the exercise is insightful. We learn to see that what first appears to be neutral and objective can have many hidden meanings and that the meaning of a sign is taken as much from what is not said as what is said – its 'silences'. At the end of the analysis we are left with the problem of how to achieve a balance between the open-ended nature of interpretation and the need to reach a view in order to influence future actions.

Issues of justice and individual rights are highlighted, and their implications for communal action and freedom are noted. However, rather than offer us a prescriptive solution, the chapter opens up the potential for different perspectives. As the author says, by rejecting the notion of definitive meanings the world is more receptive to new ways of acting. Indeed, McAulay turns the problem back on to you, 'the reader'. Individuals have the ability to engage with texts; this is a fundamental underpinning principle of semiotic analysis. Further, that in our active engagement with texts we create meaning, often without being aware of it. Since a critical research approach requires us to analyse taken-for-granted values and assumptions, it should not surprise us to note that, ultimately, McAulay challenges us to take responsibility for our own acts of reading and meaning creation. Such practices, he argues, create the possibility for improved development and design of IS and even the emancipation of individuals.

In the following chapter on Self-Ethnography, Chumer attempts to describe and evaluate a research approach that he has been using and reflecting on since 1996. Chumer argues that Self-Ethnography (or SE, for short) is a particularly useful approach to adopt when studying what he calls socially embedded phenomena. SE has emerged from the hermeneutical and phenomenological philosophical traditions as exemplified in the works of Heidegger, Husserl and others. With its focus on 'being' and 'existence', phenomenology would seem to lend itself well to an approach that seeks to engage in the role of self, or selves, in the practice of inquiry. The self-ethnographer, on the other hand, also needs to be able to distinguish between 'self' and 'other' in order to make sense of the world around them. Thus, an hermeneutic grounding contributes to the relationship between 'self' and 'other' within a research context. Further, SE seeks to bring into the light the biases of the researcher and the impacts that such biases may have on the research account. This calls for a self-reflexive process, involving the recording of the 'self' or selves, the 'other' and how they are influenced by the phenomena and context being studied, and in which they are embedded. The researcher, as researcher–author, becomes more transparent, or such is the intention.

The researcher, then, is viewed as an active participant, more or less on 'equal terms' with other participants. SE is concerned with the 'home-base' of the researcher, that is, the context within which they are already located. 'Traditional' ethnography tends to involve the researcher entering into a context in order to conduct research on or with 'strangers'. Whereas traditional ethnography involves drawing 'closer to', therefore, SE necessitates a degree of 'distancing from'.

SE offers the critical researcher the opportunity not only to recognize but also to draw upon the inscriptive effects of a research inquiry upon his or her self and the multiple identities that may emerge in the process. In essence, rather than attempt to silence or control for the role of self in the research endeavour, SE enables its celebration and contribution to enriching 'thick' description and deeper insight. Hence, Chumer recommends SE to us as an approach over and above many other forms of research noted for their positivistic tendencies.

Two examples of the application of SE are used to demonstrate its value as a framework for critical IS inquiry. The first involves information and communications technology (ICT) diffusion within a university library and the second focuses on the effects on the self of computer-based working in relation to communications and cooperative working, involving virtual environments. We see some nice examples of research data, including research diary narrative. This helps us to understand the analysis that follows. As is common to 'critical' studies of IS, the SE surfaced issues of power and politics in the case of the ICT diffusion and helped to explain why resistance to the changes was encountered by the organization. The SE also highlighted ways in which technology use in a virtual context impacted on the role of researcher\teacher; in particular, the difficulty of resisting power behaviour in oneself and in the 'other'. This insight was not surfaced by the author's peers, who omitted to include such issues in their own research into the effects of virtual environments.

Overall, the SE enabled an understanding of the relationship between experiences at the micro level and taken-for-granted assumptions pertaining to the macro level of the organization. Chumer maintains that such depth and richness of insight would not have been produced had a more 'traditional' or less 'critical' research approach been used to conduct the research.

Bill Doolin's chapter is a longitudinal case study of the implementation of a large information system within a newly corporatized hospital in New Zealand. The study focuses on the potential for IS to significantly impact work practices. Doolin's analysis is influenced by the ideas of Foucault and attempts to provide insight into and understanding of issues of power relations, and especially the role of IS in mediating and reinforcing knowledge and meaning in the workplace.

Reforms of the public health sector in the UK and in New Zealand offer us an interesting point of comparison. The emergence of 'new public management' throughout the 1980s and 1990s provided an opportunity for IS to be seen as a potential managerial control mechanism. Doolin's research, therefore, becomes focused around the ways in which IS are implicated in the exercise of such power and control.

The particular IS being evaluated is a 'casemix'. Casemix systems were first piloted in the 1980s as a way to link together patient and clinical information with their associated costs. Doolin points out that the 'problems' of health care at the case study hospital became translated into a lack of appropriate information to manage costs and enable efficiency. Similarly, this then became translated into a delegation to IS as a way of keeping track of resource use. In its early days, the system was promoted as a decision support system that would improve resource use and patient care, but its implementation proved to be problematic. Cynicism about previous experiences of health systems, together with lack of evidence of tangible benefits from the casemix system led to disillusionment amongst hospital staff.

Eventually, the casemix information system became viewed as another managerial tool for monitoring and control and, in some cases, was regarded as threatening. However, in the late 1990s the emergence of a new economic and management culture pushed the casemix system to the front again. A renewed attempt by management was then made to present the casemix system as a solution to tracking resources but this time with the added dimension of peer-to-peer comparison amongst the hospital's clinicians. The surveillance process produced some anxiety for clinicians who use their professional identity and status to resist what they saw as an attempt by management to dictate their choices and actions. The chapter goes on to unpack the ways in which the casemix system was implicated in the power relations, job roles and 'organizational reality' of staff.

Adopting a critical stance to the case study enables Doolin to explore the role of IS in terms of power and as discursive practice. The chapter claims to make two important contributions to critical IS research. Firstly, it demonstrates that organizational actors have the potential to resist disciplinary technologies and, in contrast to managerial motives, that IS can even empower them. Secondly, it is a relatively rare example of an empirical study using Foucault's ideas to gain insight into the exercise of power and IS. In closing, we are urged to consider and research the links between technological intensification and the intensification of power. The overall message is that we must do so in order to gain deeper insight into social and organizational relations.

As was indicated earlier, the last two chapters of the book (Cordoba and Brooke, and Klein, respectively) attempt a critique and review of all the preceding material. A critical approach demands a level of reflexivity; that is, it is important to regularly revisit one's own values and assumptions when presenting research so as to remain open to the possibility of new interpretations, different ways of acting, and to avoid falling into the trap of prescription and/or closure.

The penultimate chapter of the book is by Cordoba and Brooke, and it makes a contribution in two ways: through presenting a novel approach for reviewing critical IS work and by using this approach to evaluate the preceding chapters in this volume. The framework of ideas presented – referred to as the 'three lenses' – draws upon the work of the Colombian philosopher Zuleta amongst others.

Adopting ideas from Nietzsche, Zuleta proposes that the act of reading a text should be an intellectual activity involving a continuous problem-driven cycle. He is very concerned with the possibility of stagnation and uncritical acceptance of texts, arguing instead that the process of reading should not only involve production and consumption but also generate an on-going desire to question and understand.

In his exploration of the act of reading, Zuleta proposes three different types of reader: camel, lion and child. He argues that only when these three roles are combined do we reach philosophical insight. However, Cordoba and Brooke do not suggest these three lenses are combined, rather that they provide an opportunity to identify conflicts and creative tensions. In this way, dialogue can lead to the construction of new possibilities.

Inspired by Zuleta's attempt to 'idealize' different types of reader, Cordoba and Brooke go on to develop three lenses which could be said to characterize the existing research field of critical IS. The lens of 'enamouring' describes research approaches that provide theoretically rich and appealing arguments to develop alternative practice. However, they run the risk of privileging particular theories over others, by failing to be self-reflective and becoming disconnected from mainstream research. A 'provoking' lens is characterized by a strong element of 'denouncing', where a challenge is made to established or traditional ideas. Often it can involve a re-interpretation of critical IS ideals, but it can be limited by over-emphasizing its denouncing elements at the expense of practical suggestions for change. The third lens of 'imagining' calls for an act of 'forgetting' about the status quo and instead focuses on how to imagine a different future.

The authors then go on to integrate the three types of reader described by Zuleta with their own three different lenses to produce an evaluative research framework. By way of illustration and reflexive critique, they go on to look at all the preceding chapters of this book and 'read' them against their framework.

The evaluation using the three lenses is offered not as a meta-narrative or grand theory but, on the contrary, to help us adopt a more prismatic approach, opening up the possibility for new perspectives. Indeed, the chapter ends with an invitation to the reader to revisit the previous chapters using the three lenses and undertaking the journey for his or her self.

The book closes with the contribution from Heinz Klein, to whom this book is dedicated. Sadly, Heinz died before he could finish work on his last version of this chapter, although it was substantially developed. With some trepidation, and with his wife's agreement, Carole Brooke and Bernd Stahl have undertaken to complete the finishing touches to the final chapter on Heinz' behalf. We felt that his perspective was too important and interesting to leave out, and it performs an important reflexive role within this text.

This chapter addresses the nature of critical social research (CSR) and its development and application within the field of IS (referred to as CSISR) by adopting an historical-evolutionary perspective. By reviewing all the preceding chapters (including Cordoba and Brooke's) Heinz Klein seeks to answer two related questions. These are to what extent the contributions of the book assist us in identifying helpful and significant features towards a definition of CSR and to what extent they either reflect the status quo within IS research or 'break the mould'. In order to do this he first constructs a picture of the current status of CSR research in IS in general and then compares the contributions in this volume against it.

Klein proposes sets of criteria by which to identify critical research approaches in all their diversity. Basically, he extends notions previously proposed by Alvesson, Willmott, and Lyytinen and, in so doing, is able to highlight potential strengths, weaknesses and gaps within current CSISR research. In Klein's overview of CSR in IS generally, of particular importance is his distinction between meta-critical analysis and critical field studies. He also seeks to answer the question of whether or not there exists one or more (or no) 'paradigms' of critical IS.

Klein reflects on the 'invisible' quality of CSR within the IS field and urges researchers to bring their insights to the readers of more top journals. He proposes that one reason for this dearth of visibility might be the apparent lack of an agreed body of methods for CSR. He also proposes that there have been two previous fundamental research philosophies; one that reifies the enlightenment ideal in modified form, and one that remains highly sceptical of it.

In closing the chapter he notes that all the contributions in this book focus on the micro level. He leaves us with the question of to what extent future research needs to embrace both micro and macro perspectives. Overall, though, the message is an encouraging one. Even considering the small proportion of work which this volume represents in relation to CSR as a whole within IS, there is evidence of much 'lively activity'. In particular, he notes the level of engagement with the process of creating a philosophical foundation for research conduct. He, therefore, rejects recent claims that there is a 'missing discipline' in IS.

However, he seems to agree that, to an extent, critical IS activity is still under-represented in top-ranking journals. One strategy to raise the publications profile of CSR, he says, is to foster more collaboration between these schools of thought (cf. the 'lenses' presented by Cordoba and Brooke in the penultimate chapter of this volume).

1.4 SOME REFLECTIONS AT LAST

To emphasize the point once more, a key focus of this book is to challenge the hypocritical dangers of paradigmatic hegemony. My concern in 2003 was – and remains despite Walsham's reassurances to the contrary (Walsham, 2005, p. 114) – that this apparent contradiction might presage a developing trend with serious consequences for the future development of research in IS.

In reading the final chapter of this book, Klein's discussion draws me over and over again to considering the potentially ironic status of the critical re-searcher; one might also see this status more positively as 'slippy' or 'liminal'. I feel as if I am involved in a recursive mode of advance, evaluation and retreat. Perhaps a Möbius strip would be a better analogy, since there is no beginning and no end – all is inter-woven in the analysis. There is no escape, or so it seems, from the need for a road sign that alerts us to the 'critical researcher at work'. Otherwise, how can we be certain that the road users will appreciate or accept the intended 'improvements' and/or new routes that we hope will result from our (temporary?) disruption to the mainstream intellectual highway. Similarly, to remain working at the road surface without attempting an assessment of the road network, in general, might be seen as isolationist, parochial, irrelevant and even irresponsible. Yet, all these potential criticisms run counter to the very espoused (if albeit non-universal) types of claims that critical researchers tend to make.

Surely a key value of critical research resides in its ability to question the taken-for-granted, to reveal hidden things, to propose new perspectives, to enrich our understanding and, *maybe, sometimes,* to enable improvement, emancipation, or states of heightened self-awareness. How, then, can we be expected to provide street furniture to 'legitimate' our (de-construction/re-construction) project with all its apparently inherent characteristics of longevity and meta-level explanatory power, without inviting (from all direc-tions) scepticism, or even, 'God forbid', the ultimate 'insult' of imposing a *totalizing meta-narrative*?!

I propose that the final two chapters of this book provide, albeit in very different ways, responses to this conundrum.

The penultimate chapter by Cordoba and Brooke (yes, that is me), explores and re-presents the diverse nature of critical IS research such that it is not so much a particular perspective that is 'promoted' but a willingness to re-visit one's own assumptions and interpretations as well as those of others. The 'lenses' that are proffered as aids to the evaluation of research, are not intended to be like the prescription lenses of the optician but, rather, like the view one sees through a prism. It is not so much about 'correcting' one's own vision but opening up the spectrum of possibilities. This sounds more like the dialectical dance I was searching for early on in my research journey.

In contrast to Cordoba and Brooke, by getting to grips with the state of the field, Klein's chapter brings us face-to-face with the unwitting dilemma. How can a researcher remain hypersensitive (if that is, indeed, what is required) to their own criticality and yet at the same time promote their work as providing some kind of 'improvement' over and above existing circumstances and/or existing research in the area? The hypocritical dangers of paradigmatic hegemony are evident here also, are they not? Yet, these discussions are not about navel-gazing. We need to develop ways of generating self-critique, not least because such ability improves and informs our practice.

The aim of Klein's chapter, it could be argued, was two-fold: to indicate, in general, areas of potential strength and weakness in critical IS research, and also, in particular, to demonstrate what a critical approach to analysis can yield when applied to its own efforts. Klein's development and extension of earlier work on the characterization of critical research is a valiant attempt to draw our attention to both the need for, and the difficulties of a critical approach to IS. His careful distinction between issues relating to 'improvement' in the field of study and those relating to 'improvement' in the discipline of IS itself are especially pertinent. Nevertheless, for all the reasons I have outlined above, some readers will probably struggle with accepting the challenge he gives us to generate more 'meta-level' studies. Ultimately, such difficulties may remain within the sphere of critical IS; though, hopefully, no longer as an 'elephant in the room'. This book, after all, was never meant to offer set solutions or even, necessarily, to reconcile differences between positions. Above all, it was intended to be a celebration of diversity in approach.

In a world seemingly so permeated with technological endeavour, it seems reasonable to suppose that a critical perspective on the relationships between technology, organization and society will remain ever more relevant to the future understanding, evaluation and transformation of the world/s within which we find ourselves embedded. For me personally, the intellectual journey is undertaken with no expectation of closure as such. Especially from a critical viewpoint, I would encourage you, the reader, to create your own map as you embark on each excursion. It may be, then, that each time you engage with the materials presented here you will experience something differently.

In drawing these reflections to a close, I very much hope that you have a fruitful encounter with this book. A brief message from all of us who contributed to this volume: whether you find something new, re-discover something old or glimpse a surprising angle on a familiar scene (the back cover springs to mind again), our hope is that you will be encouraged and stimulated to pursue further your journey/s of inquiry.

As the writer Jeanette Winterson so poetically expresses it, every journey conceals within its lines another journey – a path not taken or a forgotten angle (Winterson, 1989).

REFERENCES

Alvesson, M., & Deetz, S. (2000). *Doing critical management research*. Sage, London.

Alvesson, M., & Willmott, H. (1992). On the idea of emancipation in management and organisation studies. *Academy of Management Review, 17*(3), 432–464.

Brooke, C. (2001). Information systems in use: A representational perspective. *TAMARA journal of Critical Organization Inquiry, 1*(3), 39–52.

Brooke, C. (2002a). What does it mean to be critical in IS? *Journal of Information Technology, 17*(2), 49–57.

Brooke, C. (2002b). Critical perspectives on information systems: An impression of the research landscape. *Journal of Information Technology, 17*(4), 271–283.

Conway, D. W. (1999). Pas de Deux: Habermas and Foucault in genealogical communication. *Foucault contra Habermas*. In Ashenden, S., & Owen, D. (Eds.), Sage, London, pp. 60–89.

Hassard, J., & Parker, M. (1993). *Postmodernism and organisations*. Sage, London.

Hirchheim, R.A. and Klein, H.K. (1994) "Realizing Emancipatory Principles in Information Systems Development: The Case for ETHICS", *MIS Quarterly*, 18, 1, pp. 83–109.

Howcroft, D., Truex, D. (Eds) (2002), *The DataBase on Advances in Information Systems, Special issue on Critical Analysis of ERP Systems: The Micro-level*, Vol. 33 No.1.

March, J., G. (1988). Rationality, ambiguity, and the engineering of choice. In Decision making: Descriptive, normative, and prescriptive interactions (D. Bell, E., H. Raiffa, and A. Tversky eds.) pp 33–57. Cambridge University Press.

Morgan, G. (1993). *Imaginization*. Sage, London.

Sauer, C. (1993). *Why information systems fail: A case study approach*. McGraw Hill, London.

Thompson, P., & McHugh, D. (2002). *Work organisations: A critical introduction*, (3rd ed.). Palgrave, Basingstoke.

Walsham, G. (2005). Learning About Being Critical. *Information Systems Journal, 15,* 111–117.

Winterson, J. (1989). *Sexing the cherry*. Bloomsbury, London.

Chapter 2

Critical Research and Ethics

Bernd Carsten Stahl

2.1 INTRODUCTION

Critical research is based on and inspired by ethics. This is the starting assumption of the chapter. Given that not all critical researchers will immediately agree with this statement, I support this argument through a review of the literature showing that critical research can be characterized through its critical intention, critical topics, critical theory and critical methodologies. All of these are closely linked to implicit and explicit ethical assumptions. After arguing for the ethical nature of critical research I point out which further questions should be asked by CRIS scholars.

2.2 CRITICAL RESEARCH IN INFORMATION SYSTEMS

Critical research in the field of information systems (IS) is usually described as an alternative to positivist and interpretivist research (Trauth, 2001). This is based on Orlikowski and Baroudi's (1991) seminal paper, which was built on Chua's (1986) work. This, in turn, can best be understood as a reaction to the dichotomous categorization of social science research by Burrell and Morgan (1979). Critical research in this context is a paradigm or a world-view that consists of beliefs about physical and social reality (ontology, social relations, human rationality), knowledge (epistemology, methodology) and the relationship between theory and practice. The value of this view of critical research as an alternative paradigm is that it allows discussing alternatives to the prevailing paradigm of positivist research. At the same time it is misleading because it implies that the three paradigms are mutually exclusive and comprehensive.

Neither implication is correct. There are large areas of overlap between individual aspects of the paradigms. Critical research, for example, can be based on a positivist ontology (Hirschheim, 1985) as well as on a constructionist/interpretivist ontology. At the same time there are also possible approaches that are not covered (cf. Niehaves & Stahl, 2006).

Because of the weaknesses of the traditional tripartition of IS research, this chapter suggests a different classificatory scheme. It argues that critical research can be characterized by its intention, topic, theories and methods. These are briefly described in the following sub-sections. It is important to note at this stage that the following characterization of CRIS is not meant to be exclusive. It complements and overlaps with other definitions as well. The reason for suggesting it here is that it may help delimiting what counts as CRIS and, more importantly, that it offers a starting point for looking at the ethical faculties and implications of CRIS.

2.2.1 Critical Intention

The arguably most important characteristic of critical research is its critical intention, the fact that critical researchers aim at initiating and promoting change. This is the heart of Chua's (1986) and Orlikowski and Baroudi's (1991) claim that critical research is a third way, next to positivist and interpretivist research. Both the latter research approaches can be purely descriptive, whereas critical research aspires to change social realities. As we see later, this normative characteristic is closely linked with critical topics, theories and methodologies. It is based on the Marxist view of history as a history of class struggles and a negative perception of capitalism (Hirschheim & Klein, 1989; Marx, 1969; Orlikowski & Baroudi, 1991). The injustices and inequities inherent in given social structures require the researcher to search for better, freer, less alienating and more emancipated ones. Few critical IS researchers would call themselves Marxist, but most share a suspicion that current social arrangements are not in everyone's interest and need to be improved. It has been remarked (Harvey, 1990) that the Marxist roots are typical for the continental European version of critical research and that the Anglo-American view of it draws its inspirations from other sources, notably pragmatism. In this chapter I will rely on the European tradition but I acknowledge that there are other views of criticality not necessarily captured by the theoretical views I outline. In particular, those readers who object to the Marxist background of CRIS should realize, however, that there is a strong and well-established school of thought for which the Marxist roots are central to critical research in general and, thus, to CRIS too.

Critical intention mirrors Marx's (1964, p. 141) view that philosophy (or – in our case – IS research) has always just interpreted the world differently, while it is important to change it. Marx was highly critical of German Idealism, the prevailing philosophy of his time. He thought that philosophy and studying the real world relate to one another like masturbation and sexual love (Marx, 1960,

p. 218). This feeling may be shared by critical IS researchers with regards to the prevailing research approach of positivism. Critical research seeks knowledge but not for its own sake. Critical research wants to be practical but in a specific way. The purpose is to change social practices in such a way that the negative effects of the way society and organizations are run will be minimized. 'The critical social theory approach was never intended to be an abstract philosophy. It was to bring about real change in the human condition' (Ngwenyama, 1991, p. 276). Critical research will, therefore, rarely aim at improving managerial tools or practices for the sake of efficiency. Instead, it tries to keep the bigger picture of the role of the economic system and individuals in society in mind.

Emancipation is a cornerstone of critical research and CRIS. This should not be misunderstood to imply that it is easy or not contentious. There are open questions concerning the possibility of even recognising the potential for emancipation.

Moreover, emancipation can become a problem in its own right, namely when it leads to critical researchers prescribing ways of action that conflict with the research subjects' own views of their best choices. It can turn into a dictatorship of the intellectual and, thereby, raise a range of new problems (Stahl, 2006). Despite these well-recognised problems (Kincheloe and McLaren, 2005) of emancipation, it is still a central defining feature of critical research. The problems should lead critical researchers to develop a sensitivity for problems involved in emancipation rather than discard the idea.

2.2.2 Critical Topics

On the basis of the critical intention to change society, or parts thereof, critical research is interested in those areas where our social structures are problematic. These areas are what we will call critical topics. Considering the importance of power structures for the individual and his or her ability to live a life accordingly, critical IS researchers discuss how IS can disempower people and how they can be used to empower individuals (Brooke, 2002a; Lyytinen & Hirschheim, 1988). Empowerment can play a role wherever IS are used, including traditional profit-oriented capitalist companies, virtual organizations (Levary & Niederman, 2003), or educational institutions (Dawson & Newman, 2002). The aim of CRIS is to 'promote liberating and empowering IS design and use' (Cecez-Kecmanovic, 2001a). Following the Marxist tradition, critical research is worried about the alienating effects of current labour relations (Orlikowski & Baroudi, 1991; Varey, Wood-Harper, & Wood, 2002).

Another critical topic, closely related, and sometimes used synonymously with, empowerment is emancipation. Emancipation is one of the most frequently cited topics of critical IS research (Cecez-Kecmanovic, 2001b; Cecez-Kecmanovic, Janson, & Brown, 2002; Klein & Myers, 1999; McAulay, Doherty, & Keval, 2002; Ulrich, 2001a). Capitalist work structures not only enslave and alienate labourers but they also systematically take away their ability to develop and prosper. Emancipation can, therefore, be said to be a slightly wider concept than empowerment because it needs to address the question of how the individual's abilities can be developed and their potential achieved. Emancipation, therefore, looks into psychological as well as organizational issues (Hirschheim & Klein, 1994). Related concepts are authenticity (Probert, 2002) and autonomy, which also describe the individual's ability to interact with their environment.

Apart from the fundamental topics of power, empowerment and emancipation, critical research is also interested in areas of IS where these basic questions lead to consequences. There is a multitude of specific questions related to the critical topics (e.g. gender, class and race; cf. Harvey, 1990) but some are sufficiently obvious to deserve being mentioned. Among them one can find problems ranging from the organizational levels, such as failure of IS (Doherty & King, 2001; Introna, 1997) to the social level, such as gender and discrimination (Adam, 2001; Robinson & Watson, 2001) and to the international level of problems such as access and the digital divide (Kvasny & Trauth, 2003; Tavani, 2003).

Furthermore, there are topics related to the underlying social structures, which tend to be critical of capitalism and demonstrate the problems resulting from capitalist social and economic structure. Some authors are interested in the fundamental contradictions and conflicts within capitalist society (Saravanamuthu, 2002a) but the majority of scholars interested in this area of critical topics look at consequences of capitalism, such as the commodification of information (Floridi, 1999; Ladd, 2000), privacy (Davison, Clarke, Smith, Langford, & Kuo, 2003), labour (Giddens, 1984; Knights & Willmott, 1999) or humans and their activity in general (Brooke, 2002b; Klein & Lyytinen, 1985).

Finally, there is the critical topic of how capitalism and its alienating conditions came to power and retain a high level of legitimacy. This question is closely linked to the relationship of economic practice and its scientific justification. The underlying problem here seems to be a certain kind of purposive rationality, which is widespread in IS and, thus, constitutes another topic of interest for critical research (Cecez-Kecmanovic et al., 2002; Hirschheim & Newman, 1991; Hirschheim & Klein, 2003; McAulay et al., 2002; Saravanamuthu, 2002a, 2002b; Varey et al., 2002; Wastell, 1996; White, 1985; Wynn, 2001).

2.2.3 Critical Theories

Interest in the critical topics is usually linked to preferences for certain theories. The reason for this is that the choice of theory influences the type of research object and method. Theory also has a large influence on possible conclusions and practical outcomes. Much critical theory goes back to Marxist theories, to historical or dialectical materialism (Brooke, 2002a). It typically shares certain aspects of Marxist theory such as the assumption of fundamental conflict between labour and capital, an emphasis on history and the idea of totality (Orlikowski & Baroudi, 1991).

The most prominent development of Marxist thought in the twentieth century is usually associated with the Frankfurt School and the names of its representatives such as Horkheimer, Adorno, Bloch and others. The close link between the Frankfurt School and historical materialism can be gathered from the fact that it was originally planned to name it *Institut für Marxismus* (Institute for Marxism) which was eventually discarded for the less contentious name *Institut für Sozialforschung* (Institute for Social Research; cf. Wiggershaus, 2001. While the original scholars of the Frankfurt School are sometimes cited in IS research, most critical research referring to it emphasizes the works of Karl-Otto Apel and, more importantly, of Jürgen Habermas.

In critical IS research Habermas (1981) Theory of Communicative Action (TCA) plays a central role. The basis of this use of TCA in IS was laid by Lyytinen and Klein (1985) and Lyytinen and Hirschheim (1988). The Habermasian framework is critical in that it allows the questioning of validity claims and requires a rational justification of such claims. That means it can be used to elicit hidden assumptions, ideologies and other bases of suppression, alienation and power inequalities. It is based on the counterfactual idea of an ideal discourse situation where there are no differences in power or ability to communicate and where only the 'forceless force of the better argument' (*der zwanglose Zwang des besseren Arguments*) determines which validity claims are upheld (Hirschheim & Klein, 1989). The TCA thus allows the description of how meaning and social reality are created. At the same time, it facilitates the critical intention because it contains a model (the ideal discourse situation) according to which social structures, and also IS, can be modelled (Lyytinen & Hirschheim, 1988; Ulrich, 2001a).

While there seems to be a strong reliance on Habermas and his theories in critical IS research, there are also other approaches. One of them is based on Michel Foucault's work. The strength of Foucault's theory is that it allows the identification of the non-rational background of so-called rational discourse (Foucault, 1971). It is critical of the self-image that business in general and IS in particular usually display. Foucault also allows the observation of the importance of the body and of physical and other means to establish discipline (Foucault, 1975). Finally, Foucault and his redescription of Bentham's Panopticon offer a fascinating basis for the description of surveillance, which is an important aspect of the use of IS (Goold, 2003). Foucault's theory is highly useful in addressing some of the critical topics but less so in realizing the critical intention. Foucault does not supply us with a framework or an ideal we could strive to realize (Stahl, 2004b).

There are, of course, other theoretical approaches open to critical researchers. One of them is critical realism (Mingers, 2001) which tries to overcome the dichotomy of positivism and interpretivism and opens up avenues for understanding critical issues. Then there are critical approaches developing from different traditions such as Rorty's neo-pragmatism or post-modern approaches. It is impossible to give a comprehensive review of these here. For our purposes it will suffice to point out that the Habermasian stream of the Frankfurt School and approaches in line with Foucault's arguments have tended to feature most centrally in critical IS research (Brooke, 2002b).

2.2.4 Critical Methodologies

The final characteristic of critical research in IS is the choice of method. Fundamentally, any method or methodology that allows the collection of relevant data concerning one of the critical topics, using a critical theory, which aims to fulfil the critical intention can be used in critical research (cf. McGrath, 2005). This includes positivist, empiricist, and quantitative approaches. Orthodox Marxist critical research would typically use such approaches to prove the subjugation of labour. In the practice of critical IS research, however, it seems to be the case that there are some methods that are typically used by critical researchers and these are generally on the qualitative and hermeneutic side. One important aspect of critical research methodologies is that they are reflexive, that is, they reflect on the role of the researcher within the research process (Cecez-Kecmanovic, 2001a). There seem to be two groups of critical methodologies; one aims at determining the social realities of people who are affected by IS whereas the other concentrates on the use of language.

The first group of research methodologies comprises those research approaches that allow developing an in-depth understanding of people's view of their situation. This will usually require intensive interaction. One can, therefore, find participative approaches (Trauth & O'Connor, 1991; Walsham, 1995) used in critical research. An example of this is ethnography, which can be used in a critical way making it 'critical ethnography' (Schultze, 2001). A research method that is based on participant observation and that openly shares the critical intent to change given situations is action research (Gergen, 1999; Mumford, 2001). The second group of research methodologies is more interested in how the use of language hides power influences, how IS produce ideologies, how discourses lead to disempowerment, and how these developments can be counteracted. Here, we find methodologies based on the concept of discourses (Ulrich, 2001b). These can be based on assumption analysis (Hirschheim & Klein, 1994), discourse analysis (Schultze & Leidner, 2002; Thompson, 2003) or ideology critique (Doherty and Keval, 2002). More generally, most hermeneutic and narrative approaches to IS research seem to be well suited to serve as methodology for critical IS research (Heaton, 2001a, 2001b; van der Blonk, 2003). There is the difficult question of compatibility of these different research methodologies (Brooke, 2002b), which we will have to leave open.

Before we come to the next part of the argument, a brief explanation of the relationship between the four characteristics is in order. Critical intention, topic, theory, and methodology define critical research. While this should allow an unequivocal description of most critical research, there are also some grey zones.

Not every piece of critical research will display all four of the characteristics. They are typically linked, but this is not necessarily always the case. As indicated earlier, critical research may use quantitative methods or be based on a positivist ontology (cf. Niehaves & Stahl, 2006). Similarly, research looking at power issues using a Foucauldian angle and a participative methodology can still be non-critical. The most important characteristic of critical research is the critical intention; that is, the wish to improve the situation of people caught up in the injustices of capitalist structures and organization.

2.3 THE ETHICAL FOUNDATIONS OF CRITICAL RESEARCH IN IS

The preceding section suggested a new way of classifying critical research. It aimed to provide an alternative to the positivist – interpretivist – critical distinction which is often misleading. In this section, the characteristics of critical research are shown to be based on or closely linked to ethics.

2.3.1 The Concept of Ethics

Since this chapter aims to show the direct link between critical research in IS and ethics, the reader will now expect a comprehensive definition of ethics. Given the complexity of the topic, however, the reader will be disappointed. The philosophical discussion of ethics is simply too extensive to be summarized in a useful way in this chapter. (Many useful introductions to philosophical ethics are available. They typically concentrate either on an exploration of the history of ethical ideas (cf. Brandt, 1959; Hinman, 1998) or an exposition of the most relevant authors (Dewey & Hurlbutt, 1978).) To avoid being drawn into ethical debates, I will use a common sense notion of ethics. Ethics will stand for doing 'the good' and 'the right'. Moral rules are part of the tacit knowledge of all agents and they guide our behaviour, usually unconsciously. Ethical theories can justify moral norms and, thereby, guide action in those cases where the moral choice is not obvious. The justification of morality can be achieved by looking at the consequences (utility) of an action and by looking at the intention, the virtue of the agent and by considering the implications for justice or for the 'other' in general. These aspects, which form the basis of some of the more prominent ethical theories, can also play a role in practice. In our context it means that critical researchers will typically have an internalized morality, which is rationalized using some or all of these terms.

The philosophically versed reader may be disappointed by this somewhat superficial introduction to ethics. (For a more comprehensive and philosophically grounded introduction to the relationship of ethics and IS see Stahl, 2004a.) The link of the current conception of CRIS with philosophical ethics is discussed in a much more detailed fashion in Stahl (2008a, 2008b). It can, nevertheless, be justified because it is the level of abstraction that one can find in social practice. Individuals working in capitalist systems typically have this level of ethical awareness. Similarly, critical researchers, while usually more philosophically interested than the average worker, are not necessarily ethicists.

For the following discussion of the ethics of critical research we will therefore restrict ourselves to an understanding of ethics as normative, as distinguishing right from wrong, and as being somehow justified. The aim of the argument is to demonstrate the relationship between, ethics and CRIS.

2.3.1.1 The Ethics of Critical Intentions

The critical intention was introduced as the most important characteristic of critical research. Critical topics, theories and methodologies all follow from the critical intention. At the same time, the critical intention is of a deeply ethical nature. The critical intention was defined as the desire to use research to initiate and promote change. Critical researchers not only want to observe but they also want to interact with their research object. This is what sets critical research apart from positivist and interpretive research in the Chua/Orlikowski and Baroudi tradition. The critical intention is ethical because it implicitly introduces a normative dimension into the discussion that cannot be deduced from traditional research approaches. Since Hume (1948), most philosophers have accepted that there is no direct line from 'is' to 'ought', that prescription cannot result from description. If critical research aims to change, then this cannot result from the observation of reality. Rather, a normative premise must be implied. That premise would read similar to the following: 'when injustice is being done, critical research should change it'. This premise is clearly of an ethical nature. While the suggested formulation may be debatable and can be replaced by another one, it will retain the ethical quality. It needs to refer to what should be done in order to justify the critical intention. The normative premise puts us in the realm of ethics. We have to consider questions of right and wrong, of good and bad and of the justification of these terms.

There are other links between the critical intention in research and ethics, such as the view that research is linked to virtue (Varey et al., 2002) or that ethics requires knowledge to be effective. The question of change also raises the issue of clarity of the definition of critical research, because it has been argued that all IS research aims at change (Keen, 1991). For the purpose of our argument (that critical research is ethically relevant research) these questions are of minor importance. Similarly, we need not worry about ethical theories and their related problems. The argument is a purely logical one: if critical research aims to change, then it is prescriptive and prescriptive statements cannot follow from observation. There must, therefore, be a normative (prescriptive) premise to critical research. Such a premise must rely on ethics, be it explicitly or implicitly.

2.3.1.2 The Ethics of Critical Topics

While the argument for the ethical quality of the critical intention was relatively straightforward, discussing the ethical quality of critical topics is much more complex due to their variety. This chapter can only offer a cursory glance at the possible arguments. For most of the critical topics introduced earlier, it is easy to argue that they are of ethical relevance.

The most important critical topic is power. Power is a complex term but in most cases it refers to the ability an agent has to influence another agent's behaviour; to make one do another's bidding. Power implies obligations, rules and norms, all of which have an ethical nature. This does not mean that power is intrinsically bad (or good), just that its exertion has ethical consequences (Giddens, 1984). This is true for political power (Rawls, 2001), economic power (Galbraith, 1958/1998) as well as information as power (Mason, Mason, & Culnan, 1995). This argument extends to the attempts to free the individual from power as summarized under the concept of emancipation. While it is arguably impossible to completely free oneself from power relationships (Gergen, 1999), critical research attempts to identify and analyse those effects of capitalist societies that alienate individuals (Myers & Avison, 2002) and limit their options.

The other critical topics introduced earlier typically refer to power or to issues equally closely linked to ethics. The digital divide, for example, is a topic of interest for critical researchers because it disempowers some, and it precludes them from living up to their potential (cf. Trauth, Howcroft, Butler, Fitzgerald, & DeGross, 2006). Britz (1999, p. 25) points out that: 'access to information is the most important ethical question in the information age [...]'. Apart from the immediate ethical importance, access is also ethically relevant because it affects the way society is organized, for example, through e-democracy or e-government (Breen, 1999). This argument leads easily to other critical topics such as the problem of gender in IT. Again, the central question relates to who gets access to which resources and on what grounds. This, in turn, determines opportunities and obligations and is, therefore, an ethical question (Adam, 2002; Stewart, Shields, & Sen, 2001; Wheeler, 2001). Similarly, questions of IS failure derive their interest to critical researchers from the ethical effects they have. Information systems failures may involve an economic or technical problem but their importance originates from the ethical impact they have. Failures waste money and other resources, limiting the freedom of the agents involved. At the same time, failure is often caused by non-technical problems, many of which are related to ethics. These include organizational politics, recognition of legitimate stakeholders, or a lack of respect for others (cf. Keil, Tiwana, & Bush, 2002; Schiller, 1999; Wilson, 2003; Wilson & Howcroft, 2002).

2.3.1.3 The Ethics of Critical Theory

The ethical qualities of some critical theories are obvious, while this is less so for others. The Frankfurt School, particularly in its Habermasian incarnation, is clearly concerned with ethics. For Habermas every speech act contains, among others, the claim to normative rightness. Amoral speech is, thus, impossible. His discourse ethics (Habermas, 1983, 1991) is a direct consequence of the Theory of Communicative Action, which is the basis of a considerable part of critical research in IS. There is little recognition of this in the field of IS and the understanding of Habermas as an ethicist is limited (for an exception to this see Yetim, 2006). For other theories, such as Foucault's, this argument is harder to support. Suffice it to say, that an interpretation of Foucault as motivated by morality is at least possible, if not univocally recognized (Stahl, 2004b).

The question of the ethical quality of critical theory is probably best addressed by looking at the common denominator: Karl Marx. The orthodox reading of Marx (at least the later Marx) suggests that he rejected ethics, and saw society as a social system in which ethics played no role. Marx's emphasis on the importance of the material world as a determinant for society and also for consciousness can be read this way (Marx, 1998). It should be noted, however, that a different reading of Marx is also possible. On the contrary, the early Marx was clearly interested in ethical questions, but one can also see the later Marx as ethical. Rorty (1998) argues that the communist manifest is an expression of hope for a better society, comparable with the New Testament, and equally based on an ethical view of human nature. Another stream of thought uses similar ideas to the ones presented here. It asks what is the relevance of property in the means of production, if not ethical? (Kambartel, 1998). Similarly, how can one explain Marx's interest in alienation and emancipation, if not on an ethical basis (Wynn, 2001)? Looking at the overall theoretical and political system based on Marx, one can conclude that '[. . .] Marxism-Leninism is not only an economic system but a moral theory; a theory of production and a system of ethics' (Vallance, 1992, p. 40).

2.3.1.4 The Ethics of Critical Methodology

The link between critical research and a specific methodology is much weaker than its link with the critical intention. It is not useful to talk about 'ethical methodologies'. Critical research can use different methodologies, which often can be used in other contexts as well. Nevertheless, there are indicators that some methodologies, which are typically used for critical IS research, are linked to ethics. This can be said for methodologies which are linked to a close and direct interaction between researcher and research subject. The close interaction between the two requires a personal relationship to be built up which, in turn, has ethical implications. The most typical research methodology for critical research is probably the one that includes the critical intention to change reality and the participative approach to the subject's reality, namely action research. Action research can be described as being explicitly based on the emancipatory intention of critical research (Mumford, 1991; Sandberg, 1985). An action researcher wants to change things, but is also, ideally 'dedicated to the pursuit of knowledge in an ethical manner' (Mumford, 2001, p. 64).

Discourse-oriented methodologies can be interpreted as being closely aligned to ethics due to their communicative nature. Following a Habermasian theory renders all communication aimed at mutual understanding an ethical endeavour, but there are also other ethical theories that see a fundamental ethical quality in communication (cf. Ricoeur, 1990). Phenomenological approaches, predominant in interpretive and also in critical research in IS, thus, can be described as inherently ethical (cf. Stahl, 2005).

2.4 CONCLUSION

The chapter has offered a new definition of critical research, based on its intention, topics, theories and methodologies. In a second step it has put forward the argument that all of the aspects are closely linked to ethics and that consequently critical research can be understood as ethical research. Which conclusions can critical researchers draw from this?

It seems to me that the most important conclusion to be drawn from this has to do with awareness. If the current argument is convincing and if critical research in IS is strongly influenced by, and possibly based on, ethical considerations, then the critical researcher needs to reflect on this. Due to the reflective capability of CRIS, this should not pose a major problem. It is, nevertheless, important for CRIS as a field of investigation to own up to its ethical roots. Critical research needs to leave its crypto-ethical status and openly engage with the problems posed by its ethical nature. This seems to be the first and foremost conclusion to be drawn from this chapter.

The choice of topic, theory and methodology should be reconsidered paying attention to the ethical aspects of each. Critical researchers need to ask whether a particular theory they are using is suitable for addressing ethical issues. This way of viewing critical research may explain the attractiveness of the Habermasian framework for critical researchers, since it explicitly includes ethical concerns. It may also explain the choice of certain methodologies, which allow scholars to actively promote their ethical concerns.

Another conclusion of the acceptance of critical research as ethical research will be that ethical theory will have to be explicitly considered by critical scholars. This will add a new dimension and a new degree of complexity to critical research. It may facilitate a clearer definition of some of the central concepts upon which critical research is built but which are, nevertheless, unclear. A good example is the concept of emancipation. It has been noted that despite its central importance, it is not clear what it means to be emancipated (Brooke, 2002a). If we concede that ethics is the main reason why critical research is concerned about emancipation, then an ethical discussion will allow better insights into what it means to be emancipated and, possibly, how emancipation is to be achieved. Similar arguments can be brought forward for terms such as 'rationality', 'power' and other topics of interest. This type of discussion will benefit from interaction with related academic fields such as computer ethics or information ethics, which are interested in similar problems including power, access, rationality, etc., and which have a history of framing these problems in ethical terms.

It is not to be expected that critical researchers will easily agree on the ethical foundations of their work or that we will be able to construct a coherent ethical framework of critical research. Ethical theories and traditions are too divergent to allow for simple summaries. This lack of simple outcomes does not, however, absolve us from the necessity of making the normative foundations of CRIS more explicit and, thereby, opening them up to critical scrutiny.

REFERENCES

Adam, A. (2001). Computer ethics in a different voice. *Information and Organization, 11*(4), 235–261.

Adam, A. (2002). Cyberstalking and Internet pornography: Gender and the gaze. *Ethics and Information Technology, 4*(2), 133–142.

Brandt, R. B. (1959). *Ethical theory: The problems of normative and critical ethics.* Prentice Hall, Englewood Cliffs, NJ.

Breen, M. (1999). Counterrevolution in the infrastructure—A cultural study of techno-scientific impoverishment. *Ethics and electronic information in the 21st century.* In Pourciau, L.J. (Ed.), Purdue University Press, West Lafayette, IN, pp. 29–45.

Britz, J. J. (1999). Ethical guidelines for meeting the challenges of the information age. *Ethics and electronic information in the 21st century.* In Pourciau, L.J. (Ed.), Purdue University Press, West Lafayette, IN, pp. 9–28.

Brooke, C. (2002a). What does it mean to be 'critical' in IS research? *Journal of Information Technology, 17,* 49–57.

Brooke, C. (2002b). Critical perspectives on information systems: An impression of the research landscape. *Journal of Information Technology, 17,* 271–283.

Burrell, G., & Morgan, G. (1979). *Sociological paradigms and organizational analysis.* Heinemann, London.

Cecez-Kecmanovic, D. (2001a). Doing critical IS research: The question of methodology. *Qualitative research in IS: Issues and trends.* In Trauth, E. (Ed.), Idea Group Publishing, Hershey, PA, pp. 141–162.

Cecez-Kecmanovic, D. (2001b). Critical information systems research: A Habermasian approach. *Proceedings of the 9th European conference on information systems, Bled, Slovenia,*, pp. 253–263.

Cecez-Kecmanovic, D., Janson, M., & Brown, A. (2002). The rationality framework for a critical study of information systems. *Journal of Information Technology, 17,* 215–227.

Chua, W. F. (1986). Radical developments in accounting thought. *The Accounting Review, 61*(4), 601–632.

Davison, R. M., Clarke, R., Smith, H. J., Langford, D., & Kuo, F.-Y. (2003). Information privacy in a globally networked society: Implications for IS research. *Communications of the Association for Information Systems, 12,* 341–365.

Dawson, R. J., & Newman, I. A. (2002). Empowerment in IT education. *Journal of Information Technology Education, 1*(2), 125–141.

Dewey, E. J., & Hurlbutt, R. H. (1978). *An introduction to ethics.* Macmillan, New York.

Doherty, N. F., & King, M. (2001). An investigation of the factors affecting the successful treatment of organisational issues in systems development project. *European Journal of Information Systems, 10,* 147–160.

Floridi, L. (1999). *Philosophy and computing: An introduction.* Routledge, London.

Foucault, M. (1971). *L'ordre du discourse*. Gallimard, Paris.

Foucault, M. (1975). *Surveiller et punir: Naissance de la prison*. Gallimard, Paris.

Galbraith, J. K. (1958/1998). *The affluent society*, (40th anniversary ed.). Mariner Books, Boston, New York.

Gergen, K. J. (1999). *An invitation to social construction*. Sage, London.

Giddens, A. (1984). *The constitution of society—Outline of the theory of structuration*. Polity Press, Cambridge, UK.

Goold, B. J. (2003). Public area surveillance and police work: The impact of CCTV on police behaviour and autonomy. *Surveillance and Society*, *1*(2), 191–203.

Habermas, J. (1981). *Theorie des kommunikativen Handelns—Band I/II*. Suhrkamp, Frankfurt am Main.

Habermas, J. (1983). *MoralbewuÔtsein und kommunikatives Handeln*. Suhrkamp, Frankfurt am Main.

Habermas, J. (1991). *Erläuterungen zur Diskursethik*. Suhrkamp, Frankfurt am Main.

Harvey, L. (1990). *Critical social research*. Unwin Hyman, London.

Heaton, L. (2001a). Preserving communication context: Virtual workspace and interpersonal space in Japanese CSCW. *Culture, technology, communication: Towards and intercultural global village*. In Ess, C., & Sudweeks, F. (Eds.), SUNY Press, Albany, NY, pp. 213–240.

Hirschheim, R. A. (2001b). Information systems epistemology: An historical perspective. *Research methods in information systems (IFIP 82 proceedings)*. In Mumford, E., Hirschheim, R., Fitzgerald, G., & Wood-Harper, T. (Eds.), North Holland, Amsterdam, pp. 13–36.

Hinman, M. L. (1998). *Ethics: A pluralistic approach to moral theory*. Harcourt, Fort Worth, TX.

Hirschheim, R., & Klein, H. K. (1989). Four paradigms of information systems development. *Communications of the ACM*, *32*(10), 1199–1216.

Hirschheim, R., & Klein, H. K. (1994). Realizing emancipatory principles in information systems development: The case for ETHICS. *MIS Quarterly*, *18*(1), 83–109.

Hirschheim, R., & Klein, H. K. (2003). Crisis in the IS field? A critical reflection on the state of the discipline *Journal of the Association for Information Systems*, *4*(5), 237–293.

Hirschheim, R., & Newman, M. (1991). Symbolism and information systems development: Myth, metaphor and magic. *Information Systems Research*, *2*(1), 29–62.

Hume, D. (1948). *Hume's moral and political philosophy (1711–1776)*. Hafner, New York Edited with an introduction by Henry D. Aiken.

Introna, L. (1997). *Management information and power: A narrative of the involved manager*. Macmillan, London.

Kambartel, F. (1998). Bemerkungen zur Politischen Okonomie. *Philosophie und Politische Okonomie—Essener Kulturwissenschaftliche Vorträge 2*. In Kambartel, F. (Ed.), Wallstein, Göttingen.

Keen, P. G.W. (1991). Relevance and rigor in information systems research: Improving quality, confidence, cohesion and impact. *Information systems research: Contemporary approaches and emergent traditions*. In Nissen, H.-E., Klein, H.K., & Hirschheim, R. (Eds.), North Holland, Amsterdam, pp. 27–49.

Keil, M., Tiwana, A., & Bush, A. (2002). Reconciling user and project manager perceptions of IT project risk: A Delphi study. *Information Systems Journal*, *12*, 103–119.

Kincheloe, J. L., & McLaren, P. (2005). Rethinking critical theory and qualitative research. *The Sage handbook of qualitative research*, (3rd edn.)., Denzin, N.K., & Lincoln, Y.S., (Eds.) Sage, Thousand Oaks, pp. 305–342.

Klein, H. K., & Lyytinen, K. (1985). The poverty of scientism in information systems. *Research methods in information systems (IFIP 8 2 proceedings)*. In Mumford, E., Hirschheim, R., Fitzgerald, G., & Wood-Harper, T. (Eds.), North Holland, Amsterdam, pp. 131–161.

Klein, H. K., & Myers, M. D. (1999). A set of principles for conducting and evaluating interpretive field studies in information systems. *MIS Quarterly, 23*(1), 67–94.

Knights, D., & Willmott, H. (1999). *Management lives: Power and identity in organizations.* Sage, London.

Kvasny, L., & Trauth, E. (2003). The digital divide at work and home: The discourse about power and underrepresented groups in the information society. *Global and organizational discourse about information technology (Ifip Tc8/Wg8 2 Conference).* In Wynn, E., Whitley, E., Myers, M.D., & DeGross, J. (Eds.), Kluwer Academic Publishers, Dordrecht, The Netherlands, pp. 273–291.

Ladd, J. (2000). Ethics and the computer world – A new challenge for philosophers. *Cyberethics—Social and moral issues in the computer age.* In Baird, R.M., Ramsower, R., & Rosenbaum, S.E. (Eds.), Prometheus Books, New York, pp. 44–55.

Levary, R. R., & Niederman, F. (2003). Managing the virtual corporation using IT. *IT-based management: Challenges and solutions.* In Joia, L.A. (Ed.), Idea Group Publishing, Hershey, PA, pp. 143–159.

Lyytinen, K., & Hirschheim, R. (1988). Information systems as rational discourse: an application of Habermas Theory of communicative action. *Scandinavian Journal of Management, 4*(1/2), 19–30.

Lyytinen, K. J., & Klein, H. K. (1985). The critical theory of Jürgen Habermas as a basis for a theory of information systems. *Research methods in information systems (IFIP 8 2 proceedings).* In Mumford, E., Hirschheim, R., Fitzgerald, G., & Wood-Harper, T. (Eds.), North Holland, Amsterdam, pp. 219–236.

Marx, K. (1960). *Deutsche Ideologie,* (4th ed.). Dietz, Berlin.

Marx, K. (1964) Karl Marx/Freidrich Engels Studienausgabe. Edited by Fetcher, B.I. Frankfurt am Main: Fischer Philosophie.

Marx, K. (1969). *Manifest der Kommunistischen Partei.* Reclam, Stuttgart.

Marx, K. (1998). *Das Kapital—Kritik der politischen Okonomie, 3 Bd, Band 1 MEW Bd 23,* (16th ed.). Dietz, Berlin.

Mason, R. O., Mason, F., & Culnan, M. J. (1995). *Ethics of information management.* Sage, London, New Delhi.

McAulay, L., Doherty, N., & Keval, N. (2002). The stakeholder dimension in information systems evaluation. *Journal of Information Technology, 17,* 241–255.

McGrath, K. (2005). Doing critical research in information systems: A case of theory and practice not informing each other. *Information Systems Journal, 15,* 85–101.

Mingers, J. (2001). Embodying information systems: The contribution of phenomenology. *Information and Organization, 11*(2), 103–128.

Mumford, E. (1991). Information systems research—Leaking craft or visionary vehicle? *Information systems research: Contemporary approaches and emergent traditions.* In Nissen, H.-E., Klein, H.K., & Hirschheim, R. (Eds.), North Holland, Amsterdam, pp. 21–26.

Mumford, E. (2001). Action research: Helping organizations to change. *Qualitative research in IS: Issues and trends.* In Trauth, E. (Ed.), Idea Group Publishing, Hershey, PA, pp. 46–77.

Myers, M., & Avison, D. (2002). An introduction to qualitative research in information systems. *Qualitative research in information systems: A reader.* In Myers, M., & Avison, D.D. (Eds.), Sage, London, pp. 3–12.

Ngwenyama, O. K. (1991). The critical social theory approach to information systems: Problems and challenges. *Information systems research: Contemporary approaches & emergent traditions.* In Nissen, H.-E., Klein, H.K., & Hirschheim, R. (Eds.), North Holland, Amsterdam, pp. 267–280.

Niehaves, B., & Stahl, B. C. (2006). Criticality, epistemology and behaviour vs design – Information systems research across different sets of paradigms. *14th European Conference on Information Systems, 12–14 June 2006,* Göteborg, Sweden.

Orlikowski, W. J., & Baroudi, J. J. (1991). Studying information technology in organizations: Research approaches and assumptions. *Information Systems Research, 2*(1), 1–28.

Probert, S. K. (2002). Ethics, authenticity and emancipation in information systems development. *Ethical issues of information systems.* In Salehnia, A. (Ed.), IRM Press, Hershey, PA, pp. 249–254.

Rawls, J. (2001). *Justice as fairness: A restatement.* In Kelly, E. (Ed.), Belknap, Cambridge, MA/ London.

Ricoeur, P. (1990). *Soi-même comme un autre.* Edition du Seuil, Paris.

Robinson, S., & Watson, J. (2001). Female entrepreneur underperformance: A puzzle for the information age. *Journal of International Information Management, 10*(1), 45–56.

Rorty, R. (1998). *Das Kommunistische Manifest—150 Jahre danach.* Sonderdruck Edition Suhrkamp, Frankfurt am Main.

Sandberg, A. (1985). Socio-technical design, trade union strategies and action research. *Research methods in information systems (IFIP 8 2 proceedings).* In Mumford, E., Hirschheim, R., Fitzgerald, G., & Wood-Harper, T. (Eds.), North Holland, Amsterdam, pp. 79–92.

Saravanamuthu, K. (2002a). Information technology and ideology. *Journal of Information Technology, 17,* 79–87.

Saravanamuthu, K. (2002b). The political lacuna in participatory systems design. *Journal of Information Technology, 17,* 185–198.

Schiller, D. (1999). *Digital capitalism: networking the global market system.* MIT Press, Cambridge, MA/London.

Schultze, U. (2001). Reflexive ethnography in IS research. *Qualitative research in IS: Issues and trends.* In Trauth, E. (Ed.), Idea Group Publishing, Hershey, PA, pp. 78–103.

Schultze, U., & Leidner, D. (2002). Studying knowledge management in information systems research: Discourses and theoretical assumptions. *MIS Quarterly, 26*(3), 213–242.

Stahl, B. C. (2004a). *Responsible management of information systems.* Idea Group Publishing, Hershey, PA.

Stahl, B. C. (2004b). Whose discourse? A comparison of the Foucauldian and Habermasian concepts of discourse in critical IS research *Proceedings of the 10th Americas conference on information systems,* New York 06-08 August 2004.

Stahl, B. C. (2005). A critical view of the ethical nature of interpretive research: Paul Ricur and the other. *13th European Conference on Information Systems 'Information Systems in a Rapidly Changing Economy',* Regensburg, Germany, 26–28 May 2005.

Stahl, B. C. (2006). Emancipation in cross-cultural IS research: The fine line between relativism and dictatorship of the intellectual. Ethics and Information Technology, 8(3). *Special issue on bridging cultures: Computer ethics, culture, and information and communication technologies.* In Ess, C. (Ed.),, pp. 97–108.

Stahl, B. C. (2008a). *Information systems: Critical perspectives.* Routledge, London.

Stahl, B. C. (2008b). The ethical nature of critical research in information systems. Information Systems Journal, 18(2). *Exploring the critical agenda in IS research (special issue).* In Brooke, C., & Klein, H.K. (Eds.),, pp. 137–163.

Stewart, C. M., Shields, S. F., & Sen, N. (2001). Diversity in on-line discussions: A study of cultural and ender differences in listservs. *Culture, technology, communication: Towards and intercultural global VILLAGE.* In Ess, C., & Sudweeks, F. (Eds.), SUNY Press, Albany, pp. 161–186.

Tavani, H. (2003). Ethical reflections on the digital divide. *Journal of Information. Communication and Ethics in Society, 1*(2), 99–108.

Thompson, M. (2003). *ICT, power, and developmental discourse: A critical analysis.* In Wynn, E., Whitley, E., Myers, M.D., & DeGross, J. (Eds.), Kluwer Academic Publishers, Dordrecht, The Netherlands, pp. 347–373.

Trauth, E. (2001). Choosing qualitative methods in IS research: Lessons learned. *Qualitative research in IS: Issues and trends.* In Trauth, E. (Ed.), Idea Group Publishing, Hershey, PA, pp. 271–287.

Trauth, E., & O'Connor, B. (1991). A study of the interaction between information technology and society: An illustration of combined qualitative research methods. *Information systems research: Contemporary approaches & emergent traditions.* In Nissen, H.-E., Klein, H.K., & Hirschheim, R. (Eds.), North Holland, Amsterdam.

Trauth, E., Howcroft, D., Butler, T., Fitzgerald, B., & DeGross, J., (Eds.), (2006). *Social inclusion: Societal & organizational implications for information systems,* Springer, Boston.

Ulrich, W. (2001a). A philosophical staircase for information systems definition, design, and development. *Journal of Information Technology Theory and Application, 3*(3), 55–84.

Ulrich, W. (2001b). Critical systemic discourse. *Journal of Information Technology Theory and Application, 3*(3), 85–106.

Vallance, E. (1992). Never the twain? Ethics and economics in eastern and Western Europe *Business ethics in a New Europe.* In Mahoney, J., & Vallance, E. (Eds.), Kluwer Academic Publisher, Dordrecht, The Netherlands, pp. 36–46.

van der Blonk, H. (2003). Writing case studies in information systems research. *Journal of Information Technology, 18,* 45–52.

Varey, R. J., Wood-Harper, T., & Wood, B. (2002). A theoretical review of management and information systems using a critical communications theory. *Journal of Information Technology, 17,* 229–239.

Walsham, G. (1995). Interpretive case studies in IS research: Nature and method. *European Journal of Information Systems, 4,* 74–81.

Wastell, D. G. (1996). The fetish of technique: Methodology as a social defence. *Information Systems Journal, 6,* 25–40.

Wheeler, D. (2001). New technologies, old culture: A look at women, gender, and the Internet in Kuwait. *Culture, technology, communication: Towards and Intercultural global village.* In Ess, C. (Eds.), SUNY Press, Albany, NY, pp. 187–212.

White, K. B. (1985). Perceptions and deceptions: Issues for information systems research. *Research methods in information systems (IFIP 8 2 proceedings).* In Mumford, E., Hirschheim, R., Fitzgerald, G., & Wood-Harper, T. (Eds.), North Holland, Amsterdam, pp. 237–242.

Wilson, M. (2003). Rhetoric of enrollment and acts of resistance: Information technology as text. *Global and organizational discourse about information technology.* In Wynn, E., Whitley, E., Myers, M.D., & DeGross, J. (Eds.), Kluwer Academic Publishers, Dordrecht, The Netherlands, pp. 225–248.

Wilson, M., & Howcroft, D. (2002). Re-conceptualising failure: Social shaping meets IS research. *European Journal of Information Systems, 11,* 236–250.

Wiggershaus, R. (2001). Die Frankfurter Schule: Geschichte, theoretische Entwicklung, politische Bedeutung. dtv, München.

Wynn, E. (2001). Möbius transitions in the dilemma of legitimacy. *Qualitative research in IS: Issues and trends.* In Trauth, E. (Ed.), Idea Group Publishing, Hershey, PA, pp. 20–44.

Yetim, F. (2006). Acting with genres: Discursive-ethical concepts for reflecting on and legitimating genres. *European Journal of Information Systems, 15*(1), 54–69.

Chapter 3

Practically Critical: Making the Critical Approach More Useful

Andrew Basden

3.1 INTRODUCTION

This chapter examines the nature of the problems that the critical approach to information systems (IS) (as distinguished by 'emancipation' and 'communicative action' approaches) encounters in its attempts to uncover problems and inconsistencies at various levels of analysis. It then suggests a way to both resolve the inconsistencies and address the problems, to make the application of both emancipation and communicative action easier in everyday IS research, design, development and evaluation. It does this by reference to philosophy. Philosophy is usually seen as a highly abstract discipline, with little direct relevance to practice in everyday experience, but here it will be demonstrated that philosophy not only has direct relevance, but can also point the way to practical tools.

Critical approaches to IS in business may be seen as a paradigmatic response to two previous approaches, which Jackson (1991) calls the hard and soft systems approaches. The hard approach was characterized by a desire for control, with information technology (IT) being the means to effect that control by making business processes more structured and reliable. The hard approach, in its extreme form, attempted to suppress individual human preferences or beliefs, and shared many fundamental beliefs and preferences with the scientific paradigm of logical positivism. The soft approach, epitomized by Checkland's (1981) *Soft Systems Methodology*, responded by emphasizing subjective opinions, values and *Weltanschauungen* (world views). The soft approach, in its extreme form, denied any possibility of a reality that transcends humanity. It held that we create our own realities by orchestrating 'appreciations' of situations (Bergvall-Kåreborn, 2001).

There are two main problems with both the hard and soft approaches. One is that neither allow for any sound notion of right and wrong, and so give no sound basis for distinguishing applications of IS that are 'good' from those that are 'evil' or detrimental. When forced to talk about right and wrong, as happens in practice, the hard approach speaks instead about costs and benefits, while the soft approach reduces them to personal preferences; both could be used, for example, to design a more efficient method of genocide. The other is that neither provides any basis for addressing the impact of social structures on the way IT has been developed and used. Society's values are structures. For example, Adam (1998) argues that IT is shaped to masculine values, and, hence, is unsuited to feminine applications, and Pacey (1996) says that IT is shaped to Western values, and so is unsuited to the application in non-Western contexts. To the soft approach, structures are dissolved in inter-individual relationships while in the hard approach, structures are reduced to immutable laws that govern life; neither provides a sound basis for critique of social structures.

The critical approach responded to these by espousing both normativity and social structures. Two main versions have arisen, both of which give priority to a major norm which is meaningful in terms of social structures and which should guide all our applications and development of IT (and indeed the rest of human life). They are 'critical' in the sense of assuming a normativity by which to criticize existing social structures and advocate changing them. In the first, the major norm is that of emancipation: social structures oppress or constrain people and IS should be designed and used in such a way as to overcome this. In the second, the major norm is open communication and discourse by which we come to understand each other perfectly and, as a result, engage together in 'rational' social action. Various factors, including power structures, distort our ability to communicate openly, and this results in irrational social action.

Both of these approaches are problematic, however, especially when employed in practical situations of everyday life and in applications outside the professional arena, such as social networking and virtual worlds. The emancipatory critical approach is unable to usefully define emancipation. While it enabled us to critique the 1970 s view of IS, of people's lives dominated by large, inflexible organizational computer systems, it is not clear what 'emancipation' means in computer games. The communicative critical approach tends to assume that all social activity must involve rational discourse and critique, and this blinds us to other types of social activity. While it has been useful in analyzing business processes of the 1980s and 1990s, in which rational communication is paramount, it is not clear how it can be applied to such applications as social networking today. We need to be critical about the critical approach.

3.2 THE PROBLEM OF EMANCIPATION AND POWER

Emancipation was a central thrust of the early Frankfurt School, partly explainable by its Marxist lineage. It is the major normativity of this branch of the critical approach. It is the 'good' that overcomes the 'evil', which is oppressive social structures and their results. The word was originally most closely associated with the issue of slavery, and then became applied to the oppression of workers. Emancipation, in this original sense, has a strong social element, and arose as a major norm because of oppressive social structures, not just because individuals acted in an evil manner. As such, the norm of emancipation transcends individual perspectives and values. Emancipation then became associated with suppression of the rights of those affected by actions and decisions outwith their control. Though still retaining a strong social aspect, it became applied to the indirect impact of inter-individual action.

The notion of emancipation is sometimes associated with, and has often been replaced by, that of empowerment in some discourses (Allen, Colligan, Finnie, & Kern, 2000; Markus & Bjørn-Andersen, 1987Markus and Bjørn-Anderson, 1987). There is a difference in connotation: emancipation speaks of the action by one person or group to remove oppressive conditions from another, while empowerment speaks of the action by a person or group to remove oppression from themselves. Walsham (2001) is one example of many who use Foucault's notion of power as a lens through which to view IS use. He does so at several levels (individual, organizational and societal) and understands power, not as accorded by status, but as a type of relationship we have with others, which is intimately linked with knowledge. Walsham demonstrates that this understanding is more useful in the analysis because relationships are more dynamic and variable than status. As an example, to which we refer below, Walsham (2001:91) comments on how a plotter engineer did not use the IS provided by his company, saying 'Gary was able to draw on his deep knowledge of plotters to leverage power over Comco'. Feminist thought also makes use of the notion of power, but as invested in the more static structure of gender. An example is given by Haraway (1991, p. 196), who views rational knowledge as 'power-sensitive conversation'.

In relation to IS, the notion of emancipation (or empowerment) leads to 'emancipatory information systems development' (EISD) (Hirschheim & Klein, 1994), to 'participatory design' (Berg, 1998) and to emancipation as a major driver of management, including organizational use of IS (Alvesson & Willmott, 1992). One concern is how the development and use of IS entrench social structures that oppress people. The notion was first applied to IT workers of the 1970s and (Ulrich, 1994) to those who are affected by IT without their having any input. More recently, for example, Ngwenyama and Lee (1997) have applied it to email, and Cordoba and Midgley (2003) have applied it to IS planning. Conversely, IS (including the Internet) can be hailed as a means to emancipation. This contrasts with hard systems thinking, in which IS is seen as a means to efficiency or control, and with soft systems thinking, in which IS is a means to self-expression or self-fulfilment. Furthermore, the notion of emancipation (in which we will include power, unless otherwise stated) exhibits problems and perhaps has proved less useful in practice than had been hoped. Several reasons can be adduced for this.

The first reason is that the focus of early emancipation-oriented IS research on workers oppressed by large, centralized IT is of diminishing interest today. Since the 1980s other issues have become much more significant in the use of IS, partly because of the advent of the personal computer, the home computer and applications like computer games, music, art or social networking. While emancipation might be useful in considering organizational IS, it is less useful for these other types of computing. There is a diversity of types of IS application for which the notion of emancipation has little meaning. Likewise, there is a diversity of IS problems that cannot reasonably be treated as emancipation, such as ease of use, affordance, learnability, attractiveness, accessibility or benefits in use. To do so, rather stretches the meaning of 'emancipation' too far. We need a critical approach that, in itself, admits a variety of problems and applications.

A second reason is that emancipation tends to focus on the negative, on the 'evils' from which we should be delivered, rather than on the positive, on 'good' already in the situation or that which IS might be able to bring. Though it could be argued that such 'good' may be treated as emancipation from constraints, this rather distorts the experience of computer users, especially when considering new possibilities. For example, in using a paint package to construct an icon, I do not feel *emancipated* from the inability to construct icons, so much as *enabled* to use the new ways to construct them.

A third reason is perhaps deeper than these two: emancipation lacks useful definition, relying instead on an intuition of its meaning being shared by us all. Emancipation has become almost synonymous with 'avoidance of problem', becoming a generic super-norm, a general 'good' over against a general 'evil'. As such, hardly ever is it questioned or its nature explored, so it gives no hint as to what might be considered 'evil'. From what should we expect to be emancipated? What means can we use? How do we recognize the need for emancipation? How do we know when it has been achieved? To none of these practical questions is a good answer forthcoming. Many books of a critical approach fail to include emancipation in their indices. It is taken for granted. A notable exception is Ulrich (1994), where we find 23 index entries, as well as a number of indirect references. He lists eight things from which we might be emancipated, but gives no basis for selecting them, nor does he discuss the other questions. Perhaps a definition of emancipation might be found in Habermas (1972), to which he frequently refers as introducing the idea of emancipatory interest. When we turn to Habermas (1972), we find no index entry of emancipation, and, again, its meaning is assumed rather than explained. So we must discuss briefly here what emancipation is and how it might be applied.

In some cases, what emancipation means is reasonably clear and its importance as a norm is uncontentious; for example, an over-weening management, which demands that employees sacrifice their home and family life for the organization. In many other cases, it is far from clear. It could be defined as 'freedom from unwarranted constraints'. This definition seems initially useful to us in that IS are very good at embodying constraints (e.g. as If–Then rules) or facilities that help users overcome constraints. However, this merely shifts the need for clear understanding to three other concepts: 'freedom', 'unwarranted' and 'constraint'. The fact that something is a constraint does not necessarily imply freedom should be sought. For instance, gravity is a constraint, but since we can do nothing about it, we tend to accept it, and often use it to our advantage. One might reply that 'nature' is to be excluded, and that the emancipatory paradigm only applies in human social situations. Even here these notions are less than helpful because there are many human 'constraints' that we might find arduous, and yet are good. In writing managerial reports or writing poetry, for example, we might be expected to use a certain style of writing. Should we be emancipated from the demand for such a style of writing; is this an unwarranted constraint?

Perhaps emancipation should be restricted to issues that are more important than language style (though workers' strikes have been called for less), such as issues of justice? Unfortunately, we then meet another problem; that one person's constraint is another person's justice. For example, the norm of justice to workers in the two-third world is a constraint on our purchasing of goods ('fair trade'), the norm of justice to future generations calls us to radically change our (Western) lifestyles so as to curb climate change, and the norm of justice to animals suggests that we should not allow more experiments on animals for cosmetics. When are such constraints warranted and when unwarranted?

These examples illustrate a number of things, which we also find in our everyday experience. One is that it seems necessary to recognize there are fundamentally distinct types of warrant or constraint and we should respond differently to each. If it is to be useful, the notion of emancipation must be enriched, to acknowledge different types of warrant, constraint and freedom. Emancipation can no longer be assumed to be a single, undifferentiated norm. Another is that constraint and freedom are intertwined. Constraints on us might be required by the freedom of others, and our freedom might impose constraints on them. As Alvesson & Willmott, 1992Alvesson and Willmott (1992:448) put it, 'Critique and liberation from old dogmas is then followed by new dogmas'. The relationship between constraint and freedom can become more nuanced than this, however. The attempt at emancipation from one 'evil' might also lead to losing a 'good': 'women emancipating themselves from dominant socialization patterns and gender roles may reduce their interest in, and capacity for, caring' (p. 447). If we assume that constraint and freedom are mutually exclu-sive of each other, then we end up with paradoxes of this kind.

Wilson (1997) discusses one particular paradox within EISD at greater length; what might be called the paradox of 'enforced emancipation'. His argument is that though we are supposed to be emancipated from positions that constrain us, to judge whether a system is emancipatory or not presupposes a position from which to make such judgements. He asks (p. 15)

> 'How do the proponents of EISD know that what they urge is in the service of all mankind and not merely a function that they themselves happen, at the moment, to desire?'

He points out (p. 20) that:

> 'the use of facilitators to ensure "that everyone contributes and is listened to" takes on slightly menacing overtones when it is suggested that their deployment of "emancipatory methodology" will be used to overcome "wilful unresponsiveness by an individual"'

It may be that the notion of empowerment is less afflicted by this paradox than is emancipation. It does exhibit its own problems; however, like most lenses, the power lens tends to determine what we see and often makes us blind to factors not explainable in its own terms. That it can distort analysis and misrepresent a situation is illustrated in Walsham's (2001) study of the plotter engineer, Gary, mentioned earlier, as 'leverage[ing] power over' his company. However, if we examine Walsham's actual report of Gary's working (p. 68–9), we find no hint of power leverage. Instead, we find someone who believes in the company, feels closely associated with it, and defends it. Gary is willing to go beyond the call of duty by, for example, keeping his own stock of spare parts and his own log book instead of relying on the IS because he wants to give a good service to the customers. Gary's generosity is 'reinterpreted' by the lens of power as its very opposite, self-interest. It is not uncommon to find blindness to generosity and self-giving love in power-centred literature. For a more de-tailed discussion of Walsham's approach, see Basden (2008). A similar blind-ness to these aspects may also be found in some feminist literature that likewise focuses on power relations, such as those that sought emancipation from male hegemony or sought empowerment for women during the 1970s to 1990s.

However, a more nuanced version of power-centred critical approaches, including feminism, seems to have emerged around the turn of the century. Walsham (2001) himself recognizes that other conceptual tools are needed, and cites Knights and McCabe as finding that those affected are not so concerned with an issue of power so much as maintaining professional self-identity. The feminist writer, Adam (1998), argues for a more sophisticated form, eco-fem-inism, which seeks to restore the aspects of reality that have been overlooked by 'masculine' assumptions when technology was developed, rather than focusing on emancipation or power. Artificial intelligence in particular, has been devel-oped according to masculine assumptions of the supremacy of logic and mind over intuition and body. In her conclusion (p. 180) she says, 'The way that a number of aspects of knowing are not reducible to propositional knowledge, but rely instead on some notion of embodied skill, points to the role of the body in the making of knowledge'. We will return to these more nuanced versions later. First, we will consider the root of the above problems in emancipation and power.

3.3 THE ROOT OF THE PROBLEM: DUALISTIC GROUND-MOTIVES

The problems with emancipation and power may be seen as arising from a deeper presupposition. Eriksson (2006) argues that the three main systems thinking approaches, hard, soft and critical are all expressions of a deep presupposition known as the nature-freedom ground-motive (NFGM). 'Ground-motive' denotes a 'spiritual driving force that acts as the absolutely central mainspring of human society' (Dooyeweerd, 1979:9). A ground-motive governs thinking in society for centuries about the nature of reality (what constitutes it), diversity (what types there are), normativity (what is 'good' and 'evil') and how to obtain the 'good' (how to solve problems and what is ethical conduct). Dooyeweerd discussed four main ground-motives, the form-matter motive, (which governed the thinking of the ancient Greeks), the creation-fall-redemption motive, (which governed that of the Hebrews and early Christians), the nature-grace motive, (which emerged as a synthesis of these and governed the thinking of mediaeval Europe, especially Scholaticism and Roman Catholic thought), and the nature-freedom motive, (which has governed thinking from the Renaissance to this day). Habermas (2002) also recognizes the form-matter and creation-fall-redemption ground-motives under the names 'Athens' and 'Jerusalem'.

Three ground-motives, those of form-matter, nature-grace and nature-freedom, are dualistic in nature. Down the centuries when a dualistic ground-motive is in force, theoretical thought swings dialectically between the two poles. At any time in a given community of thought, one pole is seen as real and 'good' (to be sought), while the other is seen as unreal and 'evil' (to be avoided). The NFGM leads thought to assume a mutual antithesis between the principles of nature and freedom: that what is controlled or operates by deterministic laws cannot be free, and vice versa. Disciplines like management, politics and IS have experienced a swing from the nature pole (around 1970s) to the freedom pole (1990s). Though in everyday experience both freedom and control are interwoven, our theoretical thinking (via science, philosophy, etc.) presuppose either a determined cosmos, or one constructed by an absolutely free human ego, and have no way of truly integrating both[1]. The influence of NFGM may be seen in many of the common dualistic oppositions of today, such as nature–culture,

---

1. The stance known as critical realism claims to integrate constructed knowledge with reality, but raises other problems; we do not discuss it here.

fact–value, rationalist–irrationalist, science–humanities, modernism–post-modernism, positivism–interpretivism etc. Thought influenced by one pole finds thought influenced by the opposing pole meaningless or inferior, as exemplified, perhaps, by the attitudes of each of positivist and interpretivist researchers, respectively.

Eriksson argued that hard systems thinking is centred on the nature pole (systems are objectively 'out there' and the aim of hard systems thinking is to control), and soft systems thinking is centred on the freedom pole (systems are a matter of subjective interpretation, and the aim of soft systems thinking is to free up interpretations). The critical approach attempts to embrace both poles (systems are socially constructed but, transcending this, they impact on people and are subject to the norm of emancipation). Laws that transcend our freedom (such that they govern us whether we recognize them or not) have traditionally been recognized only in pre-human nature (physics, biology), and, thus, the notion of something that transcends us has strong connotations of the nature pole of NFGM. Emancipation is, therefore, interesting: the word itself suggests the freedom pole, but that it transcends us suggests the nature pole. This is the root of the paradox.

Dooyeweerd (1984), on which Eriksson based his thought, argued that the dualistic ground-motives of Western thought (like that of nature-freedom) are deeply problematic and will always end in such paradoxes, since they force apart two aspects which, in reality, are intertwined (especially as experienced in everyday life). Dualistic ground-motives hide, rather than reveal, the structure of reality, including normative reality. To understand everyday experience requires a way of understanding that can embrace both poles of each dualistic ground-motive, but this cannot be done by any approach that is within the confines of the ground-motive because it pre-supposes an absolute antithesis between them. A dualistic ground-motive forces our attempts at understanding to focus on one of its poles or the other. If we attempt integration, we will be found initially to generate an antinomy, such as 'enforced emancipation' (Wilson, 1997), which can only be resolved by eventually moving to one pole or the other. Marxism gave priority to the nature pole of NFGM; Frankfurt-School critical thought gives priority to the freedom pole.

Dualistic ground-motives are also problematic in the sense of hindering critical thought, in that both poles and also their presumed opposition are taken for granted and not examined. We noted earlier that precisely this has happened with emancipation. Since freedom and constraint are seen as aligned with opposing poles, there has been little attempt to seek to understand the different types of constraint or freedom. '(Un)warranted' is largely meaningless under both poles of the NFGM because, under the nature pole, it is reduced to a mere label for deterministic processes and, under the freedom pole, it is a label for value-judgements. The reason it appears in the definition of emancipation is because we already have an intuition of what it means, outwith the confines of the NFGM. 'Warranted' speaks of 'due', of doing justice to something, but neither the nature nor the freedom poles offer a sound basis for recognizing this. To summarize,

- We need to expand the critical approach so that it acknowledges the 'good' as well as criticizes the 'evil'.
- We need a way of revealing more clearly the nature of emancipation, as diverse and as being relevant to twenty-first century applications of IS.
- We need an understanding of reality that allows both freedom and constraint or control, which can resolve paradoxes like 'enforced emancipation'.
- We need a way of acknowledging power that does not obliterate other aspects like generosity.

To make further progress, it requires moving to a non-dualistic ground-motive, and this is discussed later.

3.4 CONTRIBUTION FROM HABERMAS: COMMUNICATIVE ACTION

A second critical perspective, centred on communication, has become important over the last two decades, based on the thought of Habermas. Habermas, while initially emphasizing emancipation (1972), re-focused on communicative action as the deeper and more important issue (1984, 1987). Communicative action is a rational social activity that seeks mutual understanding between people via open dialogue. Habermas contrasted it, especially, with instrumental action, which seeks to control others and closes down dialogue. Open (or 'ideal') dialogue involves discussion and critique both of the content of what is said, by processes of argumentation, and of its claims to validity (which Habermas classified as intelligibility, propositional truth, sincerity and social and moral appropriateness). The force of the better argument should always win, so rationality is an integral part of communicative action. Various things distort open communication, including lack of information, subjective bias, unwarranted assumptions, conflicts of interest, power relations or unjust social conditions. The ideal, therefore, is communication that is free of all such distortions. This is a counterfactual ideal, though Habermas holds it up as a useful aspiration.

In Habermas' theory of communicative action (TCA), ideal dialogue replaces emancipation as the major norm. It has close links with emancipation, in that it is believed to lead to emancipation from oppressive conditions because it enables all participants to express their views without distortion, and it, itself, is emancipated from distortions by a critique of validity claims.

'Communicative action' says Habermas (1987:120) 'relies on a cooperative process of interpretation in which participants relate simultaneously to something in the objective, the social, and the subjective worlds'. In this cooperative process, participants draw upon 'a reservoir of taken-for-granteds, of unshaken convictions' (1987:124), which Habermas calls the lifeworld, a concept he adapted from Schutz & Luckmann, 1973Schutz and Luckman (1973), who, in turn, adapted Husserl's (1970) concept of 'Life-world'. The lifeworld was, to Habermas, a mysterious thing that dissolves as soon as we try to take it up with our thinking (Ray, 1993). We can think and talk about things in the three 'worlds' of objective things, inner feelings and social/moral norms because we direct ourselves towards them from the outside, as it were, but our relationship with the lifeworld is that we orientate ourselves within it (Habermas, 1987:126). The lifeworld is a stock of shared understandings that includes meanings and norms.

Habermas believed that TCA explains how modern life retains both meaning and norms despite operating by means of mechanical rules. Normativity in TCA is complex. Habermas argued that meanings and norms guide communicative action and also emerge intersubjectively from critique of validity claims. Normativity is, therefore, not ignored, as in the hard approach, nor reduced to subjective values, as in the soft approach. At first sight, TCA admits of no transcending normativity, of the kind that emancipation was in the earlier critical approach, in that all norms emerge by the processes of communicative action. A closer examination reveals, however, that there is a transcending normativity, a deeper norm which pertains, regardless of what actually emerges from communicative action. This is the norm of communicative rationality or ideal dialogue, the norm of sound argumentation and critique of validity claims.

Habermas' TCA has obvious relevance to IS and has been applied both directly and indirectly. It is used directly, for example, by Lyytinen and Klein (1985) to form a theory of IS, and by Heng and de Moor (2003) for understanding and evaluating practice on the Internet, on the grounds that Internet use might be seen as discourse. It is used indirectly via the Language Action Perspective (Goldkuhl & Lyytinen, 1982, Weigand, 2006), which incorporates Habermas' ideas. The Language Action Pespective has found use in analyzing and modelling business processes and business conversations, such as that between supplier and customer (Denning & Dunham, 2006; Goldkuhl, 2006), and in making a proposal for new research directions in data and knowledge engineering and natural language processing (Basden & Klein, 2008). There are problems in using TCA, however, which will be discussed in order of increasing depth.

One problem is whether ideal dialogue (to the extent that it is feasible) will, in practice, lead to emancipation from oppressive conditions, as has been assumed and occasionally argued in some of the literature surrounding TCA. This belief rests on the assumption that language (as employed in argument) is sufficient to capture all meaning in life perfectly and fully. This assumption may be questioned, even in the ideal, and comes about as a result of the following problems, which concern the notion of ideal dialogue.

In proposing that all issues may be resolved (in principle) by rational argument, where the 'better argument' will prevail, it depends on there being a single universal type of rationality. But Winch (1958) argued for multiple rationalities. 'In science, for example', suggested Winch (1958), 'it would be illogical to refuse to be bound by the results of a properly carried out experiment; in religion it would be illogical to suppose that one could pit one's strength against God's'. He went on to argue that the rationality of the social sciences is unlike that of the physical. Practical life turns up many examples of different rationalities, for example, when financial indicators suggest one course of action, while legal or moral reasons suggest another. While we can expect seamless reasoning within a rationality, we cannot do so between different rationalities. Any attempt to argue from one to the other involves category errors. In decision-making, when a choice must be made between them, that choice is supra-rational. There is no 'higher' rationality that tells us which type of rationality should prevail over the other. This means that TCA's notion of the 'better argument' prevailing is inadequate[2]. While it might help prepare the ground *within* each rationality, it cannot ultimately help us make choices *between* rationalities. TCA's call for openness of dialogue must be reinterpreted to include supra-rational choice between rationalities. The hidden prejudices or presuppositions that distort communicative action are not always a problem of rationality but can be a denial of other virtues like honesty and goodwill.

This leads to another problem. The focus on communicative rationality fails to recognize that it is frequently very difficult to express what is relevant to the situation being experienced. On the one hand, much knowledge is tacit, and on the other, some people are less able to express their views and thoughts than the others (for example, because of Asperger's Syndrome). So, TCA-based proposals that we should aim to improve expression of relevant ideas and views in open dialogue, merely favours the already-articulate and that which is easily expressed in words. However, there are some types of social activity in which argument or critique of validity claims as such is not appropriate. Most attempts at applying TCA have been in business decision support, where rational communication is presumed to be central. Recently, Internet applications relying on other types of social activity have burgeoned, such as social networking, social virtual worlds and computer games. Users of applications like Facebook 'poke' each other or send 'growing things' and 'snowglobes' to each other for fun, not to make business decisions. Though this might be described as communication, it is not governed by rationality (not even of multiple types). It is for the purpose of enjoyment and fun, not to enhance mutual understanding (communicative rationality), nor even to control (instrumental rationality). The same applies to computer games and social virtual worlds, and many applications outside the professional arena. Even within the professional arena there are many

---

2. Habermas [1984:53-67] does recognise the importance of this question and discusses Winch, but, arguably, the outcome of his discussion is flawed. In the end, claiming that Winch's argument was too weak, he reduced the number of types of rationality that he would discuss to two, namely instrumental and communicative rationality. He apparently resolved the problem of which type of rationality should prevail (communicative), but did so on the basis of the dogma that communicative rationality is superior. That he gathered reasons to support this dogma does not remove its status as dogma, because the reasons were largely provided by communicative rationality itself.

applications in which communicative action is not primary, such as physical simulations, mathematical calculations, route-finding software and computer music and paint packages. Recognition that critical researchers should look beyond professional applications is also reflected in Fraser's (1989) feminist critique of Habermas, cited by Ray (1993:68). Fraser emphasizes the household. That we should also look beyond the communicative aspect is echoed in her emphasis that women's unpaid child-rearing is a 'dual aspect activity' that involves a 'material' aspect and cannot and should not be reduced to the single communicative aspect.

3.5 ROOT OF THE PROBLEMS IN TCA: REDUCTION

The root of most of these problems may be traced to a tendency to reduce all aspects of life to a logical-communicative aspect, though the NFGM discussed above also plays some part. Reduction can take several forms, including methodological reduction, in which we narrow our focus in order to simplify research, and value reduction, in which only a limited range of aspects has importance for us. These are usually unobjectionable, as long as they are not taken too far and we are always aware of other aspects outside our focus. However, there are types of reduction which Clouser (2005) argues are objectionable, not only in their practical consequences but also philosophically. He identifies four main types; two strong and two weak. The weak reduction that Clouser calls 'causal dependency' pervades much of Habermas' TCA. Clouser explains (2005:359):

> '*Causal dependency.* The nature of reality is basically that of aspect X (or of aspects X and Y). It is the Xness of things which make possible the other kinds of properties and laws true of them. So while other aspects are real and can be proper objects of scientific investigation, there is a one-way causal dependency between the non-X aspects and aspect X. The non-X aspects could not exist without X, while X could exist without the others'.

The X aspect to which TCA reduces others is the logical-communicative aspect. Most kinds of social action are made possible by X (Habermas, 1991 explicitly reduces at least dramaturgical and normatively regulated action types to the communicative). The entire lifeworld (with its diverse types of meaning and normativity) could not exist without X. Though Habermas does not go to the extreme in reduction, TCA does exhibit a tendency to reduction. We will first look at the extreme version and then draw back from it.

Clouser's argument that reduction is objectionable is both philosophical and practical. It is objectionable philosophically because reduction is self-performatively inconsistent, by which Clouser (2005:85) means:

> 'a theory must be compatible with any state that would have to be true of a thinker, or any activity the thinker would have to perform, in order to have formulated the theory's claims'.

This means that to formulate TCA as a theory of social action, Habermas (or any other thinker) would necessarily function in aspects that cannot be reduced to the logical-communicative in the way assumed possible under TCA. By 'aspects' Clouser is referring to basic kinds of properties or laws that we experience and function in pre-theoretically, among which he includes such things as faith, justice, morals and aesthetics, as well as logicality and communication[3]. According to Clouser, this criterion for theories is relatively new, having been first defined and deployed by Dooyeweerd about 50 years ago, but since then advocated independently by other thinkers, such as Foucault. Clouser's argument that reduction is self-performatively inconsistent (2005:192 ff) is complex and need not be rehearsed here.

What concerns us more is that reduction is objectionable in practice. Clouser explains (2005:187) 'it lowers the status of all other aspects by making them products of, and thus less real than, the aspect(s) it favours'. This is what has led to some of the problems identified above. For instance, a problem arises from TCA assuming that logical-communicative dialogue should normally be central, and that other types are either negative (for example, instrumental action) or need not be given the same amount of attention as communicative action. In Clouser's terms, those types of action are 'less real'. As was seen above, each aspect defines a distinct type of rationality. That TCA has difficulty in recognizing types of rationality other than the logical-communicative (and the instrumental, which it treats as deficient) is explainable by causal dependency reduction, in that it assumes that the other rationalities arise from its favoured one.

Clouser can take us further, to address some of the other problems above. He argues that reduction, when taken to an extreme, accords a status of absolute self-dependence to the favoured aspect (he uses the term 'divinity' to denote this). This is what leads to the assumption lurking at the root of the notion of ideal dialogue, that language use is, in principle, able to capture all meanings, leaving nothing tacit and that, as a result, all emancipation will be overcome by rational dialogue. Clouser (2005) and Dooyeweerd (1984) claim that this is a false assumption.

However, Habermas does not go to the extreme in reduction, in that he recognizes instrumental action as distinct from communicative action, and he recognizes that there are some things that cannot be couched in dialogue: the 'stock of taken-for-granteds' that is the lifeworld. His recognition of instrumental reason as a distinct aspect is, however, only partial. In seeing it as an 'evil' that distorts communicative action, it is, thus, defined mainly in relation to communicative action, rather than as a truly distinct aspect. One might also detect the influence of the modern ground-motive of nature-freedom here, which opposes control (instrumental action) and freedom (from distortions resulting from instrumental action). Though Habermas recognized the tacit nature of the

---

3. For example, one can detect in Habermas' writing about TCA (1984, 1987) a strong vision for, and an almost aesthetic delight in, its ability to account for many things in human and social life and to resolve problems left by previous thinkers.

lifeworld, this sits uneasily with the notion of ideal dialogue, because if we cannot talk about the contents of the lifeworld, there is much that is omitted from our dialogue and, hence, it is no longer ideal. TCA offers no way to allow the contents of the lifeworld, including its diverse meaning and normativity, into our dialogue without distorting them.

To summarize,

- We need to counteract reductionist tendencies in TCA, so that it can give due regard to the non-rational types of action in which communication might occur but is not of primary importance.
- Especially, we need to recognize multiple rationalities and provide a way to facilitate supra-rational openness, such as involving honesty and goodwill.
- We need a way to give due respect to difficulties in expressing thoughts and meanings while not abandoning rational dialogue.
- We need a way to be able to bring the contents of the lifeworld into dialogue in a way that does not overly distort them.

A basis for meeting these requirements, as well as those of the emancipatory approach, may be found in the thought of Dooyeweerd.

3.6 THE CONTRIBUTION OF DOOYEWEERD: ENRICHING THE CRITICAL APPROACH

Dooyeweerd's major work, *A New Critique of Theoretical Thought* (Dooyeweerd, 1984), first published as four volumes in 1953–1955, shows Dooyeweerd to be both a critical and a positive philosopher. He both deconstructed Western philosophy and then accepted the challenge of constructing something that could itself be criticized. The latter, known as Cosmonomic Philosophy or Philosophy of the Law-Idea, should not be seen as a wholesale replacement for Western philosophy but as a means of reforming it. Here we will review a little of Dooyeweerd's critical approach, before briefly looking at sufficient of his positive proposals to allow us to address the problems above. A fuller explanation is available in Basden (2008) or Clouser (2005), and a critical discussion of how Dooyeweerd's thought 're-integrates' social theory, is available in Strauss (2006).

Dooyeweerd contended that we cannot start, in philosophy, by presupposing the possibility of taking a theoretical or critical attitude of thought, but must first establish what makes it possible. An extensive immanent critique of 2500 years of theoretical thinking revealed that it is never neutral because what we take to be 'theoretical' is itself determined by our religious presuppositions. By 'religious' Dooyeweerd meant an ultimate commitment about the nature of reality, of 'good' and 'evil', and of knowledge. The NFGM, mentioned earlier, is one such religious presupposition, which makes the antithesis between freedom and control absolute, with the result of shielding both from critical examination. In Dooyeweerd, such polar antitheses are questioned and he allows us to probe the nature of freedom and control. This can overcome the paradoxes inherent in the emancipatory critical approach.

Dooyeweerd held that all theoretical thinking, including his own, rests on presuppositions[4]. Rather than seeking presupposition-less thought, we should make our presuppositions explicit. He made his own clear: the creation-fall-redemption (CFR) ground-motive. His positive philosophy might be seen as a philosophical (not theological) exploration of what follows if we presuppose the cosmos is created. This is not a return to the dominance of the religious over the secular, as occurred under the mediaeval nature-grace ground-motive, but an exploration of implications for philosophy. Presupposing CFR enabled Dooyeweerd to tackle diversity and coherence and to begin with the lifeworld. (See Basden (2008) for a detailed discussion of this.)

So, at the very start of Dooyeweerd's *New Critique*, we find, 'If I consider reality as it is given in the naive pre-theoretical experience ...' (1984,I:3). He invites his readers to do likewise, to adopt a pre-theoretical rather than theoretical attitude of thought. In the theoretical or critical attitude, we 'stand over against' some aspect of reality (Dooyeweerd used the term '*Gegenstand*'), whereas in the pre-theoretical attitude, we engage with all the aspects instead of standing over against them. In the theoretical attitude, the chosen aspect becomes, to us, a distinct 'world' seen, as Habermas would say, from the 'outside'. Habermas' three 'worlds' (objective, social, subjective) might correspond approximately to three aspects of reality which Dooyeweerd delineated (see the analytical, social, psychic aspects below). In the pre-theoretical attitude, we are usually unaware of the aspects—echoing Habermas' notion of being 'inside' the lifeworld. A pre-theoretical attitude to reality accommodates all the aspects thereof, whereas a theoretical attitude separates aspects from each other conceptually. The aspects resist such separation, however, because each is inextricably intertwined with the others, so that what theoretical thought delivers must never be treated as 'truth'. It was, perhaps, this resistance that Habermas observed, when he said that the lifeworld 'dissolves' when we try to think about it. Dooyeweerd never used the term 'lifeworld', but it is equivalent to his notion of pre-theoretical attitude of thought.

The notion of aspects is not unique to Dooyeweerd as we have already seen in Adam (1998) Habermas also uses the term (1987:126): '...singles out above two aspects of ...the teleological aspect...the communicative aspect...'. Most thinkers speak of aspects when they want to make distinctions among things that cannot be reduced to each other. Thinking aspectually is so natural that we usually take it for granted. Dooyeweerd, however, addressed the nature of aspects, their intertwinement and the possibility of separating them out conceptually without undue distortion. He was convinced that the aspects are not mere categories, but

---

4. Dooyeweerd's notion of ground-motives is a level deeper than Habermas' [1972] notion of knowledge-constitutive interests, which are more equivalent to Dooyeweerd's notion of aspectual world-views.

have a modal character, as spheres of meaning and law. This enabled him (and us) to do what Habermas was hindered in doing; namely to probe the contents of the lifeworld in such a way that it does not dissolve in the process. The challenge is to determine what different types of meaning and law there might be. This cannot be achieved by theoretical thought alone because the *Gegenstand* relationship prevents us experiencing the lifeworld from the inside. However, the kernel meaning of each aspect may be grasped with the intuition in a way that does not involve theoretical thought[5]. This can help us distinguish the types of meaning we encounter in everyday life. For example, we might be aware of justice or frugality (see the list below) as we engage in life. Once this has occurred, theoretical thought can be employed to make various checks; for example, for possible antinomy. From a lifetime of sensitive reflection (together with some theoretically based checks, described in Basden, 2008), Dooyeweerd delineated fifteen such aspects:

- Quantitative aspect, in which amount and quantity are meaningful
- Spatial aspect, in which continuous extension and space are meaningful
- Kinematic aspect, in which flowing movement is meaningful
- Physical aspect, in which energy, matter, forces are meaningful
- Biotic aspect, in which life functions are meaningful
- Sensitive aspect, in which feeling and response are meaningful
- Analytical aspect, in which distinction is meaningful
- Formative aspect, in which creative power, instrumentality and technology are meaningful
- Lingual aspect, in which symbolic signification is meaningful
- Social aspect, in which social interaction and structures are meaningful
- Economic aspect, in which frugal management of resources is meaningful
- Aesthetic aspect, in which harmony, delight, fun are meaningful
- Juridical aspect, in which what is due (rights, responsibilities) is meaningful
- Ethical aspect, in which self-giving love is meaningful
- Pistic aspect, in which faith, vision, commitment are meaningful.

Each aspect is irreducible to all the others in respect of its meaning. So, to speak of self-giving love seems 'meaningless' when thinking economics or mathematics, and vice versa. However, all aspects are equally important in principle, so one cannot say that the meaning of one aspect has a priori priority over that of another, nor can any be set aside. Because of this, analysis should normally consider every aspect. Analysis that ignores an aspect distorts our view. Aspectual analysis is a key to defending ourselves against reductionist tendencies.

---

5. Basden and Klein [2008] suggest the lifeworld might be composed of two types of shared background understanding, of which intuition of aspectual meaning is one. It is a shared understanding of what Dooyeweerd called the law side. In addition to this, we possess a shared background understanding of actual things and happenings, which are subject to the law side, which Basden and Klein (2008) call subject-side intuition. Law-side intuition is trans-cultural, but is sometimes obscured by subject-side intuition, which is culture-dependent.

The laws of the earlier aspects (e.g. physical law of gravity) are determinative while those of the later aspects (e.g. lingual laws concerning syntax, semantics, pragmatics) are non-determinative in that they allow some freedom. The laws are normative, providing guidance for what is 'good' in the widest sense (for example, aspectual law is not an authoritarian command – 'Do X, or else!' – so much as a promise – ' If you do X, then Y will tend to result'). In this way, freedom is consistent with the idea of transcendental normativity, as required by the critical approach. Aspectual normativity must not be confused with social norms; the latter are socially constructed, while the former pertain regardless of us and, though we might be able to go against them, we cannot escape the repercussions of doing so. Thus, the syntactic laws of any actual language are socially constructed, but their very existence reflects the aspectual law that syntax is important and beneficial.

As spheres of law, the aspects provide a suite of basic types of 'good' and 'evil' that are irreducibly distinct, defining what is 'warranted' or 'unwarranted'. That which is in line with the norms of an aspect is warranted from the point of view of that aspect. Table 3.1 gives examples of this for each aspect. (Note that in

TABLE 3.1 Aspectual Good and Evil

Aspect	Good ('Warranted')	Evil ('Unwarranted')
Quantitative	Numeric order, precision	(determinative)
Spatial	Simultaneity, extension	(determinative)
Kinematic	Movement, duration, change	(determinative)
Physical	Persistence, causality, unity of whole cosmos	(determinative)
Biotic/Organic	Health, vitality, thriving	Disease, death
Psychic/Sensitive	Sensitivity, responsiveness, recognition, memory	Insensitivity, inability to respond, sensory deprivation, forgetting
Analytic	Clarity, non-contradiction	Obfuscation, false reasoning, inconsistency
Formative	Achievement, planning, construction, structure	Laziness, confused plans, destruction, messiness
Lingual	Understandability, expression of meaning	Poor pragmatics, semantics, syntax, lexics, etc.
Social	Respect, friendliness	Disrespect, enmity
Economic	Frugality, management, prosperity	Waste, excess, mismanagement, poverty
Aesthetic	Harmony, interest, surprise, fun, playfulness, leisure	Uniformness, boredom, over-seriousness, over-work
Juridical	Justice, responsibility	Injustice, irresponsibility
Ethical	Generosity, self-giving	Selfishness, self-interest
Pistic/Faith	Vision, faithfulness, commitment	Low morale, disloyalty, refusal to commit, hidden agendas

the most determinative aspects 'evil' is not possible since it is impossible to go against their laws.)

This can give crisp, diverse meaning to 'emancipation'. When seen as freedom from unwarranted constraints, full emancipation occurs when the only constraints we experience are warranted in every aspect. In any concrete situation the constraints upon us might be warranted within one aspect (e.g. the economic) but unwarranted in another (e.g. the juridical). So emancipation becomes, not freedom from constraints in general, but modification of the aspectual structure of constraints such that they become warranted in all their aspects. This helps us, in practical situations, decide which constraints we can accept, and which we cannot accept. This view also provides a basis for analysis by which we can recognize the 'good' in the situation, so as not to jeopardize it.

Is this possible in principle or might some aspects inherently work against others (e.g., will being ethical always, inherently, jeopardize prosperity)? Van der Kooy (1974, p. 40–41) argued that simultaneous realization of norms (of every aspect) is possible in principle because there is no inherent conflict between norms of different aspects if one presupposes the creation-fall-redemption ground-motive. This gives a hope and vision to aim for in IS development. It does not preclude, however, conflict between concrete (socially constructed) norms, such as the requirement mentioned earlier, of a certain writing style for reports.

The paradox of enforced emancipation as Wilson (1997) introduced, at first sight seems to be a clash between freedom and control (as seen under the NFGM). Yet does not *all* application of emancipation to others involve some control? All attempts at emancipation could, therefore, be deemed 'enforced'. Such a view is untenable. So we need a better basis for differentiating between invalid and valid emancipation. This may be provided by reflecting that, in this context, 'enforced' is not merely formative functioning, but involves at least an attitude that transgresses the norms of the ethical aspect; namely, unconcern for the other.

To the power-oriented critical approach, Dooyeweerd can offer both affirmation and critique. By asking which aspects are most important in power, we find the formative aspect (control), then the juridical (concern that rights are being suppressed by such control and should be reclaimed by gaining control), and then some of the pistic (in its link with identity (Walsham, 2001)). This reveals that power ignores certain aspects, such as the ethical aspect of self-giving which, as mentioned earlier, is distorted into its opposite when viewed through the lens of power. The utility of Dooyeweerd's suite of aspects is that it can act as a multiple lens, making every aspect visible and precluding unnecessary distortions. It is especially useful in conjunction with (eco-)feminism to reinstate aspects overlooked by a 'masculine' worldview (see Basden, 2008).

Now we can turn to communicative action. As a sphere of meaning, each aspect defines a distinct way in which things can 'make sense', or not—a distinct type of rationality. Aspectual irreducibility explains why the rationality of one aspect is irreducible to that of another. The two types differentiated in our earlier quotation from Winch (1958) are the physical and pistic rationalities.

Instrumental and communicative rationalities, as differentiated by Habermas (1984), may now be seen as those of the formative and lingual aspects. In this way, Dooyeweerd already recognizes multiple rationalities and challenges us to find supra-rational ways to bring rationalities together in the situations of dialogue that we face. Ultimately, Dooyeweerd argues such decisions have religious roots (in the sense of ultimate commitments), and it is good if these religious roots can be laid bare.

The aspects can assist us towards open dialogue among multiple aspects in three ways. Firstly, aspectual analysis of situations provides a basis for disentangling distinct basic kinds of meaning. Secondly, it was suggested earlier that open dialogue involves virtues other than rationality, such as honesty and goodwill; these can now be seen as 'good' in aspects other than the analytic. Thirdly, some distortions of dialogue arise from undue commitment to one aspect at the expense of others. Analysis of which aspects people think are important can expose this.

This has practical relevance for IS, because it would suggest that if an IS funnels its users' thinking down one path of reasoning, however good, then it provides a disservice rather than a service. In the case of an Electronic Placement System for insurance (Walsham, 2001), usage of the system remained low for many years because of its focus on the economic aspect, which overlooked what was more important in insurance trading; namely, the pistic aspect of "Utmost Good Faith". This was despite offering benefits in terms of communication (lingual aspect) and time-savings (economic).

Human activity is multi-aspectual insofar as it involves functioning in all aspects, but in many human actions one aspect is more important than others (the 'qualifying' aspect). This can open up Habermas' notion of action types approximately as follows:

- instrumental action: qualified by formative aspect
- communicative action: qualified by lingual aspect, with strong analytical flavour
- strategic action: qualified by social aspect, with strong formative flavour
- dramaturgical action: qualified by aesthetic aspect
- normatively regulated action: qualified by juridical aspect.

Since aspects are fundamentally irreducible to each other and all are of equal importance, if this view is valid, then all action types are of equal importance in human life, and it can help TCA avoid reductionistic tendencies. It can also suggest other action types not discussed by Habermas—such as ethical and faith-based action types.

That all human activity is multi-aspectual means we will find, for example, some lingual functioning (i.e. communicative action) in almost all activity. To call this communicative action, however, is misleading when the qualifying aspect is other than lingual. This makes it necessary to understand how aspects are intertwined in human activity. One type of inter-aspect relationship is dependency, and this can explain the apparent reduction of dramaturgical and normatively regulated action to communicative. Action in any aspect depends foundationally on action in earlier aspects, and also depends on later aspects to gain its full meaning (anticipatory dependency). Social action, for example, cannot occur without lingual, but, conversely, lingual action has very little meaning if it is not carried out to enable social action. Likewise, economic, aesthetic, juridical, ethical and faith-based action depends foundationally on social, and on lingual action[6]. Dramaturgical and normatively regulated actions (aesthetic and juridical) depend foundationally on communicative action. However, they are not reducible to it, because they involve other things that do not make sense in terms of the lingual or analytic aspects alone, such as surprise and retribution. Habermas did not differentiate foundational dependency from reduction in the way Dooyeweerd did.

Instrumental action is, under Dooyeweerd, not wholly negative, but has a valid place alongside communicative action. Habermas' insight that instrumental action distorts communicative action may be accounted for by the imposition by us of one aspectual norm (formative) on action that should be guided by another (lingual). It is not instrumentality as such that is the problem, but our attitude to it. Dooyeweerd's insight into this enables us to extend TCA to see as detrimental the imposition by us of *any* aspect on activity that should be guided by another. This frees us from imposing communicative action on all software design or use and allows us to recognize that Facebook 'pokes' are meaningful in the aesthetic aspect of fun, rather than the analytic aspect of argument or the formative aspect of control.

Dooyeweerd's thought can, therefore, account for some of the problems encountered in emancipatory and communicative critical approaches, as well as ameliorate the problems and enrich the approaches. How it does so is summarized in Table 3.2.

3.7 SITUATING THE CRITICAL APPROACH

As we noted earlier, Eriksson (2006) argues that hard and soft systems thinking express the nature and freedom poles of NFGM, and see themselves as opposing each other. Critical systems thinking tries to embrace both poles, but is ultimately unsuccessful in this and migrates to the freedom pole. This gives a picture of the three approaches being always incommensurable with each other. But is this correct? In good practice, we find elements of all three.

According to Dooyeweerd (1984, volume I) the opposition between nature (control) and freedom is false, when viewed from outwith NFGM. So the

---

6. Communicative action is more than simple lingual functioning. In saying, 'But communicative action designates a type of interaction that is *coordinated through* speech acts and does *not coincide with* them' Habermas [1984:101] may have been referring implicitly to what Dooyeweerd called inter-aspect dependency.

TABLE 3.2 How Dooyeweerd Enriches Critical Approaches

Issue in critical approach	Dooyeweerdian enrichment
Should acknowledge the 'good' as well as 'evil'	Aspects define types of good' as well as 'evil'
Nature of emancipation	Aspects provide diverse normativity
Paradoxes, e.g. enforced emancipation	Move away from nature-freedom ground-motive and consider ethical aspect of self-giving
Power-lens obliterates certain aspects	Give due regard to all aspects, especially that of self-giving
Reductionist tendencies in TCA	Recognize multi-aspectual nature of human action
Open dialogue with multiple rationalities	Each aspect defines distinct rationality; considering aspects ensures no aspect overlooked, and exposes hidden agendas
Problems in expressing ideas	Implicitly (not explicitly) addressed
Dialogue including contents of lifeworld	Intuitive grasp of aspectual meaning

presumed incommensurability between the approaches might also be false. If this is so, then on what basis may we differentiate between them? One answer is in terms of which aspects each deems important. Table 3.3 attempts to show this for each type of systems thinking. Hard approaches focus on the quantitative, analytic, formative and economic aspects, insofar as they try to quantify and conceptualize an objective reality and control it with reference to costs and benefits. Soft approaches focus on the sensitive, social and pistic, insofar as they pay attention to what participants feel, to their social roles and their *Weltanschauungen*. Critical approaches focus on the social, juridical and lingual aspects, insofar as they recognize the social and societal element of IS, and either promote emancipation or ideal dialogue. Feminist critical approaches add the biotic aspect of the body (as an antidote to overly mental approaches) and power-oriented approaches add the formative. This analysis is not meant to be exhaustive, but rather to provide an overall view that shows approaches as complementary rather than antagonistic. It also might suggest there are other aspects which none of these approaches give much attention to, such as the aesthetic and ethical (but see Stahl's chapter for the latter).

3.8 SOME REFLECTIONS

This chapter has examined some of the difficulties encountered in trying to turn the critical perspective into practical guidance for IS research and practice. To some extent it has blurred the boundaries between the two main versions of the critical approach, namely emancipatory and communicative, and given attention to some issues at the expense of others. Nevertheless, it offers a critical

TABLE 3.3 Aspectual Focus of Systems Approaches

Aspect	Hard systems approach (Instrumental)	Soft systems approach (Subjective)	Critical perspective (Emancipatory or Communicative)
Quantitative	Quantification		
Spatial			
Kinematic			
Physical			
Biotic/Organic			(Feminist: body)
Psychic/Sensitive		Feelings	
Analytic	Requirements analysis		
Formative	Planning, control, achieving goals		(Power)
Lingual	(Documentation)		Communicative action, Ideal dialogue
Social		Group awareness	(Intersubjectivity)
Economic	Resource management		
Aesthetic			
Juridical			Oppression, Emancipation
Ethical			
Pistic/Faith		Perspectives, *Weltanschauung*	(Power: identity)

affirmation and enrichment of both. Problems in the two versions have been highlighted and discussed. Both versions were seen as too vague to be of full practical use, and need a basis for acknowledging diverse normativity and types of application, and diverse rationality and types of human action.

These problems were addressed first by exposing their root (in the currently active NFGM) and a tendency to reductionism. These are philosophical issues, and so a philosophy was appealed to which had discussed these at length: the cosmonomic philosophy of Dooyeweerd. Not only can it help us critique the current ground-motive but it can also provide the basis for understanding diversity, as experienced in the lifeworld. This led Dooyeweerd to delineate a number of aspects (spheres of meaning and law), and his suite is employed here to discuss normativity, rationality and social action. This offers a rich, multi-aspectual picture, which accords with the lifeworld of ISD and IS use. It is possible, in principle, that an alternative suite of aspects could be employed, as long as it treats aspects not just as categories but as spheres of meaning and law.

It has been demonstrated that philosophy can have direct relevance and can point the way to practical tools. The reason it has been able to do this is because the philosophy employed (that of Dooyeweerd, 1984) self-consciously adopts a pre-theoretical (everyday, lifeworld) attitude first, rather than presupposing that a theoretical attitude is the superior route to knowledge.

This chapter has not sought to work out the relevance of this for critical research in IS in detail. Rather, it has sought to raise initial questions about critical approaches and to point out some directions in which research might proceed in order to seek answers. To draw these pointers together, the following suggestions may be made for various types of critical research in IS, most of them employing Dooyeweerd's suite of aspects as a checklist.

- To research that is critical of social structures, Dooyeweerd's suite of aspects offers a tool for analysis that is intuitively grasped and serves to make explicit what has been overlooked. Winfield (2000) worked out a practical method for 'multi-aspectual knowledge elicitation'[7]
- To research that focuses on emancipation, the normativity inherent in Dooyeweerd's aspects offer a usefully diverse and well-founded definition of emancipation.
- To power-oriented research, Dooyeweerd offers aspects that are often overlooked when using power as a lens, especially the ethical aspect.
- To feminist research, Dooyeweerd's aspects offer confirmation of the desire to reinstate long-overlooked aspects, and helps feminism avoid criticisms of reactionism.

A benefit of using Dooyeweerd's aspects is that it focuses attention as much on the positive as on the negative, so that critical action research does not destroy the former.

We seem to have presented Dooyeweerd's suite of aspects as a universal solution. It should not be seen so. Dooyeweerd himself argued that, while the aspects transcend us, our *knowledge* of them does not, because it involves analytical thinking to differentiate them. In this respect, 'theoretical thought has never finished its task' (Dooyeweerd, 1984, II:556). Dooyeweerd was not only being critical, he was being critical of criticality itself, recognising that even criticality is not absolute but itself invites critical analysis (reflexivity). This, albeit in a confined way, is what we have tried to undertake in this chapter.

REFERENCES

Adam, A. (1998). *Artificial knowing: Gender and the thinking machine*. Routledge, London.

Allen, D. K., Colligan, D., Finnie, A., & Kern, T. (2000). Trust, power and interorganizational information systems: The case of the electronic trading community. *TransLease Information Systems Journal, 10*, 21–40.

Alvesson, M., & Willmott, H. (1992). On the idea of emancipation in management and organization studies. *Academy of Management Review, 17*(3), 432–464.

Basden, A. (2008). *Philosophical frameworks for understanding information systems*. IGI Global, Hershey, PA.

Basden, A., & Klein, H. K. (2008). New research directions in data and knowledge engineering: A philosophy of language approach. *Data & Knowledge Engineering, 67*(2), 260–285.

---

7. Winfield and Basden [2006] might be a more accessible source.

Berg, M. (1998). The politics of technology: On bringing social theory into technological design. *Science, Technology and Human Values, 23*(4), 456–490.

Bergvall-Kåreborn, B. (2001). The role of the qualifying function concept in systems design. *Systemic Practice and Action Research, 14*(1), 79–93.

Checkland, P. (1981). *Systems thinking systems practice.* Wiley, New York.

Clouser, R. (2005). *The myth of religious neutrality: An essay on the hidden role of religious belief in theories,* (2nd ed.). University of Notre Dame Press, Notre Dame.

Cordoba, R., & Midgley, G. (2003). Addressing organisational and societal concerns: An application of critical systems thinking to information systems planning in Colombia. *Critical reflections on information systems: Systemic approach.* In Cano, J.J. (Ed.), Idea Group, Hershey, PA, pp. 159–208.

Denning, P. J., & Dunham, R. (2006). Innovation as language action. *Communications of the ACM, 49,* 47–52.

Dooyeweerd, H. (1979). *Roots of western culture: Pagan secular and Christian options (Original work published 1963).* (J. Kraay, Trans.) Wedge, Toronto, Ontario, Canada.

Dooyeweerd, H. (1984). *A new critique of theoretical thought, Ontario, Canada: Paideia Press, Jordan Station, Vol. 1–4 (Original work published 1953–1958).*

Eriksson, D. M. (2006). Normative sources of systems thinking: An inquiry into religious ground-motives of systems thinking paradigms. *In search of an integrative vision for technology: Interdisciplinary studies in information systems.* In Strijbos, S., & Basden, A (Eds.), Springer, New York, pp. 217–232.

Fraser, N. (1989). *Unruly practices: Power, discourse and gender in contemporary social theory.* Polity, Cambridge.

Goldkuhl, G. (2006). Action and media in interorganizational interaction. *Communications of the ACM, 49,* 53–58.

Goldkuhl, G., & Lyytinen, K. (1982). A language action view of information systems. *Proc of the 3rd international conference on information systems, December.* In Ginzberg, M., & Ross, C. (Eds.), Ann Arbor, Michigan, pp. 13–30.

Habermas, J. (1972). *Knowledge and human interests.* (J. J. Shapiro, Trans.) Heinemann, London.

Habermas, J. (1984). *The theory of communicative action. Reason and the rationalization of society (T. McCarthy, Trans.), Polity Press, Cambridge, England, Vol. 1.*

Habermas, J. (1987). (T. McCarthy, Trans.) *The theory of communicative action. The critique of functionalist reason, Polity Press, Cambridge, England, Vol. 2.*

Habermas, J. (1991). A reply. *Communicative action.* In Honneth, A., & Joas, H. (Eds.),, pp. 214–264.

Habermas, J. (2002). *Religion and rationality: Essays on reason, God and modernity.* Polity Press, Cambridge, England.

Haraway, D. (1991). *Simians cyborgs and women: The reinvention of nature.* Free Association Books, London.

Heng, M. S.H., & de Moor, S. A. (2003). From Habermas's communicative theory to practice on the Internet. *Information Systems Journal, 13,* 331–352.

Hirschheim, R., & Klein, H. K. (1994). Realizing emancipatory principles in information systems development: The case for ethics. *MIS Quarterly, 18*(1), 85–109.

Husserl, E. (1970). *The crisis of European sciences and transcendental phenomenology.* (D. Carr, Trans.) Northwestern University Press, Evanston, IL.

Jackson, M. C. (1991). *System methodology for the management sciences.* Plenum Press, New York.

Lyytinen, K. & J., Klein, H. J., (1985). The critical theory of Jürgen Habermas as a basis for a theory of information systems. In: E. Mumford, R.A. Hirschheim, G. Fitzgerald, & A.T. Wood-Harper (Eds.). *Research methods in information systems* (pp.219–231). North Holland.

Markus, K. L., & Bjørn-Andersen, N. (1987). Power over users: Its exercise by systems professionals. *Communications of the ACM, 30,* 498–504.

Ngwenyama, O. K., & Lee, A. S. (1997). Communication richness in electronic mail: Critical social theory and the contextuality of meaning. *MIS Quarterly, 21*(2), 145–167.

Pacey, A. (1996). *The culture of technology.* MIT Press, Cambridge, MA.

Ray, L. J. (1993). *Rethinking critical theory; emancipation in the age of global social movements.* Sage Publications, London.

Schutz, A., & Luckmann, T. (1973). *Structures of the life-world, Northwestern University Press, Evanston, IL, Vol. I.*

Strauss, D.F.M. (2006). Reintegrating Social Theory. Frankfurt-am-Main: Peter Lang.

Ulrich, W. (1994). *Critical heuristics of social planning: A new approach to practical philosophy.* Wiley, Chichester, England.

Van der Kooy, T. P. (1974). De gereformeerde wereld en de sociologie [The Calvinist world and sociology]. *Anti-Revolutionaire Staatkunde, 2,* 37–56.

Walsham, G. (2001). *Making a world of difference: IT in a global context.* Wiley, Chichester, England.

Weigand, H. (2006). Two decades of the language-action perspective. *Communications of the ACM, 49,* 45–46.

Wilson, F. A. (1997). The truth is out there: The search for emancipatory principles in information systems design. *Information Technology and People, 10*(3), 187–204.

Winch, P. (1958). *The idea of a social science.* Routledge and Kegan Paul, London.

Winfield, M. (2000) *Multi-Aspectual Knowledge Elicitation.* Unpublished doctoral thesis. University of Salford England.

Winfield, M. J., & Basden, A. (2006). Elicitation of highly interdisciplinary knowledge. *In search of an integrated vision for technology; interdisciplinary studies in information systems.* In Strijbos, S. (Eds.), Springer, pp. 63–78.

Critical IS Empirical Studies

Participatory and Emancipatory Information Systems Development: Principles, Practices and Pitfalls

Dubravka Cecez-Kecmanovic and Marius Janson

4.1 INTRODUCTION

Participatory and emancipatory approaches to information systems (IS) development have been classified as naive and idealistic, lacking in realism, and justifiable only in terms of a metanarrative. However, they have also been disparaged as instruments for the ideological manipulation of workers and the legitimation of economic rationalism. This chapter re-examines the notion of participatory and emancipatory IS development in terms of these criticisms by exploring, questioning and grounding the approach in practice. Based on a 14-year long study of the Colruyt company (a Belgian retail company that engages in participatory and emancipatory IS development) we search for the practical meaning of participation and emancipation beyond grand narratives or ideology. By drawing on this study, we re-examine the nature, meaning and challenges of a participatory and emancipatory IS development project. We do this through critical reflection on practice, and pragmatic questioning regarding the adoption of participatory and emancipatory ideas and ideals, their realism and practical usefulness. Finally, we revisit and discuss the conditions for emancipatory IS development practices.[1]

The history of participatory and emancipatory information systems (IS) development approaches reflects ideas and ideals of worker participation and workplace democracy. Proposed as a way to counteract a narrow functionalist focus on organizational productivity and effectiveness, participatory and emancipatory IS development assumes systematic and meaningful user involvement, open and non-distorted communication and reasoned argumentation that is based on cooperation and mutual understanding between information systems (IS) developers, managers and employees affected by the system (Hirschheim and Klein, 1994). Conceptualizing information systems as social systems with a potential to free employees from 'repressive social and ideological conditions and, thereby, contributing to the realization of human need', Hirschheim and Klein (1994, p.87) were first to articulate the concept of an emancipatory IS development methodology.

It all started with the Scandinavian participatory design and the socio-technical design movement in the UK in the 1960s in response to technological developments leading to bureaucratization and dehumanization of work. Participatory design and social–technical principles promoted humanist ideals, arguing for the use of technology to achieve both efficiency objectives and improved 'quality of working life' (Bjerknes & Bratteteig, 1995; Mumford, 1981, 2000, 2006). The belief in technological progress and human knowledge sparked enthusiasm for computer applications that would replace boring, repetitive and dehumanizing jobs, increase job satisfaction and, thereby, eliminate workers' alienation. Proliferation of projects that adopted and advanced participatory design in Norway, Sweden, Denmark (referred to as the collective resources approach) together with projects that adopted the socio-technical design in the UK, (followed by other European countries, Canada and the USA) in the 1970s and early 1980s, raised hopes in the democratizing potential of information technology. However, their promises of humanization of work, workplace

---

1. This research received financial support from the Center for International Studies, University of Missouri-St. Louis, Missouri, United States of America.

democracy and worker empowerment, to make design and work-related choices were not long lived. The economic pressures in the late 1980s and 1990s, and the rise in unemployed labour, changed market and employment conditions, leading to the revival of computer-aided neo-Taylorism (Moldaschl & Weber, 1998). The deployment of IS to cut costs, downsize workforce, increase managerial control, achieve lean and efficient production based on standardized work processes, went counter to socio-technical and participatory design principles and practices. Socio-technical design, as Mumford (2006) conceded 'moved from success to failure' as '[t]he attraction and validity of bureaucracy was seen as stronger and safer and the new humanistic approaches as over-risky' (p.321).

Despite these counter developments or perhaps because of them, research interests in participatory design did not die. Actually, an increasing reliance on IS – both internally in organizations (e.g. ERP systems) and externally (inter-organizational IS, e-commerce) – compounded with harsher conditions in IS development and deployment, increasing risks and recurring failures, have revived interests in participatory and emancipatory IS development approaches (Howcroft & Wilson, 2003; Mumford, 2006). These and other researchers are raising their critical voices against the narrow view of information systems as a means of furthering the economic rationalist agenda: the view that obscures repressive social conditions and 'the continued destruction of the human potential' (Saravanamuthu, 2002). The unrealized potential of participatory and emancipatory approaches to IS development has been re-discovered in a struggle for a more humane and socially sustainable use of technology and the creation of less inhumane and less bureaucratic organizations.

However, since the first ideas and ideals were proposed and applied, the participatory and emancipatory approaches to IS development have been criticized, and at times even condemned. User participation in IS development in practice has often served to ensure better requirement specification, user acceptance of the future systems and the achievement of performance targets. A critique from a labour process perspective by Saravanamuthu (2002) emphasizes the risks for 'participatory IS approaches to become tools of ideological manipulation, as they sidestep workplace conflict and (implicitly) legitimatize the logic of efficiency' (p. 195). Such participatory practices were accused of disingenuousness, for being instrumentalized for managerial purposes, where humanistic concerns served as a façade for economic rationalist agendas (Howcroft & Wilson, 2003). Alternatively, emancipatory IS development ideas and approaches, were dismissed as unrealistic and naive, incapable of addressing real-life power struggles or preventing colonizing effects of information technologies (Wilson, 1997). Wilson's critique of the Critical Theory foundation of emancipatory projects was particularly unforgiving, questioning their real meaning and agendas and accusing them for imposing yet another 'totalizing discourse' in IS development and organizational use of IS.

Given the critique and controversy surrounding participatory and emancipatory IS development approaches, further studies are warranted of their 'real' meaning, objectives and practical implications as well as the claims of their unrealized potential and unfulfilled promises. In this chapter we join the debate about participatory and emancipatory IS development by revisiting its assumptions and principles through an insight into IS development process in practice. We examine a case of the Belgian retail company Colruyt that practiced various forms of participatory and emancipatory IS development (without naming it as such) for more than three decades. The Colruyt company developed a unique approach to informatization as a foundation of its continuous organizational innovation and development. Based on the longitudinal study of the Colruyt company's participatory culture, decision-making and IS development practices, we aim to develop a more refined, empirically grounded, understanding of the nature and objectives of participatory and emancipatory IS development. We aim to provide insights into, and demonstrate the realism of, participatory and emancipatory IS development (thus responding to the charge that it is naive and practically impossible). We also aim to revisit the conditions for emancipatory IS development practices (Hirschheim and Klein, 1994; Alvesson & Willmott, 1992) and shed a new light on the subtle difference between IS development practices that liberate and empower, and those that colonize and disempower.

The chapter is organized as follows. We first discuss key ideas and ideals, as well as criticisms in the literature of participatory and emancipatory IS development. This is followed by the description of the research methodology—the longitudinal case study of the development of information system for information dissemination (ISID) in Colruyt, including a short description of the company history and culture. This section also includes introductory remarks about Alvesson and Willmott's (1992) framework proposed to analyse the nature of emancipatory projects. Next we tell a story of how ISID was born in the early 1970s and how its development continued till now. The discussion explores the participatory nature and characteristics of ISID development as part of the Colruyt company's organizational development, and then we question and provide insight into the emancipatory nature of ISID development through the lens of the Alvesson and Willmott framework (1992). We conclude by summarizing the chapter's major claims and contributions.

4.2 PARTICIPATORY AND EMANCIPATORY IS DEVELOPMENT

4.2.1 Idea(l)s and Criticisms

Participatory and emancipatory ideas with respect to IS development originated with the socio-technical design approaches of the 1960s and 1970s which were inspired by workplace democracy and quality of working life (QWL) movements in Europe. Among the first was the Norwegian Industrial Democracy Program that included experiments conducted by the Tavistock Institute of Human Relations between 1964 and 1967 and which examined the introduction of manufacturing technologies and the subsequent change in job distribution and wage systems for workers (Emery & Thorsrud, 1976). The ideas that arose from this inspired two different research programmes: the 'collective resources' approach in Scandinavia and the 'socio-technical systems design' in the UK.

The collective resources approach – advanced by projects such as NJMF, DEMOS and DUE[2] – aimed at increasing workplace democracy by ensuring that those affected by the introduction of new technologies have the right to influence their work situation and to take part in decision-making (Bjerknes & Bratteteig, 1995). Given the assumed antagonistic relationship between labour and capital, the collective resources approach relied on trade unions as the key guarantor that workers' interests were respected and incorporated in the process of technological change process. However, collective demands were rarely met. Workers did not participate in designing technological change and their concerns regarding technology deployment and workplace transformation seldom featured in the bargaining processes.

Parallel to the Scandinavian participatory design ideas and projects, Tavistock Institute researchers developed the socio-technical system design concept that was inspired by the QWL movement, initially in the UK, and subsequently embraced by academics in the US, Canada, Australia, etcetera. By conceiving of labour processes as organic entities in which humanistic and economic concerns are simultaneously considered and negotiated, the socio-technical system design aimed to 'revolutionize the way we live and work' (Mumford & Weir, 1979; Mumford, 2006, p. 320). It promoted workers' interests through higher quality and a satisfying work environment, more interesting work, personal development and up-skilling, and the practical application of autonomous work groups. Socio-technical design was based on an important democratic principle: 'employees who use the new systems should be involved in determining the required quality of working-life improvements' (Mumford, 2006, p. 318). By adopting socio-technical design, it was believed, workers were granted 'direct control over the nature of the technology encountered in their day-to-day job' (Asaro, 2000, p. 269).

By the mid-1980s the collective resources approach and the socio-technical design converged and became accepted by companies throughout Europe (Asaro, 2000; Mumford, 2006). Benefits such as increasing efficiency and productivity (in manufacturing as well as services sectors) achieved through collaboration and without major resistance by employees, were valued by managers. Some successes with autonomous work groups, improving quality of working life, and remedying employee redundancies due to automation, were valued by employees. However, despite notable successes and many reported achievements of both economic and social objectives, the ideas and the ideals of

---

2. For a detailed description of these and other projects as part of the Scandinavian tradition see Bjerknes and Bratteteig (1995), Ehn and Sandberg (1983), Kyng and Mathiassen (1982).

participatory IS development, did gradually lose their appeal and during the 1990s faded away from IS practices (Mumford, 2006).

To re-examine and compare key ideas, practices and pitfalls throughout the history of user participation in IS development, we will focus our discussion on several key dimensions. Namely, how, and in what form, did users actually engage in IS development processes, informed by different conceptions of work and work organization, different views of technology and different ideologies.

4.2.2 User Participation and Emancipation in IS Development

The most contentious issues are the purpose and objectives of promoting user participation in IS development processes. User participation is thought to lead to a higher quality system, achieve a better fit between organization and system and, ultimately, increase performance and productivity, and result in efficiency gains. Even though a causal link between user participation and system success has been extensively examined, the empirical findings are inconclusive (Cavaye, 1995; Hawcroft & Wilson, 2003; Markus & Mao, 2004).

On the one hand, socio-technical design promoted user participation in order to achieve both economic benefits as well as social improvements, such as job satisfaction, quality of working life and workplace democracy. The collective resources and trade union approach, however, was more radical, aiming for more substantive democratic changes, employee empowerment, and increasing worker autonomy. On the other hand, social improvements and democratic change were never objectives in their own right. Rather, they served the purpose of 'enrolling users', creating an impression of involvement and influence, defusing user resistance, providing a 'safety valve', as well as legitimizing the changes arising from the system and increasing user acceptance (Hawcroft and Wilson, 2003). Both socio-technical design and collective resources approaches are accused of the instrumental use of humanist rhetoric and democratic language to achieve performance and efficiency gains, and to ultimately entice employees to accept systems that worsen their working conditions and increased exploitation. These observations motivated IS researchers to explore further the neohumanist approach that furthers user participation, inspired by the emancipatory ideals and principles aimed at genuine democratic changes in workplace and organization.

A distinctly critical approach to IS development was influenced by Critical Social Theory (Lyytinen & Hirschheim, 1985; Lyytinen & Klein, 1985). Building on Alvesson and Willmott's (1992) seminal paper on emancipation in management and organization studies, Hirschheim and Klein formulated four conditions for an emancipatory IS development methodology (1994, pp. 87–88)

1 Providing support for an active process of individual and collective self-determination,
2 Providing support for critical self-reflection and associated self-transformation,

3 Inclusion of a broader set of institutional issues relating particularly to social justice, due processes and human freedom, or, more concretely in ISD, to employees' ethical needs, quality of work life, personal autonomy, and the linkage between participation and democracy, and

4 Inclusion of the principle for critical evaluation of claims or rational discourse during the systems development processes.

The emancipatory ideas in IS development and, more broadly, in management, however, have been criticized for neglecting the reality of business conditions, the pre-eminence of shareholders' interests and robustness of organizational power structures. The alleged utopian nature of emancipatory projects was a reason for claiming their disconnection from reality and the mundane practices of management (Alvesson & Willmott, 1992). Moreover, Wilson (1997, p. 196) contends that emancipatory IS development implies an arbitrary ideological position, which can be articulated and evaluated 'only in terms of a metanarrative'. Wilson, (1997, pp. 195–201) further asserts that an IS development process conceived of as a rational discourse that counteracts distorted communication, can be seen as a formula for totalizing discourses, that view organizations as homogeneous entities. In short, emancipatory ideas in both management and IS development leave open questions concerning power, the possibility of autonomous subjects capable of self-reflection and self-transformation, and many others. However, Wilson's (1997) paper added more to their obscuring and distorting rather than to clarifying and critiquing, thus assisting the decline of an already fragile and marginalized research into emancipatory IS development.

In contrast to the aforementioned negative opinions, it is our premise that ideas and ideals of participatory and emancipatory IS development do have as yet unrealized potential for improving both development processes and results, such as IS designs that make an economic and social contribution. However, the critique of their utopian nature and disconnectedness from the reality of business and IS practice must be addressed seriously. Instead of starting from the grand enterprise of participatory and emancipatory project based on Critical Theory ideals – a metanarrative criticized for advancing yet another ideology and totalizing discourses – a more modest and pragmatic approach is considered here. That is to say, our aim is to follow in the footsteps of Alvesson and Willmott (1992) who argue for reorienting participatory and emancipatory studies in organizations and management towards practice and 'micro-emancipation'. Thus, in this paper we focus on both 'critical' and 'non-critical' concerns in the IS development processes of the Colruyt company, a Belgian retail company that views its business performance and efficiency as inseparable from employees' discretion and autonomy, their self-realization, creativity and critical self-transformation. By drawing on a longitudinal study that reflects the company's organizational development and its processes and practices of IS development, we aim to (1) re-examine the nature, meaning and challenges of a participatory and emancipatory IS development project through a critical reflection on practice, (2) raise pragmatic questions regarding the adoption of participatory and emancipatory ideas and ideals, their realism and practical usefulness and (3) revisit the conditions for participatory and emancipatory IS development practices (Hirschheim and Klein, 1994; Alvesson & Willmott, 1992).

4.3 RESEARCH METHODOLOGY

While conducting a longitudinal case study of informatization processes and organizational development in the Colruyt company (from 1993 to 2006), we observed unique practices of user participation in the development of IS with explicit democratic and emancipatory intent. Intrigued by these observations we decided to study more in-depth the meaning and nature of user participation as it emerged and continued throughout the company's history. We focused on the ISID, which is a groupware and document management system that was developed by the company's IT department. ISID's development commenced in the mid-1970s and it has been under continuous development ever since (Resseler, 1986). ISID proved to be an essential component of participatory decision-making and the cooperative culture that the company developed at its inception and which it continued to support subsequently. It was, therefore, particularly intriguing to investigate how the Colruyt company actually developed ISID, how it attracted and engaged users and how users felt about their participation in systems development and use. Given the criticisms and controversies found in the literature, we were particularly interested in examining the practice of, and to define theoretically the nature of, participatory IS development and, specifically, the space between non-emancipatory and emancipatory practices.

4.3.1 The Colruyt Company

The Colruyt company was founded in Brussels, Belgium, in 1965 as a single food discount store—a revolutionary concept in Europe at that time. The company offered its customers prices on all products below those of competing stores, friendly service, the ability to make informed purchasing decisions by providing extensive product information and a choice from a wide-ranging number of quality products. Competing on product price and quality, while paying employees above-industry average wages, was, and still is, the company's major business strategy. A former IS manager summarized it like this:

> 'The business strategy was concise, that is -10%, +10%, and 1%. It means that we charge customers 10% below our competitors, we pay employees 10% above average industry rates, and we realise 1% return on sales'. (IS Manager, Interview 1993, 2000)

Starting with a single discount store in 1965, the Colruyt company became the third largest food retail chain in the early 1980s, and in 2006 operated 228 food discount stores in Belgium and 44 stores in France, with annual sales revenue of US $6.3 Billion (company 2005–2006 Annual Report).

Contrary to the standard practice of a hierarchical organization, the company's founder (until 1993) CEO, late Mr. Jo Colruyt and members of upper management, developed a flat organizational structure characterized by decentralized decision-making, reducing power differences among employees and between company management and employees, and encouraging personal responsibility and initiative. Mr. Jo Colruyt held that any issue or topic, including corporate norms, was open for discussion by all staff. With respect to the results of practicing these ideals he stated:

> '[Employee] commitment to the company? Yes, but under the condition that the company is willing to change. If many employees attend training sessions, the company has to adjust. . . The company cannot maintain the same philosophy [as before the training]. The company is a [collection of] employees, and when they change the company has to change.. . . company philosophy has to change to integrate the employees who now have different ideas. Members of top management have to attend these training sessions also, so that they know what ideas exist among the employees. Members of top management have to change as well, otherwise they cannot relate to [the] employees'. (Jo Colruyt, Interview 1993).

Jo Colruyt's most important decision at the company's inception, and which set the company apart from all its competitors, was to base all business processes on Information Technology (IT) and its possibilities to automate tasks, support workers in their operations and improve efficiency (e.g., Colruyt was first in Belgium to introduce bar codes). Stated Jo Colruyt:

> 'On opening our first discount store we decided to organise all retail related processes around the possibilities of information technology. We resolved to accept the positive as well as the negative aspects [concerning] information technology. [Thus], we elected to not sell any product that could not be handled by information technology. We also realised that our employees could not be the 'traditional lady at the cash register' because they are not used to operate a computer [based checkout system. [All] this means that Colruyt is totally different from its competitors'. (Mr. Jo Colruyt, Interview, 1993)

However, Jo Colruyt was acutely aware that implementing IT throughout the company affects people and influences social conditions of work. As he often emphasized, 'Existing conditions, social structures, relations between individuals, and relations between social classes in a company change when new technologies are introduced' (Jo Colruyt, Interview 1993). To enable workers to accept IT and to engage in bringing about the necessary changes themselves, the company invests heavily in staff training and education. Seminars are available in communication, self-actualization, self-empowerment, self-expression, decision-making and assertiveness. The seminars have minimal theoretical content but focus instead on building communicative competence under practical day-to-day conditions. Attending these training seminars is entirely voluntary. The skills acquired in seminars form the basis from which employees participate and (re)create the company's social structure. The seminar programme is complemented by courses with coverage on specific job skills and the application of information technology.

4.3.2 The Longitudinal Study

The longitudinal study of the Colruyt company started in 1993 when one co-author first visited company headquarters in Brussels and conducted the first interview with Jo Colruyt (Janson, Joshi, & Taillieu, 1998). The visit established a research relationship which continues today. Regular visits to company headquarters involved informal discussions and interviews with employees and managers, and attending and observing official meetings in stores, warehouses and headquarters, and observing the use of ISID.

On-site audio-taped interviews were conducted with him, and then his son (Jef Colruyt) after becoming CEO, and also with the chief information officer, the marketing manager, middle level managers, IS personnel, workers, and union representatives (Table 4.1). Semi-structured interviews were conducted in the Flemish language, the native language of interviewees, which were later transcribed and translated for further analysis. The interviewees were encouraged to tell their own story without feeling limited by our interview guide.

TABLE 4.1 Colruyt Interviewees

Roles	1993	2000	2001	2003	2006
Founder, Former CEO, member of the board of directors (Jo Colruyt)	X				
Checkout clerk	X				
Store manager	X				
Former chief information officer	X	X			
Manager marketing	X		X		
General director of distribution	X			X	
Director warehousing 1993/general director distribution 2003	X			X	
Union steward			X		
Union official			X		
Manager information systems development located in user group			X	X	X
Current CEO, member of the board of directors (Jef Colruyt)				X	
Information systems analyst				X	
Chief information officer				X	X
Systems analyst					X
Systems developer					X
Manager outsourcing					X
Human relations department					X
Manager information systems development located in IS department					X

Furthermore, data collection also included researcher's observation notes, company documents, policy statements, work procedures and rules, meeting documents (most available via ISID) as well as company annual reports (1975, 1985, 1988 and 1990–2006), union reports, and newspaper articles.

On-site enquiry into the company's IS development processes was part of the broader study of the Colruyt company's informatization and democratization as a key development strategy. The study traces the emergence of company participatory culture and decision-making processes and its strategic reliance on IT to support these processes and achieve both social and commercial objectives. ISID plays a central role in enabling and supporting distributed and participatory decision-making. In-house development and use of ISID exemplifies Colruyt's informatization approach and participatory practices. Our examination of ISID development focuses on user involvement throughout the development process (since the mid-1970s), the ways and forms of user engagement in and influence on development, the ways ISID was used in decision-making, and the implications on user-developer and employee–manager relationships.

4.3.3 Data Analysis: Exploring Participatory and Emancipatory IS Development

Our examination and interpretation of the nature, meaning and challenges of ISID development drew on the narratives of actors, employees, managers and IS specialists, and the ways these individuals made sense of, and reflected on, events and on-going changes. The narratives and meaning-making processes were an integral part of their social construction of reality, their social actions as well as social and cultural (re)production (Czarniawska, 1998; Weick, 1995). As actors engaged in different phases and tasks of ISID's development process, they constructed their views of the process, together with their identities and roles within the broader cultural and organizational context. Through their narratives, actors made sense and reflected, both individually and collectively, on their jobs and the role of information in performing their jobs and decision-making, their needs and requests for information, and the vision of ISID to meet these needs. The narratives reflected what was important to these actors and what was problematic and challenging in ISID development. Furthermore, during the course of ISID development, implementation and use, the narratives revealed increasing consciousness concerning participants' rights and participation in decision-making.

We draw from interviews, ISID documents, published reports and company Annual Reports to reconstruct the story of ISID development since the first ideas emerged in the mid-1970s. By tracing narratives and identifying themes of user involvement and participation we analysed and critically interpreted ISID development. Our analysis first probed the nature of user participation, including forms, types and degree of involvement and influence. We also examined to what extent user participation in ISID development was based on consensus or dissensus assumptions, and what the implications were for the development process.

To explore the purpose of user participation, and especially the emancipatory character and scope of ISID development, we adapted Alvesson and Willmott's (1992) two-dimensional framework as a guide for analysis and critical reflection presented in Table 4.2. The framework proposes a distinction between the *type of emancipatory project* and the *focus of its intent* in order to enable a more refined analysis and understanding of emancipatory projects in practice. The type of emancipatory project may range from questioning, to incremental transformation or reformist type, to utopian. Questioning involves critiquing, challenging and, at times, resisting dominant forms of thinking and social arrangements, without proposing the desired (the ideal). The utopian type advocates alternatives to existing conditions. The utopian element is important, as Alvesson and Willmott (1992, p. 450) explain, when participants envision alternative arrangements, social relations or ends. Between these two opposites, an incremental, or reformist, type of emancipation involves gradual change towards the desired forms or systems. Table 4.2. Alvesson and Willmott's framework – type and foci of emancipation (1992, p. 449).

TABLE 4.2 Alvesson and Willmott's framework – type and foci of emancipation (1992, p. 449)

| Type of emancipatory project | | | |
Foci of Emancipatory intent	Questioning	Incremental transformation	Utopian
Means			
Social relations			
Ends			

Concerning emancipatory intent, a distinction is made between means, social relations and ends. The emancipation of means concerns distorted discourses and oppressive organizational practices that are assumed to be necessary to achieve organizational and managerial ends. The emancipation of ends, on the contrary, 'is concerned with unfreezing institutionalized priorities and, thereby, opening up debate about the practical value of economic growth, consumption, the quality of life and so on' (Alvesson & Willmott, 1992, p. 450). Finally, the focus on social relations draws attention to social and power structures, relations of domination and control, and the ways these limit autonomy, creativity, self-determination and self-realization.

The Alvesson and Willmott (1992, p.450) framework introduces analytical distinctions that are relevant for examining and clarifying the nature and scope of participatory and emancipatory IS development. The framework reflects the idea that an emancipatory project does not need to be a grand enterprise of liberation and that even small-scale projects can have an emancipatory effect (which Alvesson and Willmott call micro-emancipation). However, the authors also suggest that any narrow focus of emancipatory intent (such as focus on means) cannot be assessed without understanding the implications within a broader context of social relations and ends. The adaptation of the framework informed our analysis by sensitizing us to subtle differences among employees, managers and IS personnel narratives that prove essential for exploring the space between emancipatory and non-emancipatory discourses and practices.

4.4 A STORY OF ISID DEVELOPMENT

Since its inception in the mid-1960s the Colruyt company had instilled a cooperative culture that was particularly evident in the way meetings were organized and managed. The topics of meetings, their content and outcomes were expected to be known to all employees, not only participants. Employees were interested to find out 'What did they talk about during this meeting? What actions will be taken? Did my name come up? How did they see my responsibility?' As a result meetings were taped and transcribed, and memos from meetings distributed.

Thus, as the company grew and employed more individuals, the need for a software application for capturing, processing and distributing messages and documents became an issue:

> 'I am responsible for information within the company. But I am also responsible for personnel relations, these two are somehow connected, how can I resolve the issues with a computer technology? . . . We struggled with the question how to support information handling from a programming point of view' (Lengeler, Former CIO, Interview 2000).

In early 1970s they got the idea to use of an IBM software package that was used by IT personnel to transmit documents:

> '[The IBM software] was originally implemented for communication between very few individuals in the IS department. I don't recall any longer whether there was a meeting but I remember that the question was posed "what if we expand the system so that it can be used by more people in more departments and throughout the entire organization'. (Lengeler, Interview 1993)

This marked the birth of interactive system for information dissemination (ISID) – at that time, a pioneering concept of an information system to assist organization-wide communication:

> '. . . we really created the embryo of an information network, which became immensely important later. I sense that we at the Colruyt company were forerunners'. (Lengeler, Interview 2000)

ISID captured information, documents, memos, reports, messages, etcetera. It performed very basic functions such as storing, sending and printing, using a passive network of terminals connected to mainframe computers in headquarters only. The number of documents grew to such an extent that the company installed a carousel of optical disks each with exceptionally large capacity that made it possible to retain all of 120 000 documents created per year and enable their efficient retrieval (today employees are able to retrieve documents from 1975 onwards).

The growing document base raised the question of information distribution, namely, not every document is of interest to each and every employee. For example, reports on meetings are primarily of interest to meeting attendees and secondarily to non-attendees. Thus, employees who met to discuss specific issues of problems formed so-called infogroups, members of which would be sent meeting summaries automatically. Other employees were then able to search meeting reports and other information by keywords (each database document being assigned several keywords according to a company-designed thesaurus).

In the early 1980s, IBM withdrew support for its software, and the Colruyt company decided to develop its own information-sharing software package. In his interview, Lengeler (2000) recalled how the second phase of ISID project started with a steering group:

> 'We formed a steering group with a membership originating from the various departments, also of the various levels of the hierarchy. . . . we wanted in the first place to see if the project would be possible. But that is a normal way to take hold of a project. It was also remarkable that work groups were formed in a multidisciplinary way. People came from the user's environment despite belief [at] that time that information projects were just the concern of IT people. However, [with multidisciplinary working groups] the voices [the requests] came from the base...'

Pressures to expand ISID and develop new functions came from various quarters. On the one hand, there was a visionary leader, Jo Colruyt, (then CEO) with 'a personal belief in the possibility of IT' for enhancing not only business processes but also company communication and cooperative forms of work. As a leader who promoted a cooperative organizational culture and decentralized decision-making, he saw an opportunity to use IT more innovatively 'as a tool for enabling power distribution and for sharing power'. In the book 'There are No Gentlemen Here Sir' (1985) Jo Colruyt explained the connection between information and power:

> 'Information is power – when management wants to practice power decentralization then it has to practice information decentralization. Power decentralization has the enormous advantage arising from organizational flexibility to instantly adjust the organization to new situations. Hundreds of employees obtain the power to take [the] initiative. They will experience this in their personal life, and consider it an enrichment of their professional life'. (p. 74)

There existed much enthusiasm about ISID among employees:

> '[ISID] a fantastic system for storing information and for communication [it was] built because the company considers it imperative that everyone becomes

informed to the degree necessary to do his/her job . . . The Colruyt company has its unique [organizational]atmosphere that is not limited to form – there is content as well. For me the unique aspect is the extensive and wide-ranging use of information technology and a simplified bureaucracy. Every document is accessible in a short time [via ISID], everything proceeds speedily and effectively'. (Marcel de Broyer, 1985, p.180)

However, not all managers were enthusiastic with the development and implementation of ISID because the system heralded company-wide, open access, and, at the same time, ISID fostered the emergence of cooperative ways of working, participatory decision making and a participatory culture. The intertwined development of ISID and organizational culture produced continuously emerging user expectations and increasing user demands. The more employees used ISID, and the more they realized its potential, the higher were their expectations and their demands. Evidence of the company's continued building of its specific 'cooperative culture', 'democratic work environment' and 'participative decision making' is demonstrated by ISID's history, company documents and interviews:

'[Colruyt] has a democratic work environment. Everyone gets the chance to express his thoughts. To enable this we have regular meetings, e.g., shift meetings, workgroup meetings for warehouse workers, etc. One gets the chance to advance on the job even if you lack [a high school] education. There is honesty and correctness among employees. You can participate even as a warehouse worker. For example, several years ago I made a proposal [via ISID] to gain more space in the warehouse by rearranging the way fresh food is collected. Several weeks later my proposal was implemented. I received the chance in three years to advance from unschooled worker to shift foreman. This is only possible in a healthy and dynamic company'. (Rene Vermeren, a warehouse worker, 1985, p. 163)

Cooperative culture and participative decision-making, in turn, create more pressure to inform employees concerning the company's economic situation, market conditions as well as numerous internal events and processes relevant for employees doing a good job. This also creates further demands on, and expectations of, ISID to support cooperative problem-solving, a democratic work place and employee participation. In spite of its intended purpose, namely, cooperative problem solving, ISID occasionally caused friction among employees. Thus, as various departments used ISID to raise and discuss critical problems (such as, for example, lack of store inventory) they tended to accuse one another instead of overcoming deficiencies. Commented the former CIO manager, it seemed that 'because of the extensive delegation of responsibility and the decentralization of power, one ends up with more power conflicts' (Lengeler, Interview 2000). Thus, to enhance collaborative culture employees participated on a continuous basis in sensitivity, groupwork and personal development training. This resulted in greater openness within the firm, employees with better people skills, and more effective ISID use.

An interesting implication of what they call 'the meeting culture' in Colruyt is 'a particular atmosphere of trust, . . ., as management was forced to create a certain level of openness concerning the release of information that creates and maintains trust' (Lengeler, Interview 2000). Starting from early 1970s, throughout ISID development and use, employees have seen their relationship with management changing. There was a sense of 'growing together with the company', 'feeling of enormous responsibility and power', 'the spirit of enterprise and excellence', 'freedom to make decisions and to share responsibility within your company', 'full commitment to the job and the company', 'shared interest between managers and workers' ('after all it's profit that pays our salaries'), and 'belonging to a winning company' (only 5% of food retail firms were expected to survive). These views were expressed by a checkout clerk, delivery truck driver, shop clerk, sales representative, stock boy, purchasing agent and other workers. The use of ISID, it is believed, helped to a great extent in building such trust among workers and management, and was seen as assisting the development of their relationships.

The Colruyt company is heavily unionized with workers belonging to a Socialist, Christian or Liberal Union. As is evident from the previous ISID description, the system greatly enhanced trust among and the flow of information between management and employees. This proved to be a challenging condition for the Unions, with the result, that, in 1984, the Socialist Union aired a TV programme and published a book severely criticizing the Colruyt company. Jo Colruyt, then CEO, viewed these events as a breach of trust and misuse of open access to company information:

> 'Union stewards [names deleted] need to recognize the right to privacy for managers and employees of the company. Management, managers, and employees should be able to communicate with one another without the risk that the information is made public. It is an essential component of an open system of communication, . . .Misusing of the company's information systems such as ISID, places the company at risk'. (Jo Colruyt, ISID document, July 1985)

The reactions were mixed, with some requesting the perpetrators be sacked and others arguing for strict control of access to information. However, Lengeler recalls, Jo Colruyt was not in favour of controlling ISID access either. Instead, he said 'we should educate workers to use information responsibly instead of making information inaccessible'. However, the event made it obvious that completely open employee access to ISID created too high a risk for the company. Therefore, access to highly confidential information in ISID was restricted. Currently:

> '70% of ISID documents are not confidential and 30% are confidential. Anyone in the company has access to non-confidential ISID documents whether he was recipient or not. 20% confidential ISID documents can only be read in their entirety by recipients and non-recipients can only read the keywords [and with special permission the whole document]. The remaining 10% are accessible to recipients only'. (Walter den Hertog, Marketing manager Interview, 2006)

This, and several other incidents of ISID misuse, prompted discussions on the appropriate use of information, and contributed to the development of, not only new features of the system, but also new norms and rules governing the system's use.

A further phase of ISID development was triggered in 2004 by a necessity to rebuild the web-based version of the system to operate on a new technological infrastructure. A typical ISID working group was formed consisting of representatives from all stakeholders—warehousing, human relations department, work simplification group, IS professionals from the IT department as well as from the user community, translation department and employee representatives from various sections of the company. Phase 3 of ISID development is currently underway.

4.5 DISCUSSION: THE PARTICIPATORY AND EMANCIPATORY NATURE OF ISID DEVELOPMENT

4.5.1 Exploring ISID's Participatory Nature

At first during the early 1970s participation in the ISID's development project was seen from a rather pragmatic and technical perspective. Stated the former IT and Personal manager 'I thought it would be useful to have a network [with the ability] to inform all company employees'. (Lengeler, Interview 2000). At this time there existed no formal procedures for user participation or representation. Rather, the development process was informal and basically included employees in the IT department who conceived of the original design and who assisted in resolving practical problems of capturing, storing and retrieving information. The initial ISID infrastructure consisted of a mainframe and approximately fifteen terminals located in the IT department.

Concerns for participation emerged in employee narratives during the late 70 s when ISID was designed as a distributed system in company headquarters. After experiencing how they could use information available from ISID, employees became interested in its further development. Getting the right information was important to employees in performing their jobs. Furthermore, being informed about current problems, meeting schedules and outcomes became prerequisites for meaningful and equitable participation in workgroups. At this time the Colruyt company was widely practicing self-nominated workgroups for problem-solving using ISID. Employees were aware of the relationship between information and decision-making:

> 'Decisions are based on information. Thus, once you have a structured way to make the information immediately available it makes the decision procedure easier'. (Lengeler, Interview 2000)

The ability or inability to obtain the necessary information from ISID was enabling or limiting factors in decision procedures. Therefore, user demands and expectations became a driving force for ISID development. User participation became more explicit and formalized during ISID's second development phase and was governed by a steering group comprising employees, managers of different departments and representatives of IT. During the first phase, the development team consisted predominantly of 'people concerned with IT', whereas the second and third phases were characterized by 'multidisciplinary working groups' enabling 'the voices [the requests] ... from the base' to be heard (Lengeler, Interview, 2000). User participation became valued and recognized as important, not only in terms of technical (IT or user process-related) knowledge but also in a political sense—hence, the term 'voices from the base'. While attending meetings during the third ISID development phase, one of the authors observed users, (including managers and workers) actively and effectively participating in discussions, convincingly arguing their proposals and objections, and providing and responding to counter arguments. The observed meeting practices during ISID development were similar to other problem-solving groups; namely, attendees engaged competently in rational discourse. These experiences raised the question as to how Colruyt achieved such effective collaboration among IT and user communities?

First, as Lengeler explains, collaboration was part of an overall Colruyt approach to informatization that had been supported by continued training programmes:

> 'It is necessary to prepare workers to embrace the computer in a sensible way. At Colruyt we do it as follows: First, Colruyt has a corporate learning centre that instructs employees to assume roles in computer-based business applications. 1) Employees learn to take charge of the informatization phenomenon instead of being overwhelmed by it; 2) Colruyt practices company-wide information access and conducts job-oriented training courses that, taken together, lead to more creative employees. [These efforts] result in employees being able to recognize the possibilities for reducing job complexity [using information technology and other technologies]; 3) Rapid change creates much employee anxiety. [Through training] Colruyt teaches employees to understand and master these feelings'.
> (Lengeler, ISID document, May 1984)

Second, collaboration between the user and IT communities is further enhanced by close two-way communication. One author attended a 2006 meeting of an ISID workgroup during which IT department members explained how they saw their role vis-à-vis the user community. These views do not necessarily reflect official job descriptions but, rather, how IT members conceptualize their services to the user. The outcome of the exercise was quite remarkable in that the user community had views that differed from those expressed by members of the IT community with respect to needed IT services. These differences became the topic of in-depth discussions that also led to adjustments and better understanding by users about what to expect from IT members and vice versa.

Employee participation in IS development was a component of a broad role as 'change agents', responsible for job or process improvements and reduction of job complexity. Employees were trained to make substantive contributions and 'take charge of the informatization phenomenon' or, in other words, to influence decisions of IS development processes. User participation in the Colruyt company's context meant 'taking initiative' and 'acquiring power' to make a contribution, together with 'taking responsibility' for outcomes. Such participation in IS development also reflects the Colruyt company's norm that during any problem-solving process those interested in, and affected by, its outcome had the right to participate in the problem-solving working group.

Our findings suggest that participatory management and employees' participation during ISID development do share similarities with the socio-technical design. For instance, at least with its ideals and principles of simultaneous focus on improvements of business performance and quality of working life, the use of technology to increase both efficiency and democracy, and delegation of responsibility to workgroups that are trained to cooperate and coordinate work processes with others (Mumford, 2006). The concerns for employee competence in participative decision-making and IS and the many Colruyt behavioural and IT training programmes are reminiscent of the Tavistock Institute's emphasis on workgroup training. While there are similarities between Tavistock Institute's and the Colruyt company's approaches, the participative practices of ISID development are more complex and conflictual giving rise to several interesting new problems.

The Colruyt company's lack of strict hierarchical management control has resulted in participative practices prone to conflicts arising from different personal interests and points of view that are not always business focused. Comments a systems analyst:

> '[Conflicts occur regularly] however, I do not immediately consider differences of
> opinion [conflict] wrong – at least as long as one [does not try] to settle conflict
> solely [by] using ISID. [In that case] one individual writes one thing while the
> second individual writes a contradictory message. Such conflict needs to be
> solved during a meeting attended by the two challengers together with a mediator
> who could be a CEO'. (Schaarbeek, Interview 2006)

To decrease the risk of unproductive conflict the Colruyt company introduced specialized training for its employees to develop communicative skills and to be competent in dealing with conflicting interests and situations. Particular emphasis was placed on resolving conflicts arising from different interests, views, knowledge and personalities of the participants. Through communicative training, employees mastered skills to better present their ideas, provide and respond to arguments, respect others' views and to engage in a fair and rational debate. In fact, they learned to apply principles of rational discourse which they practiced in workgroups, public debates (face-to-face and via ISID), and meetings. While rational discourse practices gave evidence of increasing communicative rationality, different interests were still possible, and conflicts were brought into the open. Rational discourse became possible due to decreasing power differences, even though such discourse remains open to dissensus, as assumed by Hirschheim and Klein (1994). This is contrary to Wilson (1997) who equates rational discourse with 'totalizing tendencies'.

To better understand the nature of ISID development we also need to explain the role of the late Jo Colruyt, company founder and CEO until 1993. Jo Colruyt envisioned a decentralized and democratic company in which open communication would be key:

> 'Open communication between employees means that each one of us does not remain limited to our own way of thinking or our own intellectual capability, but that there exists a constant exchange with other employees'. (Jo Colruyt, ISID document, April 1984)

The vision of open communication was realized by learning how to communicate, practicing a particular meeting culture, and by developing ISID to enable and support effective communication:

> 'An efficient and effective communication system is an important source for each employee who needs information to carry out his job. Having information means having power to act in an informed manner, that is to say having participative rights'. (Jo Colruyt, ISID document, June 1984)

As a charismatic leader Jo Colruyt influenced and motivated his employees. He exemplified high working and ethical standards that he, in turn, expected from all company employees. He advocated the participative rights of employees but he also believed in the company's responsibility for providing a democratic work environment, and the conditions – most importantly access to information – that enable employees to exercise these rights. This vision, combined with the belief of decentralized decision-making, motivated ISID's development.

It is interesting to observe that the Colruyt company's culture described above, caused Unions to question their traditional role and relationship with their constituents. On the one hand, the Union's traditional role was to promote worker interests such as wages, benefits, and work rules. On the other hand, worker benefits at the company were good, thus rendering the Unions' traditional role and power basis problematic. States a Socialist Union Official:

> 'There are no complaints concerning salaries, they are higher than the industry norm, workers enjoy profit sharing, receive one additional month's pay at the end of the year, and good overall working conditions. When we [the Union] represent worker interests company management consistently responds with "worker conditions at the Colruyt company are excellent, why always push for more?"' (Union Official, 2001)

The Unions' views with respect to informatization and especially ISID were ambivalent and Union officials did not have a unified view. For instance, several Union officials, together with a professor from the University of Louvain, published a book (Adele et al., 1984[3]) in which they accused the company of employing ISID to increase management control over workers. These authors further suggested that ISID enables management to assemble dossiers on employees which can be damaging to their careers. They claimed that the Colruyt company's culture is not genuinely democratic but is a form of indoctrination and manipulation aimed at increasing efficiency and control.

However, during his interview a Union steward[4] mentioned that the Colruyt company has an open communication culture and that employees have the freedom to raise and discuss any question:

> 'Within the Colruyt company there is communication within and between all [management] levels, from top to bottom and from bottom to top. It is possible to pose and discuss all possible questions or [requests]. That is not a problem; one will never be looked at askance for asking whatever question'. (Union Steward, Interview 2001)

He further claimed that informatization leads to greater efficiencies and easier work processes. For example, the automated daily store inventory management reduces the stress experienced by store employees (Union Steward, Interview, 2001).

These ambivalent views of Union officials indicate political sensitivity and the controversial nature of employee participation in informatization and democratization processes. Informatization that enables decentralized decision-making and increased levels of employee control is not a smooth and conflict-free process. Nurturing open communication, rational discourse and democratic culture involves struggle on a daily basis. While the history of ISID's development provides ample evidence of both democratic breakthroughs and setbacks, overall it shows a successive movement towards a genuinely participatory culture and IS development.

In summary, ISID's development exhibits several key ideals and realizes promises of the socio-technical design. However, the development of ISID in Colruyt went a long way in furthering the participative ideas and redefining the meaning of participatory development in practice. Examples include:

- The development of the company's cooperative culture and participatory management practices largely determine IS development processes and practices;
- Employee participation in ISID's development is a right (the same as the right to participate in decision-making); the employee role in IS development is seen as a component of their broader role as 'agents of change',

---

3. In this book professor Adele and Union officials published several documents obtained from ISID. It was later discovered that some documents were illegally obtained and manipulated (text slightly changed) to create the negative image of the company, its practices and its culture.

4. Union stewards are employees who represent worker interests in cases of disputes between employees and management.

which assumes individual's rights to participate as well as their responsibility for the outcomes;

- Meaningful involvement of all stakeholders in an IS development, from corporate strategy to shop floor employees, is assisted by autonomous workgroups, self-nominated and self-managed problem solving groups, a particular style of meetings and the debates via ISID;
- Managers and employees are competent participants that 'take charge of the informatization phenomenon'; this is achieved through continuous behavioural, IT and other training that support and assist the development of IS, driven by company ideals, philosophy, culture and strategy;
- IS development in the Colruyt company is practiced as rational discourse characterized by free and open communication among participants, not distorted by power relations; however, different and sometimes conflicting interests are expressed and dealt with; rational discourses makes room for both dissensus as well as consensus;
- Democratic and participative communication and decision-making throughout the development process (e.g. delegation of responsibility to work groups that have both knowledge and authority to make decisions) that are enabled and assisted by ISID (a condition envisaged by Mumford, 2006);
- Visionary leadership, commitment to democracy and moral authority of Jo Colruyt.

User acceptance of ISID was never an issue in Colruyt. In fact, users were requesting and expecting more than the technology and IS developers were able to provide at any point in time. This study confirms that when users are in charge of IS development and when they can exercise their rights to influence decisions about the nature and content of an IS (within the context of democratic work environment) they will choose the options that benefit both their personal work satisfaction and company performance. This includes job responsibility and also a broader sense of responsibility for the company.

4.6 EXPLORING ISID'S EMANCIPATORY NATURE

We now explore ISID development within the Alvesson and Willmott's (1992) emancipatory framework (presented above in Table 4.2) as a mode of engaging the empirical material. To do this we reinterpret the framework in the context of IS development. The emancipatory IS project can be of the following type:

- **Questioning, challenging and critiquing** now work and information practices as well as *arguing* and *requesting* new and higher quality of information, for instance, better access to information, user-developer and worker-manager power relations, and articulation of ends;
- **Incremental changes and transformation** of discourses and processes of IS development; worker-manager and user-developer social and power relations; and individual or organizational ends;

- **Utopian views and vision** of discourses and practices of IS development (means), social and power relations and the ends to be achieved with IS development.

In terms of emancipatory intent an IS development project can focus on:

- **Means** refer to discourses and practices of IS development and use that enable achievement of individual, group and organizational ends;
- **Social relations** affected by IS development including those between developers and users, and workers and managers;
- **Ends** supported and enabled by IS development including individual performance and job satisfaction, a democratic workplace and participative decision-making, and organizational performance and community building.

We now follow these reinterpreted dimensions of Alvesson and Willmott's (1992) framework to examine ISID development practices from an emancipatory perspective within Colruyt's culture, social context and history.

4.6.1 Questioning, Challenging, and Critiquing

Discourses during the first phase of ISID development were characterized by Mr. Lengeler (Interview 2000) and IT personnel questioning severely limited and paper-based information and work practices. The questioning and critiquing during the second, and especially during the current third, phase of ISID development reflected new levels of consciousness and sensitivity to equity, participative rights and responsibilities. Rights to open access to information, it was argued, should be coupled with responsibility for their use. Questioning the unrestricted access to ISID (following the misuse of information) included self-reflective debates about the conflicting demands between completely open access to information and preserving confidentiality of sensitive information in the interest of all.

Misuse of information available from ISID triggered a wide-ranging debate concerning the need and inherent risks of totally open access as well as a necessity to protect confidential information. Thus, if ISID was going to realize the Colruyt principle of 'access to information as a right' for all employees, the question was, on what bases this right could or should be curtailed? An anti-emancipatory step was taken – considered necessary but regrettable by the majority of employees – to restrict access to confidential information. Jo Colruyt was among those who preferred to train the community of users in responsible ISID use, but he also realized that protecting confidential information was inevitable:

> 'It will always remain a delicate balance between confidential ISID documents and a broad access to information. I prefer to keep the number of confidential documents small in relation to non-confidential documents. It appears useful to teach employees to use information judiciously and to instruct them in normative behaviour with respect to information. Employees have the right to a very broad range of information [stored in ISID]'. (Jo Colruyt, 1984)

There was a belief that democratic rights and emancipatory intent needed to be balanced against the risks of misuse and the harmful disclosure of confidential information outside the company. Jo Colruyt maintained that such was a temporary limitation and when 'each of us shoulders [his/her] responsibility for being discrete, we will be able to preserve [complete] communicative openness'.

Questioning the means, (i.e. ISID development discourse and practices) in addition to the ends to be achieved with ISID, implied user-developer and worker-manager social and power relations. Open access by anyone to ISID led to equalization of power that some managers felt threatening and pockets of resistance surfaced more or less overtly. This 'relational friction' can be seen to arise from an inherent labour-capital conflict that lies in the foundation of any capitalist company. By supporting and enabling more effective management and control of processes and employees, information systems often exacerbate this conflict. However, Colruyt's distinctive feature is its continuous effort to reveal and openly confront labour-capital conflict manifested in various relations and processes. By way of questioning, challenging, arguing, critiquing and requesting changes, ISID development and implementation led to *incremental transformation* of discourses and practices (means), power relations and ends, to which we turn next.

4.6.2 Incremental Changes and Transformation

Starting during the early 1970s, ISID development impacted on, and was impacted by, changing relationships between users and developers as well as workers and managers. An indication of changing user–developer relationships can be seen beyond users' official participation in the development team. There was an awareness among the workers that 'having information means having power to act in an informed manner'—which was initially articulated by Jo Colruyt (1984). With IT training and with experience in ISID development and use, workers became increasingly aware of their role in the ISID development as part of their participative rights. Furthermore, incremental changes were experienced in worker-manager relations. Due to access to ISID and workers' informed participation in decision-making, power relations became less hierarchical and more cooperative. However some managers resisted information-sharing and devolution of power. Transformation occurred as part of culture change and personal development took place through training:

> 'We have a culture of [personal] growth within the company. I, myself, have experienced these [culture and personal growth] at all managerial levels, it is evident, and you know this. I think that only individuals who can accept sharing information with subordinates and with others are promoted to managers'.
> (Walter de Hertog, Marketing Manager, Interview 2003)

Transformations towards sharing of information – primarily through ISID – and devolution of power were not without conflicts, but, ultimately, the few managers who obstructed these processes retired.

An important question concerns the emancipatory transformation of ends, that is to say, the extent to which IS development and implementation contributed to the articulation/transformation of ends and their achievement. Transformation of ends was directed toward a more balanced articulation of economic versus social or humanist aims. Marcel Lengeler and other employees mentioned increasing individual performance, job improvement, and commitment to hard work, while at the same time emphasizing enhancement of job satisfaction and enjoyment of work. Similarly ISID is seen as a major contributor to both better company performance and community building. In fact, the economic and social/humanist ends are often seen as conditioning and supporting each other. One employee, for instance, pointed out that ISID enabled him to enjoy 'freedom to make decisions and to share responsibility within [his] company'. Furthermore, the value of workplace democracy and power decentralization enabled by ISID is also understood as contributing to organizational flexibility. Jo Colruyt stated that:

'Power decentralization has the enormous advantage of organizational flexibility to instantly adjust the organization to new situations'. (ISID document, April, 1984).

He further emphasized greater satisfaction from work:

'To communicate [via ISID] means that as a group we are capable of greater achievements. Moreover, in this way we experience greater satisfaction from our work and experience the joy of an increased work engagement'. (ISID document, April 1984).

In short, the transformation of ends achieved through ISID exhibits a continuous struggle to balance personal and organizational achievements, to combine personal performance and enjoyment of work, and to harmonize the Colruyt company's economic prosperity with community building.

4.6.3 Utopian Vision of ISID Development

In order to avoid misunderstanding, we first discuss the sense in which the utopian concept is used with respect to ISID development. Alvesson and Willmott (1992, p. 450) introduced the utopian vision as comparing existing conditions against a new ideal and, in so doing, elect for conscious engagement with a broad repertoire of alternatives. Thus, rather than referring to impractical perfection, the utopian concept as defined by Alvesson and Willmott (1992) has a distinct realistic focus.

This reminds us of the debate surrounding Habermas' (1984) ideal speech situation. Wilson's (1997) critique of emancipatory IS development methodology is based on the interpretation of rational discourse as 'a power-independent, and, therefore, extra-social, state of ideal communication which will not be distorted by the interference of power relationships' (p. 198). He criticizes the notion of rational discourse as a condition for emancipatory IS development defined by

Hirschheim and Klein (1994), for implying 'a superior rationality', independent of 'the frameworks of power and influence operating in an institution' and also a conflict-free, unitary organization. By exaggerating and misinterpreting the ideal speech situation, defined by Habermas (1984) as social interaction that 'excludes all force . . . except the force of the better argument' (Habermas, 1984, p. 25), and the related notion of rational discourse, Wilson ridicules these concepts and makes them look silly and embarrassingly naive. Such critique is misleading as it obscures rather than reveals the complexity of these concepts and potential problems involved in understanding and applying them.

    We detect a utopian element in the vision of the ISID development process at Colruyt as a rational discourse. Being very pragmatic, Colruyt company members do not talk about the ideal of rational discourse. This was demonstrated during the ISID development team meetings that one of the authors attended, where participants showed excellent questioning skills, providing arguments and counter-arguments, and conducting an open and well argued debate[5]. The outcomes of ISID meetings were made public via ISID, thus increasing company-wide awareness of its results and seeking responses and involvement by others.

    An important utopian view of ISID at Colruyt focused on company ends. Ideally the development and use of ISID was seen as enrichment of professional and personal life of all members, contributing to democratic work environment, work enjoyment, individual and collective self-realization. This enabled freeing up the creative capacities of employees, opening up company opportunities and improving performance. This vision of ISID was essential to realize the company's philosophy and to implement in practice its ideals, principles, and strategies.

    The utopian vision of ISID and its role in determining and achieving company ends can be criticized, especially from a post-structuralist perspective, as totalizing, possibly excluding other voices. There is the risk, a post-structuralist would claim, that the utopian vision of participatory culture, open communication and the ideal of ISID development as rational discourse may degenerate into ideology with anti-emancipatory implications. While such a risk cannot be excluded, our in-depth analysis of micro-emancipatory events and situations (grounded in the narratives by actors expressed in interviews, documents, ISID transcripts) suggests that the utopian element in ISID development stimulated critical thinking and opened up novel alternatives as envisaged by Alvesson and Willmott (1992).

    The utopian vision of open communication inspired and opened up desirable models of ISID that drove its technological development. Rather than imposing a solution, the utopian vision released creative capacities of employees, motivating them to search and continue searching for innovative ways of communicating, working and decision-making.

---

5. Due to a limited space it is not possible to provide a detailed analysis of meeting records.

4.6.4 Theoretical Contribution and Lessons Learned

Colruyt did not invent participatory and emancipatory IS development, but its members dared to experiment with an ideologically and practically controversial concept. Colruyt's superior performance and continuous market success makes it an exemplary case from which to understand participatory and emancipatory IS developments. Our analysis of ISID's development forms the basis for revisiting Hirschheim and Klein's conditions for an emancipatory IS development methodology and practice (1994, pp. 87–88). Learning from Colruyt, we propose the following organizational and material conditions for participatory and emancipatory IS development:

1 Emancipatory IS development is an active process and, at times, a struggle for individual and collective self-determination within the broader context of corporate culture. While management support is conducive to participatory and democratic processes, as is the case in Colruyt, emancipation cannot be bestowed upon the employees. For meaningful emancipation to come about, it is necessary that employees are conscious of their rights to access information, that they are communicatively competent and ready to take up power, and determine individual and collective aims. However, benevolent management and top-down introduction of participatory and emancipatory IS development, is not unproblematic, and it runs the risk of instrumental use for corporate performance ends.

2 Emancipatory IS development involves norms, forms and discourses of critical self-reflection and associated self-transformation that are not narrowly focused on the means but, instead, centre on broader issues of social and power relations, labour-capital conflicts, company economic and profit objectives, as well as its social and community aims.

3 Emancipatory IS development depends on, and is embedded in, a broader set of institutional conditions relating particularly to corporate culture, social structure and management processes, employees' rights, equality and social justice, quality of work life and democratic workplace and the like. Emancipatory IS development 'is not something that can simply be plugged into existing systems to improve their emancipatory performance' (Alvesson & Willmott, 1992).

4 The concept of emancipatory IS development is based on the assumption of dissensus in organizations; that is, existence of different interests, views and perspectives by various stakeholders. Participatory and emancipatory IS development increases risks of conflict and may be a cause of prolonged and ineffective decision-making. To counteract these risks, company members need to continually improve their communicative, conflict resolution and negotiation skills and learn to deal with different interests and conflicts; or, stated differently, increase communicative rationality.

5 Emancipatory IS development practices are characterized by principles of rational discourse, involving reasoned argumentation, non-distorted

communication, articulation of, and a search for, solutions acceptable to different stakeholders, and reaching agreement free from the coercive use of power. It should be understood that even though rational discourse seeks consensus, this does not imply universal and lasting agreements and, further- more, the possibility of dissensus remains. In fact, sometimes in contentious situations a limited and tentative agreement is all that can be achieved. The practice of participatory and emancipatory IS development that is character- ized by communicative rationality and rational discourse also involves risks of failure and risks of manipulation.

6 Emancipatory IS development constitutes collective sense-making and inno- vation, is part of organizational development (e.g. self-nominated and self- managed groups; problem solving workgroups; public debates via ISID; a particular democratic style of meetings) and organizational learning; it also requires conscious, systematic and continuous training and personal and collective development.

7 Emancipatory IS development endorses and relies on the nexus between rights to information and democratic rights, between information decentral- ization and power decentralization, and between participation and motivation for change, and personal and collective improvement. These complex rela- tionships emerge in a non-linear way, with recurrent obstacles and set-backs.

8 Emancipatory IS development involves vision, incremental transformation and questioning of the ends to be achieved by IS implementation. Perfor- mance and efficiency objectives are not necessarily in conflict with work- place democracy and participative decision-making; on the contrary, Colruyt demonstrates employee discretion and autonomy, self-realization, and job satisfaction are in fact contributing to creativity, organizational flexibility, and innovation that lead to consistently higher performance compared with similar retailers.

Derived from the in-depth analysis and critical reflection on the Colruyt longitudinal case study, the proposed conditions for, and characteristics of, participatory and emancipatory IS development address both theoretical and practical concerns. They are intended to summarize the learning from the Colruyt study and make the participatory and emancipatory IS development more relevant and accessible to IS practitioners.

4.7 (UN)CONCLUDING REFLECTIONS

This chapter, based on our longitudinal study of ISID in the Colruyt company, has re-examined the nature, meaning and challenges of a participatory and emancipatory IS development project. Through an in-depth analysis and critical reflection guided by insights suggested by Alvesson and Willmott (1992), our chapter has identified instances of micro-emancipation and discussed their meanings and implications for practice. The chapter provides convincing em- pirical evidence testifying to the realism and practical usefulness of participatory and emancipatory IS development. Based on both empirical and theoretical argument, the chapter revisited the conditions for emancipatory IS development practices (Hirschheim and Klein, 1994; Alvesson & Willmott, 1992). We also make several key contributions.

Our chapter demonstrates the reality of participatory and emancipatory ISD practices and their meaning in context, however, local or controversial they might appear. We dispel the mistaken notion that emancipatory ideas are abstract and idealistic without practical meaning or relevance. The Colruyt company's vision as both an industry leader in customer service, efficiency and democratic social relations required novel forms of work (such as self-selected and self-managed workgroups) and information availability. This necessitated that the company developed and experimented with novel IS as well as novel ways of designing them. The participatory and emancipatory ISID development practices in the Colruyt company reflects its organizational culture of devolved decision making, autonomy and responsibility of workgroups, and individual and collective striving for excellence and superior performance. The company's IS development processes were equally driven by concerns for work improvement, efficiency, effectiveness, and sound technical solutions, as they were for improvement of working conditions, employees' work satisfaction, individual and collective self-realization and community well-being.

An IS development cannot be seen in isolation from company philosophy, culture, social relations, and management processes and practices. The more an IS permeates organizational processes and relations the more IS development becomes intertwined with these processes and relations. This intertwining, however, can in principle reinforce or transform existing structures and relations. In the case of ISID development, we saw evidence for both. On the one hand, ISID development reflected and reinforced company philosophy of open communication, cooperative and inclusive culture, participatory decision making and equitable relations. On the other hand, ISID development and implementation also continually transformed company culture, processes and practices, as well as social and power relations.

Increasing efficiency and effectiveness of business processes and overall company performance are not, as is widely assumed, unavoidably opposed to social and humanist objectives such as worker participation, their greater autonomy, responsibility and emancipation. Similarly, increasing levels of economic performance do not unavoidably lead to increased control, diminished worker autonomy, and stringent worker subordination. In fact, by acquiring greater autonomy and responsibility, and by increasing their participation in decision-making practices, Colruyt employees became more innovative in simplifying work processes and more successful in increasing efficiency and effectiveness. Participatory privileges, access to information, and employee empowerment, have been practiced as values in their own right, which, in turn, became the drivers of the Colruyt company's economic prosperity. Continuous improvements in performance and economic success can go hand-in-hand with continuous empowering. Emancipatory processes did not just remain the vision of the late CEO Jo Colruyt but, more importantly, it became a lived experience and the conviction of the workers and managers at all levels. Not withstanding his humanistic and philosophical values, Jo Colruyt was also an extraordinarily pragmatic manager under whose guidance the company expanded to Belgium's third largest food retail discount; and presently expanding into France. Our longitudinal study of the Colruyt company demonstrates not only the realism of participatory and emancipatory IS development practices but also confirms the reality of Hirschheim and Klein's (1994) contention that emancipation produces:

> 'Stable, self-confident personalities [who] are the pillars of a stress-resistant work force; individuals confidently expressing ideas [who are] the bedrock of creativity to meet competitive demands; and only people accustomed to autonomous, responsible action can be expected to take the initiative when things go wrong, which increases organization's flexibility and capacity to deal with uncertainty' (1994, p. 98)

A major lesson from the Colruyt company is, perhaps, that to advocate participatory and emancipatory IS development, one can use not only a humanist argument but also an economic one. In fact, the participatory and emancipatory approach to ISID development was characterized by equalizing developer-user and manager-employee power relations and, moreover, the company succeeded in achieving emancipatory change. Importantly though, the company's emancipatory transformation produced significant commercial successes. In almost every aspect of its performance – sales per store, sales per square meter or per employee, profit per employee or square meter, etcetera—the Colruyt company consistently showed superior results compared to other similar retail chains. Linking participatory and emancipatory ISID development practices with company success, and, more broadly, linking the practices of workplace democracy and employee participation in decision-making (enabled and supported by ISID) to the Colruyt company's superior performance and commercial success, should capture the attention of managers and IS practitioners alike.

By pointing toward the potential for economic benefit we may draw managers' and companies' attention to the unrealized potential of emancipatory IS development projects. Rather than advocating yet another form of instrumental use of humanist values, we raise awareness of the emancipatory project as liberating, as unleashing individual and collective creative potential for humane and more democratic forms of work and social relations and as contributing to a company's economic success. The participatory and emancipatory IS development implies critical self-reflection of employees, IS professionals and managers, and that is not limited to improving working conditions and employees' work satisfaction, proposed by the socio-technical approach. By critically assessing and continually advancing the participatory and emancipatory IS development paralleled with equalizing power relations and increasing employees' discretion and autonomy, and by nurturing critical self-reflection and associated self-transformation, the company achieved both emancipatory transformation and economic success.

While a distinction between truly emancipatory and falsely emancipatory discourses and practices is not always obvious and clear cut, this chapter provides an empirical and theoretical argument for making such a distinction. It advances knowledge that enables one to recognize emancipatory IS development processes and practices, while being sensitive to the risks of distortion and deception, and careful to understand the inherent contradictions and frailty of emancipatory discourses and practices, while resisting the allure of apparently emancipatory and idealized discourses and practices. The chapter contributes to a better, empirically grounded conception of participatory and emancipatory IS development by defining (theoretically and practically) a space between non-emancipatory and emancipatory IS development processes and practices. It, therefore, opens up this space for further examination and critical assessment by IS researchers and practitioners.

REFERENCES

Adele, B., Martens, A., Tordeur, G., Van der Smissen, E., & Muelenaer, G. (1984). *Dossier Colruyt.* EPO, Antwerp, Belgium.

Alvesson, M., & Willmott, H. (1992). On the idea of emancipation in management and organization studies. *Academy of Management Review, 17*(3), 432–464.

Asaro, P. M. (2000). Transforming society by transforming technology: The science and politics of participatory design. *Accounting, Management & Information Technology, 10,* 257–290.

Bjerknes, G., & Bratteteig, T. (1995). User participation and democracy: A discussion of scandinavian research on system development. *Scandinavian Journal of Information Systems, 7*(1), 73–98.

Cavaye, A. L.M. (1995). User participation in system development—Revisited. *Information and Management, 28*(5), 311–323.

Colruyt, J. (1985). Communication. There Are No Gentleman Here Sir. Penneman, T. (Ed.), Druco Publishing, Belgium, Halle, pp. 73–5.

Czarniawska, B. (1998). *A narrative approach to organization studies.* Chicago University Press, Chicago.

de Broyer, M. (1985). Response to TV Program. There Are No Gentleman Here Sir. Penneman, T. (Ed.), Druco Publishing, Belgium, Halle, p.180.

Ehn, P., & Sandberg, A. (1983). Local union influence on technology and work organization: Some results from DEMOS project. *Systems Design for, with and by Users.* In Briefs, U., Ciborra, C., & Schneider, L. (Eds.), North Holland, Amsterdam, pp. 427–437.

Emery, F., & Thorsrud, E. (1976). *Democracy at work: The report of the Norwegian industrial democracy program.* Martinus Nijhoff, Leiden, Norway.

Habermas, J. (1984). *The theory of communicative action—Reason and the rationalisation of society,* Beacon Press, Boston, MA, Vol I.

Hirschheim, R., & Klein, H. (1994). Realizing emancipatory principles in information system development. *MIS Quarterly, 18*(1), 83–110.

Howcroft, D., & Wilson, M. (2003). Participation: Bounded freedom or hidden constraints on user involvement. *New Technology, Work and Employment, 18*(1), 2–19.

Janson, M., Joshi, K., & Taillieu, T. (1998). The evolving organization: An interview with Jo Colruyt. *The Journal of Leadership Studies, 5*(3), 141–151.

Kyng, M., & Mathiassen, L. (1982). Systems development and trade union activities. *Information Society for Richer, for Poorer.* In Bjorn-Andersen, N. (Ed.), North Holland, Amsterdam, pp. 247–260.

Lyytinen, K., & Hirschheim, R. (1985). Information systems and emancipation: Promise or threat? *System Development for Human Progress.* In Klein, H.K., & Kumar, K. (Eds.), Elsevier Science Publishers, B.V., North Holland, pp. 115–139.

Lyytinen, K., & Klein, H. (1985). The critical theory of Jurgen Habermas as a basis for a theory of information systems. *Research Methods in Information Systems.* In Mumford, E., Hirschheim, R., & Wood-Harper, T. (Eds.), Elsevier Science Publishers, North Holland, Amsterdam, pp. 219–236.

Markus, M. L., & Mao, J. Y. (2004). Participation in development and implementation—Updating an old, tired concept for today's IS contexts. *JAIS, 5*(11–12), 514–544.

Moldaschl, M., & Weber, W. G. (1998). The three waves of industrial group work: Historical reflections on current research on group work. *Human Relations, 51,* 347–388.

Mumford, E. (1981). Participative systems design: Structures and methods. *Systems Objectives Solutions, 1*(1), 1–11.

Mumford, E. (2000). Socio-technical design: An unfulfilled promise or a future opportunity. *Organizational and social perspectives on information technology.* In Baskerville, R., Stage, J., & DeGross, J. (Eds.), Kluver, London, pp. 33–46.

Mumford, E. (2006). The story of socio-technical design: Reflections on its successes, failures and potential. *Information Systems Journal, 16,* 317–342.

Mumford, E., & Weir, M. (1979). *Computer systems in work design—the ethics method.* Associate Business Press, London.

Resseler, K. (1986). *Organizational communication. Ph.D. dissertation.* University of Louvain, Belgium.

Saravanamuthu, K. (2002). The political lacuna in participatory systems design. *Journal of Information Technology, 17*(4), 185–198.

Vermeren, R. (1985). Response to TV Program. There Are No Gentleman Here Sir. Penneman, T. (Ed.), Druco Publishing, Belgium, Halle, p. 163.

Weick, K. (1995). *Sensemaking in organizations.* Sage, Thousand Oaks, CA.

Wilson, F. A. (1997). The truth is out there: The search for emancipatory principles in information systems design. *Information Technology and People, 10*(3), 187–204.

FURTHER READING

Alvesson, M., & Deetz, S. (2000). *Doing critical management research.* Sage Publications, London.

Barki, H., & Hartwick, J. (1989). Rethinking the concept of user-involvement. *Management Information Systems Quarterly, 13*(1), 53–63.

Barki, H., Rivard, S., & Talbot, J. (2001). An integrative contingency model of software project risk management. *Journal of Management Information Systems, 17*(4), 37–68.

Bodker, S., Ehn, P., Kammersgaard, J., Kyng, M., & Sundblad, Y. (1987). A utopean experience: On design of powerful computer-based tools for skilled graphical workers. *Computers and Democracy—A Scandinavian Challenge.* In Bjerkins, G., Ehn, P., & Kyng, M. (Eds.), Avebury, Aldershot, pp. 251–278.

Carmel, E., Whitaker, R., & George, J. (1993). PD and joint application design: A transatlantic comparison. *Communications of the ACM, 36*(4), 40–48.

Ehn, P., & Kyng, M. (1987). The collective resource approach to systems design. *Computers and democracy: A Scandinavian challenge*. In Bjerknes, G., Ehn, P., & Kyng, M. (Eds.), Avebury, Aldershot, UK, pp. 17–57.

Franz, C. R., & Robey, D. (1984). An investigation of user-led systems design: Rational and political perspectives. *Communication of the ACM, 27*(2), 112–126.

Hedberg, B. (1980). Using computerized information systems to design better organizations and jobs. *The human side of information processing*. In Bjorn-Andersen, N. (Ed.), North Holland, Amsterdam, pp. 19–33.

Hirchheim, R. A., & Klein, H. K. (1994). Realizing emancipatory principles in information systems development: The case for ethics. *MIS Quarterly, 18*(1), 83–109.

Jarvenpaa, S. L., & Ives, B. (1991). Executive involvement and participation in the management of information technology. *MIS Quarterly, 15*(2), 205–227.

Jiang, J. J., Klein, G., & Chen, H. G. (2006). The effects of user partnering and user non-support on project performance. *JAIS, 7*(2), 68–90.

McGrath, K. (2005). Doing critical research in information systems: A case of theory and practice not informing each other. *Information Systems Journal, 15*, 85–101.

Mumford, E. (1983). *Designing human systems: The ethics method*. Manchester Business School, Manchester, UK.

Newman, M., & Noble, F. (1990). User involvement as an interaction process: A case study. *Information Systems Research, 1*(1), 89–113.

Nielsen, J. F., & Relsted, N. J. (1994). A new agenda for user participation: Reconsidering the old Scandinavian prescription. *Scandinavian Journal of Information Systems, 6*(2), 3–20.

Nygaard, K., & Sorgaard, P. (1987). The perspective concept in informatics. *Computers and democracy: A Scandinavian challenge*. In Bjerknes, G., Ehn, P., & Kyng, M. (Eds.), Avebury, Aldershot, UK.

Olerup, A. (1989). Socio-technical design of computer-assisted work: A discussion of the ethics and tavistock approaches. *Scandinavian Journal of Information Systems, 1*(1), 43–71.

Verlinden, T. (2003). Colruyt: Profit sharing increases bond between company and employees. *Scope on People and Work, 1*, 26–29.

Wood, J., & Silver, D. (1989). *Joint application design: How to design quality systems in 40% less time*. John Wiley & Sons, New York.

Chapter 5

ERP Adoption – What Do They Say About It?

Dave Oliver and Celia Romm

5.1 INTRODUCTION

This chapter presents a critical approach to the way organizations justify adopting Enterprise Resource Planning (ERP) systems. The perspectives on social activity put forward by Max Weber and Jürgen Habermas provide the basis from which the themes of communication, rationality, legitimacy and domination are explored. The data used in the study are electronically mediated justifications of ERP adoption presented by universities. A model of ERP adoption is developed using grounded theory, which is then critiqued. The themes underlying ERP adoption discerned in the study are a mix of technical, value-driven and strategic influences. The conclusions reached in this chapter are that despite the difficulty of identifying and measuring domination and emancipation, there is some evidence to suggest that people occupy a subservient role to technology, process and organization.

Western society has been strongly focused on the deployment of technology for a substantial period of time. Centred on mechanical systems during the Industrial Revolution, the impetus has more recently been directed towards electronic systems including the use of information technology (IT). There is a strong performative influence in the desire not only to adopt technology but also to control. Beniger (1986) sees the 'information revolution' as an expression of management's desire for increased control, by extending control over systems of administration in addition to those of production. ERP systems are a specific type of information technology, deployed extensively over the last 15 years, particularly by large and medium-sized organizations, so, following Beniger's thinking, ERP systems would be expected to be directed towards the attainment of increased administrative control.

ERP systems are packaged software applications that provide a range of applications required by most businesses within a single framework, using a modular approach. Each module serves a distinct business activity such as Human Resource Management or Purchasing. An organization can select the modules it chooses to implement from those available, and these will be presented as a single integrated solution. Integration of systems, based upon standard business applications or modules with a common database and operating style, is the essence of the ERP approach. Integration facilitates the production of reports that require data from different functional units, which, using the previous non-integrated solution would have required the difficult task of reconciling data from different sources. Prior to the advent of ERP systems, applications were created to serve specific business functions only.

The widespread adoption of ERP systems by large and medium-sized organizations has been described as the 'ERP revolution' by Ross (1999). In many organizations, it has resulted in the replacement of a considerable quantity of disparate information systems with one single ERP system. The financial impact is significant: 'By early 2000 the ERP revolution generated over $20 billion in revenues annually for suppliers and an additional $20 billion for consulting firms' (Willcocks & Sykes, 2000, p. 32). ERP systems have now been adopted by the majority of the Fortune top 500 firms and, as the high end of the market became saturated, these systems have filtered down to medium-sized organizations such as universities, and to regions beyond those initially penetrated in Europe and North America (Kumar & Van Hillegersberg, 2000).

Although it is only the most senior people in the organization who possess the authority to instigate a course of action with such extensive financial, technical and organizational ramifications as the adoption of an ERP system, the implementation of an ERP project requires the acceptance, compliance and commitment of a broad range of people. 'Implementing any integrated ERP solution is not so much a technological exercise but an 'organizational revolution'. Extensive preparation before implementation is the key to success' (Bingi, Sharma, & Godla, 1999, p. 9).

King and McAulay (1997) argue that how change is received is as important as the nature of the change itself. Because ERP deployment has such broad impact it is important for management to create a climate that will encourage acceptance and even enthusiasm for it. The most important staff are those who will need to adapt to new work patterns imposed by the new systems, but more peripheral employees and other stakeholders are also on management's radar as constituencies to be influenced.

5.2 CRITICAL SOCIAL THEORY

Choosing a critical approach opens up a range of perspectives from which to view and analyse the data available. These perspectives encourage both deep and broad thinking around the object of attention. Critical social theory (CST) assists the researcher to move beyond an understanding of what is being done, to why it is being done. Being 'critical' in IS research does not only mean commitment to a certain set of assumptions and values that determine a third path in IS research. Being 'critical' also means having a much broader historical, social and political view of the IS discipline. (Cecez-Kecmanovic, 2005, p. 42) As Cecez-Kecmanovic indicates, CST provides a further direction, beyond those found within mainstream IS, from which a framework to aid analysis may be sought. This chapter draws on the ideas of Weber and Habermas, to inform the analysis of the underlying forces within which managers of organizations are acting, as they seek to legitimize the introduction of ERP systems.

A critical approach may also contrast the compatibility of specific operational objectives with the stated aims and intentions of the organization. It is possible that the pursuit of one specific objective, in this case the adoption of an ERP system, could create a conflict with broader institutional goals. A critical approach should, therefore, explore the possibility of a conflict between a specific tactic and overall goals. Domination, legitimation and communication are also key elements of social theory (Giddens, 1984). The emancipatory interest, which is how release from domination is to be achieved, forms another dimension to critical approaches. For Habermas, emancipation works via self-reflection, 'emancipating people from the illusions and ideologies that distort their perceptions of themselves' (McClure, 1991, p. 37). As domination is effected through power, self-reflection may not be an adequate mechanism for a complete release from all forms of domination. Lyytinen and Klein (1985) observe in their study of how the ideas of Habermas could be applied to IS research, that emancipation is a complex issue. Nevertheless the liberating and emancipatory intent of CST in identifying inhibitors to human potential in the social context is a lofty objective that should not be dismissed simply because the emancipated state is one that is difficult to prescribe. Cecez-Kecmanovic (2005, p. 24) writes 'critical IS researchers believe that such objectives are worthy of pursuit even if they are only partially achieved'.

Habermas (1971) suggests that technology can exert a form of domination, and as technology is inherent in information systems, we need to be conscious of potentially adverse effects. Marcuse (1970) also argues that technology may exercise forms of control over society, contrary to its apparent purpose as a tool. In a context of technological domination, managers and workers alike become servants of the needs of technical systems of production (Schroyer, 1975). However, technical systems of production must be legitimated by the societies in which they operate, otherwise they would fall into disuse as a result of their failure to meet socially constructed expectations. Even if they do exert a dominating role, that dominance has to be tacitly accepted by social actors in order for it to not only continue but to develop and thrive. Hill (1988) argues new technologies diffuse through a society, and transform it, more because the technologies align with people's desires, than because of the singular power of repressive interests to enforce ownership and participation. Hill further argues that the technological context, once created, limits and focuses the future social developments that are likely to follow, and, thus, creates a particular *shape of demand* for subsequent technologies. From this perspective ERP systems can be seen as an evolutionary development from earlier types of information technologies.

5.3 RATIONALITY TYPES AND THEIR APPLICATION

Exploring the rationality types underlying the statements relating to ERP adoption provides an insight into issues beneath the surface justification. As mentioned, an objective of critical analysis is to expose both broader and deeper meanings to a context. At the surface this study is a study of the justifications for ERP adoption, but at a deeper level of meaning we seek to connect this event to attitudes and values held in the broad social setting. This deeper level of understanding can provide unifying threads that form on-going themes within society across a variety of contexts and it is finding and linking these themes that are of interest to critical social theorists. Cecez-Kecmanovic and Janson (2000, 2001) and Cecez-Kecmanovic (2005) present a case for the analysis of developments in IS using a rationality framework based on the ideas of Weber and Habermas. *Instrumental rationality* relates to the determination of the most appropriate means for achieving a given end. A key issue identified by Weber is the precise calculation of alternative means (Habermas, 1984). This requirement seems to suggest a preference for formal rationality, where quantitative techniques are used to rank alternatives, compared to informal rationality where the ordering of alternatives is elaborated using language. Ultimately, in whatever terms it is expressed, a rationale based upon grounds of efficiency, effectiveness, timeliness or cost exhibits instrumental rationality. Instrumental rationality is one of the underlying rationality types that we use to decorate the model presented later in the chapter. The consideration of ends involves issues of *substantive or value rationality*, which, as they are based on values, are usually not as amenable to calculation or formal expression as those relating to means (Weber, 1978). As Weber points out orientation towards values is crucial in determining alternative courses of action, since this is how fundamental priorities are established. Marcuse (1970, p. 122) observes:

> 'Values may have a higher dignity (morally and spiritually, but they are not *real* and thus count less in the real business of life—the less so the higher they are elevated *above* reality'

and

If the Good and the Beautiful, Peace and Justice cannot be derived either from ontological or scientific-rational conditions, they cannot logically claim universal validity and realization.

These arguments suggest there is a tendency for value-based action in society to be repressed. In Western societies, instrumental and substantive rationality has become conflated as the following observation by Avgerou and McGrath (2005, p. 302) indicates:

'In the substantive sense, the modern Western economic rationality in which people orient their decisions towards maximizing efficiency and weighing costs and benefits, conveys one particular set of values that historically came to dominate over others. These values involve the ethical sanction of acquisitive activity and a propensity to seek new solutions to problems rather than adhere to traditions. Other societies subscribe to different values and, hence, strive to attain different ends. Such ends may include ethical, political, or utilitarian considerations, such as social equity, social justice or the furtherance of power of a political unit.'

Pfeffer (1981, p. 15) argues that 'consensus on technology is more readily achieved than consensus on values and preferences, at least in this culture'. When we find that a preference for a technological solution of some type is expressed, but there is no accompanying justification for it other than it being technological, we may assume that technology is itself valued and, therefore, the underlying rationality type of the justification is substantive. Substantive rationality is another of the underlying rationality types that we use to decorate the model presented later in the chapter.

Strategically directed action is based upon the behaviour of others. The type of behaviour generated by strategic necessities may be imitative of others or it may involve viewing other human actors as opponents (Habermas, 1984). Language can also be used as a means of strategic action (Lyytinen & Klein, 1985). Applying the analysis of the rhetorical situation by Blitzer (described in Yates & Orlikowski, 1992) to the justification of ERP adoption, we have an exigency in the form of an ERP system that needs to be implemented; an audience, the employees in the organization where the ERP system is to be deployed; a constraint, those with the power to influence the situation – the managers. Willcocks and Smith (1995) have pointed to this tactic of attempting to develop attitudes and behaviours that will foster co-operation and commitment to process and IT changes, through the use of rhetoric. Resistance to change, writes Robbins (1993), can be reduced by education and communication. Generally accepted norms induce organizations to provide explanations that are viewed as rational in order to be perceived as legitimate (Meyer & Rowan, 1977). This tendency is emphasized for public institutions where objective measures of efficiency tend not to operate, so the creation of perceptions of efficiency become extremely important. This would appear to be especially true of educational bodies such as universities, which are both public institutions and purveyors of rationality (Langley, 1989). Justifications for a course of action that are based on the behaviour of others, or justifications that tend towards influencing others, are strategically orientated and are underpinned by *strategic rationality*. Strategic rationality is the final underlying rationality type that we use to decorate the model presented later in the chapter.

5.4 RESEARCH APPROACH

March (1988) asserts that there are two approaches to building theories that attempt to describe the behaviour of social institutions: prescriptive theories which describe optimal behaviour, and behavioural theories that describe actual behaviour. Pfeffer (1981) makes a further distinction in approaches to behavioural analysis and theory building. One involves analysing and predicting substantive outcomes, the other is the analysis and prediction of how organizational activities are perceived, interpreted and legitimated. A critical theory approach is possible from this perspective.

In common with other types of investment activity the adoption of an ERP system is a purposive intervention by an organization, to bring about a new state of affairs judged to be superior to the current state. In presenting a rationale for this course of action, the organization makes statements about the existing and desired states of affairs. These claims may be assessed using the four components of communicative competence defined by Habermas (1984), namely their truth, rightness, appropriateness and intelligibility.

The purpose of this research is not to assess whether the statements made are grounded in reality, which can only be achieved from knowledge of each case, but to identify common themes (conceptual categories) and from these develop a conceptual model of how ERP adoption is justified. A grounded theory analysis is used to construct these conceptual categories (Strauss & Corbin, 1998). What organizations value, or consider important in the context of ERP adoption can be revealed. The language, which forms the conceptual categories and their relative importance, constitutes descriptive data that are then discussed from a CST perspective. Also the conceptual categories are analysed to detect their underlying rationality type(s).

Universities were chosen as cases for the study for a number of reasons. Firstly, universities are substantial and experienced users of IT and a significant number have emerged as purchasers of ERP systems. Secondly, Rands (1992) and Weill and Olson (1989) argue that the requirements for software acquisition vary considerably across different industries. The demand for software varies across industries, so, too, does the source of supply. Universities are a specific vertical market targeted by ERP vendors, which provides stability on the supply side as well as the demand side. Restriction to a particular industry and market segment prevents industry and market effects – that might be uneven across industry sectors – from distorting the analysis.

Finally, the direction given by Eisenhart (1989) that the process of interest must be transparently observable confirms the use of universities as suitable

TABLE 5.1 Sources of Data

Universities Studied	Abbreviation	Number of documents	Word count	Number of coded statements
California State University	CSU	7	8680	121
Central Queensland University	CQU	5	2994	82
University of Colorado	UoC	6	30847	204
Duke University	Duke	5	15700	144
University of Michigan	UoM	7	36114	219
University of Minnesota	Minne	11	6863	91
University of Nebraska	UoN	8	10116	59
University of New South Wales	UNSW	8	32555	106
Total		57	143869	1026

candidates. Universities have formal approaches to action and consequently their activities are habitually documented. Also, many universities have placed material relevant to this research programme in an accessible form on their Web sites. This varied collection of documents includes Requests for Proposal (RFP), publicity statements and committee reports relating to the ERP project. A multiple case-study approach was used to develop the model, which provides greater potential for empirical generalization than does a single case study. Table 1 illustrates the sources and volume of data analysed in this study. Columns one and two show the universities studied and the abbreviations used for them. Only those universities that made their rationale for adopting ERP systems accessible in an electronic form were considered. Column three shows the number of documents analysed from each university. The word count is shown in the fourth column and the number of statements that were coded (identified and classified) in the fifth column.

5.5 DEVELOPMENT OF THE MODEL

Grounded theory development cannot proceed from a vacuum, but neither should its direction be prescribed at the outset. A point of departure is, however, needed to provide initial focus. Information systems define a territory within organizations inhabited by processes, technology (hardware, software, and databases) and people (Khazanchi & Munkvold, 2000), (Laudon & Laudon, 1984). The domains *Organization*, *Process*, *Technology* and *People* provide a basic framework as shown in Figure 1. These groupings are sufficiently broad to presuppose any formative outcomes. Conceptual categories may be grafted onto this basic framework.

Language is the primary means used to derive conceptual categories and gives these form and substance. The first author performed the task of searching

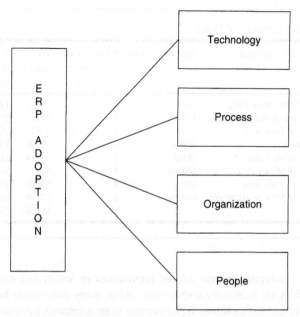

FIGURE 5.1   The basic model of ERP justification.

for, reading and analysing the source documents to identify and classify statements that justified the adoption of an ERP system. These activities took place in an iterative fashion, as with grounded theory conceptual categories emerge from the data progressively. Several iterations of the documents that had been assembled took place before stability was reached. In this way the tree depicted in Figure 1 became adorned with the branches (conceptual categories) that appear on the extended tree of Figure 2.

A conceptual category may be viewed from a number of perspectives. The breadth of each conceptual category is determined from the number of dimensions within it. At the extremes a dimension has a high level of agreement if it surfaces in all eight cases or a low level of agreement if it surfaces in a minimum of two. Dimensions of conceptual categories are represented in tabular form as illustrated in Table 2. The size with which conceptual categories are depicted in Figure 3 gives an indication of their comparative importance. In addition, each conceptual category is decorated to depict the underlying rationality types attributed to it as shown in Figure 2.

FIGURE 5.2   Legend for tree decoration.

TABLE 5.2 *Process Improvement* – Dimensions

Dimension	CSU	CQU	UoC	Duke	UoM	Minne	UoN	UNSW	Level of agreement
Improved/streamlined processes	Yes	Yes	Yes	Yes	Yes	Yes	Yes	Yes	8
Adopting 'best practices'	Yes	Yes		Yes			Yes	Yes	5
Reducing costs			Yes	Yes	Yes	Yes			4
Efficiency improvements	Yes				Yes		Yes	Yes	4
Reducing administrative workload		Yes	Yes			Yes			3
Level of agreement	3	3	3	3	3	3	3	3	24

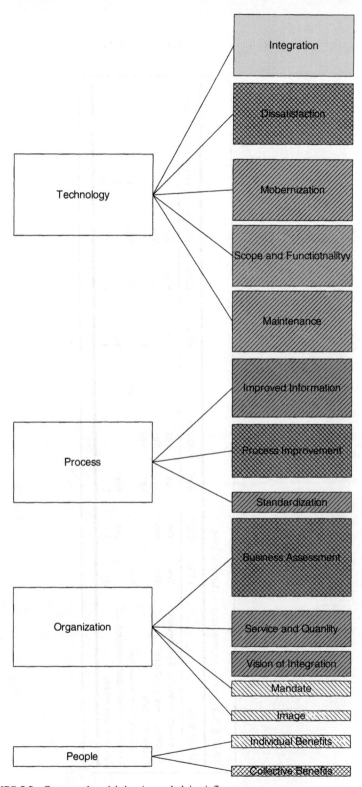

FIGURE 5.3 Conceptual model showing underlying influences.

After coding the data into conceptual categories, Nvivo software was used to compute their frequencies. Although we agree with Krippendorf (1980) that quantitative indicators obtained from a content analysis are insensitive and shallow in providing insight, they are of some value in assessing the relative importance of different domains and conceptual categories. Whilst this measure is not central to grounded theory, it provides additional evidence. Although a precise measurement of the strength of each conceptual category cannot be given using this methodology, the statements used to create the conceptual categories, the number of dimensions within a conceptual category, the level of agreement within those dimensions and the frequency of reference within each conceptual category provide an indication of their actual and relative strength. In the following sections we expand upon how the model shown in Figure 3 was developed using a grounded theory approach.

5.5.1 The Process Improvement Conceptual Category

For the purposes of this chapter, the *Process Improvement* conceptual category is chosen as an illustration of how a conceptual category emerged.

Table 2 shows the dimensions and the level of agreement derived from the data and Table 3 the percentage references. *Process Improvement* has five dimensions and a level of agreement of 24 as shown in Table 2. Note the level of agreement is the sum of all of the dimensions within a conceptual category. Also the reader should note that from this section onwards domains are emphasized in the text by an underline, conceptual categories by bold italics and dimensions by normal italics.

All universities examined expressed their justification for new systems using the rationale of *Process Improvement,* which is the second most important conceptual category in the Process domain. Justificatory statements for ERP adoption in the *Process Improvement* conceptual category belong to two main categories.

These are rationale for improved or streamlined processes and those that relate to the adoption of 'best practices'.

The rationale of improved or streamlined processes is adopted by each of the universities studied. Business Process Reengineering (BPR) rhetoric is discernable in many of the justifications put forward by universities for ERP adoption. The radical nature of BPR (in which the complete removal of processes predominates) is evident at the University of Michigan which stated that 'Policies,

TABLE 5.3 *Process Improvement* by Percentage Reference

University	CSU	CQU	UoC	Duke	UoM	Minne	UoN	UNSW	Mean
Content	14.0	20.7	14.7	10.4	18.3	20.9	16.9	10.4	15.78

processes, and procedures that do not add value to the institution will be eliminated.' (University of Michigan, 1995, p. 25). *Process Improvement* rationales
exhibit instrumental rationality. The University of Colorado, indicating that they
had studied a large number of HR and Financial processes, included in the
rationale for their ERP system the proposition that as many as half of these
could be automated, simplified or eliminated. The objective of implementing
improved processes becomes part of the rationale for ERP adoption:

> 'A.S.P. flowcharted (or "mapped") the HR and Financial processes of over 360
> University units. When analyzing those flowcharts, it was determined that over
> 50% of the steps that are completed for a transaction could either be handled
> efficiently through automation, simplified, or eliminated.' (University of
> Colorado, 1998, p. 7)

Some universities did not conduct a detailed analysis of their current policies,
processes, and procedures but assume they contain inefficiencies yet to be
identified and use ERP adoption as a vehicle for reviewing them. This is indic-
ative of substantive rationality since it embraces the belief that the processes
built into the ERP system are inherently superior. Central Queensland University, in this latter category, expresses the intention of reviewing processes during
ERP adoption:

> 'We are looking at reforming the ways we conduct every significant aspect of our
> internal and external business' (Chipman, 1999)

BPR also proposes that organizations should organize around processes as
opposed to functions. The historical tendency to organize administrative affairs
on the basis of function emphasizes hierarchies and division of work activity.
The University of Michigan articulates this approach as follows:

> 'These current systems, built originally to support an organizational view, should
> be systematically replaced with systems supporting a process view.' (University
> of Michigan, 1995, p. 13)

In addition to BPR the ERP systems are also associated with the idea of 'best
practices'. The rationale of adopting best practices is provided by a number of
universities:

> 'Perform administrative functions in concert with a common set of administrative
> 'best practices' approaches.' (California State University, 1999)

> 'We will be implementing best business practices wherever possible, as part of
> this effort, on all campuses. The University of Nebraska' (Sieber et al., 1999, p.
> 634)

> 'Ensure that the University takes maximum advantage of available 'best practices'
> embedded in the software solutions being acquired and implemented.' (University
> of New South Wales, 1998, p. 10)

The term 'best practices' has become part of the discourse of BPR and ERP. It
invokes impressions of efficiency and good management and has become part of

the value system. Although it appears to represent a form of instrumental rationality there is also substantive and strategic dimension to its use. Its conformity with prevailing management theories presents ERP adoption as an appropriate solution, thereby providing legitimation to the ERP system. The claim that the 'best practices' embedded in ERP systems actually are superior does not appear to have met serious challenge. Soh, Kien, & Tay-Yap (2000) have claimed the reference models that espouse industry 'best practices' are at too high a level for an effective assessment of how an ERP system would actually affect organizational processes:

> 'We must conform our processes to the systems we are purchasing, and not the other way round.' (Chipman, 1999)

The notion that current business practices must change to suit the ERP system is a clear indication of the domination of technique over organization. It is inconsistent to decry legacy systems for not meeting organizational requirements, but at the same time encouraging the deployment of an ERP package whose compatibility with organizational needs is uncertain. One incompatibility is a cause for dismissing systems, the other a cause for welcoming them.

Process Improvement is a vehicle though which the general aim of reducing costs is to be achieved. Improved processes are assumed to require less work and, therefore, to be a type of efficiency improvement. Staff savings are not promoted explicitly, although reducing costs, improving efficiency and reducing administrative workload might be considered to have this consequence. By focusing on the more positive aspects of *Process Improvement* ERP adoption is presented in a more acceptable fashion to employees, who could feel the new systems pose a threat to their jobs. This may be why, as shown in Table 2, all the universities studied referred to improved/streamlined processes, but only half of them referred to reducing costs. The *Process Improvement* conceptual category is aligned with technical, substantive and strategic rationality.

5.5.2 The Technology Domain

As shown in Figure 3 and Table 4, a significant proportion of the justifications for adopting ERP systems are founded upon technology. Whilst the analysis suggests rationales in this domain are based principally on instrumental rationality, a preference for a technological solution may indicate value is placed on technology per se, which reflects substantive rationality. The Technology domain conceptual categories are summarized in Table 4.

Integration is the most important rationale in the Technology domain. Expressions promoting the desirability of integration are presented strongly. The need to eliminate redundant data, integrate databases and systems, increase consistency and eliminate shadow systems are presented as rationales for ERP adoption. There is some inconsistency between the desire for integrated systems and the failure of existing systems to meet end user needs expressed in the

TABLE 5.4 Technology Domain Conceptual Categories

Conceptual category	Number of dimensions	Level of agreement	Percentage reference	Underlying rationale
Integration	7	29	10.3	Technical
Dissatisfaction	6	28	9.0	Technical, substantive, strategic
Modernization	4	20	7.8	Technical, substantive
Maintenance	3	10	2.1	Technical, substantive
Scope and Functionality	2	9	3.6	Technical, substantive
Total	22	96	32.8	

Dissatisfaction conceptual category. Clearly one reason shadow systems have arisen is because the needs of end users were not met by the central systems. As a replacement central system, an ERP system may not meet these decentralized needs for information either. In the perception of the central administration, shadow systems are seen as an unnecessary cost factor and an inhibitor to flexible information provision.

Modernization complements *Dissatisfaction* and provides a rationale based on new techniques and practices. The desire to modernize and extend automation through ERP adoption is expressed through a will to introduce a greater degree of electronic communication. There is a desire to introduce web interfaces to extend the capacity of users (staff and students) to access administrative information. Some universities want to introduce client/server technology via ERP adoption. ERP adoption is presented with the rationale of reducing maintenance costs and avoiding the need to maintain old and complex systems. Some universities present the prospect of transferring maintenance costs to the vendor. The *Maintenance* conceptual category also raises questions of consistency with respect to the desire for increased flexibility and control. Although vendor supplied maintenance appears convenient, it may not be flexible enough to meet changing information requirements. If ERP functionality does not meet user requirements, modifications and adaptations will need to be implemented locally. Also, it is quite likely that vendor-supplied upgrades, which an adopter may feel compelled to accept in order to retain currency and support, may not provide any useful functionality, despite the cost of implementing them.

Finally, the *Scope and Functionality* conceptual category demonstrates that ERP systems are presented as a means of extending the scope of IT into new application areas not currently automated and also as a means of improving the functionality of IT applications. As shown in Figure 3, technical, substantive and strategic rationality types are evident in the *Technology* domain. Most conceptual categories in the *Technology* domain exhibit a mix of instrumental and substantive rationality. The strong presence of instrumental rationality indicates that rationalizing influences are strongly evident in the *Technology* domain. The

TABLE 5.5 Process Domain Conceptual Categories

Conceptual category	Number of Dimensions	Level of agreement	Percentage reference	Rationale
Improved information	5	27	16.4	Technical, substantive
Process improvement	5	24	15.5	Technical, substantive
Standardization	3	10	2.6	Technical, substantive
Total	13	61	34.5	

intrinsic value attached to technological solutions demonstrated in the *Modernization* and *Dissatisfaction* categories, indicates substantive rationality is also an underlying influence. Strategic rationality is evident in the rhetoric of the *Dissatisfaction* conceptual category.

5.5.3 The Process Domain

As Figure 3 and Table 5 depict, the Process domain is important in ERP adoption. The Process domain conceptual categories and their underlying rationales are summarized in Table 5. *Improved Information* is the most important rationale in the Process domain. Expressions promoting the need for improved information are presented strongly. The desire for *more accessible information, more accurate information, more reliable information, more flexible information* and *more comprehensive information* are the dimensions that form this conceptual category. The underlying intent to increase control over operations is evident in the rationales for *Improved Information*.

As the *Process Improvement* conceptual category was discussed extensively earlier in this chapter, it is not dwelt on here. *Standardization* is the least important conceptual category in the Process domain. The rationales of *standardize processes and policies, use community standards/best practices* and *common software/systems* constitute this conceptual category. The dominant positioning of the business process in the ERP system over existing business practices is very significant. Also the ideas of conforming to industry standards, evident in the idea of best practices in the *Process Improvement* and the *Standardization* conceptual categories, indicate a subservient attitude towards externally defined processes. The conformity requirement, that is a normal consequence of using computers, and clearly evident in ERP software, is given strong support in these rationales.

5.5.4 The Organization Domain

As Figure 3 and Table 6 depict the *Organization* domain is important in ERP adoption. The *Organization* domain conceptual categories are summarized in Table 6.

TABLE 5.6 Organization Domain Conceptual Categories

Conceptual category	Number of dimensions	Level of agreement	Percentage reference	Rationale
Business assessment	12	43	8.5	Technical, strategic
Service and quality	3	14	6.2	Technical, substantive
Vision of integration	2	8	10.8	Technical, substantive
Mandate	2	8	2.0	Strategic
Image	1	4	1.0	Strategic
Total	20	77	28.5	

Business Assessment is the most important rationale in the Organization domain. *Business Assessment* is a composite conceptual category consisting of *Vendor Assessment, Formal Assessment, Business Contingencies and Risk Assessment*. The organizational view includes a number of pragmatic aspects that relate to dealing with investment opportunities. It is partly underpinned by instrumental rationality but strategic rationality is also strongly evident. In the *Vendor Assessment* conceptual category, the importance of the producer is emphasized. ERP adoption is viewed as establishing a relationship with the vendor as well as conducting a transaction. This can be explained by the long-term nature of the ERP commitment and, therefore, vendor stability, a strategic issue, is valued. Some evidence of a formal assessment of the ERP investment opportunity is presented, but it has a relatively low profile. *Formal assessment* exhibits instrumental rationality. Attention is given to similar projects at other universities which demonstrates the strategic dimension of organizational behaviour. Organizations gain security and legitimacy from knowing their behaviour is consistent with their peers. Purchasers of a software product do not want to become technologically isolated. They seek a product that is widely used, thereby helping to secure the on-going viability of both the vendor organization and their own.

Risk is focused upon avoiding the technical risks associated with continuing to operate legacy systems, enhancing existing systems or developing in-house systems. Universities justify ERP adoption as the most viable of a set of alternatives, which is a strategic assessment. Some universities acknowledge the financial risk of diverting a large proportion of the institution's resources towards the venture. Financial risks are apparent due to the size of the ERP investment relative to the overall organizational budget. It is possible that universities and other poorly resourced organizations that implement ERP may find themselves over extended.

Organizational risk, known to be applicable in IT adoption contexts, was not evident in this analysis. This suggests that organizations either chose to ignore it for strategic reasons or felt it was of little consequence. The lack of attention to organizational risk appears inconsistent with the magnitude of the change involved in ERP adoption, particularly given the serious outcomes of failed ERP projects that have been reported from at least as early as 1996 (Bulkeley, 1996).

The dimensions of Service and Quality are improved service levels, improved access to student information and greater ability to meet regulatory requirements. Service and Quality relates to the administrative activities of the organization. The rationale is mainly that savings in administration achieved from ERP adoption will improve teaching, learning and research outcomes. One efficiency-related aspect of ERP adoption, presented as a service gain, is the ability of students to view their results and enrol in courses on-line. Whilst this is a convenience to students it is also a saving of administrative labour. Pollock (2003b) writes on this driver for ERP adoption. Instrumental rationality underpins rationalizing activity such as this. In addition, aspiration to a higher level of service is a substantive rationale, as it places value on customer satisfaction.

The dimensions of *Vision of Integration* are *unified and integrated operations*, and *teamwork and synergy*. The *Vision of Integration* captures the aspiration of a more cohesive enterprise. Universities want to mould themselves into more unified entities and they represent the ERP system as a way of drawing the various units of the university together in order to achieve this. The *Vision of Integration* represents an organizational ideal, which ERP adopters have accepted with enthusiasm.

The dimensions of *Mandate* are *use of consultants* and *senior management consensus* and *commitment*. The rationales in the *Mandate* conceptual category are of a strategic nature. Support from both senior managers and an external consultant provides strong endorsement to the ERP project.

Image has a single dimension, which is *improve external perceptions*. This conceptual category may be more influential than these summary measures indicate. Enhanced respect and standing may be an unstated justification for an organization through adopting ERP, because it is aware that ERP adoption is consonant with the technological values held in society. Strategic rationality underlies *Image*.

5.5.5 The People Domain

The *People* domain depicted in Figure 3 and Table 7 is of limited extent. This suggests that the interests of people are subordinate to other considerations, which, in itself, is a significant finding of this study.

TABLE 5.7 People Domain Conceptual Categories

Conceptual category	Number of dimensions	Level of agreement	Percentage reference	Rationale
Individual benefits	4	10	2.4	Strategic
Collective benefits	2	5	1.8	Strategic, Substantive
Total	6	15	4.2	

Individual Benefits is the most important conceptual category in the People domain. *Professional development, empowerment, job satisfaction, improved conditions* and *job security* are presented as rationales for ERP adoption. *Individual Benefits* accrue to those involved with installing and operating the new systems. The acquisition of new skills, greater job satisfaction and empowerment are presented as employee benefits of ERP adoption. It is suggested that by participating in the ERP project or working in areas that make use of new administrative systems, staff will acquire new skills to enhance employment prospects or promote job security. It is also suggested that staff empowerment will result as a consequence of the need for more varied and responsible roles required in the implementation of revised business processes.

The other conceptual category in the *People* domain is *Collective Benefits*, which applies to those working less closely with the new systems. Increased resources for activities central to the mission of a university provide a powerful rationale for ERP adoption for the institution as whole and appeals to a broader community. It is proposed that a more efficient administrative framework supported by an ERP system will release people to engage in more interesting work, more closely related to the core business of the organization. Given the tendency of large IT projects to exceed cost expectations, and ERP implementation being larger than most, this prospect is likely to remain unrealized. There is also the proposition that the ERP system will inspire greater teamwork, which articulates an ideal similar to that found in the *Vision of Integration* conceptual category.

The overall significance of this domain may be higher than the model suggests because of the more direct influence of the rationales in this domain. For those who feel threatened, the prospect of increased job security as a consequence of a more effectively operating university provides some reassurance. These arguments are intended to enhance acceptance of the ERP implementation. Strategic rationality is evident in the *Individual Benefits* conceptual category, and substantive and strategic rationality in *Collective Benefits*.

5.6 REVIEWING THE MODEL

Some major issues are now discussed further. The general principle of rationalization is present in the justifications for integrated systems and improved processes. Integration in all its forms, *Improved Information,* and *Process Improvement,* account for the majority of all justificatory statements, indicating an underlying agenda of increased managerial control. This observation moderates any tendency to view the Technology and Process domains as acting autonomously on the Organization domain. Integration, comprising the conceptual categories in the Technology and Organization domains, is the pre-eminent rationale presented for ERP adoption. Integration is also identified as an important issue in ERP adoption by Ross (1999), Ross, Vitale, & Willcocks (2003), Alvarez (2000), Alvarez and Urla (2002) and Markus and Tanis (2000). Whilst it is evident in this study that integration is regarded as an ideal, Hanseth, Ciborra, & Braa (2001) puts an opposing view, namely that integration may impede flexibility and adaptability in an organization. This is because when systems are integrated, a change in one part of the system requires change to the whole system. His preference is for loosely coupled software architectures. A difficulty that the integration move may encounter is in regard to shadow systems. Shadow systems are a contentious issue in the move to implement ERP systems, as is evident in the writing of Wagner (2002, p. 433), who reports on an ERP study at a university where the implementation team 'at the time of writing ... remain unable to break the hold of shadow systems'. If shadow systems which have functionality that is not embedded in the adopted ERP system are eliminated, some degradation in organizational performance may occur in the short term as shadow systems are forced out. In the medium term it is likely that new shadow systems, which are complementary to the ERP solution, will emerge. In fact Wagner and Newell (2004) report that this phenomenon is already manifesting. This suggests that shadow systems will remain important as a means of addressing requirements beyond those met by ERP systems.

The issues of accessibility to data and information currency need to be re-examined in future studies of the post-implementation ERP environment. There is a need to establish whether ERP systems are able, in practice, to meet the information requirements of accessibility, flexibility, accuracy, reliability and completeness claimed for them, and also to ascertain if they are able to adapt to changed information needs in a way older systems were not. Writers including Ward (1994), Ward, Taylor, & Bond (1996), Sheppard (1990) and Ballantine and Stray (1999) have identified process improvement as a motive for investing in information systems. Process improvement in organizations is a move towards increased rationalization of operations through introducing efficiencies of various kinds that reduce costs and simplify work. The underlying rationale of process improvement is instrumental rationality. IT is the most recent in the line of technologies that have been used to reduce the manpower component of processes to make them faster and cheaper to operate (Zuboff, 1988).

In the 1990s the notion of BPR emerged as a new expression of the general rationalization objective. Whilst BPR was clearly not a totally new idea, it injected a greater degree of radicalism into the efficiency agenda. Its originators, Hammer and Champy (1993), advocate a 'clean slate' approach, placing the idea of radical change firmly on the agenda. BPR is revolutionary not evolutionary, and is, therefore, highly compatible with the 'ERP revolution'. The ideology of BPR is relatively undefined, leaving room for ERP vendors to portray ERP systems as the way to fill the BPR void. As computerized information systems were integral to the majority of significant business processes by the 1990s, it seemed impossible to envisage radical change to business processes without a radical change to the information systems that underpinned those processes. Davenport and Short (1990), Davenport and Stoddard (1994) and Coleman (1995) assert that IT is a key enabler of re-engineering. Powell (1995) suggests an IT investment may be made to create a suitable climate for change. Bancroft, Seip, & Sprengel (1997) suggest ERP usually instigates, or is instigated by, BPR.

As an integrated package, an ERP system offers a generic solution to which an adopting organization must adapt (Davenport, 1998; Pozzebon, 2000, 2001). The purchaser of a software package such as an ERP system does so in the knowledge that organizational practices will need to be modified to suit the package. The idea of conforming to a package appears more acceptable by presenting this as a move towards the incorporation of 'best practices'. The struggle of re-orienting an organizations' processes to those required by the ERP package is made more palatable if it is presented as a policy of improvement. It seems inevitable that there will be clashes between what the package offers and how the organization would like to conduct business operations. Kien and Soh (2003), Soh, Sia, Boh, and Tang (2003), Soh and Sia (2004), Pollock (2003a), Siau and Messersmith (2003), Wagner and Newell (2004) and Scott and Wagner (2003) all consider the issue of 'fit' as it relates to ERP adoption. Pollock (2003a) illustrates the difficulties of generalizing ERP packages but does not propose strategies for dealing with misfits. Wagner and Newell (2004) and Scott and Wagner (2003) also describe issues of misfit and problems caused by inadequacies in the ERP package. Soh stresses the need for early detection of misalignment between organizational practices and package implementations so that adequate resources can be made available to address them in a timely manner. Siau and Messersmith (2003) consider the issue of fit, not so much as a threat, but as an opportunity for staff to be creative in their implementation of ERP. The fact that these issues of fit are not exposed until implementation may indicate that a longer and more intensive appraisal of packages of this complexity is warranted, prior to making a decision to adopt. On the other hand, there is a belief that this may be an impossible task, as is suggested in the following observation made in relation to an ERP implementation:

> 'The chief executive's retrospective reflections indicate that the system was of sufficient size and complexity to make it virtually impossible for decision-makers to understand the implications for the company. It could not, therefore, be rationally analyzed or planned.' (Rose & Pernille, 2002, p. 452)

The maintenance of existing systems is viewed as costly and problematic whereas vendor-supplied maintenance is seen to contain a secure prospect of future enhancement at a known cost. In practice, much systems maintenance reflects changing requirements, and the responsiveness of ERP systems in dealing with these is, so far, unknown. The onus for maintenance falls on the ERP vendor, so there is no certainty that the nature and timing of upgrades will be advantageous to the user. Moreover, failure to keep pace with vendor-supplied upgrades can result in a loss of vendor support. The inflexibility of legacy systems is augmented in ERP systems by a new type of inflexibility caused by the pressure to conform to successive upgrades. The cost of maintenance appears to be more predictable but it may result in unwanted or belated change. The investment decision, in so far as it is reflected in these rationales, illustrates the complexity of the investment context. There are many underlying themes: integration, dissatisfaction, improved information access, maintenance, best practices, modernization, image, similar projects and so on, which make a formal assessment of the investment context extremely complex. However, in spite of this complexity, since a formal assessment was presented by one of the eight universities studied here, it does appear to be possible to perform one.

A number of studies of investment in IT have addressed the issue of the use of generic financial appraisal techniques. This perspective expresses an economically rational view of investment, a type of instrumental rationality. However, findings from a number of studies, Hochstrasser and Griffiths (1991), Farbey, Land, and Targett (1992), Bacon (1992) and Ballantine, Galliers, and Stray (1999) suggest that this economically rational approach does not, in practice, dominate IS/IT investment decisions. Ross et al. (2003, p. 111) report the 'business cases for the ERP system implementation tended to be vague' and Gosain (2004, p. 152) referring to a 2003 article by Umble, Haft and Umble writes: 'In spite of the substantial investment and length of time needed to implement ERP systems, companies have generally proceeded to implement ERP without a rigorous financial case'. This has been the case in spite of the fact that the 'level of investment has the potential to increase the risk position of even the wealthiest organizations' (Scott & Wagner, 2003, p. 286). To further illustrate this potential outcome, it is reported that one Australian University experienced severe financial consequences from its failed ERP systems and 'had written off its failed computer system after allocating $48.6 million for its implementation and repair' (Bucknell, 2003).

An explanation for the relatively minor role played by formal analysis in many investment decisions is provided by Steiner (1979) who states that the likelihood of quantitative criteria being employed diminishes as the importance of an issue rises, and the higher up the organizational hierarchy a decision is made. Similarly Symons (1990), Hochstrasser and Griffiths (1991), and Powell (1992) report that the greater the expense and strategic importance of an IS, the weaker the role of formal evaluation methods. It appears that the more extensive the scope of the IS/IT investment, the more complex is the task of conducting a formal analysis and the less convincing are its conclusions. Whilst this finding is seemingly paradoxical, it emphasizes the difficulty of conducting a formal analysis in what appears to be the most significant contexts. From a critical theory perspective this evidence does not indicate the rigorously applied, instrumentally rational form of organizational behaviour that the Weberian and Habermasian analyses propose.

The importance of legitimacy and trend following, principally discussed in this chapter in the *similar projects* sub-category of *Business Contingencies*, is also brought out by Gosain (2004), Wagner and Newell (2004) and Scott and Wagner (2003). Gosain suggests the tendency to follow trends is accentuated by the complexity of an ERP acquisition, which makes the task of assessing an ERP investment too difficult for many organizations. Scott and Wagner (2003) report that the Vice-President at the university they studied, justified the move to ERP on the basis of what was happening at other universities. For Iacono and Kling (2001), the issue of why so many organizations at similar points in time attempt to implement the same technology is largely unexplained. The reference to similar projects occurring at other universities suggests that the concept of mimetic isomorphism (Oliver, 1991) has a strong influence in this 'ERP revolution'. Tingling and Parent (2002) provide a good explanation for this imitative behaviour, which seems applicable in the ERP context. Since transitioning from one technology-based system to another is costly, organizations find security in the knowledge that they are not isolating themselves. Continued support and upgrading is more likely to be ensured if many organizations adopt the same technology. If few organizations adopt the technology, an organization may find support for the system difficult and costly to acquire. Consequently, the herding behaviour we perceive in ERP adoption is highly rational in the strategic sense.

The notion that a university believes it can enhance its image by adopting a particular information technology illustrates the importance of information technologies in cultural congruence. Compliance with both accepted and emerging norms of instrumental rationality becomes a way of legitimating planned activities. Universities use instrumental rationality to legitimate the new ERP system and, in turn, anticipate that legitimacy will be conferred on them by the society in which they exist, by demonstrating conformity to these technological norms.

Pollock (2003b) focuses on the issue of self-service and customer empowerment enabled by ERP systems, which, as noted earlier in this chapter, provides a rationale for cost-cutting enabled by ERP that aligns with consumer preferences. He also refers to the image and status-conferring aspects of ERP adoption noted in this chapter in the *Image* conceptual category. Ross et al. (2003) and Scott and Wagner (2003) also identify the role of image and status in ERP adoption.

5.7 CONCLUSION

This study took justifications used by universities for the adoption of an ERP system as a basis from which to explore issues of communication, rationality, legitimacy and domination. The ideas of Habermas, who links communication and rationality, provided a framework for exploring these rationales for ERP adoption. Whilst Habermas' thoughts are directed mainly to broad social questions, we have found his ideas can be applied successfully in this more limited social context.

Grounded theory was used to develop the major themes presented in this study. Grounded Theory is a qualitative, investigative approach to research that endeavours to find the truth through a series of consecutive data collection steps, and may use a variety of data sources, such as interviews or different types of textual materials. The approach is referred to as "grounded theory" because the investigation produces a theory that is grounded in the data - not one that precedes the data, which is the case with positivist, quantitative and statistically based research. Critical theory is non-prescriptive with respect to research approach or methodology and is weak as regards empirical grounding. Whilst grounded theory is often employed in interpretive studies, its grounding in data is a quality that can prove valuable when taking a critical approach. We observed earlier that grounded theory cannot proceed in a vacuum. The same might also be said of critical social theory, for evidently it requires a society or social practice to criticize. As demonstrated in this study, grounding in data provides a basis from which a critical social theory approach can be pursued.

The commonalities in the justifications that enabled the development of the model, lead us to conclude that the rationales and the themes that underpin them provide an insight into broadly held attitudes towards the deployment of information technology in administrative settings. Other writers in the information systems field who have taken a critical stance have also explored the issue of the rationalities that underlie the deployment of IT and have reached conclusions similar to ours. This further illustrates the usefulness and importance of rationality to the critical social theory approaches. In addition, the rationales that accompanied the introduction of new ERP systems presented an opportunity to examine the underlying values held by these organizations. Although this study is limited to universities, the cultural values they reveal are likely to correspond to those of the societies from which they are drawn.

Instrumental rationality is strongly evident in justifications based on improved technologies, processes and information in the Technology and Process domains. The predominance of technical rationale suggests that the ideals of instrumental rationality are deeply entrenched. We suggest that although instrumental rationality underlies ERP adoption, it is more a value than an expression of the calculation and comparison of means. Organizations claim that ERP systems will enable various efficiencies but the lack of precision to these statements renders them more as assumptions than clear expectations. Along with Wagner and Newell (2004) and Gosain (2004) we consider that instrumental rationality is an inadequate explanation for the adoption of new technologies, as in this study we have identified multiple rationality types underlying ERP deployment. Technology has become part of the social value system and, as this study confirms, its deployment is based on a substantive or value rationality, which has emerged from origins in instrumental rationality. As mentioned earlier, Avgerou and McGrath (2005) have also noted this tendency. We have suggested in this chapter that instrumental rationality can reflect substantive rationality. Gosain, (2004, p. 174) expresses a similar view:

'As the decisions around enterprise systems implementations become typified or de-personalized, procedures devised for instrumental value may become valued ends in themselves as a standardized organizational response'.

The substantive value of technology detected here is evidence that the life-world has been further colonized by technology as suggested by Habermas. The privileging of technology over people, also evident in the writing of Zuboff (1988) and Brooke (2001), is an issue that deserves further critical reflection. The value placed on technology is partly for efficiency reasons (the instrumental rationales), partly because technology is valued intrinsically by western societies, and partly because it appears to satisfy the aspirations for increased managerial control. Strategic rationality plays an important role in ERP justification because of the need to form favourable attitudes towards ERP adoption and, thereby, create a climate favourable to implementation. Communicating in ways intended to influence others towards the acceptance of a desired outcome is what Habermas calls strategic rationality. Strategic rationality may also be discerned in justifications based upon the actions of others, evident here in the trend-following rationales. The extent to which these rationales exhibit communicative rationality, the type of rationality which is, perhaps, Habermas' most well known contribution in the field of communication, is not explored here. Whether communicative rationality was exercised in the ERP adoption decision, as opposed to the rationale for the decision, was beyond the scope of this study. We were also interested in exploring the aspect of domination and emancipation, another key area of interest for critical theorists. In the context we studied, the issues of domination and emancipation were examined by exploring how the introduction of an extensive technological system for administration is presented in relation to the people who are affected by it.

We are now able to comment on indications of domination by comparing the relative size of the domains. Using this measure we can observe that issues relating to people are of lesser importance than those from the Technology, Process and Organization domains. People appear as objects to be influenced by the application of strategic rationality both within and beyond the People domain. Emancipation is the converse of domination and implies release from it. A barrier to emancipation would seem to be the general support of the rationalizing and technology agendas which, as we have seen, are used to legitimize ERP adoption, thus indicating its social acceptance. This conclusion emphasizes, as others have noted, how difficult it is in many contexts to identify what actually constitutes domination and, therefore, emancipation.

In the university context in which this research was situated, this apparent dominance of *Technology* and *Process* would seem to pose a threat to both the values and aspirations of the organization, (namely the knowledge creation, teaching and research objectives) and the people who work in them. Only a minimal impact on organizational performance in these key areas appears to be anticipated as a consequence of ERP adoption. This is emphasized by the relatively scant references to the core activities of universities, which are teaching and research. The impact of ERPs on the mission of organizations, therefore, deserves continued examination.

Acknowledgements

The ideas and assistance of Associate Professor Greg Whymark in the conduct and presentation of this study are gratefully acknowledged by the authors. This chapter is developed from a number of earlier writings, in particular D. Oliver, C. Romm, (2002), Justifying ERP Adoption, Journal of Information Technology, 17 (4) pp. 199–213 and Dave Oliver, Greg Whymark, Celia Romm (2005), Researching ERP adoption: an Internet-based grounded theory approach, Online Information Review 29(6), pp. 585–603.

REFERENCES

Alvarez, R. (2000). Examining an ERP implementation through myths: A case study of a large public organization. *Paper presented at the Americas conference on information systems (AMCIS),* Los Angeles.

Alvarez, R., & Urla, J. (2002). Tell me a good story: Using narrative analysis to examine information requirements interviews during an ERP Implementation. *The DATA BASE for Advances in Information Systems, 33*(1), 38–52.

Avgerou, C., & McGrath, K. (2005). Rationalities and emotions in IS innovation. *Handbook of critical information systems research: Theory and application.* In Howcroft, D., & Trauth, E.M. (Eds.), Edward Elgar, pp. 299–324.

Bacon, C. J. (1992). The use of decision criteria in selecting information systems/technology investments. *MISQ, 16*(3), 335–350.

Ballantine, J. A., Galliers, R. A., & Stray, S. J. (1999). Information systems/technology: Evaluation practices. *Beyond the IT productivity paradox.* In Willcocks, L.P., & Lester, S. (Eds.), John Wiley, pp. 123–150.

Ballantine, J. A., & Stray, S. J. (1999). Information systems and other capital investments: Evaluation practices compared. *Logistics Information Management, 12*(1–2), 78–93.

Bancroft, N. H., Seip, H., & Sprengel, A. (1997). *Implementing SAP R/3. How to introduce a large system into a large organization.* Prentice-Hall.

Beniger, J. R. (1986). *The control revolution.* Harvard University Press.

Bingi, P., Sharma, M. K., & Godla, J. K. (1999). Critical issues affecting an ERP implementation. *Information Systems Management (Summer)* 7–14.

Brooke, C. (2001). Information systems in use: A representational perspective. *Tamara, 3*(1), 39–52.

Bucknell, J. (2003). Fortunes favour uni boss, for now. *The Australian* 6.

Bulkeley, W. M. (1996). Technology (a special report): Working together – when things go wrong: Foxmeyer drug took a huge high-tech gamble; it didn't work. *Wall Street Journal Eastern Edition* 25.

California State University (1999). *Why CMS? Retrieved 4/5/2000.* http://cms.calstate.edu/ T6_Documents/NewsAndPublications/General/Why%20CMS102099.doc.

Cecez-Kecmanovic, D. (2005). Basic assumptions of the critical research perspectives in information systems. *Handbook of critical information systems research: Theory application.* In Howcroft, D. (Eds.), Edward Elgar, pp. 19–46.

Cecez-Kecmanovic, D., & Janson, M. (2000). The rationality potential of information systems: A critical approach. *Paper presented at the Australian conference on information systems,* Brisbane.

Cecez-Kecmanovic, D., & Janson, M. (2001). Doing critical IS research: The question of methodology. *Qualitative research in IS: Issues and trends*. In Trauth, E.M. (Ed.), Idea Group Publishing, pp. 141–162.

Chipman, L. (1999). *From the Vice-Chancellor's Desk: Systematic Changes, Vol. #266* Central Queensland University, UniNews Weekly.

Coleman, T. (1995). IT value for money: Going beyond financial analysis. *Hard money–Soft outcomes*. In Farbey, B., Targett, D., & Land, F. (Eds.), Alfred Waller, pp. 59–67.

Davenport, T. H. (1998). Putting the enterprise into the enterprise system. *Harvard Business Review* 121–131.

Davenport, T. E., & Short, J. E. (1990). The new industrial engineering: Information technology and business process redesign. *Sloan Management Review* 11–27.

Davenport, T. H., & Stoddard, D. B. (1994). Reengineering: Business change of mythic proportions? *MISQ*, *18*(2), 121–127.

Eisenhart, K. M. (1989). Building theories from case study research. *Academy of Management Review*, *14*(4), 532–550.

Farbey, B., Land, F., & Targett, D. (1992). Evaluating investments in IT. *Journal of Information Technology*, *7*, 109–122.

Giddens, A. (1984). *The constitutition of society: Outline of the theory of structuration*. Polity Press.

Gosain, S. (2004). Enterprise information systems as objects and carriers of institutional forces: The new iron cage? *Journal of the Association for Information Systems*, *5*(4), 151–182.

Habermas, J. (1971). *Toward a rational society: Student protest, science and politics*. (J. Shapiro, Trans.) Heinemann.

Habermas, J. (1984). *The theory of communicative action: Reason and the rationalization of society*. (T. McCarthy, Trans.) Beacon Press.

Hammer, M., & Champy, J. (1993). *Reengineering the corporation*. Harper Collins.

Hanseth, O., Ciborra, C. U., & Braa, K. (2001). The control devolution: ERP and the side effects of globalization. *The DATA BASE for Advances in Information Systems*, *32*(4), 34–46.

Hill, S. (1988). *The tragedy of technology: Human liberation versus domination in the late twentieth century*. Pluto Press.

Hochstrasser, B., & Griffiths, C. (1991). *Controlling IT investment strategy and management*. Chapman & Hall.

Iacono, S., & Kling, R. (2001). Computerization movements: The rise of the Internet and distant forms of work. *Information technology and organizational transformation: History, rhetoric, and practice*. In Yates, J., & Van Maanen, J. (Eds.), Sage Publications, pp. 93–135.

Khazanchi, D., Munkvold,, & Erik., B. (2000). Is information systems a science? An inquiry into the nature of the information systems discipline *The DATA BASE for Advances in Information Systems*, *31*(3), 24–42.

Kien, S. S., & Soh, C. (2003). An exploratory analysis of the sources and nature of misfits in ERP implementations. *Second-wave enterprise resource planning systems*. In Shanks, G., Seddon, P. B. (Eds.), Cambridge University Press, pp. 373–387.

King, M., & McAulay, L. (1997). Information technology investment evaluation: Evidence and interpretations. *Journal of Information Technology*, *12*, 131–143.

Krippendorf, K. (1980). *Content analysis*. Sage.

Kumar, K., & Van Hillegersberg, J. (2000). ERP experiences and evolution. *Communications of the association for computing machinery*, *43*(4), 22–26.

Langley, A. (1989). In search of rationality: The purposes behind the use of formal analysis in organizations. *Administrative Science Quarterly*, *34*, 598–631.

Laudon, K. C., & Laudon, J. R. (1984). *Management information systems – Organization and technology.* McMillan.

Lyytinen, K. J., & Klein, H. K. (1985). The critical theory of Jurgen Habermas as a basis for a theory of information systems. *Research methods in information systems.* In Mumford, E., Hirschheim, R., & Wood-Harper, T. (Eds.), Elsevier Science Publishers B.V./North-Holland, pp. 219–236.

March, J. G. (1988). Rationality, ambiguity, and the engineering of choice. *Decision making: Descriptive, normative, and prescriptive interactions.* In Bell, D., Raiffa, E.H., & Tversky, A. (Eds.), Cambridge University Press, pp. 33–57.

Marcuse, H. (1970). *One dimensional man.* Sphere Books.

Markus, M. L., & Tanis, C. (2000). The enterprise systems experience – From adoption to success. *Framing the domains of IT research: Glimpsing the future through the past.* In Zmud, R.W (Ed.), Pinnaflex Educational Resources.

McClure, J. (1991). *Explanations, accounts, and illusions: A critical analysis.* Cambridge University Press.

Meyer, J. W., & Rowan, B. (1977). Institutionalized organizations: Formal structure as myth and ceremony. *American Journal of Sociology, 83*(2), 340–363.

Oliver, C. (1991). Strategic responses to institutional processes. *Academy of Management Review, 16*(1), 145–179.

Pfeffer, J. (1981). Management as symbolic action: The creation and maintenance of organizational paradigms. *Research in Organizational Behaviour, 3,* 1–52.

Pollock, N. (2003a). Fitting standard software packages to non-standard organizations: The 'biography' of an enterprise-wide system. *Technology Analysis and Strategic Management, 15*(3), 317–332.

Pollock, N. (2003b). The 'Self-service' student: Building enterprise-wide systems into universities. *Prometheus, 21*(2), 101–119.

Powell, P. (1992). Information technology evaluation: Is it different? *Journal of the Operational Research Society, 43*(1), 29–42.

Powell, P. (1995). Fuzzy strategy–Crisp investment. *Hard money–Soft outcomes.* In Farbey, B., Targett, D., & Land, F. (Eds.), Alfred Waller, pp. 173–192.

Pozzebon, M. (2000). Combining a structuration approach with a behavioral-based model to investigate ERP usage. *Paper presented at the Americas conference on information systems (AMCIS),* Long Beach, California.

Pozzebon, M. (2001). Demystifying the rhetorical closure of ERP packages. *Paper presented at the 22nd international conference on information systems,* ICIC, New Orleans.

Rands, T. (1992). The key role of applications software make-or-buy decisions. *Journal of Strategic Information Systems, 1*(4), 215–223.

Robbins, S. P. (1993). *Organizational behaviour concepts controversies and applications,* (6th ed.). Prentice Hall.

Rose, J., & Pernille, K. (2002). Dominant technological discourses in action: Paradigmatic shifts in sense making in the implementation of an ERP system. *Global and organizational discourse about information technology.* In Wynn, E.H., Whitley, E.A., Myers, M.D., & DeGross, J.I. (Eds.), Kluwer Academic Publishers, pp. 437–464.

Ross, J. W. (1999). *The ERP Revolution: Surviving Versus Thriving, Sloan School of Management* (pp. 1–13). Working Paper. Cambridge, Massachusetts: Center For Information Systems Research, Massachusetts Institute of Technology.

Ross, J. W., Vitale, M. R., & Willcocks, L. P. (2003). The continuing ERP revolution: Sustainable lessons, new modes of delivery. *Second-wave enterprise resource planning systems.* In Shanks, G., & Willcocks, L.R. (Eds.), Cambridge University Press, pp. 102–134.

Schroyer, T. (1975). *The critique of domination*. Beacon Paperback.

Scott, S. V., & Wagner, E. L. (2003). Networks, negotiations, and new times: The implementation of enterprise resource planning into an academic administration. *Information and Organization, 13*, 285–313.

Sheppard, J. (1990). The strategic management of IT investment decisions: A research note. *British Journal of Management, 1*, 171–181.

Siau, K., & Messersmith, J. (2003). Analyzing ERP implementation at a public university using the innovation strategy model. *International Journal of Human–Computer Interaction, 16*(1), 57–80.

Sieber, T., Siau, K., Nah, F., & Sieber, M. (1999). Implementing SAP/R3 at the University of Nebraska. *Paper presented at the international conference on information systems (ICIS),* Charlotte.

Soh, C., Kien, S. S., & Tay-Yap, J. (2000). Cultural fit and misfit: Is ERP a universal solution. *Communications of the Association for Computing Machinery, 43*(4), 47–51.

Soh, C., & Sia, S. K. (2004). An institutional perspective on sources of ERP package-organisation misalignments. *Journal of Strategic Information Systems, 13*, 375–397.

Soh, C., Sia, K. S., Boh, W. F., & Tang, M. (2003). Misalignments in ERP implementation: A dialectic perspective. *International Journal Of Human–Computer Interaction, 16*(1), 81–100.

Steiner, G. (1979). *Strategic planning*. Free Press.

Strauss, A., & Corbin, J. (1998). *Basics of qualitative research*, (2nd edn.). Sage.

Symons, V. (1990). Evaluation of information systems: IS development in the processing company. *Journal of Information Technology, 5*, 194–204.

Tingling, P., & Parent, M. (2002). Mimetic isomorphism and technology evaluation: Does imitation transcend judgement? *Journal of the Association for Information Systems, 3*, 113–143.

University of Colorado (1998). *Administrative streamlining project business plan retrieved 22/02/ 2000.* http://www.cusys.edu/~asp/busplan/Master.html.

University of Michigan (1995). *Strategic data plan report retrieved 2/5/2000.* http://www.mpath-ways.umich.edu/overview/pplsoft.html.

University of New South Wales (1998). *Request for information for the supply of an integrated administrative system retrieved 3/3/2000.* http://nss.admin.unsw.edu.au/html/projects/softrfi.rtf.

Wagner, E. L. (2002). Interconnecting information systems narrative research: An end-to-end approach for process-oriented field studies. *Global and organizational discourse about information technology.* In Wynn, E.H., Whitley, E.A., Myers, M.D., & DeGross, J.I. (Eds.), Kluwer Academic Publishers, pp. 419–436.

Wagner, E. L., & Newell, S. (2004). 'Best' for whom?: The tension between 'best practice' ERP packages and diverse epistemic cultures in a university *Journal of Strategic Information Systems, 13*, 305–328.

Ward, J. (1994). *A portfolio approach to evaluating information systems investments and setting priorities. Information management: The evaluation of information systems investments.* Chapman & Hall pp. 81–96.

Ward, J., Taylor, P., & Bond, P. (1996). Identification, realisation and measurement of IS/IT benefits: An empirical study of current practice. *Paper presented at the 2nd European conference on information technology evaluation,*.

Weber, M. (1978). *Economy and society*. Berkeley.

Weill, P., & Olson, M. H. (1989). Managing investment in information technology: Mini case examples and implications. *MIS Quarterly, 13*(1), 2–17.

Willcocks, L., & Smith, G. (1995). IT-enabled business process reengineering: Organizational and human resource dimensions. *Journal of Strategic Information Systems, 4*(3), 279–301.

Willcocks, L. P., & Sykes, R. (2000). The role of the CIO and IT function in ERP. *Communications of the Association for Computing Machinery, 43*(4), 32–38.

Yates, J., & Orlikowski, W. (1992). Genres of organizational communication. *Academy of Management Review* 299–326.

Zuboff, S. (1988). *In the age of the smart machine.* Basic Books.

Chapter 6

Distortions in the Media: A Critical Analysis of Learning Technology Macro Discourse

Wendy Cukier and Sara Rodrigues

6.1 INTRODUCTION

In this chapter, we link two traditions of scholarship in information systems (IS) – Habermasian critical theory and critical discourse analysis. These are applied to a critique of public discourses about technology. Building on institutional theory, we suggest that distortions in technology discourse can significantly affect organizational decision-making processes. Habermas' notion of communicative rationality provides a normative framework for analysis. We review current approaches to discourse analysis and ways in which the validity claims can frame discourse analysis in a way that is both theoretically sound and empirically grounded. This chapter responds to some of the criticisms that have been levelled at IS research based on critical theory (Klein, 1999).[1]

Our motivation for investigating media discourses about technology stems from the observation that there is often a gap between the promise of technology and the reality it delivers. In spite of the dominant notions of systematic analysis and design, many technology developers and adopters do not appear to behave 'rationally'. There have been debates concerning 'the productivity paradox' in which scholars have questioned if investments in technology 'for competitive advantage' have actually delivered on their promise. Studies in behavioural finance have shown a gap between the models of rational investors and actual investor behaviour. There is often a gap between the promise and the reality, and much has been written about the failure of 'hyped' technologies such as ERP to produce the benefits that justified their excessive costs. The consulting firm Gartner Group has coined the term 'hype cycle' to describe the pattern of escalating enthusiasm about new technologies from the 'peak of inflated expectations' to the 'trough of disillusionment' tapering off into the 'plateau of productivity' (cited in le Roux, 2002).

Abrahamson (1996) and others have documented the process through which a promising new idea rapidly becomes fashionable through 'excessive optimism, aggressive marketing, media hype and popularization by gurus'. Scholars have explored the rise and fall of management fashions through media analysis and have examined the cycle of the fashions and the patterns within those cycles (Abrahamson, 1996; Eccles, Nohria, & Berkley, 1992). Benders and van Veen (2001, p. 33) proposed that management fashions are best conceptualized as 'the production and consumption of temporarily intensive management discourse, and the organizational changes induced by and associated with this discourse'. Several studies have explored the 'guru industry' and cycles of management fashions with respect to issues such as 'culture', 'excellence', 'total quality management', 'empowerment', 'business process reengineering', 'downsizing', 'knowledge work', and 'globalization' (Collins, 2000; Furusten, 1995; Jackson, 2001).

'Rhetorical recycling' may add value by enabling proven methods to be reintroduced repeatedly as if they were innovations (Eccles et al., 1992). When best-selling books, business magazines, business sections of daily papers, corporate newsletters, etc. reinforce a specific management approach such as 'business process reengineering' or 'total quality management' (TQM), 'empowerment' or 'effectiveness' or 'the learning organization', they turn technical concepts and methods into rhetorical tools (Collins, 2000; Jackson, 2001). Certainly some scholars (Drury & Farhoomand, 1999) have noted the vital importance of marketing in the transfer and commercialization of technology.

---

1. thanks to our research assistants Sara Rodrigues, Eva Nesselroth, Ravindra Mohabeer and Rashaad Bhamjee.

However, technology fads and fashions may have substantial implications in terms of long-term investments of private and public money. While we accept that technology is, in large part, socially constructed and that technology decisions are influenced by institutional environments, we believe that technology decision making should still be as reasonable as possible (Abell, 1991). One way to improve the reasonableness of decision making is to gain a better understanding of the limits to rationality that may be imposed by an institutional environment. Discourse is an important part of the institutional environment of organization and, as such, analysing institutional discourse offers a means of revealing societal norms, and making explicit the implicit assumptions about the nature of the institutional environment. Our interest in developing a method for critical analysis of public discourses about IT stems from an understanding that such discourses have a powerful influence on the trajectory of information technology and its impact on all levels of society. Through texts, social identities, social relations and systems of knowledge and beliefs are simultaneously constituted in ways that either reproduce/reinforce prevailing patterns or create pressures to transform them. Calling attention to what has been obscured or invisible in previous texts resists, destabilizes and helps transform prevailing social practice (Fletcher, 1998). As critical social theorists, we are interested in finding ways to conduct empirically grounded analyses of channels of public communication and debate about IT. Here, we focus specifically on discourse in the media, which is an important carrier of popular discourses but also incorporates political, practical and academic discourses. We provide some anecdotal evidence concerning the role of various actors in the production and reproduction of the discourse.

There is a tradition of critical IS research framed in Habermasian communicative rationality (Cecez-Kecmanovic, 2001) which has been used to explore how technology impacts communicative ethics or how communicative ethics can be applied to improve IS development. However, research on exploring ways in which Habermas can inform the analysis of discourse about technology is limited. In spite of the long tradition of technology criticism which focuses attention on the construction of reality, there has been limited attention to the media discourses which, as noted above, frame technology decision making in organizations. In this chapter, while we do not specifically examine the impact of media discourse on technology decision making, we argue, based on previous research on institutional behaviour, that distortions in media discourse may promote decisions which are not 'rational'. Our goal is to link two traditions of scholarship in information systems – critical discourse analysis and critical theory in the Habermasian tradition – and to extend its reach to the critique of public discourses about technology. We explicate techniques for CDA based on Habermas' validity claims and focus on the macro- and institutional-level discourses that reflect deeper social and political processes and provide a context for technology decision making.

This chapter is divided into four parts and proposes an approach to an empirically grounded analysis of channels of public communication and debate about IT. First, we review current approaches to discourse analysis and their application in IS research. In the second section, we examine how Habermas' validity claims can frame discourse analysis. In the third section, we outline our methodology for case studies on media discourses which concern e-learning. We then consider the overall shape of the discourse through citation analysis and conduct a detailed examination of some of the content of the discourse using Habermasian validity claims.

6.2 DIVERSITY IN APPROACHES TO DISCOURSE ANALYSIS

'Discourse' refers to the institutionalized language codes or 'talk' for articulating the social construction of reality. The discourses that we are interested in here are the 'talk' about information technology, which represent 'institutionalized forms of conversation' that mirror dominant power relations and ideology (Parker, 1992) and shape the way technology is understood and enacted (Feldman & March, 1981). Discourse is one of the principal ways in which reality is socially constructed.

Discourse analysis has long been the subject of scholars in sociology, psychology and cultural studies (see for example, Fairclough, 1995; Fiske, 1982; Hansen, Cottle, Negrine, & Newbold, 1998; Hirsch, 1986; Inglis, 1990; Jensen & Jankowski, 1991; Van Dijk, 1991; Wodak, 1989) and has more recently become a subject of interest in the management of IS (see for example Chiapello & Fairclough, 2002; Cecez-Kecmanovic, 2001; Cecez-Kecmanovic & Janson, 1999; Cecez-Kecmanovic, Janson, & Brown, 2002; Thomas, 2003). Some IS scholars have looked at the development and diffusion of information technologies throughout organizations and society. They often examine the relationship between IS and the organizations and societies within which they are embedded (Howcroft & Trauth, 2005) but the link between societal discourse and organizational behaviours has been largely unexamined.

There have been attempts to categorize approaches to discourse analysis using the concept of 'paradigms' (e.g., Heracleous & Barrett, 2001; Philips & Hardy, 2002). Existing typologies of discourse analysis distinguish, among other things, interpretative approaches from critical discourse analysis. Slembrouck (2001), for example, explores many of the tensions which surround critical discourse analysis in linguistics and the challenges to 'descriptivism' which, he argues, was seen as serving the status quo.

Discourse analysis is often undertaken from an 'interpretative' stance and is focused on 'reading' texts, artefacts or practices in order to understand their social construction. Interpretative approaches, for the most part, are grounded in the notion that reality is socially constructed, and as such draw on a wide range of philosophical and linguistic theories of language and approaches to reading 'texts' (which can include the written word or social practices). A number of scholars have applied these approaches to 'reading' organizational texts (Boland, 1991; Lee, 1994), to analysing metaphor or genre (Orlikowski & Yates, 1994) or deconstruction (Calás & Smircich, 1991). These are modes of address that imply specific social uses of communication in relation to particular political and cultural practices (Jensen, 1991). According to Burrell and Morgan's (1979) framework for paradigm analysis, the interpretative paradigm is subjective and focuses on examining the status quo rather than effecting change.

Phenomenological methods examine lived experience, interpretations and understanding in order to explore the way in which social practices are constructed through language, signs and metaphors. The 'interpretative' approach can be identified in studies that draw on phenomenological or hermeneutic traditions. As such:

> the act of interpretation may be thought of as a phenomenological reduction, extracting a textual essence, the steps of the reduction are not made explicit. (Jensen, 1991, p. 31)

Ricoeur (1976) attempted to differentiate semiotic from semantic approaches, analysing language as discourse by focusing, not just on signification, but, on meaning as well. Hermeneutic approaches have also been applied in management studies (Boland, 1991; Lee, 1994). The analysis of genre, narrative and interpretive repertoires are yet another approach to analysing discourses (Orlikowski & Yates, 1994). These are modes of address that imply specific social uses of communication in relation to particular political and cultural practices, and, as Jensen suggests, 'define subjectivity in collective rather than individual terms' (Jensen, 1991, p. 43).

The more formalist approaches associated with semiotics purport to study the formal 'objective' aspects of signs (Jensen, 1991, p. 19). Semiotic approaches focus on the analysis of language, signs and sense-making without supposing that they are related to an objective reality. This tradition is well established in communications scholarship (Fiske, 1982). For example, Barthes stresses the importance of understanding connotative as well as denotative meanings of signs, arguing that connotation is the principal way in which mass media communicates ideological meaning (as cited in Seiter, 1999) an approach which has been applied to 'reading' visual as well as textual media (Hansen et al., 1998). Notably, Levi-Strauss used linguistic structural analysis to examine complex relationships in society (as cited in Berger & Bradac, 1982). Deconstruction, for example, is another technique which examines generic elements and conventions by taking them out of their original context in order to expose them. Based on Derrida's notion (1982) of *différance*, in which the meaning of a sign is dependent on its opposite, deconstruction has been applied to a wide range of contexts (e.g., Calás & Smircich, 1991). While this technique provides interesting useful insights, it can create a cycle of deconstructing the deconstruction, which is difficult to apply to improve practice.

Foucauldian analysis in some ways defies simple categorization. To Foucault, 'discourse' is defined as a combination of text, artefact and social practice which reflects and reinforces power structures in a particular context. He examined the discourses of systems of punishment, medicine, institutions and routines in order to expose the underlying political structures which construct them (Foucault, 1971, 1979, 1980). A Foucauldian analysis of social and cultural practices is inherently political. It asks who does the speaking, what are the positions and viewpoints from which they speak, which institutions prompt people to speak on what subjects and which institutions publicize the things that are said? It also examines how one discourse connects to other discourses and how a discourse allows dominant groups to tell their stories while silencing the discourse of others (Parker, 1992). Although it is often defined as a 'critical' approach to discourse analysis because of its interest in power, the epistemology underlying Foucault's approach leaves little room for normative or ethical analysis (Inglis, 1990).

The Marxist tradition focuses on exploring the underlying superstructures reflected (or obscured) in discourse. Mainstream culture, like religion, is viewed as the opiate of the masses, and is used to suppress consciousness. Feminist scholars have also applied critical discourse analysis to reveal the systemic biases in the portrayal of women managers in media. Fondas (1997), for example, undertook a feminist analysis of management writings. Krefting (2001) analysed the portrayal of women executives in mass media. Generally, the approach to discourse associated with Marxist scholars from the Frankfurt school is 'critique', the reading of texts, artefacts or social practices to reveal underlying ideology (Hardt, 1992). For Kracaueur (as cited in Larsen, 1991), qualitative content analysis is synonymous with exegesis.

Even while media texts are thought of as complex and indeterminate, they are also said to be historically determined to the extent that they express the general ideological trends (*zeitgeist*) of a given period, which minimizes the danger of 'subjective' interpretations. Crucially, following the knowledge interests of the Frankfurt School, the deciphering of latent meanings through qualitative content analysis implies a deconstruction of ideology and critique of its social origins (Larsen, 1991, p. 123).

Critical discourse analysis (1) exposes the deep structures which underlie discourse, particularly power structures; (2) is grounded in normative or ethical standards (Fairclough, 1995); and (3) has an emancipatory interest (Brooke, 2002). 'Critical [discourse] analysis cannot remain indifferent to questions of truth, be it a matter of omissions or falsifications for persuasive purposes' (Fairclough, 1995, p. 18). Critical discourse analysis is a particular epistemological orientation to discourse and tends to be associated with a qualitative 'reading' or analysis of artefacts (Fairclough, 1995).

While many researchers (Hardy, 2001; Slembrouck, 2001) suggest that theory which underpins critical discourse analysis is broad and can include Marx, Gramsci, Baudrillard, Bernstein, Bourdieu, Giddens, Habermas, Harvey,

TABLE 6.1 Communications Research Paradigms

Epistemology	Assumption regarding texts	Question	Examples of theory
Interpretive	Socially constructed	How is meaning constructed through signs and language?	Derrida, Barthes
Functionalist	Manifest meanings	What is the measurable content of communications?	Chicago School
Radical structuralist	Discourse reflects economic and ideological structures	What economic and political interests underlie communications?	Frankfurt School, Adorno, Marcuse
Radical humanist	Discourse should satisfy the four validity claims	Use power of reason to expose distortions and emancipate.	Habermas

etc., we suggest that there are significant differences in the implications of these theoretical approaches and that Habermas provides a unique conceptual framework. Following Burrell and Morgan (1979), we would differentiate between approaches which rely on structural change – radical structuralism – from those that are based in radical humanism which allows for individual human agency (see Table 6.1). While radical humanism focuses, like radical structuralism, on effecting change, its means are different. The change envisaged can occur at the individual level with enlightenment and emancipation as the path. Habermas' (1981) emphasis on the emancipatory power of reason distinguishes him from neo-Marxists. He also explicitly distanced himself from Foucault. Specifically, the epistemology underlying Foucault's approach leaves little room for normative or ethical standards (Inglis, 1990). Habermas has criticized these approaches as 'presentistic, relativistic and cryptonormative' (Habermas, 1985, p. 324).

Habermas' theory of communicative action offers a strong and unique conceptual framework for understanding communications distortions and for improving practice (Forester, 1983). The theory of communicative action and the concept of communicative rationality in particular (Habermas, 1981) can be seen as the 'technical' centrepiece of the comprehensive 'critical social theory' laid out in Habermas' oeuvre.[2] From an analysis of the formal pragmatics of speech acts – 'a rational reconstruction of individual, highly idealised speech acts' (Habermas, 1981, p. 440) – Habermas derives universal conditions of

---

2. an introduction to early Habermas please see McCarthy (1978); for a recent treatment with specific attention to IS see Klein and Huynh (2004).

communicative action. In order to study empirical pragmatics these idealiza-
tions must be relaxed in a controlled fashion (Habermas, 1981, p. 441). It is this
challenge – moving from formal to empirical pragmatics, from universal principles of discourse to tools for discourse analysis – that is addressed in this
chapter. Generally, the approach to discourse associated with the Frankfurt
School is 'critique', the reading of texts, artefacts or social practices to reveal
underlying ideology (Hardt, 1992; Horkheimer, 1937, 1947). While we do not
suggest that empirically based work is preferable to theoretically based work, we
propose that an approach to discourse analysis framed by Habermasian communicative rationality is both theoretically sound and empirically based.

6.2.1 Levels of Discourse Analysis: Macro, Meso and Micro

Discourse operates at different levels. Slembrouck (2001) suggests that there are
different 'strata' of discourse analysis: micro (text in situation), meso (institutional) and macro (socio-cultural). A review of management and IS literature
suggests that most of the work to date has been at the micro-level and focuses on
discourses within organizations (Alvesson, 2000; Czarniawska-Joerges &
Joerges, 1988; Doolin, 2003; Drake, Yuthas, & Dillard, 2000; Fairclough,
2005; Grant, Keenoy, & Oswick, 2001; Hardy, 2001; Kets de Vries & Miller,
1987; Philips, Lawrence, & Hardy, 2004). Researchers have also conducted
discourse analyses at the organizational level, specifically focusing on information technology. For example, Robey and Markus (1984) suggest that elements
of the systems design process can be interpreted as rituals that enable actors to
appear overtly rational while negotiating to achieve their private interests.
Orlikowski and Yates (1994) examined genre repertoires in organizational communications, and Päivärinta (2001) applied the concept of genre to critical IS
development. Murray (1991) examined discourses of power among IS specialists. Bloomfield and Vurdubakis (1994) examined the discourse reflected in
information technology consultancy reports. Also, Heracleous and Hendry
(2000) have examined discourse and the study of organizations. Heracleous
(2001, 2004, 2006) has also examined organizational change as discourse,
organizational discourse as symbolic action as well as analysed dominant,
strategic and marginalized discourses in organizations. Others have applied
hermeneutic analysis to aspects of technology discourse (e.g., Boland, 1985,
1991; Boland & Day, 1989; Butler, 1998; Gopal & Prasad, 2000; Myers, 1995).

   Social sciences researchers have generally focused on macro-level discourses, particularly on the role of media in shaping perceptions of social reality
(Lazarsfeld & Merton, 1948; Lippmann, 1992; McLuhan & Fiore, 1968), as well
as the structural forces shaping discourse (Chomsky, 1989; Foucault, 1980).
There is also a well-established tradition in the social sciences of exposing the
broad societal discourses which surround technology. For example, Ellul (1977)
and Winner (1986) have examined aspects of the technological imperative which
has enveloped society and suppressed technology criticism. Ellul (1977, p. 325)

argued that 'the human being who uses technology today is by that very fact the human being who serves it'. Nardi and O'Day (1999) examined 'the rhetoric of inevitability', a language which represents technological change as unstoppable and unavoidable (Postman, 1992; Rose, 2003; Stoll, 1995).

While the relevance of media discourse as part of an organization's institutional environment has, with varying degrees of explicitness, been acknowledged in the organization theory literature (e.g., DiMaggio & Powell, 1984; Meyer & Rowan, 1977; Meyer & Scott, 1983) the analysis of macro-level discourse has not received much attention. The role of media discourse in the diffusion of management knowledge has been examined by Clegg and Palmer (1996) as well as by Alvarez (1996). The popularization of entrepreneurial ideas not only involves intellectual merits, but also political, social and ideological positions and dispositions. Abrahamson (1996, 2001) and others (e.g., Furusten, 1995; Kieser, 1997) examined the role of management fads and fashions and their influence on uninformed or irrational organizational decision making. In the information technology literature, societal discourses are seldom considered.

An understanding of macro-level (societal) discourse, as reflected in the media, is important to the study of IS as it forms part of the institutional environment of organizations and organizational decision-making. While media do not create attitudes and behaviours in a direct cause-and-effect manner, but media can set the agenda for what the public thinks is important. As such, it is likely that the more attention a particular phenomenon receives in the news media, the more likely it will be perceived by the public as important (McCombs & Shaw, 1972). Media discourse influences organizational action in two different yet related ways. First, decision making involves 'sense making'. It is an act of interpretation rather than a choice between ex ante given alternatives (Weick, 1969, 1995). The language decision makers use to frame their reasoning and its outcomes is not neutral to the content of decision making, but inevitably reflects collective experience, shared purposes and previous choices made by the members of a specific (sub)culture. Discourse enters decision making through taken-for-granted assumptions that, while unnoticed, shape the outcome in powerful ways. The second type of impact of macro-level discourse on organizational decision making stems from organizations' tendencies to conform to their institutional environments (DiMaggio & Powell, 1984; Meyer & Rowan, 1977). Discourse mirrors the views perceived as commonly held, and therefore it is the centre towards which conformity gravitates. An idea perceived as shared by the majority becomes influential regardless of its merits. Public opinion can come to represent a kind of social consensus, silencing those outside the consensus (Cantril, 1991; Herbst, 1993; Noelle-Neumann, 1994). The perception of an idea as mainstream (e.g. as a result of repeated expression of this idea through a variety of media channels) endows it with normative power. Weick (1969, 1995) notes that decision making involves 'sense making'; it is an act of interpretation rather than a choice between alternatives. The language decision makers use to frame their reasoning and its outcomes is not neutral; it inevitably reflects collective experience, shared purposes and previous choices made by the members of a specific (sub)culture. As Attewell and Rule (1984, p. 1190) note '[al]though planners may believe they are acting rationally in adopting new technologies, their decisions actually reflect a pervasive mystique that what can be developed, must be developed'. Macro-level discourse also partially establishes the institutional environment of organizations and, in turn, shapes the tendencies of managers to conform to their institutional environments (DiMaggio & Powell, 1984; Meyer & Rowan, 1977).

While the relationship between the media and audiences is complex, recent research suggests that even though audiences are not passive receptors of ideas, media has a series of small effects which, in aggregate, have significant influence. Agenda setting, framing, priming, demobilization and partisan reinforcement all affect sense making (Davis, 2006). Scholars examining financial markets have documented 'thought contagion' and 'herding behaviours' (Lynch, 2000) which reflect institutional isomorphism and show the link between the media and the perceptions and behaviours of investors (Valliere & Peterson, 2004; Wheale & Amin, 2003). Consequently media discourse is an important subject of enquiry.

6.3 HABERMASIAN VALIDITY CLAIMS AND DISCOURSE ANALYSIS

Habermas (1981) maintains that communicative action, in general, achieves higher levels of rationality than strategic action because it reaps the full potential of rational argumentation. With the dissolution of a theologically founded form of substantive ethics, a new form of secular, procedural morality emerges 'based on moral agreement that expresses in rational form what was always intended in the symbolism of the holy' (Habermas as cited in Cannon, 2001, p. 101). The basis of this morality is communicative ethics, which involves procedural ethics concerning how speakers participate in the discourse. 'Discourse ethics', as advocated by Apel (1995), asserts that morality is grounded in a pattern inherent in mutual understanding based on language. This position avoids relativism by invoking a standard for communication which is universal and unconditional (Cannon, 2001) yet at the same time dynamic and grounded in the social world (Duquenoy, Thimbleby, & Torrance, 1998). If this ethical standard for rationality is met, then the result is comprehension, trust, knowledge and consent; by contrast, standard violations result in systematically distorted communication, which, in turn, lead to misrepresentation, confusion, false assurances and illegitimacy.

6.3.1 Applying Habermasian Validity Claims to Textual Analysis

Habermas' theory of communicative action provides a strong conceptual basis for assessing the (communicative) rationality of societal and organizational discourses. Difficulties in linking 'discourse ethics' with practical concerns have been explored (e.g., Blaug, 1999; Cannon, 2001). However, Habermasian communicative rationality has evolved as the foundation of a significant body of IS research that is critical of the currently dominant functionalist and rational-choice approaches to system development. For instance, IS development methodologies based on the principles of ideal speech treat systems analysis and design as a communication and learning process. In order to achieve emancipatory rationality, these methodologies focus on diagnosing distorting tendencies in communication (e.g., Klein & Hirschheim, 1993; Lyytinen & Klein, 1985; Ngwenyama, 1991; Päivärinta, 2001; Ulrich, 2001). Ngwenyama and Lee (1997) studied the managerial use of e-mail within a company applying Habermasian validity claims to e-mail messages. Truex and Klein (1991) outline an interpretation of IS as formalized language games based on Habermas. Cecez-Kecmanovic (2001) discusses how communicative practices embedded in public discourse via computer-mediated communication influence the rationalization of organizational processes. Finally, Stahl (2003) examines the impact of computers on discourse using Habermas' theories.

While the application of the standard of communicative rationality has been discussed in the context of IS development, it has not been applied to public discourses about information technologies. Drawing upon Forester (1983, 1989) we propose an approach to Critical Discourse Analysis which is grounded in Habermasian validity claims (see Table 6.2). Forester (1983, p. 236) suggests that Habermas' theory of communicative action allows for (1) empirical analysis of communicative interaction and structural settings; (2) interpretive analysis of meaning; and (3) normative analysis of systemic distortion and violation of the free discourse of humans implicit in the most ordinary communications. Writing about urban planning, Forester (1989) maintains that exposing dominant 'ideologies' and power structures to the standards of 'rational' discourse may provide a means of reducing their influence on decision making, thereby 'undistorting' communications and improving the human condition. However, to our knowledge, no such efforts have been made thus far to apply communicative rationality to the textual analysis.

To assess the communicative rationality of media discourse about technology, we develop a series of questions that facilitate the identification of claims to truth, sincerity, legitimacy and clarity in published texts. These questions form the basis of a coding scheme to identify the elements of ideal speech acts present in the discourse. Through a careful analysis of the texts, using a combination of quantitative and qualitative techniques, we provide a concise assessment of the speech elements associated with each claim. Subsequent analysis allows for considerations of communication distortions by examining the instances where the ideal speech situation is not realized. Our focus is on understanding the overall patterns of communicative rationality in the discourse, rather than on detailed analyses of specific passages.

Truth claims are assessed by examining the degree to which claims made in the texts are correctly linked to accurate, relevant facts about the objective

TABLE 6.2 Approaches to Discourse and Textual Analysis

Approach to textual analysis	Focus	Examples of applications
Semiotics	Signs and signification	Hansen et al., 1998; Seiter, 1999
Deconstruction	Meaning is derived from 'difference' sign and its opposite. Focus on gaps and silences to expose hidden structures	Calás & Smircich, 1991; Bowring, 2000
Interpretative reading or hermeneutic analysis	Exegesis of underlying meaning; explication of world-views, analysis of metaphor, narrative, genre	Boland, 1989, 1991; Fondas, 1997
Foucauldian genealogical analysis	How language and social practices create power and limit knowledge	Townley, 1993
Content analysis	Measure frequency of terms	Gerbner, 1977; Herman & Chomsky, 1988
Citation analysis	Measure frequency of citations	Abrahamson, 1996, 2001
Critical discourse analysis	Make explicit what is implicit in the text or cultural practice in order to expose the underlying ideology and ways in which it reinforces social, political and economic superstructures	Fairclough, 1995; Krefting, 2001; Ngwenyama & Lee, 1997

world. As this correspondence cannot be observed directly, it needs to be judged indirectly, based on the information provided in the sampled texts. In particular, we examine whether or not referenced facts are consistent across articles and we apply Michalos' (1986) tests to examine the logical consistency of arguments. Our reading of the texts is guided by the following questions: Have the claims been stated unambiguously (i.e., are issues and options clearly defined)? What evidence has been provided to support these arguments? Has reasoning been provided that leads from the data (observations) to the conclusion (claim)? Have alternative lines of reasoning and explanation been explored, and if so, what were the results? Or, by contrast, has information been distorted or omitted, and were (ideological) claims left unexamined?

Sincerity claims are examined through the analysis of the rhetorical devices used. As Habermas (1981) notes, intentions cannot be observed directly. Hence, sincerity must be assessed based on indirect observation to assess whether or not what is said is consistent with *how* it is said. In textual analysis, this corresponds to examining the consistency between denotation and connotation. Analysing the choice of connotative vocabulary used in the texts may reveal nuances not apparent on a cursory reading. 'Stylistic choices also have clear social and ideological implications, because they often signal opinions of the reporter about news actors and news events as well as properties of the social and communicative situation' which are not directly expressed (Van Dijk, 1991, p. 116). Metaphors have a subtle and often unexamined impact on understanding. 'Metaphor permeates all discourse, ordinary and special, and we should have a hard time finding a purely literal paragraph anywhere' (Goodman as cited in Sterman & Wittenberg, 1999, p. 324). Metaphor involves a 'transfer of scheme' from one area to another, and metaphors filter reality. 'Yet metaphors are imperfect models, and if pushed too hard crack and fail' (Goodman cited in Streman and Wittenberg, 1999, p. 324). In the context of innovations, metaphors can mark a 'departure from sense-making' (Ramiller, 2001, p. 133).

The sincerity claims can help identify instances in which the use of connotative language can influence interpretation or understanding of the text in ways that defeat its content, thereby (consciously or not) promoting a hidden agenda. We pay particular attention to three aspects: emotionally charged adjectives and nouns, and metaphors that might suppress understanding or create false assurances. Our reading of the text is guided by the following questions: Is what is stated consistent with what is assumed or implied in the discourse? Are the tone and the emotional colouring of the text in accordance with its content?

The claim to legitimacy links communicative rationality to the normative standards of the community in which a speech act is embedded. Applying this claim to textual analysis, we focus on identifying textual elements that indicate general participation in the discourse. The right to participate, and, in particular, the right to speak and be listened to, are pre-conditions to communicative rationality and, in turn, to democracy and justice (Habermas, 1991; Apel, 1973). Hence, in the interest of preserving Habermas' spirit of universality (Habermas, 1976) and of achieving greater future generalisability of our methodology, we choose participation (i.e., inclusion/exclusion, voice/silence) as the focus of our examination of legitimacy. The claim to legitimacy reflects the right of all stakeholders to speak out and put their arguments forward, which coincides with the right of the readers to hear and gain knowledge of all perspectives and arguments involved in order to arrive at their own informed judgement. The following questions guide our reading of the text: Who speaks? To whom is legitimacy accorded? Who is considered an expert, and on what basis? How were decisions legitimized? Once these questions are answered, it is then possible to consider questions of absence, including which groups and viewpoints are marginalized or excluded from the discourse. What is missing or suppressed?

The theoretical status of the clarity claim differs from the other validity claims, which refer to the pragmatic dimension of language. Clarity and comprehensibility of codes must not be taken for granted. Questions that guide the assessment of the claim to clarity and comprehensibility are: Is what is said or written audible or legible, respectively? Is the text grammatically correct, and is the usage of terms in accordance with common practice within the respective community? Is the terminology familiar to the audience (i.e., restricted to shared meaning)?

6.4 METHODS IN ACTION

Our study explores technology fads and fashions through citation analysis and discourse analysis of 'e-learning'. This term is widely used in the media and is consistent with what Fairclough (1995) refers to as changes in discursive patterns. In post-secondary institutions, a range of technologies is used to support learning, including electronic mail, presentation systems, multimedia and computer-based applications, audio and video-conferencing, and Web-based applications (Bates, 2000). Although much has been written on the benefits of these technologies (e.g., improved learning, reduced costs, and improved access), the empirical evidence to support such claims is mixed and the outcomes seem to be tied to particular applications. Yet, despite the lack of clear evidence demonstrating the value of adopting technology to support learning, use of and expenditure on, learning technology in the higher educational sector continues to increase (Green, 2001).

Advocates of technology in education maintain that 'higher education is becoming part of a knowledge and learning industry in which competition forces every institution to rethink its products and markets', and suggest that 'half of all of education beyond high school will soon be online' (Finkelstein, Frances, Jewett, & Scholz, 2000) Some institutions (e.g., Athabasca University) do offer a substantial portion of their curriculum entirely online although at most universities distance-learning activities retain a small proportion of their enrolments (Green, 2001). In addition, a number of universities have established mandatory requirements for students to acquire laptop computers (Burg & Thomas, 1998).

Although learning technology was not new ('telelearning' had emerged in the late 1970s and 'on-line learning' in the 1980s), the information highway and e-business boom led to a re-labelling of learning technology as 'e-learning' and an escalation of hype. Advocates of the technology maintained that a revolution was imminent, claiming: 'Today's production and distribution of information are undermining the traditional flow of information and with it the university structure, making it ready to collapse in slow motion once alternatives to its functions become possible' (Twigg & Miloff, 1998). 'Higher education is becoming part of a 'knowledge and learning industry' in which competition forces every institution to rethink its products and markets.' Some believe that 'half of all of education beyond high school will soon be online' (Finkelstein et al., 2000). Distance education through e-learning was labelled 'a killer application' offering universities competitive advantage (Fornaciari, 1999).

In an environment where learning technology is widely used, those who resist it are characterized as technophobes or neo-Luddites. These 'resisters' warn that 'digital diploma mills' might destroy the foundations of education by promoting an uncritical or sub-critical 'corporate agenda' (Noble, 1998; Robertson, 1998), but they receive little attention as their resistance is considered futile in the face of this learning revolution (Oblinger & Rush, 1997). Others have argued that the benefits of learning technology are overstated and have not been demonstrated empirically (Feenberg, 1999). Apart from the 'paucity of empirical evidence that interactive learning technologies are any more effective than other instructional approaches', there are questions about the quality of much of the research, in part because studies often confound media with methods (Phipps & Merisotis, 1999; Reeves, 1993, 1998, 1999). Others maintain that the results achieved by using technology to enhance learning are affected by a wide range of variables including the type of learning technology, the type of course, the type of learners, the instructional design, and the nature of support services (Bates, 2000). Thus, while learning technology may be a useful tool, it is no panacea. However, as has been noted above, post-secondary institutions continue to invest in learning technology, even without clear evidence of its benefits.

The purpose of this research is to explore the shape of media discourse concerning e-learning, using discourse analysis framed within Habermas' validity claims. We are particularly interested in identifying communications distortions which result from violating these validity claims and that may shape decision making at the organizational and political levels. We are not interested in the technologies and their advantages or disadvantages per se but rather how these are constructed.

For the citation analysis, we used ProQuest, a bibliographic database which provided us with the data for our period of study (1992–2005). Using standardized search terms we first conducted a citation analysis to examine the overall shape of the discourse. We conducted an analysis of selected high-circulation publications including examples of popular, trade and academic publications.

Traditionally, critical discourse analysis relies primarily on qualitative methods. Fairclough notes that 'Critical discourse analysis is a particular epistemological orientation to discourse and tends to be associated with a qualitative 'reading' or artefacts' (1995). Kracauer (in Larsen, 1991) also insists that a reading of a text necessarily involves an act of interpretation which, like other readings, is based on specific assumptions to be made explicit in the reading. However, we find little guidance concerning the mechanics of conducting the analysis. In fact, one of the major criticisms levelled at discourse analysis is that it is selective or lacks rigour (Philips & Hardy, 2002). Following Creswell (1994), we combine qualitative and quantitative approaches to textual analysis in a way that reflects Habermasian principles or the epistemological foundations of critical theory (Ngwenyama & Lee, 1997). A multi-method approach for certain purposes is defensible so long as the 'reflective limits' of the positivist philosophy of science are recognized (Habermas, 1988). Different approaches to 'reading' text are not mutually exclusive and applying multiple perspectives to texts may address the limitations of individual techniques in isolation.

To use the validity claims as the basis for our analysis, we applied a two-stage coding method. Preliminary coding was conducted to identify texts linked to validity claims. This coding was based on identifying the speech dimensions that signify each validity claim, as outlined in Table 6.3. Given the particular interest in technology decision-making, we placed an emphasis on the reporting of perceived costs and benefits or advantages and disadvantages. Each article was coded twice for the following:

1. Statements regarding the advantages and disadvantages of the technology;
2. Terms used to describe the project, such as adjectives, metaphors and other associative language;
3. Experts and spokespeople cited in the discussions of technology, etc.;
4. Specialized language or jargon.

Texts were read and re-read to refine the categories which emerged. Ultimately, the principal categories were organized around advantages and disadvantages, costs and benefits, and positive and negative word associations. Subcategories also emerged concerning types of costs and benefits and to whom they would accrue.

6.5 FINDINGS

The citation analysis shows the overall trends and patterns consistent with other management fashions. The dot.com bust in 2000 seems to have precipitated a boom and bust in the discourse as well. While references to the generic 'instructional technology' are relatively flat through the period, references to on-line learning increase sharply between 1997 and 2005, when they begin to level off. The overall patterns of media coverage of learning technology are of interest.

6.5.1 E-Learning

The term 'e-learning' saw little usage in the media between 1992 and 1999. Then, suddenly, the term spikes dramatically until 2002 with 1163 occurrences in the press that year. In 2005, we see that the term 'e-learning' soars to new levels, and this may indicate the institutionalization of the term, where its use has penetrated popular discourse.

6.5.2 Distance Learning

The term distance learning climbs steadily, peaking in 1999. After 2000, the term makes a marked decline. This pattern shadows the rise and fall of the dot.com era, where the crash of online enterprises in 2000 proved that ventures on the World Wide Web were not fail-safe investments.

TABLE 6.3 Summary of Validity Claims and Corresponding Speech Dimensions

Validity claim	Result	Distortion	Validity test	Speech dimensions
The propositional content of what is said is factual or true. Argumentation	Truth	Misrepresentation	Is the evidence and reasoning provided sufficient?	Is the evidence and reasoning provided sufficient?
The speaker is honest (or sincere) in what she says.	Sincerity	False assurance	Is what is said consistent with how it is said?	Connotative words; metaphors
What the speaker says (and hence does) is right or appropriate in the light of existing norms or values.	Legitimacy	Illegitimacy	Are competing 'logics' (e.g., stakeholders) equally represented?	Use of 'experts' and 'authorities' silences
What is said is audible (or legible) and intelligible.	Clarity	Confusion	Is the physical and linguistic embodiment of the message sufficiently unambiguous?	Physical representation: syntactic and semantic rules jargon

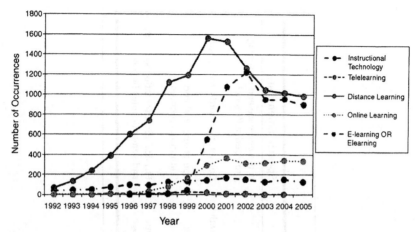

FIGURE 6.1   Citation analysis (all ProQuest databases).

6.5.3 Telelearning

The term telelearning marks the earliest rise and fall of all the terms under study. While used relatively infrequently, its occurrence peaks in 1999 and drops sharply thereafter, falling into disuse with no occurrences in 2005.

6.5.4 Online Learning

By contrast, the term online learning saw a steady increase in occurrences, peaking in 2000. From 2000 to 2005, the term has levelled, averaging 335 citations annually for the last 5 years of the study (Figure 6.1).

6.6 ANALYSIS

6.6.1 Truth Claims: Argumentation and Evidence

Truth claims, in which the propositional content is true, are assessed by considering argumentation and evidence in the discourse. Specific questions that we applied to understand the truthfulness of the discourse include the following:

- What is said about the technology?
- Are the issues and options clearly defined?
- What costs and benefits have been identified and assessed?
- What evidence has been provided to support these arguments?
- Has the relevant information been communicated without distortion or omission? (here, frequencies are of value)
- Are there ideological claims which are unexamined?

The changes heralded with the new technology are far-reaching:

> The sweeping technological advances in learning technologies, now in the prototype phase, will be the substantive achievements of the twenty-first century. The educational equity and access to knowledge that this represents is much like the invention of the printing press. (EM 11)

One of the major arguments made in support of Learning Technology is improved efficiency and cost savings. In announcing plans to develop a virtual university in the western states, Colorado's Governor Roy Romer focuses on 'the potential for increased learning productivity. Technology can be an effective and cheaper way to help people learn' (EM 24). Among the major benefits suggested are 'improving instructional quality and effectiveness, increasing students' access to higher education by making access more convenient, promoting greater productivity and accountability in the use of public funds' (EM 50). Particularly in the early stages, the promise of the technology to improve productivity and reduce costs is paramount (EM 16). What is perhaps most interesting, however, is that even in academic journals there are very few articles that actually provide any empirical evidence to support their claims of benefits; rather, most the benefits are simply asserted.

A number of claims are made that online learning is more interactive and also more appealing to students (EM 6). 'It has the power to change where, when, how and with whom, learning takes place' (EM 32). 'Improving accessibility by supporting distance education and making education more convenient is a major incentive for technology-enabled learning' (EM 31). 'Anytime/anyplace learning saves students time and improves accessibility' (EM 30).

The enthusiasts argue that technology improves learning and some go as far as to suggest that, in some ways, learning technology is superior to traditional classroom education. They claim that the Internet is more *interactive* than the traditional classroom:

> Compared with the traditional lecture method, the Internet can be a much more interactive learning medium which encourages discussion and collaboration. In on-line classes, students can discuss ideas, conceptualise and problem-solve through chat groups. In cyber-courses, more emphasis is put on 'project learning' or 'discovery learning' and can be more demanding and difficult than just listening and taking notes.(EM 6)

Of course, there is nothing to prevent discussion or problem solving in traditional classes. It is merely a matter of instructional design. Nevertheless, throughout the discussion, there seems to be an assumption that use of the Internet automatically promotes more interaction. As a result, the role of the traditional lecture has been diminished, while out-of-class activities, such as discussion groups, on-line tutorials and the use of the Internet, play an increasingly significant part in the learning process (EM 47). The most enthusiastic of the proponents suggest that online learning is superior to face-to-face communication. Some suggest it is 'more convivial' or 'intimate', and that online courses 'may even create a kind of tutorial intimacy that most students and teachers have never known' (EM 30). Indeed, one proponent goes so far as to suggest that it can improve communication:

> face-to-face interaction can often hinder communication,

Ms. H counters:

> On-line, the social barriers of race, appearance, gender, and class evaporate, and women in particular say they can finally make themselves heard. Students have said to me that for the first time, they can focus on the message instead of the messenger, (EM 6)

Very occasionally, however, there are suggestions that one motivation for investing in technology is market positioning: Queen's University President William Leggett said that the high-tech business classroom is only one of several initiatives to position his institution as 'a leader in the use of technology'. The impacts on learning or utility are not discussed (EM 33). Disadvantages are mentioned much less frequently than advantages, and are not really part of the dominant discourse.

Some observers question the notion that technology will save costs and also raise issues related to quality. A textbook is not a course, whether it is in print or electronic:

> You can't just put 15 weeks' worth of lecture material onto the Web. You have to plan the experience so that it makes sense on the Web. It absolutely means more planning if you want quality. And planning is time and time costs money. Unfortunately, you can't build virtual classrooms with virtual dollars. (EM 35)

Some acknowledge the labour intensiveness and expense of producing quality learning technology experiences, suggesting that interactive course development is expensive:

> He estimated that it takes about 40 hours of work to develop one hour of useful interactive programming for students – the equivalent of $100,000 if developed by a full professor for a 30-hour course. (EM 33)

Very occasionally, questions are raised about the very nature of education and attempts made to distinguish it from training. Observers also question whether or not the emphasis on developing computer-related skills or the focus on 'education as product for market' is appropriate. One should not make too much of these developments, however. They could be to education what decaf is to real coffee: a miracle of science, but one best employed as an occasional replacement, rather than a full-time substitute. The great value of the university is the opportunity to meet face-to-face with other students and to have one's own ideas challenged; deliberately in seminars and laboratories and midnight arguments, incidentally just by the act of being on campus, poised to encounter the unexpected. A university devoid of large and sustained doses of this sort of personal contact is, to borrow from John Kenneth Galbraith, like fornicating through a mattress. It lacks a certain *je ne sais quoi* (EM 1).

Several things are noteworthy. First, there is virtually no evidence presented to support the claimed advantages. Even in the academic literature, most of the articles make assertions without any empirical evidence. The benefits were for the most part simply asserted. Second, there are clear omissions. Costs are generally not mentioned or they are only partially addressed. For example, while several articles mention that students of the Acadia Advantage laptop programme at Acadia University in Nova Scotia must pay $1400 per year for a mandatory laptop computer lease, few mention the $24 million investment in infrastructure that was needed to support the programme, much of it donated by vendors. Certainly no one raised the question of the impact on financing this would have on a system-wide basis. When they are mentioned, the assumption that the costs are outweighed by the benefits is also reflected in the early articles (EM 39). In the entire period, only four of the academic articles made any reference to the costs of the technology.

Overall, the discourse focused on the advantages of technology rather than on the disadvantages. Statements concerning the advantages of the technology outnumbered statements concerning the disadvantages, costs or risks associated with the technology by a factor of 2:1. There also seems to be a shift in focus through the period – what begins with an emphasis on cost savings, improved productivity, among other things, gradually shifts. Early stages focus almost exclusively on its positive impact on the 'quality of education', 'increased interactivity', and 'changing teacher/student relationships'. There is almost no discussion of costs until the later part of the period. Not only are disadvantages rarely discussed, there is often little evidence put forward to support assertions concerning the advantages offered by the technologies.

6.6.2 Sincerity: Metaphors and Descriptors

If communication is sincere, the speaker is honest (or sincere) in what he or she says. Sincerity claims are assessed by considering metaphors and connotative words in the discourse. Specific questions that are applied to understand the sincerity of the discourse include the following:

- Do metaphors and connotative words promote/suppress understanding?
- Do metaphors and connotative words create false assurances?

For example, the discourse enthusiastically proclaims:

(N)owhere does the information revolution fall with greater force than in the academic community. (EM 43)

The metaphors of *revolution* and *paradigm shift* recur again and again, as is evident in the following examples: 'The Revolution in Electronic Technology and the Modern University' (EM 24); it is 'A New Paradigm for University Teaching and Learning' (EM 29); the university of 'convergence' (EM 24); the 'global classroom' (EM 20). Information technology is 'tearing down traditional boundaries'. These are 'large scale, revolutionary projects', a 'revolutionary innovation' and 'the digital revolution promises to swell a tide of change of historic proportions in our cultural sea'. The invocation of the larger discourses of the technological imperative recurs over and over again:

> The time seems right to seize the moment and attempt to shape forces that will be irreversible in any event. Computers are far and away the most flexible tools ever created by mankind and, as such, they will eventually revolutionize how most subjects are taught. (EM 5)

This use of associative language creates meaning and reinforces both the positive aspects of the technology. This is a common rhetorical technique – 'the appeal to novelty in a culture that values progress, newness, and change can be as powerful as it is invisible' (Michalos, 1986, p. 95). The technological imperative is almost palpable.

With e-learning, the virtual university is the *term du jour* and 'infrastructure' enters the lexicon in a big way:

> 'This infrastructure is a re-engineered vision of a university's educational processes. Distance education has taken on a new meaning that emphasizes interactivity in learning technology as an enabler of a re-engineering of the educational process itself. An electronic infrastructure supporting these processes should not impose technology restrictions on the players. (EM 10)

There is invocation of the religion of technology: 'A few educators and their benefactors see technology itself as a saviour: buy the hardware and save the college. We know what matters most is how you use the technology' (EM 13). ' [He] had a religious experience, technically speaking. . .Multimedia development is a passion. It feeds our interests and has a dramatic, positive effect on our students' (EM 3). Other authors suggest cynical motives propel all those 'except for a relatively small number of true believers' (EM 19). Technology 'evokes passion' from devotees (EM 45). The birth of these technologies is heralded like the birth of another saviour: 'we do know that computing's most exciting gift has been the birth of new communications technologies and their ability to open undreamed-of opportunities for extending the humanities knowledge base' (EM 27). They paint a vision of the future where collaboration will be a dominant form of teaching, learning and research.

There is also invocation of the broader societal discourses on corporatization and an emergence of the view of education as business, which is both explicitly and reflected in the use of metaphors. According to a number of the writers, education is in crisis (EM 26; EM 12) and as such, 'knowledge is [their] business' (EM 43). It is emphasized that 'students will view education as a consumer good, investing time as well as money based on comparative value' (EM 38). 'Society expects higher education to become more flexible in its course and curriculum offerings in order to meet the new educational needs of a learning society. . .consumers of instruction' (EM 21). For example, one article is actually titled 'Business Designs for the New University: What Happens if the

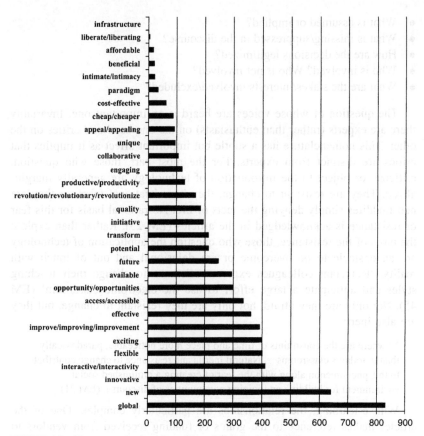

FIGURE 6.2   Frequency of selected metaphors in articles on e-learning.

Institution with the Obsolescent Business Design is a University?' (EM 12). As a business it is often touted as inevitable, statements such as: 'it's a market that is not just desirable but inevitable', are not uncommon (EM 7). Content analysis reinforces our analysis of the patterns (see Figure 6.2).

6.6.3 Legitimacy: Whose Interests?

Legitimacy claims consider whether what the speaker says (and hence does) is right or appropriate in the light of existing norms or values. Legitimacy claims are assessed by considering the inclusivity of the discourse, and by assessing the extent to which the discourse relies upon 'experts' and 'sources'. Specific questions that are applied to understand the legitimacy of the discourse include the following:

- Who is speaking, who is silent, what are their interests?
- What is privileged? What is not said about the technology?

- What is assumed or implied?
- What is missing/suppressed in the discourse?
- How are the decisions legitimized?
- Who is involved? Who is not involved?
- What are the stakes/interests involved/excluded?

The question of whose voices are heard is an important one. Invariably there are experts (rather than enthusiasts) on the one hand and critics on the other. This nomenclature has a subtle but important effect as it implies that critics are distinct from experts. For the most part, those who question, criticize, or object to the introduction of technology are generally marginalized. They are resistant to change, they have irrational fears, or they are neo-Luddites simply denying the facts of life. No rational basis for this fear or resistance is acknowledged in the articles (EM 25). Rather than explore the basis of the resistance, those who question the application of technology are an obstacle to be overcome or are delusional and out of touch with reality. 'Reluctant colleagues express resistance to change their teaching styles and anticipate a large effort to use the electronic classroom' (EM 45). Not only are they afraid, not only are they resistant to change, but they are also inert:

> Nowhere are the constraints of time and place more noticeable, paradoxically, than in today's classrooms. . . Natural inertia and resistance to change contribute to this phenomenon along with the fear of creating a diminished social environment for building and joining communities of discourse. (EM 21)

With e-learning, the relationships are particularly complex. One of the articles makes reference to the grants or funding received from vendors to implement the projects (EM 20). Generally, however, vendors' motives are stated or assumed to be focused on improving education. IBM is often cited speaking on the benefits of educational technology without any questions raised about their objectivity or interests. Little reference is made, for example, to the size or importance of educational markets or the obvious market value of showcasing technology. The interests of suppliers may not be synonymous with the interests of educators or governments. Similarly, the impact of vendor funding on research into technology in education is beyond the scope of this chapter but is a dimension of the (re)production of the discourse that could be explored.

When experts are cited who criticize technology, they are generally marginalized. David Noble's anti-technology essay on 'digital diploma mills' notes:

> Beneath that change [technological transformation] and camouflaged by it, lies another: the commercialization of higher education. For here as elsewhere technology is but a disarming disguise. . .they [the champions of computer-based instruction] ignore. . .the fact that their high-tech remedies are bound only to compound the problem, increasing further, rather than reducing, the costs of higher education. (EM 46)

However, Noble's article was published with not one but three accompanying critiques. Shneiderman resorts to ridicule:

> Does he [Noble] think professors publishing books and universities requiring texts from commercial publishers are also examples of 'commoditisation'? Is the university requirement to publish in journals (run by companies or professional societies) an example of monopolistic practices? Does he fear that purchases of chairs and desks results from 'interlocking directorates? (EM 46)

The imbalance in argument and in language is reinforced by the choice of and presentation of experts.

6.6.4 Clarity

Clarity requires that what is said is linguistically intelligible and comprehensible.

There is no doubt that clarity is one of the more difficult standards to apply. There are a number of ways in which confusion may be created in specific speech acts (Michalos, 1986, p. 38). For the purposes of this study, we did not examine clarity in detail – our assumption was that published texts are syntactically correct – however, we do note that there is extensive use of jargon which, at times, seems to obscure as much as it illuminates.

6.7 CONCLUSIONS AND IMPLICATIONS FOR FURTHER RESEARCH

This chapter has proposed a method for applying Habermasian validity claims in critical discourse analysis, by translating universal principles of communication into specific tools for discourse analysis. It illustrates our method by applying it to the media discourse on an information technology project revealing a number of distortions. Following institutional theory, we suggest that such public discourses about technology are part of the institutional environment of organizations that may influence and, as in the case we analysed, potentially distort organizational decision-making.

This chapter also provides evidence that public discourse on technology often follows a predictable pattern of the technology hype cycle. Citation analysis on e-learning shows an overall pattern which suggests that new technologies are often greeted with intense enthusiasm and media attention (often driven by intense marketing efforts), but that, over time, interest drops and declines. In some cases, there is evidence that the same technology is repackaged under a different label and its 'reintroduction' is again accompanied by a similar flurry of attention which then drops off.

A close examination of the media discourse not only shows changes in intensity but also in content, with the initial phase focused almost entirely on the benefits, the second phase with more attention on the costs and challenges, and a final phase with less interest in the promises of the technology, and more balanced and realistic expectations. Habermasian validity claims can provide a standard for media discourse which helps to separate hype from reality. The truth claim allows us to examine argumentation. The sincerity claim frames our analysis of the use of connotative language. The legitimacy claim places focus on 'who' is speaking while clarity leads to an examination of the comprehensibility of the use of language.

Although our efforts to apply the Habermasian validity claims to textual analysis are imperfect, they are defensible as a proposed framework for the exposure of explicit and implicit distortions in media discourse. The study illustrates how this method could be applied to the media discourse on e-learning to reveal the ways in which communications distortions contribute to the hype cycle. We do not profess an opinion on the nature of these technologies, but rather on the media discourse about them. The information provided in the published texts places its emphasis on benefits rather than costs. There are general claims about the benefits of the technologies based on limited evidence. Improvements are claimed with little effort to establish causal links.

In particular, the costs of the technologies and their implementations as well as the risks are downplayed. Silences about the costs of technology can result in communications distortions and poor decision making. The metaphors and images used reinforced discourses of the technological imperative and progress. In this way, connotative language reinforces the benefits of the project. The overwhelming use of positive adjectives and metaphors suggests that, regardless of the argumentation, the positive aspects of the technology are reinforced through the choice of language. Although it is not examined in this chapter, previous work has suggested that the academic literature is not significantly different from the non-academic literature, using much of the same loaded language associated with the technology 'revolution' (Cukier, Bauer, & Middleton, 2004). More reflection on our own discourses as researchers is clearly needed.

Examination of the authorities cited also shows that the dominant voices are from those who support the technology; critics and sceptics are marginalized both subtly and overtly. The relative power of the various actors engaged in this discourse, their complex inter-relations and the role of the suppliers of technology in promoting it cannot be ignored.

Media hype may be motivated by a number of things including corporate agendas (Gerhard and Mayr, 2002). These can be direct, especially when a private enterprise, like a hardware or software supplier, stands to gain from the proliferation of technologies. They can also be indirect, for example, with consultants or 'gurus' for hire, paid to advise companies on how to respond to the new developments. Government also plays a critical role in the institutionalization of the information highway (King et al., 1994) as well as related concepts such as e-learning and e-business. In Canada, a range of public/private partnerships include the Information Highway Advisory Council (IHAC), the Canadian E-business Opportunities Roundtable (formed in mid-1999) and an E-learning Council (established by Industry Canada in 2000; Arms-Length Committee, 2000). Media producers, like local and national newspapers, may also gain from the diffusion of hype, as stories about e-learning and catchy headlines promising a revolution or a paradigm shift help to sell newspapers and fill columns. They are often funded, at least in part, through advertisements by the vendors of the technology, in 'special issues' dealing with aspects of the technology. The interactions among the various actors or producers of discourses are an important part of the analysis.

Scholars have insisted on the importance of applying standards of communicative rationality to IS development at the organizational level. We suggest that it is equally important to apply such standards to societal level discourses as manifest in media. These media discourses provide part of the institutional environment of organizational decisions about technology and there is broad consensus that organizations tend to conform to their institutional environment (e.g., DiMaggio & Powell, 1984; Meyer & Rowan, 1977; Meyer & Scott, 1983). We did not empirically explore the extent to which the media discourses shape and reflect the organizational discourse, and this needs further investigation, as do the ways in which the discourse is produced and reproduced. However, institutional theory suggests that organizations actively seek conformity with their institutional environment in order to gain legitimacy (Powell & DiMaggio, 1991). In addition, discourse enters organizational decision making through taken-for-granted beliefs and assumptions (most importantly, the language that decision-makers use to frame their reasoning and its outcomes). This influence often goes unnoticed, yet it shapes decision outcomes in powerful ways. We agree with Forester's (1983) claim that Habermasian communicative rationality is an appropriate standard to apply in order to expose the communications distortions that 'suppress common sense'. Further work examining the relationship between public discourses, as reflected in the media and organizational discourses, would be a productive area of investigation. Given that both levels of discourse have been analysed in terms of communicative rationality, we expect the link to be an area for future critical analysis in the Habermasian tradition.

What is particularly striking, and unexpected, is the absence of any significant differences in the patterns revealed in the three-part discourses that were analysed. While much has been written about the problems of resistance to technology and the neo-Luddites who plague efforts to introduce innovation, this chapter suggests that there may be value in paying equal attention to the problems associated with uncritical and unreflective technology enthusiasm. Rather than dismissing technology critics, or, as we have seen throughout the analysis of the discourse, marginalizing them, allowing them more play may produce a healthier decision-making process.

Although the study did not explicitly examine organizational decision-making, previous work on institutional isomorphism and the role of norms shaping organizational behaviour suggests that the findings regarding the nature of discourse on learning technology are relevant to the understanding of technology planning. Although the results are not conclusive, the enthusiasm about learning technology seems to be particularly pronounced at the beginning of the period, coincident with the rise in discussions of the information highway.

Other studies on management fashions and fads (e.g., Abrahamson, 1996) have suggested that the unbridled enthusiasm at the beginning of a trend fuels hype, often resulting in the benefits being oversold. Many of these fads achieve broad acceptance and lead to large expenditures, only to suffer a backlash when they fail to live up to their promises (Abrahamson & Fairchild, 1999; Sterman & Wittenberg, 1999). The process of learning technology that has been described would seem, at one level, to parallel the life cycle of management fads. While further research is needed, there is some evidence to suggest that the pattern is not unique to learning technologies but probably applies to other technologies as well. While at one level, it seems absurdly obvious, both the review of the academic literature and the systematic analysis of discourse suggest that there is little consideration given to the costs of learning technology. Often, the benefits are assumed not demonstrated. The questions implied by communicative rationality, can surely help reduce uncertainty, regardless of the basis upon which the decision is ultimately made. What *are* the benefits? What evidence is there to support the claims? What do we really know and what do we not know? What are the costs? What other impacts might the technology have? What do the acronyms really mean? Are there taken-for-granted assumptions that should be questioned? Who should be involved? What perspectives should be considered? Not only should paying attention to communicative rationality improve decision making, but, arguably, the success of technological innovations in the long term might actually be enhanced by also moderating the positive feedback processes including the marketing media hype and extravagant claims of efficacy. In other words, a critical perspective may reduce the chances of technology being oversold and, thereby, ironically, enhance its diffusion. In order to achieve rational decisions, a critical perspective is essential because it enables decision makers to separate the broader societal hype about technology from what is in the best interest of universities and the principal stakeholders in post-secondary education.

REFERENCES

Abell, P. (1991). *Rational choice theory.* Edward Elgar, Brookfield, VT.

Abrahamson, E. (1996). Management fashions, academic fashions and enduring truths. *Academy of Management Review, 21*(3), 616—619.

Abrahamson, E. (2001). Words into Numbers. *Paper presented at the Academy of Management Conference Report,* Washington, DC.

Abrahamson, E., & Fairchild, G. (1999). Management fashion: Lifecycles, triggers and collective learning processes. *Administrative Science Quarterly, 44,* 708—740.

Alvesson, M. (2000). Varieties of discourse: On the study of organizations through discourse analysis. *Human Relations, 53*(9), 1125—1149.

Apel, K. O. (1973). *Transformationen der Philosophie.* Suhrkamp, 2 Bände, Frankfurt a-M.

Apel, K.-O. (1995). The rationality of human communication: Between consensual, strategic and systems rationality. *Graduate Faculty Philosophy Journal, 18*(1), 1—26.

Arms-Length Committee (2000). *To advise governments. Universities and colleges on reaping benefits of online learning.* Industry Canada, Ottawa.

Attewell, P., & Rule, J. (1984). Computing and organizations: What we know and what we don't know. *Communications of the ACM, 27*(2), 1184—1191.

Bates, A. W. (2000). *Managing technological change.* Jossey-Bass, San Francisco.

Benders, J., & van Veen, K. (2001). What's in a Fashion? Interpretative viability and management fashion *Organization, 8*(1), 33—53.

Berger, C. R., & Bradac, J. J. (1982). *Language and social knowledge: Uncertainty in interpersonal relations.* E. Arnold, London.

Blaug, R. (1999). *Democracy real and ideal: Discourse ethics and radical politics.* State University of New York Press, New York.

Bloomfield, B., & Vurdubakis, T. (1994). Re-presenting technology: IT consultancy reports as textual reality constructions. *Sociology, 28*(2), 455—477.

Boland, R. (1985). Phenomenology: A preferred approach to research in information systems. *Research methods in information systems.* In Mumford, E., Hirschheim, R.A., Fitzgerald, G., & Harper, T.W. (Eds.), North Holland, Amsterdam, pp. 193—201.

Boland, R. J. (1991). Information system use as a hermeneutic process. *Information systems research: Contemporary approaches and emergent traditions.* In Nissen, H.E., Klein, H.K., & Hirschheim, R.A. (Eds.), North Holland, Amsterdam, pp. 439—458.

Boland, R. J., & Day, W. F. (1989). The experience of system design: A hermeneutic of organizational action. *Scandinavian Journal of Management, 5*(2), 87—104.

Bowring, M. A. (2000). De/construction theory: A look at the institutional theory that positivism built. *Journal of Management Inquiry, 9*(3), 135—137.

Brooke, C. (2002). What does it mean to be 'critical' in IS Research? *Journal of Information Technology, 17,* 49—57.

Burg, J. J., & Thomas, S. J. (1998). Computers across campus. *Communications of the ACM, 41*(1), 22—25.

Burrell, G., & Morgan, G. (1979). *Sociological paradigms and organizational analysis: Elements of the sociology of corporate life.* Heinemann, London.

Butler, T. (1998). Towards a hermeneutic method for interpretive research in information systems. *Journal of Information Technology, 13*(4), 285—300.

Calás, M., & Smircich, L. (1991). Voicing seduction to silence leadership. *Organization Studies, 12*(4), 567—601.

Cannon, B. (2001). *Rethinking the normative content of critical theory: Marx, Habermas and beyond.* Palgrave, New York.

Cantril, A. H. (1991). *The opinion connection: Polling, politics and the press.* Congressional Quarterly Press, Inc, Washington, D.C..

Cecez-Kecmanovic, D. (2001). Critical information systems research: A Habermasian approach. *Paper presented at the Global Cooperation in the New Millennium, The 9th European Conference on Information Systems,* Bled.

Cecez-Kecmanovic, D., & Janson, M. (1999). Communicative action theory: An approach to understanding the application of information systems. *Proceedings of the 10th Australasian Conference on Information Systems ACIS'99,* Wellington, New Zealand, pp. 183—195.

Cecez-Kecmanovic, D., Janson, M., & Brown, A. (2002). The rationality framework for a critical study of information systems. *Journal of Information Technology, 17,* 215—227.

Chiapello, E., & Fairclough, N. (2002). Understanding the new management ideology: A transdisciplinary contribution from critical discourse analysis and new sociology of capitalism. *Discourse and Society, 13*(2), 185—208.

Chomsky, N. (1989). *Necessary illusions: Thought control in democratic societies.* House of Anansi, Concord, ON.

Clegg, S. R., & Palmer, G., (Eds.), (1996). *The politics of management knowledge,* Sage, London.

Collins, D. (2000). *Management fads and buzzwords: Critical-practical perspectives.* Routledge, New York.

Creswell, J. (1994). *Research design: Qualitative and quantitative approaches.* Sage, Thousand Oaks, CA.

Cukier, W., Bauer, R., & Middleton, C. (2004). Applying Habermas' validity claims as a standard For critical discourse analysis. *Information systems research relevant theory & informed practice.* In Kaplan, B., Truex, D.P., Wastell, D., Wood-Harper, A.T., & DeGross, J.I. (Eds.), Kluwer Academic Publishers, Norwell, MA, pp. 233—258.

Czarniawska-Joerges, B., & Joerges, B. (1988). How to control things with words: Organizational talk and control. *Management Communications Quarterly, 2*(2), 170—193.

Davis, A. (2006). Media effects and the question of the rational audience: Lessons from the financial markets. *Media, Culture and Society, 28*(4), 603—625.

Derrida, J. (1982). *Margins of philosophy.* University of Chicago Press, Chicago.

DiMaggio, P. J., & Powell, W. W. (1984). The iron cage revisited: Institutional isomorphism and collective rationality in organizational fields. *American Sociological Review, 48,* 147—160.

Doolin, B. (2003). Narratives of change: Technology, discourse and organization. *Organization, 10*(4), 751—770.

Drake, B., Yuthas, K., & Dillard, J. F. (2000). It's only words: Impact of information technology on moral dialogue. *Journal of Business Ethics, 23,* 41—59.

Drury, D. H., & Farhoomand, A. (1999). Information technology push/pull reactions. *Journal of Systems and Software, 47*(1), 3—10.

Duquenoy, P., Thimbleby, H., & Torrance, S. (1998). *Towards a synthesis of discourse ethics and Internet regulation.* Middlesex University, London.

Eccles, R. G., Nohria, N., & Berkley, J. D. (1992). *Beyond the hype: Rediscovering the essence of management.* Harvard Business School Press, Boston, MA.

Ellul, J. (1977). *The technological system.* (J. Neugroschel, Trans.) Continuum, New York.

Fairclough, N. (1995). *Critical discourse analysis: The critical study of language.* Longman Group, New York.

Fairclough, N. (2005). Discourse analysis in organization studies: The case for critical realism. *Organization Studies, 26*(6), 915—939.

Feenberg, A. (1999). Distance learning: Promise or threat? *Crosstalk, 7*(1), http://www-rohan.sdsu.edu/faculty/feenberg/TELE3.HTM.

Feldman, M. S., & March, J. G. (1981). Information in organizations as signal and symbol. *Administrative Science Quarterly, 26*(2), 171—186.

Finkelstein, M., Frances, C., Jewett, F., & Scholz, B. (2000). *Dollars, distance, and online education: The new economics of college teaching and learning. Series on higher education.* American Council on Education, Washington, DC.

Fiske, J. (1982). *An introduction to communication studies*. Methuen Press, London.

Fletcher, J. (1998). Relational practice: A feminist reconstruction of work. *Journal of Management Inquiry*, 7(2), 163—186.

Fondas, N. (1997). Feminization unveiled: Management qualities in contemporary writings. *Academy of Management Review*, 22(1), 257—282.

Forester, J. (1983). Critical theory and organizational analysis. *Beyond method*. In Morgan, G. (Ed.), Sage, Beverly Hills, CA, pp. 234—346.

Forester, J. (1989). *Planning in the face of power*. University of California Press, Berkeley, CA.

Fornaciari, C. J. (1999). Distance education as strategy: How can your school compete? *Journal of Management Education*, 23(6), 703—718.

Foucault, M. (1971). *The order of things: An archaeology of the human sciences*, (1st American edn.). Pantheon Books, New York.

Foucault, M. (1979). *Discipline and punish: The birth of the prison*. Vintage Books, New York.

Foucault, M. (1980). *Two lectures: Power/knowledge*. Random House, New York.

Furusten, S. (1995). *Popular management books: How they are made and what they mean for organizations*. Routledge, London.

Gerbner, G. (1977). Comparative cultural indicators. *Mass media policies in changing cultures*. In Gerbner, G. (Ed.), Wiley, New York, pp. 199—205.

Gerhard, J. & Mayr, G. 2002. Competing in the E-learning environment: Strategies for universities. Paper presented at the *35th Hawaii International Conference on Systems Science (HICSS), Hawaii*, January 7–10.

Gopal, A., & Prasad, P. (2000). Understanding GDSS in symbolic context: Shifting the focus from technology to interaction. *MIS Quarterly*, 24(3), 509—546.

Grant, D., Keenoy, T., & Oswick, C. (2001). Organizational discourse: Key contributions and challenges. *International Studies of Management and Organization*, 31(3), 5—25.

Green, K. (2001). *The 2001 national survey of information technology in U.S. higher education*. Campus Computing Project, Encino, CA.

Habermas, J. (1976). *Communication and the evolution of society*. (T. McCarthy, Trans.) Beacon Press, Boston.

Habermas, J. (1981). *The theory of communicative action (2 Vols.) (1984)*. (T. McCarthy, Trans.) Beacon Press, Boston.

Habermas, J. (1985). *The philosophical discourse of modernity (1990)*. (F. G. Lawrence, Trans.) MIT Press, Cambridge, MA.

Habermas, J. (1988). *On the logic of the social sciences*. (S. Nicholsen, & J. A. Stark, Trans.) MIT Press, Cambridge, MA.

Habermas, J. (1991). *Justification and Application: Remarks on Discourse Ethics*. (C. P. Cronin, Trans.). Cambridge: MIT Press.

Hansen, A., Cottle, S., Negrine, R., & Newbold, C., (Eds.), (1998). *Mass communications research methods*, New York University Press, New York.

Hardt, H. (1992). *Critical communication studies. Communication. History and theory in America*. Routledge, New York.

Hardy, C. (2001). Researching organizational discourse. *International Studies of Management and Organization*, 31(3), 25—48.

Heracleous, L. (2006). A Tale of Three Discourses: The Dominant, the Strategic and the Marginalized. *Journal of Management Studies*, 43(5), 1059—1087.

Heracleous, L., & Barrett, M. (2001). Organizational change as discourse: Communicative actions and deep structures in the context of information technology implementation. *Academy of Management Journal*, 44, 755—778.

Heracleous, L., & Hendry, J. (2000). Discourse and the study of organization: Towards a structurational perspective. *Human Relations, 53*(10), 1251.

Herbst, S. (1993). *Numbered voices: How opinion polling has shaped American politics.* University of Chicago Press, Chicago.

Herman, E. S., & Chomsky, N. (1988). *Manufacturing consent: The political economy of the mass media.* Pantheon, New York.

Hirsch, P. M. (1986). From ambushes to golden parachutes: Corporate takeovers and an instance of cultural framing and institutional integration. *American Journal of Sociology, 91,* 800—837.

Horkheimer, M. (1937). Traditional and critical theory, 1972. *Critical theory: Selected essays.* In Horkheimer, M. (Ed.), Continuum, New York, pp. 152—188.

Horkheimer, M. (1947). *Eclipse of reason.* Oxford University Press, New York.

Howcroft, D., & Trauth, E. M. (2005). *Handbook of critical information systems research: Theory and application.* E. Elgar, Northampton, MA.

Inglis, F. (1990). *Media theory.* Blackwell, Oxford, UK.

Jackson, B. (2001). *Management gurus and management fashions.* Routledge, New York.

Jensen, K. B. (1991). Humanist scholarship as qualitative science: Contributions to mass communication research. *A handbook of qualitative methodologies for mass communication research.* In Jensen, K.B., & Jankowski, N. (Eds.), Routledge, London, pp. 17—43.

Jensen, K. B., & Jankowski, N. (1991). *A handbook of qualitative methodologies for mass communication research.* Routledge, London.

Kets de Vries, M. F.R., & Miller, D. (1987). Interpreting organizational texts. *Journal of Management Studies, 24*(3), 233—247.

Kieser, A. (1997). Rhetoric and myth in management fashion. *Organization, 4*(1), 49—74.

King, J. L., Gurbaxani, V., McFarlan, K. L., Raman, K. S., & Yap, C. S. (1994). Institutional factors in information technology innovation. *Information Systems Research, 5*(2), 139—199.

Klein, H. K. (1999). Knowledge and methods in IS research: From beginnings to the future. *New information technologies in organizational processes.* In Ngwenyama, O., Introna, L., Myers, M. D. (Eds.), Kluwer, Boston, pp. 13—25.

Klein, H. K., & Hirschheim, R. (1993). The application of neo-humanist principles in information systems development. *Human, organizational and social dimensions of information systems development.* In Avison, D., Kendall, T.E., & DeGross, J.I. (Eds.), Elsevier, Amsterdam, pp. 263—280.

Klein, H. K., & Huynh, M. Q. (2004). The critical social theory of Jürgen Habermas. *Social theory and philosophy for information systems.* In Mingers, J., & Willcocks, L. (Eds.), Wiley, Chichester, UK, pp. 157—237.

Krefting, L. A. (2001). Re-presenting women executives: Valorization and devalorization in US business press. *Paper presented at the European Group on Organizational Studies (EGOS) Conference,* Lyon, France.

Larsen, P. (1991). Textual analysis of fictional media content. *A handbook of qualitative methodologies for mass communication research.* In Jensen, K.B., & Jankowski, N. (Eds.), Routledge, London, pp. 121—148.

Lazarsfeld, P. F., & Merton, R. K. (1948). Mass communications, popular taste, and organized social action. *Mass communications.* In Schramm, W. (Ed.), University of Illinois Press, Urbana, IL, pp. 492—512.

le Roux, I. (2002). *E-learning at the University of Pretoria: Has the plateau of productivity been reached?* Working paper. University of Pretoria.

Lee, A. S. (1994). Electronic mail as a medium for rich communication: An empirical investigation using hermeneutic interpretation. *MIS Quarterly, 18*(2), 143—157.

Lippmann, W. (1992). *Public opinion.* Macmillan, New York.

Lynch, A. (2000). Thought contagions in the stock market. *Journal of Psychology and Financial Markets, 1*(1), 10—23.

Lyytinen, K. J., & Klein, H. K. (1985). The critical theory of Jurgen Habermas as a basis for a theory of information systems. *Research methods in information systems.* In Mumford, E., Hirschheim, R., & Wood-Harper, T. (Eds.), North Holland, Amsterdam, pp. 219—237.

McCarthy, T. (1978). *The critical theory of Jürgen Habermas.* Hutchinson, London.

McCombs, M. E., & Shaw, D. L. (1972). The agenda-setting function of mass media. *The Public Opinion Quarterly, 36*(2), 176—187.

McLuhan, M., & Fiore, Q. (1968). *War and peace in the global village.* Bantam, New York.

Meyer, J., & Rowan, B. (1977). Institutionalized organizations: Formal structure as myth and ceremony. *American Journal of Sociology, 83,* 157—179.

Meyer, J., & Scott, R., (Eds.), (1983). *Organizational environments: Ritual and rationality,* Sage, Newbury Park, CA.

Michalos, A. C. (1986). *Improving your reasoning.* Prentice Hall, London.

Murray, F. (1991). Technical rationality and the IS specialist: Power, discourse and identity. *Critical Perspectives on Accounting, 2,* 59—81.

Myers, M. D. (1995). Dialectical hermeneutics: A theoretical framework for the implementation of information systems. *Information Systems Journal, 5*(1), 51—70.

Nardi, B. A., & O'Day, V. L. (1999). *Information ecologies: Using technology with heart.* MIT Press, Cambridge, MA.

Ngwenyama, O. K. (1991). The critical social theory approach to information systems: Problems and challenges. *Information systems research: Contemporary approaches & emergent traditions.* In Nissen, H.E., Klein, H.K., & Hirschheim, R.H. (Eds.), North Holland, Amsterdam, pp. 267—280.

Ngwenyama, O., & Lee, A. (1997). Communication richness in electronic mail: Critical theory and the contextuality of meaning. *MIS Quarterly, 21*(2), 145—167.

Noelle-Neumann, E., Schulz, W., & Wilke, J. 1994. *Publizistik, Massenkommunikation* (Aktualisierte, vollstèandig èuberarbeitete Neuausg). (Ed.). Frankfurt a-M: Fischer Taschenbuch Verlag.

Oblinger, D. G., & Rush, S. G., (Eds.), (1997). *The learning revolution: The challenge of information technology in the academy,* Anker Publishing, Bolton, MA.

Orlikowski, W., & Yates, J. (1994). Genre repertoire: The structuring of communicative practices in organizations. *Administrative Science Quarterly, 39*(4), 541—574.

Päivärinta, T. (2001). The concept of genre within the critical approach to information systems development. *Information and Organization, 11,* 207—234.

Parker, I. (1992). *Discourse dynamics: Critical analysis for social and individual psychology.* Routledge, New York.

Philips, N., & Hardy, C. (2002). *Discourse analysis: Investigating processes of social construction.* Sage, Thousand Oaks, CA.

Philips, N., Lawrence, T. B., & Hardy, C. (2004). Discourse and institutions. *Academy of Management Review, 29*(4), 635—652.

Phipps, R., & Merisotis, J. (1999). *What's the difference? A review of contemporary research on the effectiveness of distance learning in higher education.* The Institute for Higher Education Policy Report, Washington, DC.

Postman, N. (1992). *Technology: The surrender of culture to technology.* Vintage, New York.

Powell, W. W., & DiMaggio, P. J. (1991). *The new Institutionalism in organizational analysis.* Chicago University Press, Chicago.

Ramiller, N. C. (2001). The "textual attitude" and new technology. *Information and Organization*, *11*, 129—156.

Reeves, T. C. (1993). Pseudoscience in computer-based instruction: The case of learner control research. *Journal of Computer-Based Instruction*, *20*(2), 39—46.

Reeves, T. C. (1998). *The Impact of media and technology in schools: A research report*. Bertlesmann Foundation.

Reeves, T. C. (1999). *E-learning the professoriate: The issue of productivity*. In ED_MEDIA Keynote Address. University of Georgia.

Ricoeur, P. (1976). *Interpretation theory: Discourse and the surplus of meaning*. Texas Christian University Press, Fort Worth, TX.

Robertson, H. J. (1998). *No more teachers, no more books: The commercialization of canada's schools*. McClelland and Stewart, Toronto.

Robey, D., & Markus, M. L. (1984). Rituals in information system design. *MIS Quarterly*, *8*(1), 5—15.

Rose, E. (2003). *User error: Resisting computer culture*. Between the Lines, Toronto.

Seiter, E. (1999). *Teleivison and new media audiences*. Clarendon Press, Oxford.

Slembrouck, S. (2001). Explanation, interpretation and critique in the analysis of discourse. *Critique of Anthropology*, *21*(1), 35—57.

Stahl, B. C. (2003). When does a computer speak the truth? The problem of it and validity claims *Global and organizational discourse about information technology*. In Wynn, E.H., Whitley, E. A., & DeGross, J.I. (Eds.), Kluwer, Norwell, MA, pp. 91—108.

Sterman, J. D., & Wittenberg, J. (1999). Path dependence, competition, and succession in the dynamics of scientific revolution. *Organization Science*, *10*(3), 322—341.

Stoll, C. (1995). *Silicon snake oil*. Anchor Books, New York.

Thomas, P. (2003). The recontextualization of management: A discourse-based approach to analysing the development of management thinking. *Journal of Management Studies*, *40*(4), 775—801.

Townley, B. (1993). Foucault, power/knowledge, and is relevance for human resource management. *Academy of Management Review*, *18*(3), 518—545.

Truex, D. P., & Klein, H. K. (1991). A rejection of structure as a basis for information systems development. *Collaborative work, social communications and information systems*. In Stampler, R.K., Kerola, P., Lee, R., & Lyytinen, K. (Eds.), North Holland, Amsterdam, pp. 213—235.

Twigg, C., & Miloff, M. (1998). The global learning infrastructure. *Blueprint to the digital economy*. In Tapscott, D., Lowry, A., & Ticoll, D. (Eds.), McGraw-Hill, Toronto, pp. 179—201.

Ulrich, W. (2001). A philosophical staircase for information systems definition, design, and development: A discursive approach to reflective practice in ISD (Part 1). *Journal of Information Technology Theory and Application*, *3*(3), 55—84.

Valliere, D., & Peterson, R. (2004). Inflating the bubble: Examining dot-com investor behaviour. *Venture Capital*, *6*(1), 1—22.

Van Dijk, T. A. (1991). The interdisciplinary study of news as discourse. *A handbook of qualitative methodologies for mass communication research*. In Jensen, K.B., & Jankowski, N. (Eds.), Routledge, London, pp. 104—120.

Weick, K. E. (1969). *The social psychology of organizing*. Addison-Wesley, Reading, MA.

Weick, K. E. (1995). *Sense making in organizations*. Sage, Thousand Oaks, CA.

Wheale, P. R., & Amin, L. H. (2003). Bursting the dot-com 'bubble': A case study in investor behaviour. *Technology Analysis and Strategic Management*, *15*(1), 117.

Winner, L. (1986). *The whale and the reactor*. University of Chicago Press, Chicago.

Wodak, R., (Ed.), (1989). *Language, power and ideology: Studies in political discourse,* John Benjamins Publishing, Philadelphia, PA.

FURTHER READING

Heracleous, L., & Marshak, R. J. (2004). Conceptualizing organizational discourse as situated symbolic action. *Human Relations, 57*(10), 1285.

Chapter 7

Semiotics and Information Technology Strategy

Laurie McAulay

7.1. Introduction

7.2. Structuralism: A Structural Approach to Understanding Texts

7.3. Post-Structuralism and Post-Modernism

7.4. Conclusion References

7.1 INTRODUCTION

Semiotics is the study of signs. Signs include written materials such as stories, poems, manuals, strategic statements and financial reports but also encompass visual artefacts such as paintings, photographs, road signs and advertisements. Semiotics provides a language, concepts and an approach to meaning that reveals the world around us as taken for granted yet at the same time constructed in ways that are malleable and which are built upon assumptions with ethical and political foundations. As a consequence of not challenging these foundations, there is potential to privilege particular personal or group interests over others through the ways in which some interpretations are considered to be legitimate whilst others are stigmatized.

The process of challenge is one that can be equated with the art of critical thinking. Being critical can take many forms, as is evident from the other chapters within this book. One way to be critical is to think about its difference from acting according to utilitarian principles (Mingers, 2000). Utilitarianism is here taken not from its meaning as an ethical underpinning based upon seeking 'the greatest happiness for the greatest number', but from its association with 'use'. 'Use' tends to be equated with contemporary norms, particularly in relation to the role of business in our lives. That which is utilitarian is all too often taken to be that which furthers the corporation, as opposed to the broader interests of society, and supporting utilitarianism implies an unquestioning acceptance of current corporate practices. To be critical thereby implies being sceptical of a single dominating and authoritative view (Mingers, 2000). From a utilitarian standpoint, information technology is concerned with the use of information technology to enhance organizational strategy, operations and corporate performance, irrespective of whether this is beneficial from the broader perspectives of society or alternative ways of being and living. To be critical is to challenge current information technology practices.

Challenging current practices appears to be the motivation behind Stamper et al.'s (2000) study of signs as representations of organizational activity, where signs can be 'used to get things done' (Stamper et al., 2000, p. 22). Stamper et al. (2000, p. 26) describe a semiotic approach that 'offers advantages over traditional architectures, especially in the consistency, integrity and maintainability of systems' (p. 26). This amounts to adopting semiotics as a structural practice based upon a primary concern for truth and scientific certainty. Stamper et al.'s motive can be compared with Lévi-Strauss' (1993, p. 65) conjecture that semiotics can provide a science that might lead us to a position where 'we are much closer to understanding the fundamental characteristics of social life'. The motive here is knowledge and understanding which is aimed at definite and immutable truth. What makes Stamper et al.'s (2000, p. 23) work critical is that they adopt a structural approach in order to progress beyond existing practice and they claim that, 'Signs have no value unless they produce some social change'. Their motive is critical, in the sense that they seek to understand existing practice in order to move away from the status quo, towards an improved state of affairs.

Simply moving away from existing norms and practices may not be sufficient where the ultimate aim lacks a radical departure from the utilitarian aims of effectiveness, efficiency and economy. For some, being critical is concerned with freeing up individuals from false consciousness in order to emancipate them and to support individual liberty. Ngwenyama and Lee (1997) take the example of individuals communicating with each other by means of electronic mail and show that individuals can emancipate themselves from error, variously referred to as 'distorted communication' or 'false consciousness'. Distorted communication, in this case, is shown to be corrected by challenging the validity or rightness of text as represented by a series of electronic mail messages. Ngwenyama and Lee take a critical perspective by drawing attention to the ability of individuals to actively engage with the messages and, in so doing, they begin to move beyond structuralism towards post-structuralism and post-modernism.

This chapter pursues a study of structuralism, post-structuralism and post-modernism at three levels. At the most basic level, the chapter provides a primer in semiotics. Structuralism, post-structuralism and post-modernism are explored and the concepts and language of semiotics are explained. At a second level, the chapter illustrates how the study of semiotics can be applied to the world of information technology. A statement is taken from the financial statements of J. Sainsbury PLC to illustrate the different ways in which information technology can support corporate strategy. The statement is considered in the next section.

This section presents a structural approach to the understanding of texts. At a third level, the chapter illustrates the possibilities opened up by critical thinking through what Mingers (2000, p. 226) calls 'being sceptical of one dominant view – the critique of authority'. This aspect of the chapter is pursued in a section which is devoted to post-structuralism and explores ways in which interpretations of information technology can be complex and involve numerous stakeholders. Certain elements of post-structuralism are concerned with distributive justice and the chapter finally raises initial questions about individual rights that have implications for personal and communal opportunities and liberty. These are difficult issues. The chapter seeks to do no more than to open up ways of thinking about issues such as justice, concepts such as signs, and artefacts such as texts in such a way as to encourage readers to take responsibility for their own readings.

7.2 STRUCTURALISM: A STRUCTURAL APPROACH TO UNDERSTANDING TEXTS

Semiotics pursued through structuralism is concerned with creating the kinds of knowledge which are associated with biology, chemistry and physics. Through foundations laid by de Saussure, Peirce, Hjelmslev and others, structuralists have developed typologies which explain language in analytical ways which are similar to the periodic table in chemistry or the classificatory schemes of biology. Just as in biology we can make sense of the world by classifying land-based species as birds, reptiles or mammals, or in chemistry we might differentiate metals, metalloids and non-metals, so in semiotics typologies have been established. For instance, these can be used to explain plots in dramas (Eco, 1994), a poem by Baudelaire (Jacobson and Lévi-Strauss, 1962) or social norms amongst tribes of people (Lévi-Strauss, 1993).

Through typologies and laws structuralism has given us ways of making sense both of signs in general and of an individual sign in particular. Let us take the example given in Figure 7.1 to see how we might begin to understand the contribution of structuralism to the determination of meaning. Structuralism can help us to respond to a number of questions. What does the series of words in this example mean? How might we use structural semiotics to support a systematic and scientific approach to the sign represented by this text? What might we learn about information technology strategy? What insights might specific instances of signs give to our understanding of signs in general?

We completed the insourcing of IT systems and the transfer of 470 colleagues, all assets and third party contracts back into Sainsbury's in April, just six months after announcing our decision to terminate our contract with Accenture. We expect to recoup the costs involved in ending this outsourcing agreement within the next two years.

FIGURE 7.1   Extract from the financial report of J. Sainsbury PLC for the year ended 2006.

The words in Figure 7.1 point to formal outsourcing arrangements for IT (information technology) which involve Sainsbury's (a major retailing company), Accenture (a consultancy, technology and outsourcing firm), information technology professionals (colleagues), contracts pertaining to information technology and information systems (third party contracts) and information technology itself (assets). Responsibility for information technology within Sainsbury's has been contracted to Accenture through an agreement in which Accenture took responsibility for day-to-day and strategic operations within a contractual arrangement designated by the word 'outsourcing'. In other words, information technology systems and services were 'sourced' from outside Sainsbury's but the insourcing decision described by Figure 7.1 signals a change. Responsibility has been taken away from Accenture and the outsourcing agreement has been terminated. Sainsbury's will, in future, take responsibility internally for operational and strategic arrangements. It has been decided to insource information technology.

The sign represented by Figure 7.1 points to something beyond the words, a state known within Saussurian analysis as the 'signified'. For de Saussure (1916), the signified represents a 'concept', a kind of reality which is formed within an individual's mind. The signified in this case is a complex concept based upon the relationships between different elements, and summarized by the decision to insource. How does Sainsbury's present this sign? Sainsbury's chooses a set of words and phrases, which are the very substance of Figure 7.1. This set of words is termed the 'signifier' within Saussurian analysis.

This level of analysis can be applied both to combinations of words, as in Figure 7.1, and also to individual words. So, the word 'colleagues' is a signifier for which the signified will appear in your, the reader's, mind, as a physical object; possibly a person who sits next to you.

Barthes (1972) uses the term 'language' to describe the production of the sign through the signified and the signifier. One of Barthes' major contributions to semiotics is to show that there is a second level of analysis which goes beyond 'language' to the level of 'myth'. At the level of myth, the sign becomes a signifier which is joined with a further signified to produce a second level of signification. 'Colleague' may become 'friend' at the level of the myth. In the case of Figure 7.1, the sign which is made up of the signifier 'insourcing' becomes a myth within a wider system.

We can explore this wider system by thinking through the concept of 'we' in Figure 7.1. The careful reader asks, who are these 'we' who 'completed the insourcing of IT systems', who decided to terminate the contract with Accenture, who announced that decision, and who expedited the transfer of responsibility in 'just six months'. At the level of myth, Figure 7.1 is an account which centres upon these 'we' and these people appear to be none other than Sainsbury's leaders. Further, the key word 'just', in 'just six months', indicates that these leaders are not just any leaders. These leaders are capable of completing strategic acts, of acting quickly in matters of importance, of expediting strategic issues on behalf of shareholders and their advisers, who, we presume, are the intended readers of this block of text. Figure 7.1 can, thus, be argued to present us with the myth of successful leadership. Figure 7.1 shows us that successful leaders make decisions about the information technology strategy of insourcing and act upon those decisions.

We can now move beyond the myth of successful leadership and explore the kind of strategy that is implied by Figure 7.1. To do this we need to extend our analysis. Within Saussurian analysis, signifiers are arbitrary in the sense that there is no unquestionable relationship to the signified. Shakespeare expressed this point in the saying that 'A rose by any other name would smell as sweet'. A rose is a rose (at the level of the signified) whatever it is called (whatever the signifier). Meaning does not, therefore, come directly from the word itself, but comes from its relationships with other words. We now need to consider these relationships.

The relationships between signifiers within the same sentence, paragraph or text are developed by means of syntagmatic analysis. This is concerned with the relationships between words in a sentence, or between words, sentences and paragraphs and other words, sentences and paragraphs which come together within larger texts. The alternative to syntagmatic analysis is paradigmatic analysis, where we look beyond the text to other choices that might have been made in terms of the selection of words, phrases and concepts. The words within Figure 7.1 have been selected to create a particular effect, and we can explore that effect by contrasting Figure 7.1 with other ways of presenting information technology strategy.

Figure 7.2 presents us with an alternative way of presenting information technology strategy to that presented in Figure 7.1.[1] If we look at the penultimate verse of the poem, we see four lines each of which presents two opposed signifiers. For instance, 'Information' and 'creative energy' in line 1 of the verse and 'converged systems' and 'personal services' in line 2. It is from the opposition of these signifiers that the verse takes its meaning. In each case, technology (for instance, 'information' or 'converged systems') is opposed to the human (creative energy or personal services). Syntagmatically, that is, by considering the ways in which signifiers interact within the verse, we can say that the meaning of technology is established as the non-human, or as the negative of the term which follows on each of the lines. These opposing terms are brought together within the verse, and this bringing together provides the meaning of

---

1. It must be emphasised that the extracts from the financial reports of Cisco are used for no other reason than to provide a basis for interpreting Sainsbury's announcement of its insourcing decision as presented in Figure 7.1. There is no intention to place either Sainsbury's or Cisco in a positive or negative light. It must be remembered that the motivation for this chapter, as expressed in the final sentence of the introduction, is 'to open up ways of thinking … to encourage readers to take responsibility for their own readings'.

A new way...
... to connect. To interact,
open a dialogue, spark an idea,
or nurture a society.

The power of individual imaginations
coming together in the network.

At the point where technology and people
touch, Cisco invents new ways to multiply
and enhance the power of the network.

Information and creative energy.
Converged systems and personal services.
Universal links and close relationships.
Communication and community.

The network powered by Cisco
is changing the way we work, live, play and learn.
Everywhere you look.

FIGURE 7.2   Extract from the financial report for Cisco for the year ended 2006.

the sign. There is a dynamic within the poem which takes the basic binary opposition of people and technology and gives it a twist.

This dynamic is developed throughout the entire poem. At the start of the poem, 'A new way ... to connect' signifies technology, whilst 'to interact', 'dialogue', 'idea' and 'nurturing society' signify the human, but the connection is loose; it has not yet been made. Verse 2 introduces the idea of 'coming together' but this connection is between people, and technology (the network) is no more than a context within which this happens. Verse 3 establishes Cisco's strategic priority as the intersection of technology and the human: 'the point at which technology and people touch'. Verse 3 presents the key idea Cisco's strategic intent centres on bringing together the opposing ideas of technology and people in support of progress and expansion: 'Cisco invents new ways to multiply and enhance the power of the network'. The fourth verse reinforces this connection and the opposing terms are brought together through the use of the 'and' word. Finally, the move from technology to people is completed in the final verse, as the dynamic is given its twist and human lives are transformed: 'changing the way we work, play and learn'.

Figure 7.3 provides yet another way of thinking about information technology strategy. We are provided with two broad scenarios in mimetic form. We are taken close to the experiences of a police department and a small business in a

A police department relies on a citywide Cisco wireless network to deliver fingerprint files, mug shots, and voicemail to each mobile unit. Officers use the same technology to file their reports from the field, instead of having to return to the station. Broadband video applications can even let them see what's happening at emergency scenes before they arrive. With the added efficiency the network provides, the officers now have more time to leave their patrol cars and interact personally with the community.

A boutique winery opens a virtual tasting room tour that attracts a national clientele using Cisco solutions designed especially for growing businesses. Wine lovers can survey the ripening vineyards through a video link, read about the latest vintage, and order bottles right from the winery's Website. And every employee—from the cellar master to the office manager—can tap into business applications wirelessly, wherever they are. The forecast: continued growth, and a rich harvest.

Safer streets and riper revenues.

FIGURE 7.3 Extract from the financial report for Cisco for the year ended 2006.

way that presents experience as it is lived. Here we are faced with a form of writing, which, like the poem before it, defamiliarizes. It surprises us by the original way in which the communication of performance is presented in the financial report. Yet, despite the unexpected form of presentation, the message remains the same as in Figure 7.2. Both Figures 7.2 and 7.3 show the coming together of technology and people. These signifiers stand for the signified of socio-technical co-determination. It is not technology alone which drives Cisco's strategy, it is the way in which the technology and the social are combined which gives Cisco a competitive advantage.

Figure 7.3 presents us with words which force us beyond syntagmatic analysis to the paradigmatic or the associative level. Whereas the syntagmatic looked inwards within the sign, the associative or paradigmatic level of analysis takes us to the meanings which can arise when we look outside the text. The use of the word 'riper', for instance, in the final line in Figure 7.3, has been chosen from many alternative signifiers. Words such as 'growing', 'expanding', 'increasing' would convey the same meaning. This kind of thinking takes us beyond what is literally presented within the example of Figure 7.3; beyond what Barthes (1974) called the denotative. We are now interested in connotations and what Figure 7.3 might mean, not so much in terms of what it says at face value, but in terms of alternative ways in which it might have been expressed, or even what it does not say – its silences. The choice of the word 'riper' is at once surprising but also important to the message that Cisco is conveying.

We can see this most particularly when we contrast a word like 'riper' with the apparently 'neutral', 'business' and 'professional' terminology presented in Figure 7.4. 'Riper' in Figure 7.3 conveys the 'human' side of Cisco. This is an organic word. In contrast, the words of Figure 7.4 are instantly recognisable as technical. In Figure 7.4 we can recognize the kind of language used by Sainsbury's in Figure 7.1. Whereas Cisco gives us examples of the poetic and the mimetic in Figures 7.2 and 7.3, we can recognize the creation of the apparently 'objective' in Figures 7.1 and 7.4.

There is a further level of paradigmatic analysis, beyond comparing and contrasting Figures 7.1–7.4, which will provide further insights into Sainsbury's insourcing statement as presented in Figure 7.1. This arises from strategic theory based upon the work of a leading academic and consultant, Michael Porter. For Porter (1980, 1985), strategy can be based upon a typology with two contrasting ways of positioning the firm: in relation to differentiation or in relation to cost leadership. Differentiation is the kind of strategy where firms seek to create unique and identifiable positions in terms of any of a range of strategic forces. A firm might, for instance, develop a product or product range which differentiates itself from competitors in terms of the facilities which are offered. This is what we see in Cisco's claims to growth achieved from a product-leadership perspective; a claim made in both the first and final sentences of Figure 7.4. Cisco is pursuing a differentiation strategy based upon product leadership. And this product leadership is the subject of the statements of strategic intent given by

Fiscal 2005 was a year of continued solid, balanced growth for Cisco from both a product- and market-leadership perspective. We achieved an outstanding financial performance with record profits and cash generation, year-over-year growth in our core routing and switching products, and very strong growth in our six advanced technologies. Our enterprise, service provider, and commercial customer market segments all experienced solid year-over-year growth. However, the highlight for the year was the balance that we achieved across our geographies, customer market segments, architectural evolutions, and product families. We believe our financial strength, product leadership, and global reach uniquely position Cisco as a company not only built to last, but built to lead.

FIGURE 7.4 Extract from the financial report for Cisco for the year ended 2006.

Figures 7.2 and 7.3. Information technology is central to Cisco's strategy, but it is the specific way in which Cisco expresses the relationship between technology and people that allows it to pursue a strategy of differentiation.

So what is not said when Cisco positions itself in terms of a strategy based upon differentiation? In order to understand differentiation, we must understand the alternatives, including the binary opposite of differentiation within Porter's framework: cost leadership. If the statements made by Cisco say nothing about cost leadership, cost leadership is nevertheless entailed in Cisco's presentation of its strategy. The meaning of the sign is taken both from what it is and what it is not – its silences.

Cost leadership entails aiming towards least cost production or least-cost provision of services within an industry. Figure 7.1 shows that Sainsbury's is motivated by cost in pursuing a strategy of insourcing. The cost motivation is explicit in the final sentence. The termination of the contract with Accenture is seen, not in terms of enabling technology leadership, which may be one reason to move away from external contractors, but in terms of the time taken to 'recoup the costs' involved in the change.

There is further evidence that Sainsbury's is pursuing a least-cost strategy in the next figure. Figure 7.5 presents us with a motivation for investing in information technology. We are told that a new information technology system has been introduced. We are told that this system supports 'colleagues on the shop floor' by 'helping them to monitor and respond to stock levels faster'. Where is the strategy in this case? The final sentence provides the answer. Information technology supports Sainsbury's in reducing 'wastage and, therefore, cost'. The focus is on cost and the strategic intent is to be more cost effective than competitors; in this case, in terms of reducing levels of waste. Note the silence here. In emphasising waste, Figure 7.5 is signifying cost leadership, and, as a result, there is no attempt to argue for differentiation. Figure 7.5 does not seek differentiation, for instance, in terms of providing market leadership through levels of availability (although this may follow logically from Sainsbury's aspiration to 'improve even further' beyond the situation where 'availability is now back in line with other supermarkets').

We can now summarize our analysis of Sainsbury's decision to insource its information technology provision. The statement given in Figure 7.1 has the effect of creating a myth of successful leadership. This leadership is based upon a strategy of cost leadership. The role of information technology in this case is to support efforts to reduce costs through, for instance, reducing waste. Structuralism has provided the tools to enable us to propose clear and definitive statements about the meaning of Sainsbury's insourcing decision.

Other meanings may be possible and this will now be considered in the next section, which introduces post-structuralism and post-modernism. We will see that it is possible to mount a critical analysis that enables us to move beyond the interpretations which structuralism can provide.

Like the majority of our supermarkets, [our Moortown] store now has a night shift in operation to replenish shelves ready for the morning. Back in 2004 availability was cited as our number one performance issue, but we've improved significantly. Our night shift colleagues are the unsung heroes of this change. Together with our new store processes, they've helped reduce the gaps on our shelves by 75 per cent, and our availability is now back in line with other supermarkets.

We're now working on the other 25 per cent as we want to improve even further. In March 2006, for example, we completed the roll-out of a new hand-held stock and sales system. This provides up-to-the-minute sales and supply data to colleagues on the shop floor, helping them to monitor and respond to stock levels faster. At the same time we have a more accurate picture of the stock we have versus stock we need and this has helped reduce our wastage and therefore cost.

FIGURE 7.5   Extract from the financial report of J. Sainsbury PLC for the year ended 2006.

7.3 POST-STRUCTURALISM AND POST-MODERNISM

The related movements which have been labelled 'post-structuralism' and 'post-modernism' share a reluctance to pursue definitive and authoritative accounts of the kind that we developed in the previous section. Post-structuralism has become associated in Europe with the later writings of Barthes and Derrida and is dated to the publication by Derrida in 1976 of his book 'Of grammatology'. It is also associated with a circle of writers in the United States, including de Man, Miller and Hartman. Post-modernity can be argued to be the historical period dominated by a new range of experiences including Disney, the knowledge-based company, information technology, mass culture, mass consumerism and globalization. Post-structuralism and post-modernism are related, and Best and Kellner (1991, p. 20) summarize their essential point of departure from structuralism and modernism in the following way:

> The poststructuralists attacked the scientific pretensions of structuralism which attempted to create a scientific basis for the study of culture and which strove for the standard modern goals of foundation, truth, objectivity, certainty and system.

Belief in the possibility of certainty and objectivity is replaced in post-structuralist and post-modernist thinking by indeterminacy and undecidability. Drawing upon some leading thinkers, for instance:

- Jameson (1991) describes postmodernism as 'the end of that and the now open space for something else' as though the 'something else' cannot yet be known.
- Baudrillard (1983) writes, 'Of the same order as the impossibility of rediscovering an absolute level of the real is the impossibility of staging an illusion'. This draws attention to the possibility that in the postmodern age we can no longer take for granted that which we consider to be real: but neither is the illusory possible.
- Derrida (1991) in seeking to explain the meaning of the word, 'deconstruction', writes, 'When I chose this word, or when it imposed itself upon me . . . I little thought that it would be credited with such a central role' and, 'What deconstruction is not? everything of course! What is deconstruction? nothing of course.' In other words, there is no foundational definition and certainty even at the level of central terms within the post-structuralist canon such as deconstruction. Its entry into the centre of post-structuralism was a surprise, even to him. Even the way that deconstruction entered into post-structuralist thinking is ambiguous (for instance did Derrida choose the word or was it imposed upon him?).

To explore the possibility and potentiality of indeterminacy and undecidability we can return to Sainsbury's insourcing statement presented in Figure 7.1. By acknowledging post-structuralist and post-modernist insights, we can see that what at first sight might appear to be neutral and objective can be shown to disguise multiple meanings.

The following seven possibilities are involved in Sainsbury's arrangements for the insourcing of its information systems and represent a sample of views drawn from internet sources.

(1) Changes in Sainsbury's corporate strategy announced in October 2004 led to a change in information technology focus leading Sainsbury's to decide 'that it is the right time to rebuild its expertise back in-house'. Sainsbury's and Accenture announced the intention jointly on 27 October 2005, to the effect that 'IT services currently provided by Accenture will be migrated back to Sainsbury's together with a number of Accenture employees (http://www.jsainsburys.co.uk/index.asp?pageID=418&subsection=&Year=2005&NewsID=605).

The following view develops the link between changes in strategy and the consequences for information technology by explaining the basis for the previous strategy:

(2) The outsourcing contract originally supported a strategy of differentiation begun by the previous chief executive officer, Sir Peter Davis. The company established a strategy at the end of 2000 with six objectives, the first of which was to 'establish a differentiated market position and deliver sustainable shareholder value'. This necessitated both information technology, and business transformation, and it was believed that such change could not be achieved without the assistance of Accenture (http://www.postalproject.com/documents.asp?d_ID=2504). 'Customer focus' was a part of this transformation, enshrined in the themes of 'faster, simpler, together', so that 'all of Sainsbury's divisions should be working together to provide a faster and simpler experience for customers'. Accenture supported a knowledge management project that was initiated to implement this strategy (Miller et al., 2003).

Despite the apparently clear strategy of differentiation, Sainsbury's also appeared to pursue a strategy of cost reduction. Two opposing views of the success of the outsourcing contract are evident in this regard:

(3) The outsourcing contract supported a successful strategy of cost reduction. Immediate savings of £35 million were achieved and information technology 'running costs' were halved (http://www.computing.co.uk/computing/news/2070647/sainsbury-halves-running-costs?vnu_lt=ctg_art_related_articles and http://whitepapers.zdnet.co.uk/0,39025945,60081713p-39000488q,00.htm).

(4) The outsourcing contract failed to support a successful strategy of cost reduction. Information technology costs in 2004 were a greater percentage of sales than in 2000. Additional costs of £290 million in 2004 resulted from obsolete information technology systems, equipment associated with information technology initiatives and stock write-offs resulting from disruptions caused by information technology systems. Profits were adversely affected due to Sainsbury's failure to 'properly stock its shelves because of

faulty distribution systems caused by the so-called IT upgrade' and Sainsbury's reported the first ever loss in its history (http://newsvote.bbc. co.uk/mpapps/pagetools/print/news.bbc.co.uk/1/hi/business/4078151.stm and http://www.compterwire.com/industries/research/?pid=37D7367A-9430-4019-9BB5-A186943E95/D&type=CWNews).

Recovering from the failure as represented by the financial loss, Sainsbury's turned away from its business transformation project towards a strategy based upon a range of strategic objectives, centring both on the customer and cost reduction.

(5) The business transformation project 'distracted the company from its "customer offer" ' necessitating 'plans to "fix the basics" '. Simplifying information technology systems, and in some cases replacing information technology systems with manual processes, in order to achieve cost reductions provided the justification for renegotiating the contract with Accenture. This happened in October 2004, a year before the announcement that the contract would be terminated. The renegotiated contract 'will see it rebuild its in-house IT team' (http://management.silicon. com/itdirector/0,39024673,39125085,00.htm; http://www.computerworld. com/industrytopics/retail/story/0,10801,96890,00.html and http://www. theregister.co.uk/2004/10/19/sainsburys_v_accenture/print.html).

This series of interpretations throws into question firstly, the nature of the strategy being pursued by Sainsbury's, and, secondly, whether the company was successful in achieving its stated aims. Further, it is possible to see Sainsbury's insourcing decision not so much as a response to a changing strategy but as a simple failure to manage the outsourcing contract successfully:

(6) The termination of the contract illustrates 'what can go wrong in any outsourcing relationship'. Douglas Hayward, described as a 'senior analyst at research Ovum', is reported as stating in a research note, 'The problems included poor decision-making by Sainsbury [sic] executives, weak outsourcing governance, political in-fighting at the retailer...'. He is also reported as claiming that 'The connection between the IT infrastructure and the customer-facing business was poorly managed – both sides share the blame here' (http://www.sharedservicesbpo.com/file/2905/sainsburys-scraps-accenture-contract-brings-it-back-in-house.html; http://services. silicon.com/itoutsouring/0,3800004871,39153723,00.htm and http:// www.computing.co.uk/computing/news/2144898/sainsburys-dumps-7bn-outsourcing)

What makes this view particularly surprising is that the outsourcing arrangement had previously been deemed a success:

(7) The Sainsbury's–Accenture contract represented a successful outsourcing arrangement which went beyond cost reduction in its ambitions. Information technology outsourcing for Sainsbury's went beyond the aim of cost reduction because of the need to develop 'IT-enabled business

transformation' designed to 'achieve a step change in … business performance … to get people to do things differently'. As such, Sainsbury's might
be considered to be representative of 'some of today's most innovative
outsourcing buyers' (http://www.cbronline.com/article_cbr_print.asp?
guid=E2A7BDEB-3F69-4E09-B0A7-E35D206AFAFA).

These various comments render undecidable a range of questions relating to
Sainsbury's strategy, the strategic use of information technology to support
business strategy and the success or failure of the outsourcing arrangement
which led Sainsbury's to the decision to insource. Was Sainsbury's business
strategy centred on differentiation or cost leadership or a combination of objectives? If the strategy changed to one of cost leadership when the new chief
executive officer, Justin King, arrived, why was the outsourcing contract renegotiated in October 2004 but then terminated only one year later in October
2005? Was the outsourcing arrangement a success or a failure?

Post-structuralism gives the reader an important role in working through
these questions. Sainsbury's insourcing decision can be approached as a 'writerly text' (Barthes, 1974) that involves the reader in the interpretation of the
signifiers of Figure 7.1 and the interpretations listed as statements (1)–(7) above.
The reader becomes a producer, rather than a mere consumer of the text. The
writerly text invites readers to interpret, where 'interpret' is used in the sense of
thinking through, producing, challenging or writing the many meanings which
might apply to the text. The writerly text is plural, according to Barthes, in the
sense of possessing many possible meanings. At the extreme it might even be
argued that the meanings are infinite and indefinite.

If we treat the insourcing decision and Figure 7.1 as a writerly text, we might
interpret its meaning in several ways. We might, for instance, see it as an attempt
to pass off lightly an embarrassing episode in Sainsbury's development. What
was once seen as an essential outsourcing arrangement, necessary to a strategy of
differentiation, became an unnecessary encumbrance which could not be aligned
with a new strategy of cost reduction and which was, therefore, terminated.
Alternatively, it may be an attempt to minimize the damage caused by poor
senior management decision making. Or we might see it as a sign of increasing
confidence, as Sainsbury's sought to take responsibility for the strategic implementation of its information technology through in-house developments. Or it
may be a sign that senior managers were turning to a simplified information
technology strategy in order to turn around the previous poor business performance resulting from ineffective information technology systems. Or it could be
that previous successful information technology initiatives were no longer relevant to a business which had new business priorities.

This may seem to be too open-ended for some readers. If texts are undecidable, then the danger is that at the extreme we are left with nothing but 'a cult of
ambiguity or irresponsible anarchism' (Eagleton, 1996, p. 130). If texts and the
world they describe are fundamentally indeterminate, then this in itself is a form
of closure which takes away responsibility for taking any kind of action; it may

be argued that there is no basis for rational action and that any action might be just as good as any other kind of action.

Some commentators have drawn back from the full force of open-endedness that typifies certain approaches to post-structuralism and post-modernism, whilst also rejecting a foundational position based upon an authoritative and singular meaning. Eco (1994), for instance, argues that although it may not be possible to determine that one of a number of interpretations is best, it is, nevertheless possible to decide that an interpretation is unjustifiable. In the case of Sainsbury's financial reports, for instance, we could not say that the text shows that Justin King, the Chief Executive Officer of Sainsbury's, likes ice cream. This interpretation does not rule out the possibility of showing in some inspired way that the use of particular statements in Sainsbury's financial reports indicates that Justin King does, indeed, like ice cream. The point is that such an interpretation is not appropriate given the context of the text. Additionally, Eco argues that it is possible for a community of interpreters to reach agreement about a particular text. This agreement could limit the interpretations to a finite number, where the community agrees that the text remains relatively open and, thus, not reducible to a single, closed meaning.

The concept of community draws attention to our responsibility towards each other and the spaces within which we live. Certain readings deny this responsibility (Popke, 2003). One such reading is implicit in the comments numbered (1)–(7) above, and is centred upon the assumption that the dominant role in decision making on Sainsbury's strategy and use of information technology is taken by the senior management team together with the chief executive officers (Sir Peter Davis and Justin King). This assumption marginalizes the potential contribution of others to decision making, strategy and information technology implementation. Yet Sainsbury's explicitly acknowledges the important role of others in the achievement of strategy (the 'unsung heroes' who stock shelves overnight as described in Figure 7.5).

There is a social justice issue here in terms of the sharing of the wealth created by strategy and information technology. In the financial year ending 2006 Justin King is reported as receiving £1 471 000 (2005: £1 131 000) against an average benefit to all employees of £18 600. (Employee costs are reported as £1793m and full-time equivalent staff as 96 200; 2005: £18 000 on average – £1753 employee costs – 97 400 full-time equivalents). It might be argued that strategy and information technology decisions conceived as the sole province of the chief executive officer supports this division of wealth. Strategy, which acknowledges the important role of others, including recognising that strategic implementation may depend upon the knowledge of others at all levels of the organization, implies a more equitable sharing of organizational wealth (Pant, 2001).

Deconstruction is the means through which the singular, definite or univocal meaning of a text is exposed in its multiplicity, its indeterminancy and its undecidability, with consequences for the kind of distributive justice entailed in discussions about relative salaries. Associated with the work of Derrida, deconstruction 'is concerned with the lucid, patient attempt to trace what has not been read and what remains unread or unreadable' (Royle, 1995). According to Derrida (1991), deconstruction is not a method, a set of rules, a procedure or an analysis. Derrida consistently refuses the possibility of a single, authoritative and definitive meaning of any signifier (including the word 'deconstruction'). This is important because definitive meanings may simply be the views and ideas imposed by powerful interests, and such meanings close down interpretations which are important to those who are less powerful. By accepting the status quo that the chief executive officer is solely responsible for strategy and information technology, we close off consideration of the contribution of those who are perceived as lower down in the organizational hierarchy. By rejecting definitive meanings, the world is opened up to new ways of acting. Derrida (1990, p. 45) says that 'deconstruction is justice':

> That is what gives deconstruction its movement, that is, constantly to suspect, to criticize the given determinations of culture, of institutions, of legal systems, not in order to destroy them or simply to cancel them, but to be just with justice .... (Derrida, 1997, p. 18)

Deconstruction, thereby, destabilizes the status quo through its willingness to be critical of that which is accepted and taken for granted. There is an objection, in particular, to authority where this is associated with the use of routines, calculations and procedures which, we might argue, take away from justice the concept of individual and collective responsibility. Derrida (1995, p. 273) writes:

> If I speak too often of the incalculable and the undecidable it's not out of simple predilection for play nor in order to neutralise decision: on the contrary, I believe that there is no responsibility, no ethico-political decision, that must not pass through the proofs of the incalculable or the undecidable. Otherwise everything would be reducible to calculation, program, causality.

In other words, we must take responsibility for action, and not allow institutionalized certainties, norms, science, systems, procedures and so forth, to take responsibility away from us. Institutional arrangements allow for a challenge to potential inequities such as salary differentials, and individuals and communities must act if these arrangements are to support justice.

7.4 CONCLUSION

Semiotics, the study of the sign, suggests implications well beyond the analysis and interpretation of texts. By moving beyond a passive acceptance of texts, or simplistic readings which take meaning at face value, we challenge assumptions and taken-for-granted values. As indicated in the introduction to this chapter, such challenges might lead to the improvement of the design and development of information technology as in the case of Stamper et al.'s (2000) work. Or we may support the emancipation of individuals from distorted communications by challenging texts in particular ways, as in the case of Ngwenyama and Lee's (1997) study of electronic mail messages. Or we may open up new meanings for taken-for-granted texts so as to move towards a society where there is a more equitable basis for the sharing of wealth and the broader rights and responsibilities created by strategy and information technology.

This chapter has illustrated how semiotics can be practised. It takes as its general topic the question of information technology strategy and addresses this topic in terms of a specific example of Sainsbury's insourcing decision. In seeking to practise semiotics through this example, there is no intention to provide a finalising discourse which occludes alternative meanings or interpretations, or even to cover the totality of that which has come to be associated with semiotics. Exploring information technology strategy at the level of signs, helps us to see the ways in which we actively create meaning, without always being aware that we do so, and reveals possibilities for the discovery of a potential infinity of new meanings. Semiotics ultimately becomes a practice which creates the possibility for change through a more open dialogue about the meanings which impact upon our lives.

REFERENCES

Barthes, R. (1972). *Mythologies* (Lavers, A., Trans.). New York: Noonday Press (1993, London: Vintage). Originally published as Mythologies, Paris, Editions du Seuil, 1957.

Barthes, R. (1974). *S/Z* (Miller, R., Trans.). New York: Farrer, Strauss and Giroux.

Baudrillard, J. (1983). *Simulacra and Simulation* (Foss, P., Patton, P. & Beitchman, P., Trans.). New York: Autonomedia, Semiotexte.

Best, S., & Kellner, D. (1991). *Postmodern theory: Critical interrogations*. Macmillan, London.

Derrida, J. (1990). Force of Law: the mystical foundation of authority. *Cardozo Law Review, 11*, 919–1045.

Derrida, J. (1991). A Derrida Reader: Between the Blinds. *Irvington*. In Kamuf, P. (Ed.), Columbia University Press, NY.

Derrida, J. (1995). *Points: Interviews, 1974–1994*. In Weber, E. (Ed.), Stanford University Press, Palo Alto, CA.

Derrida, J. (1997). *Deconstruction in a nutshell: A conversation with Jacques Derrida*. In Caputo, J. (Ed.), Fordham University Press, Bronx, NY.

Eagleton, T. (1996). *Literary theory: An introduction*. Blackwell, London.

Eco, U. (1994). *The limits of interpretation*. Indiana University Press, Bloomington, IN.

Jacobson, R. & Lévi-Strauss, C. (1962). *Les Chats de Charles Baudelaire*. L'Homme, 2.

Jameson, F. (1991). *Postmodernims, or, the cultural logic of late Capitalism*. Duke University Press, Durham, NC.

Lévi-Strauss, C. (1993). *Structural anthropology*. Penguin, London.

Miller, M., Mallors, R., Chapple, A., & Ives, W. (2003). Building a foundation for Innovation at Sainsbury's. *Knowledge Management Review, 6*(3), 12–15.

Mingers, J. (2000). What is it to be critical? Teaching a critical approach to management undergraduates *Management Learning, 31*(2), 219–237.

Ngwenyama, O. K., & Lee, A. S. (1997). Communication richness in electronic mail: critical social theory and the contextuality of meaning. *MIS Quarterly* 145–166.

Pant, L. (2001). The growing role of informal controls: does organization learning empower or subjugate workers? *Critical Perspectives on Accounting, 12*(6), 697–712.

Popke, E. J. (2003). Poststructuralist ethics: subjectivity, responsibility and the space of community. *Progress in Human Geography, 27*(3), 298–316.

Porter, M. (1980). *Competitive strategy.* Free Press, Washington, DC.

Porter, M. (1985). *Comptetitive advantage.* Free Press, Washington, DC.

Royle, N. (1995). *After Derrida.* Manchester University Press, Manchester, UK.

de Saussure, F. (1916). *Cours de linguistique générale* (Trans.). In: Bally, C., Sechehaye, A. and Riedlinger, A. (eds.). Paris: Payot. (W. Baskin, Course in General Linguistics, Fontana/Collins, 1977.).

Stamper, R., Liu, K., Hafkamp, M., & Ades, Y. (2000). Understanding the roles of signs and norms in organizations—A semiotic approach to information systems design. *Behaviour and Information Technology, 19*(1), 15–27.

FURTHER READING

An extensive explanation of semiotics suitable for reading at an introductory level can be found at:
http://www.aber.ac.uk/media/Documents/S4B/semiotic.html.

Web based sources, including material from financial reports shown as figures, were accessed on 28th July 2006.

http://www.j-sainsbury.co.uk/.

www.aber.ac.uk.

http://www.cisco.com/web/about/ac49/ac20/ac19/ar2006/index.html.

The Self-Ethnography as a 'Critical' Approach to Researching ICT Diffusion

Michael J. Chumer

8.1 INTRODUCTION

I view research methodologies and research approaches as tools in an epistemological tool chest that researchers have at their disposal. Many of the common everyday tools (such as hammers, screwdrivers, power saws) and the more sophisticated ones (including information systems, information technologies) contain the promise of improving the things that we do and the tasks that we perform. When the tasks are in support of scholarship, research methodologies and approaches contain a similar promise, where 'improve' implies gaining deeper 'insight' and 'knowledge' about the objects or phenomena under investigation and, in turn, 'improving' understanding. I argue that in developing a deeper and richer understanding of phenomena, especially phenomena embedded in the social studies. This includes organizational studies (theory, communication, behaviour, misbehaviour), management (processes, control), and ICT (information and communication technology diffusion and use), to name a few. The richness of these phenomena can be surfaced and understood by academic openness to a variety of research methods and approaches. However, academia seems to suffer from a form of research myopia that results in positing one type of research methodology/approach over another, as is the case in the widespread use of positivism to investigate socially embedded phenomena (Burrell & Morgan, 1979). Certainly knowledge created through positivistic methodologies has value but can be enhanced by using qualitative approaches especially ethnographies to include the emergent self-ethnography (SE).

I think the use of SE as a research approach is best exemplified by the words of Mills (1959):

> The most admirable thinkers within the scholarly community you have chosen to join do not split their work from their lives. They seem to take both too seriously to allow such dissociation, and they want to use each for the enrichment of the other.

I argue that SE is a research approach that uses the home base of the researcher to collect data that can be either subsequently analysed or explicated in a Gertzian fashion using 'thick' description by providing examples of both. For ICT research based upon the SE the researcher is in the thick of things experiencing the 'inscriptive' effects on body and mind on a 'self' that often toggles between several identities (researcher and practitioner). The inscriptive effects on others is also investigated by taking into account the effects of ICT phenomena, to include diffusion and use, on the 'self' of the researcher by these 'others' gained through interaction and discourse.

This chapter provides an overview of the SE as a research approach that I use, have used since 1996, and am continually refining. This chapter begins by reviewing some of the philosophical roots of SE. It then toggles between what SE is by contrasting it to other research approaches and methodologies to include ethnographies in general. The work conducted by Alvesson that focuses on 'close up' studies is also reviewed to deepen the understanding of the SE. Two examples of SE explications are introduced. One performed while investigating the diffusion of ICTs within a large university research library and another (that is still a work in process) designed to investigate the effects on the 'self' of ICTs used in computer-mediated communication (CMC) and computer-supported cooperative work (CSCW), including virtual environments and virtuality. The chapter then continues by surfacing 'Critical Issues in SE' and concludes by framing the criticalness of the SE.

8.2 PHILOSOPHICAL ROOTS OF THE SE

From a philosophical perspective, the SE is grounded in the hermeneutical and phenomenological traditions (Heidegger, 1962; Husserl, 1931, 1969, 1990; Schutz, 1982). The reason I make this assertion is that hermeneutics suggests that an object of investigation reveals, and, at the same time, conceals itself from the eye of the observer. This revealing and concealing property of objects and constructs implies the existence of events that, in turn, provide ethnographic and self-ethnographic insight and relatedness to the object and/or construct under investigation. Each observable event becomes a source of rich empirical data that reveals different parts of the object or construct but simultaneously can conceal other parts. When research approaches, such as the SE, are used to investigate complex constructs, such as ICT diffusion and the role of the end user during diffusion, those constructs assume different forms and dimensions. They suggest different implications as certain constituent elements of the constructs reveal themselves to the self-ethnographer. These constituent elements are the phenomena that the self-ethnographer identifies during the day-to-day micro-processes of everyday life. The transcendental nature of objects and constructs in general lends itself to a process of reduction. This is what the self-ethnographer does. They reduce the phenomena into its key features and constituent elements through processes of deconstruction.

The focus on 'being' or 'existence' is central to the phenomenological tradition. Phenomenologists tend to focus upon objects of the world as intentional by conscious thought (Husserl), and on self-awareness and re-flection or, rather, self's place in the world (Heidegger). The phenomenologist engages the world through the objects of 'intention', attempts to isolate the 'essence' of these objects as well their meaning, and often, through reflexivity, relates this meaning to a 'self' situated in the context of a specific lifeworld. Phenomenologists are primarily concerned with how individuals come to understand the world. Without a good sense of the self and a clear sense of the other, interaction becomes problematic and local sense making begins. For phenomenologists, the problem is confusion resulting in diffi-culty in making sense of the world.

Enter the self-ethnographer, grounded in an understanding of hermeneu-tics and phenomenology, investigating phenomena within a lifeworld in which they are embedded, concerned about their 'being' within that life-world as well as the nature of how their 'being' relates to and is affected by the 'other'. This 'other' may take on the form of both animate and inanimate objects see Latour (1993). In addition, as a living, breathing, organic instru-ment that senses the environment and interprets the results of the sensing, the self-ethnographer must be acutely aware of their biases and how those biases may affect the account of the investigation that is eventually produced. Armed with this philosophical understanding and functioning, in a reflexive manner, the self-ethnographer enters a process of 'inscription' designed to record not only the phenomena but also the 'self' as 'self' and 'self' as 'generalized other' affecting and being affected by the phenomena in which they are embedded and researching.

At the onset my suggestion is that researchers embarking upon a SE should be aware of the following:

- The transcendental nature of objects or phenomena;
- Intentionality;
- Transcendental reduction;
- The concept of the 'lifeworld' and its relation to researcher subjectivity;
- The 'self' in its various constructions to include the 'generalized other'.

8.3 SE IN CONTRAST

This section navigates research techniques and methodologies, and provides some insight into the assumptions that drive sociologically based research in general. This is done to contrast the SE from other research methods and approaches so that it begins to stand out as a critical approach to research and the subsequent building of knowledge.

I suggest that in the functionalist paradigm emphasis is on 'methodology' whereas in the SE the emphasis is on the 'approach'. The SE as an approach has embedded within it hermeneutical processes as well as phenomenology, thereby emphasizing the role of the 'self' in identifying and analysing research.

Sociological research was methodically investigated by Burrell and Morgan (1979) resulting in a taxonomy that is still commonly referred to and referenced today. Burrell and Morgan concisely and comprehensively classify and categorize sociological research. In so doing, they suggest that a researcher's assumptions about ontology, epistemology and human nature (by human nature they mean the relationship between human beings and their environment) form the foundation for a taxonomy. Their taxonomy is presented in the form of a grid. This grid is based upon two major axes. The first axis ranges from a research orientation concerning the nature of science and goes from a highly 'subjective' orientation to a highly 'objective one'. The second axis is based on the nature of society and ranges from 'regulation' to 'radical change'. The two axes yield four quadrants which Burrell and Morgan call 'research paradigms'. The paradigms are listed as follows:

(1) Functionalist
(2) Interpretive
(3) Radical humanism
(4) Radical structuralism

Therefore, present-day research can be related to the Burrell and Morgan paradigmatic grid, which provides insight to the research in terms of the researcher's assumptions about both the nature of science as well as the nature of society.

There have certainly been debates concerning the Burrell and Morgan paradigmatic grid. Many of these debates concern the ontological and epistemological isolation that they posit between each grid. In other words they make a point of suggesting that because of the nature of assumptions underlying the formulation of each grid, it is a cognitive impossibility for a researcher to function in more than one grid at the same time. Gioia and Pitre (1990) recognize this paradigmatic isolation and suggest that bridging can, and should, exist between the paradigms. Their underlying concern is that in performing organizational research (which certainly has its base in sociology); theory can suffer from paradigmatic isolation. Theory-building movement between the Burrell and Morgan paradigms is viewed as a positive thing.

What is clear from Burrell and Morgan as well as Gioia and Pitre is that the great majority of sociological research falls into the functionalist paradigm (referred to as logical positivism). According to Burrell and Morgan, 'the functionalist paradigm generates regulative sociology in its most developed form'. By 'developed' they mean that the methods are highly developed and function to serve the research interests and accepted methods of the researcher. Further, Gioia and Pitre (1990) also mention that the 'dominant' science theme or paradigm revolves around functionalism and positivism. Evidence of the dominance of the functionalist paradigm can also be found in the work of Audet, Landry, and Dery (1986) and Behling (1980).

When organizational research is investigated, its most common form falls within the functionalist paradigm and is performed under the cloak of logical positivism. Most of the theory building, as it pertains to ICT diffusion and information systems within organizational settings, is survey-oriented. Data are collected with survey instruments, often analysed using the statistical tools common to analysing data in the natural sciences. This is the hallmark of quantitative research. It is this structured form of developing sociological theory that permits the term 'methodology' to be woven into much of sociological research jargon. Methodology suggests that there are specific 'hows' and techniques that can be employed to both gather data and to analyse that data. The kind of data that is obtained and the instruments used for the collection are specified in advance. Therefore, this kind of thinking underlies the 'dominance' of the functionalist paradigm and gives the semblance that sociology and the humanities, in general, can be researched and analysed using 'methods' drawn from research in the natural sciences.

SE research does not reside within the functionalist paradigm. It is critical in nature (due to its reliance on hermeneutics and phenomenology), but can also inform (as well as be informed by) positivistic research. So I do not agree with Burrell and Morgan when they suggest that there can only ever be paradigmatic isolation. A good SE researcher must be versed in quantitative techniques and methods which can assist in the ethnographic explication of ethnographic data.

8.4 THE ETHNOGRAPHY AND SE

It is clear that different research techniques are used when investigating organizational phenomena. These techniques can be placed within one of the four paradigmatic grids in Burrell and Morgan's model. It is also clear that organizational phenomena fall within the overall category of sociology in terms of the identification and application of accepted research methods. Logical positivism was mentioned as being the most common and pervasive in terms of its use in building theory. However, there are cautionary voices (Alvesson, 2003a, 2003b; Alvesson & Karreman, 2000a, 2000b; Gioia & Pitre, 1990 2000b). The series of papers developed by Alvesson and colleagues suggest that there are benefits to building theory based on the researcher's actual involvement with the research setting (the field). Alvesson speaks about ethnography in general and then the SE specifically. Alvesson does this to show that in performing an ethnography a researcher gets as close to the field as possible, but in the SE, the researcher is much closer to the field of inquiry, because he/she is already there.

Scholars (e.g. Geertz, 1973, 1988, 1997; Wolcott, 1995) emphasize the cultural component of the ethnography. Geertz specifically suggests that the ethnographic account should result in a 'thick description' that reveals the meaning underlying the social phenomena being investigated. Alvesson further suggests that some scholars such as Baszanger and Dodier (1997) and Miller (1997) 'talk about ethnographies of institutional discourse'. Here the emphasis is on 'discourse in social settings' where community closeness, culture and discourse orientation are salient features. Furthermore, Van Maanen (1995) divides the ethnography into two parts, focusing on the actual process of performing fieldwork and the text of the ethnographic account. It is this dichotomous nature of ethnographies in general, that is of particular interest to the self-ethnographer.

As with any research the ethnography has its advantages and disadvantages. The advantages according to Alvesson (2003a) centre on the ability of the researcher to observe behaviour (individual and collective) in naturally occurring settings, using the informality of the relationships developed by the researcher throughout their involvement within the field. The disadvantages of the ethnography relate to the issues of time (being time consuming), the production of an 'account' that adequately explicates the fieldwork done, and the risk of going native (losing research perspective). What begins to surface here is a very subtle reference to creation of text that is 'faithful' to the reality being investigated. This is what Geertz refers to as the 'thick description'. In the same breath, Alvesson refers to fiction and, in doing, ties the notion of text (the ethnographic account) written as 'thick description' to the notion of fiction. Later, Alvesson posits the concept of 'grounded fictionalism'. Yet in all these references he is actually talking about the ethnographic account; that is, the ethnographer's explication of what is going on with social phenomena. The basis for the creation of this text (this grounded fictionalism) becomes critical to the self-ethnographer.

Alvesson states that:

> A SE is a study and a text in which the researcher-author describes a cultural setting in which s/he is an active participant, more or less on equal terms with other participants.

This implies that the researcher performing the SE is already in the field actively working as a member of a 'cultural setting'. Such was my case, which is why the concept of a SE seemed well suited to my research. As the researcher I: '...use the experiences, knowledge, and access to empirical material for research purposes'. This suggests that access to empirical material is rather easy due to the 'position' of the researcher. Alvesson further states, 'This research is, however, not a major preoccupation, apart from at a particular time when the empirical material is targeted for close scrutiny and writing'.

8.5 SPECIFIC APPLICATION OF THE SE LIBRARY I AND VIRTUAL I

Some background follows at this point concerning the movement from theory to actual research using the SE. My original research project did not begin with the SE in mind. The project which I will call Library 1 had its roots when I was appointed in May of 1998 to the position of Head of Media Services (a multimedia librarian position). The position was in a large academic library giving me day-to-day access to emerging organizational phenomena. My research focus was to identify the factors that affect successful diffusion of ICTs. My position allowed me to be involved with various ICT diffusion projects that ranged from those that affected the entire library system to those that affected various groups and sub-groups.

As I laboured over how to approach my research given a full-time position, what assisted in making the movement to SE was receiving four papers from Mats Alvesson, 2003a, 2003b (Alvesson & Karreman, 2000a, 2000b) that addressed close-up studies. One of the papers (Alvesson, 2003a) described SE, and it immediately resonated with my situation, because it suggested that the research site should be the one in which the researcher was already embedded. I reviewed the four papers and made the decision to use SE to perform my research. After all I would probably never again get the opportunity to be surrounded by such rich empirical data on a daily basis. Now I had an approach that validated the use of my own work environment or 'home base' for my research.

Since conducting the Library 1 study, I have used SE as an approach in studying virtual communities and 'virtuality'. For reference purposes I will call this ongoing study Virtual 1. I will share some of Virtual 1 narratives in this chapter. However, because of the scope of Library 1, all the specific data that the SE surfaced will not be addressed in this chapter. Chumer (2002) provides detailed information about the heuristic used to analyse the data that was surfaced by the SE in that study.

In Library 1 and Virtual 1 the single approach was that of the SE, yet it resulted in two separate accounts. The following is an extract drawn from Library 1 as an example of the explication of one of six specific ICT diffusion 'cases' surfaced during a 3-year SE.

8.5.1 Case 1, The Serials Backlog

When I was assigned managerial responsibilities for Technical Services the growing backlog of actual serials (journals) that needed processing by the staff using the newly-implemented ILS (Integrated Library System) was visually evident. Journals that needed to be processed were placed on movable carts aligned physically one after the other. The carts were loaded with journals awaiting input into the system as well as journals rejected by the system as not being able to be processed for many reasons. Upon further investigation the major reason was that the serials master record contained errors and the process in place suggested that the master record corrections should occur after normal serials check-in. The shelving of the journals could not be accomplished until a satisfactory check-in had occurred. As manager, I converted the backlog into the time required to process using the average time to check-in a journal with existing resources. This backlog time was calculated to be approximately four months and, when coupled with the current processing of journals arriving on a daily basis, suggested the backlog would incrementally increase if everything remained the same. As a manager, the serials backlog needed to be fixed but as a researcher it required investigation into the reasons for the backlog, as well as relevant theories that might explain what was going on. Wearing the hat of a researcher, investigation suggested that the following examples could be identified, not as final causes, but as reasons for the serials backlog.

8.5.2 Specific Case 1 Example, Graphical User Interface

This was the first example that resulted from the Serials Backlog case and surfaced as a separate example when investigating the reasons for the backlog. In meeting with the staff involved in the serials check-in process and the first line supervision of that process, it became clear that in order to perform the most basic input of serials data, the graphical user interface of the system required the user to move among many screens. This, in turn, caused the most basic of transactions to be input using multiple key strokes and multiple screens. Each screen had a different purpose in the process and in a very short time caused the monitor to be cluttered with between 5 to 8 open screens. Each screen represented a specific function unique to the serial/journal being checked in. When the check-in process was successfully completed, resulting in an elapsed time of between 5 to 8 minutes, the process was started for the second serial/journal. The previous screens needed to be cleared before the next transaction could begin. The staff and supervisors were open in their comments that were grounded in a very real frustration about the multiplicity of these screens and the resulting time-consuming process.

The process was verbalized by the staff, managers, and the end users, as being cumbersome, and the frustration suggested that there was little they could do about the technology but 'bend' to its design and create local work processes and their associated tasks accordingly.

This narration process was also followed for the remaining five cases of the Library 1 study.

Relevant theory was necessary for my work and I used Dervin's (a communication scholar) individual sense making (Dervin, 1983, 1992, 1995) and Weick's organizational sense making (Weick, 1988, 1993, 1995) in two ways. First, the common thread between both theories is their assumption about the nature of the reality that faces the individual and the collective. Both scholars make the assumption that reality is 'gappy' and 'discontinuous' but that the 'gap' and the 'discontinuity' (both cognitive in nature) become occasions for sense making (individual and organizational). If the nature of reality applies to all individuals, then I as manager and researcher will be confronting a 'gappy' reality space, laced with discontinuities. I reconstruct these discontinuities taking on the form of some micro- or macro-discourse as sense-making occasions that caused me (as manager) to stop, reflect, and then reconstruct the discourse as a situation that required some sort of managerial intervention. At the same time, these 'discursive' sense-making occasions became researchable objects (cases) that were fodder for further analysis. My cognitive switching mechanism, in full swing at the end of the 3-year project, allowed me to view the cases from the perspectives of both manager and researcher.

I made the assumption that both sense-making theories (Dervin, 1983, 1992, 1995; Weick, 1988, 1993, 1995) should apply to the objects of my research, individuals and collectives, embedded in the organizational ICT diffusion process. Indeed, if a 'gappy' reality faces all individuals then that assumption seems valid. The analysis that I performed on the micro- and macro-discourses to which I attended as sense-making occasions, was, over time, deconstructed into the data I used for further analysis. This was not planned at the outset of the research, but evolved while the SE was conducted (Chumer, 2002). The specific analysis of the data that I identified in Library 1 can be found in Chumer (2002). In my research, I integrated my analysis of the data along with my particular use of the SE. This approach and as the basis for analysis alone may be different to some reader's understanding of ethnographic accounts as relying upon only particular genres (confessional, realist).

8.5.3 Virtual 1 Narration

This research (Virtual 1) is currently a work-in-progress and, as previously mentioned, is being researched by the SE approach. It differs in 'account only' from Library 1 and aligns itself with a thick description as suggested by Geertz. In Virtual 1, I am researching the effects of virtual ICTs and virtuality on different constructs of the self, using the works of Mead, Gergen, Castells,

Husserl and Schutz as theoretical backdrops. Some samples of the SE as thick description follow. The reader will quickly see how this account differs from Library 1. This account suggests the use of 'thick' description such that a high level of self-inscription is included.

It also suggests that the researcher is embedded in the day-to-day phenomena being researched and uses that to construct the beginning of a detailed account. We begin to see an illustration of the phenomenological approach.

It is 6:30 AM and today, like every day, upon awaking I go into my home office and turn on my computers (plural). Since it takes time for them to 'boot up' I go into my kitchen to make a pot of coffee, nothing like caffeine to get me properly 'wired' in preparation to addressing the multiplicity of symbols and messages that will present themselves with each mouse click as well as those that will have managed to escape the wrath of my 'pop up' blockers. My attention will be pulled, pushed, and in many instances overloaded by the objects vying for that attention, all as a result of the mediating affect of technology. As I sip my coffee I open up in sequence three separate e-mail 'accounts' and begin processing those messages that arrived overnight. As usual one account is laced with annoying 'spam' reminding me (if I open those messages) of my dwindling manhood, my need for drugs and medications, the growing loneliness of housewives who just happen to live in my geographical vicinity, the 'good' news that I 'might' have won some lottery prize, the fact that I am so lucky because I still qualify for a low interest loan, and the really good news that if I can just click on 'this' url I can get the college degree I need to be successful in life. Indeed. What ever happened to the days where 'acceptable use' governed the communications that occurred over the Internet? However the really good news is that this was just the first e-mail account and I still had 2 others to go. I am making progress in these early hours of the morning! These 2 remaining e-mail accounts have good anti-spam controls that, overall, make a good attempt at filtering out those unwanted and invasive messages. Time for a second cup of coffee as I continue my journey in this seemingly wonderful virtual world that is mediated by my computer screen.

Continuing in this reflexive mood I recalled my discussions about the concept of virtuality where virtuality can be a 'represented' or 'mediated' space or place within which the 'self' through interactions with others embarks upon a process that results in a 'symbolized unity'. To my mind, when Mead refers to the 'generalized other,' he is referring to this 'symbolized unity.' My curiosity peaks around the emergence of this 'generalized other' when both 'virtual reality' and the symbols used in 'virtual' interaction tend to be more like simulacra (their referential nature does not have a physical referent). I begin to think about the 'generalized' other that surfaces from interactions in the physical world where the symbols used during interaction tend to be more real in their referential nature, in that the computer screen is not an actor or participant in developing this 'symbolized unity'.

In being reflective about my early morning interaction with the technologies of information and communication (ICT), I saw myself being 'bombarded' by computer-mediated messages, displayed with a variety of colors, sounds, and animation all filling my senses and in turn affecting the meaning that I construct when I interact with them. On the surface it seems that I am interacting with a series of symbols that have brief often times fleeting meanings (buy Viagra, enroll in on-line courses, get a mortgage while the rates are low). Continuing in my reflection I came to realize the invasiveness of ICTs to my 'lifeworld' (Schutz) and if my perception of a lifeworld is being so affected what about the others with whom I interact with through ICTs? A lifeworld that is not totally 'behind the screen' as suggested by Turkle but one that includes life on the screen (virtual interaction) as one part of my lifeworld. However I see my lifeworld as having a physical reality part in addition to the virtual where I can toggle almost effortlessly between the two. It does appear that I am being pulled very seductively by ICTs into communicating and interacting in a virtual more so than in a physical space. I begin to wonder what effect this 'colonization' is beginning to have on the 'symbolized unity' that I enjoyed and understood during many years of physical interaction. Interaction that for the most part occurred not with simulacra but with symbols that had clear physical referents, clear construct referents, and had well understood indexical properties. All symbols being used within rules of interaction that seemed clear as well as the roles of 'others' with whom interaction was occurring.

Now enter the emerging age of virtuality where simulacra prevails, placing symbolic interaction in constant contention and tension affecting both the rules of interaction and the roles of inter-actants. The total effect tends to result in behavior that is different than behaving in a physical world. From a post-modern perspective behavior in a virtual space emerges as quickly as the contexts within which the behaving occurs. The suggestion is that in ICT mediated communication the virtual space that is created is emancipating in nature and perhaps more democratic than interactions in a physical reality space but it seems that both (emancipation and 'situated' democracy) is fleeting. Witness the cohort of lurkers who are reluctant to engage in listserve communication being content to listen rather than engage others. They tend to still be imprisoned by their own hegemony. When some form of temporal stability occurs whether in a chat, listserve, or blog type of virtual space, rules tend to emerge as well a certain roles. This is not dissimilar to behavior within groups occurring in a physical reality space. As I interact with the ICTs as well as 'others' interacting with me through different configurations of ICTs the interactions take on meaning within very specific contexts. For example listserves may have different rules (implicit or explicit) that govern posting of messages and the nature of topics that can be discussed and blogs may have rules that vary from one context to another. These rules become internalized over time as well as certain roles of others suggesting 'general otherness' and symbolic unity.

The following text resulted from a staff meeting where a faculty member's actions surfaced as an activity that was, indeed, relevant to developing an understanding about the nature of 'virtuality'.

This inability to separate both worlds was evident during several of the faculty meetings in the IS Department at NJIT. An area of research in the IS Department is pervasive and ubiquitous computing. Both reside as program elements within Human Computer Interaction, an area that ranges from concepts of a techno-being armed with wireless PDAs, twiddlers, chording devices, and in some instances goggles and other haptic gadgets to interface design for computer applications. A faculty member who lives and breaths all things technologically pervasive and ubiquitous enters the meeting late armed with his trusty laptop. Oblivious to the meeting that is going on he turns on his laptop and soon the entire meeting hears the symphonic melodies of Microsoft Windows. Next is heard a series of beeps, gongs and similar sounds all disruptive and intrusive to the meeting. Still the faculty member is oblivious to the interactions at the meeting, his own interaction with the laptop is what is most important. This faculty member seems lost in his little virtual world where constantly being online takes precedence to everything else. It appears that the instant gratification provided by being connected and wired is paramount and self appeasing. The rules of the meeting within which this disruptive activity is occurring and the roles of other faculty at the meeting seem secondary to the needs of a self that has become isolated in its connectivity from the real world of the meeting. This to me is an example of trying to function in the virtual at the expense of interacting in the physical world. This type of behavior is most fearful to me because it suggests that there seems to be a growing difficulty in society in separating the virtual world from the physical.

From a theoretical standpoint I know that Turkle's 'interactionism' resonates well with others but Turkle seems to view the world as becoming more and more virtual and mediated and this is both inevitable and good. On the other side of reason there is Castells who seems to view the virtual as part of a total Schutzian lifeworld not the lifeworld itself. Now enter Gergen who cautions that he is seeing the 'wired' and 'online' self becoming isolated, insulated, and disorganized in a way where the locus of control is shifting in mediated environments from the mediated to the technology as mediator. The cure appears to be the ability to move between worlds and perhaps in so doing become less isolated, open to others, and in control rather than allowing the technology to control behavior.

Symbolic unity or Mead's 'generalized other' emerges in both the virtual and physical but if exit from the virtual is what is required to provide focus and control then perhaps the stabilizing effect of the 'generalized other' is more salient in a physical reality. This does not suggest that a symbolic unity cannot be reached in the virtual and for many a virtual existence does provide meaning. Perhaps the symbolic unity that has taken decades to form through face to face interactions in a physical reality provides a deeper sense of connectivity than all the wireless and wired mediations can ever hope for and a better sense of focus as well.

We can note here that the Virtual 1 text is an example of 'thick' description whereas the Library 1 text is not. However, both texts emerging from a SE are entirely appropriate to the study.

8.6 THREE CRITICAL ISSUES IN SE

8.6.1 Closeness\Subjectivity

As my account unfolded in Library 1, the tension I initially felt was due to the deep level of experience that I possessed. For over 30 years I was intimately involved with the ICT diffusion phenomena that was also the topic of IT/MIS scholarly research that I reviewed. I was very close to the phenomena of ICT diffusion as I was, indeed, part of it during those 30 years. This closeness left me with a tacit, and, perhaps, biased understanding of the importance of the user in the diffusion process. Closeness is an issue in performing qualitative research (Alvesson, 2003a; Adler & Adler, 1987; Kirk & Miller, 1986; Van Maanen, 1988). The closer one gets to the phenomena one is researching, the more insight should be expected into those phenomena. Certainly a researcher espousing the paradigm of positivism is not as close to the object of study as is the researcher spending a good deal of time 'in the field' attempting to understand the meaning that is created by the actors in specific situations and specific contexts. The researcher qua positivist is concerned with constructs embedded within pre-defined instruments, where the emphasis is on how the instruments construct phenomena. The cautionary note here is that, with the focus on the instruments, an arm's length, or distancing approach to researching phenomena is implied. This is not to suggest that insight is not gained into phenomena through survey instruments, rather that additional knowledge can be obtained by getting close to the actors as they are involved with phenomena.

An assumption underlying 'close up' studies is that the closer a researcher gets to the object(s) of investigation, the more insight should be gained about those objects, and/or their interaction within some phenomena. Adler and Adler (1987) suggest that researcher closeness to the objects of investigation occurs in three basic stages equating to the level of membership. The researcher may be a peripheral, active or complete member of what is being investigated. In citing the 'Chicago School of Sociology' Adler and Adler suggest that closeness is also indicated by the kind of observation being done, which can range from casual observer to participant observer, the latter suggesting that the researcher is both observing phenomena, as well as participating in that phenomena. Krathwohl (1993) follows the observation metaphor of researcher closeness with a higher degree of granularity, suggesting that the range is from non-participant observer to covert participant observer.

The focus of the qualitative researcher performing an ethnography is to get as close to the objects of study as possible so that there is acceptance of the researcher by the field. This acceptance implies that the objects of investigation (the actors or subjects) will act normally and not be influenced by the presence of the researcher (the Heisenberg Effect). In other words, the researcher blends into the environment being studied so that the reality of the phenomena can be observed in as naturalistic a setting as possible. On the surface this blending in or 'going native' might appear attractive. However, it is not without its own set of cautions. One of those cautions has to do with 'obtaining perspective on lived reality'. Getting too close to the object(s) of study may taint the perspective of the researcher so that an unrealistic research account is conducted. The research-er may begin to think, act, and create meaning, similar to the actors being studied. This closeness can be equated to the forest and trees metaphor, where the researcher cannot see the forest (the larger picture) being too close to the trees (the objects of investigation). A form of 'critical distance' is required by the researcher, as well as an awareness of getting too close and losing perspective. This is not easy, and is one of the reasons that qualitative, ethnographic research is not conducted more often, or is done poorly. I will say more about the issue of critical distance in the last section of this chapter.

8.6.2 Split Cognition

It was unclear at the onset of both projects (Library1 and Virtual 1) when the researcher (myself) entered into different modes of cultural activity. Being a manager in a work situation, or a faculty member at a faculty meeting could turn into being a manager or faculty conducting research upon phenomena in which the manager (me) or faculty (me) is actively engaged. This manager qua manager, or faculty qua faculty, at some point becomes a manager qua researcher or faculty qua researcher, attempting to perform both tasks at the same time. This becomes a case of split cognition, requiring a duality of thought and a sense of reflexivity that, in turn, requires a high level of cognitive discipline. Each cultural activity, which in the case of organizations may be work tasks or processes, is viewed from two distinctly separate cognitions. If the cultural activity is ICT diffusion (which was one research focus) or a faculty meeting, (which later turned into a research venue), then manager qua manager is, indeed, involved in the diffusion process, and is in a position to observe and influence events within the process itself. The same can be said for faculty qua faculty who can, likewise, point out the disruptive behaviour during the meeting in an attempt to correct it. However, manager qua researcher is in an investigative mode researching the process, setting, subjects and use of language in which she/he is actively engaged. It is as if the researcher has built into her/his cognition a switch that can toggle between self and self-identities such as 'manager' and 'researcher' or 'faculty' and 'researcher' automatically.

The nature of the switch and the how(s) and why(s) of its activation caused me to reposition the SE as an 'approach' rather than as a 'methodology'. As an approach, when in a 'manager' cognition, its use caused me to focus upon certain micro-processes in the workplace that required managerial attention. As a 'researcher' these micro-processes represented analysable data selected from which 'cases' could be extracted for further analysis. This required some theory or theory component to serve as the basis for analysis. As an approach when in a 'faculty' cognition it caused me to be constantly vigilant of my environment as if I were scanning my environment (the meeting) for discontinuities, like blips on a radar screen that could be reflexively analysed. When coupled with appropriate theory (such theory and its use being integrated into the account of the SE) SE becomes the data identification component of an emerging methodology. Yet the emerging methodology (approach and analysis) is unique to the individual researcher because of the theory(s) selected as the analysis basis. What can activate the cognitive 'switch' (manager to researcher or researcher to manager) is the ability to identify the emergent nature of events underlying phenomena (such as library ICT diffusion) when they occur. However, this cognitive switch can also be activated later while the self-ethnographer is in a reflexive mode. Typically, reviewing minutes of meetings (a form of empirical data) can trigger cognition, reflexively, which can identify a unique emergent element of phenomena that may have gone unnoticed while the actual event was occurring.

8.6.3 Cultural Setting

A major difference between the ethnography and SE is the location of the cultural setting, or, as Alvesson puts it, the 'home base' of the study with respect to the positioning of the researcher. In traditional or 'conventional' ethnographies, the researcher is investigating the 'home base' of others. Such was the case of Schultze's confessional account (Schultze, 2000) that resulted from her 8-month field experience. These 'others' are the subjects or natives that the researcher is attempting to understand, the setting within which they operate, and the language used to create meanings and develop a sense of their reality. Conventional ethnographies suggest that the researcher moves close to those being researched but not so close as to lose perspective. Schultze (2000) used her evolving closeness to the objects of study to iteratively interpret the emerging data, employing the confessional account 'genre' as the interpretive filter. I did something different. I integrated four theoretical perspectives in my Library 1 project (Chumer, 2002) and used salient portions of theory to both filter and then analyse the data, which led to identifying the user, management, and organizational culture and context as 'critical' factors affecting ICT diffusion. Further, I was already in the field or cultural setting I was investigating, while Schultze was moving closer to the objects of investigation. For me it was a distancing from, for Shultze it was distancing in reverse, or getting 'close to'.

In the SE the 'home base' of the researcher becomes the focus of study. In Library 1 the setting was the local library work location as well as the workspace of the entire library system that spanned across multiple campuses. The cultural setting surrounded me as researcher. The subjects were my subordinates, peers and superiors. The language used in the creation of meaning and sense was ingrained in the lexicon of me as self-ethnographer. In a similar manner, the study addressing the effects of virtuality on different constructions of the 'self' caused my 'home base' to be the faculty and the academic space within which I taught and performed research. According to Alvesson:

> While conventional ethnography is basically a matter of the stranger entering a setting and 'breaking in', trying to create knowledge through understanding the natives from their point of view or their reading of acts, words and material used, self-ethnography is more of a struggle of 'breaking out' from the taken for granted ness of a particular framework and of creating knowledge through trying to interpret the acts, words, and material used by oneself and one's fellow organizational members from a certain distance. (Alvesson, 2003a, p. 178)

This certain distance (critical distance) has been nicely articulated by Mingers (2000). In the following section I discuss this and show how I addressed it in my own projects.

8.7 FRAMING SE CRITICALITY

Critical distance is addressed by Mingers (2000). He introduces the following as its constituent elements. They are as follows:

(1) Scepticism towards taken-for-granted assumptions
(2) Wariness towards ultimate authorities
(3) Sensitivity to the impact or effect of phenomena
(4) Concern over the relationships between knowledge, power and interests

These four elements also frame what it means to be critical when conducting SE research. Specifically, what it means to be critical in conducting ICT research is outlined below.

8.8 SCEPTICISM TOWARDS TAKEN FOR GRANTED ASSUMPTIONS

Questioning the assumptions that each individual actor and collectives of actors make about the world, about what is important, and what advice should be offered is one way of adopting such a critical stance. Within organizations individuals and collectives make certain sets of assumptions which determine how they view the world. The self-ethnographer must be aware of his/her specific assumptions and how they differ from assumptions made by those being studied. The tendency towards going native suggests that there might be a blending of these assumptions. The implication is that the researcher, because of closeness to the actors, begins to adopt their assumptions as part of her/his own. Original perspective could become lost and, in so doing, affect the researcher's view of the reality being investigated. Critical distance implies that the researcher enters into a reflexive mode.

In the Library 1 diffusion study it became important to identify the taken-for-granted assumptions that governed the behaviour of management both locally and system wide. These assumptions were explicated and surfaced around the topical areas of organization, management, people, and technology. For the self-ethnographer, it becomes important analytically to identify, if possible what is taken for granted by analysing both individual and collective behaviour at meetings and behaviour during the work day. That is also possible through communication patterns, whether verbal, non-verbal, inter-personal or through written documents and other material. This suggests a critical investigative 'dig', which is an underpinning of the SE approach.

In the Virtual 1 project the taken-for-granted assumptions surfaced again during behaviour patterns at meetings and through daily contact with other departmental faculty.

8.8.1 Wariness Towards Ultimate Authorities

Authority structures are certainly present in organizations and may affect the phenomena under investigation which was evident in Library 1 and which is also becoming evident in Virtual 1. The self-ethnographer should be wary of what we might call 'the Moses Effect'. This means being sceptical of 'cook book' approaches which assume that the fullness and richness of constituent elements of phenomena can be understood and quickly managed. The Moses Effect is unchallenged, prescriptive communication viewed as infallible or uncontestable, flowing from a source or sources to an audience (normally the workers of an organization) and assumed to be waiting for the 'commandments' upon which to act. The power of the Moses Effect in organizations 'resides in the perception by workers and managers alike that two conditions are present: source infallibility and intermediary legitimacy' (Chumer, Hull, & Prichard, 2000). In relation to ICT and its diffusion, the source of the 'Word' must be identified by the self-ethnographer. This means that as the SE proceeds, the formal and informal sources of 'indisputable' knowledge must be uncovered and the 'verisimilitude' of the knowledge and the bases of the knowledge assumptions underlying the project phenomena need to be identified. Implicit in the knowledge assumptions are assumptions pertaining to the people, objects, and hybrids (in the sense that Latour uses the term, Latour, 1993).

In Library 1, the bureaucratic nature of the organization placed value on top–down authority structures, where decisions were mostly made at the top through consensus. Authority at local levels was limited, often requiring approval from higher levels. For example, lower level managers had the ability to change local procedures to interface with the ICTs that were diffused, but the authority and decision-making structures prevented the actualization of local decision making, causing delays that ultimately negatively affected service provision to library patrons. The basic assumption was that 'senior management knows best'. It was based upon a 'leviathan' power structure. In Virtual 1, the organization of the faculty was similar to anarchy but, even though it differed from the library organization where the authority structure was explicit, the faculty authority was implicit, suggesting that the professor, associate professor, assistant professor and lecturer structure was in vogue. Authority resided in senior faculty, along with a host of tacit assumptions about how the department should function. In both projects I had to be aware of hegemony and how it affected the selection of data to be analysed, as well as its influence in the writing of an honest and factual account of emerging phenomena.

8.8.2 Sensitivity to the Impact or Effect of Phenomena

Elsewhere, I have argued that organizations, or more correctly organizational practices, have social, environmental, historical and political effects (Chumer et al., 2000). This implies that phenomena uncovered in Library 1, such as ICT diffusion do not affect just themselves but have organization-wide ramifications. Rogers (1995) suggests that these effects surface as consequences of ICT diffusion. The self-ethnographer must be alert to how these effects manifest themselves in the different parts of the organization being studied. These consequences may not be planned or expected, but researching in detail the lived experiences of organizational actors as the diffusion of ICT is occurring, permits 'critical distance' to be maintained during the entire SE process.

In Library 1, significant ICT success surrounded the diffusion of projects that surfaced locally and were diffused locally. Global ICT diffusions often met with local resistance that caused time and effort to resolve. This resistance phenomenon was explicated in the SE. In Virtual 1, the effects of phenomena (virtuality and self-construction) were more subtle. As researcher I was required to be attentive to cues that emerged from the workplace, both during formal meetings and in informal settings.

8.8.3 Concern over the Relationships Between Knowledge, Power and Interests

Marsden and Townley (1996) suggest that in maintaining 'critical distance' the self-ethnographer should be wary of such items as the locus and bases of knowledge and power, as well as the intra-organizational interests and interest formations. It may not be easy for a researcher who is an employee of an organization to avoid being affected by the power and politics inherent in the organization. The invasive nature of power on the subject is described by Clegg (1994) and its formative effects for the subject (organizational actor) under its influence are explained by Foucault (1980). The self-ethnographer must be particularly wary about the effects of power on the ethnographer qua ethnographer, and ethnographer qua organizational member. This requires a high degree of cognitive discipline as well as an understanding of the value of reflexive thought, to include the ability to be reflexive about one's own reflexivity. (For an account of reflexive reflexivity see Lander, 2000.)

I felt the same tension during the day-to-day activities as felt by my peers and subordinates while conducting Library 1. I had to be reflexive about the effects of this tension (often caused by power differentials) on the managerial self as well as the self that emerged as researcher. This did require cognitive discipline, in that I could not allow the 'self' as researcher to be influenced by the authority structure in terms of data selection, analysis and explication. Yet at the same time, it was difficult to resist the effects of power in my own behaviour and the behaviour of the organizational entities I managed. You develop a Jekyll and Hyde personality that you must be wary about. In Virtual 1, though, there were power differentials they were not readily apparent and had to be learned through trial and error. The effects of virtual technologies were researched by other faculty in the department but they did not include in their research how their peers were using virtual environments. They also did not include how these virtual environments were affecting them as researchers and as teachers. This omission emerged during the SE.

8.9 CONCLUSIONS: THE VALUE OF THE SE

What is the value of SE in the development of theory? How does SE bring insight into the phenomena under investigation that is unique, compelling, and furthers scholarship? The value of SE will be deconstructed in two ways. The first will be a listing of the benefits of SE as explicated by Alvesson (2003a). The second will be a brief discussion of its value in theory development.

According to Alvesson the following 'advantages' collectively represent the value of SE. It can

(1) provide good research economy;
(2) facilitate the production of rich empirical accounts;
(3) develop reflexivity in relation to one's own organizational practice;
(4) avoid the problem of the other, that is, constructing the natives as clearly different from oneself (as it is 'we' rather than 'they' that are the targets of research);
(5) reduce the political-ethical problem of doing research that is focused 'downwards' or targeted at groups of people with whom we (as social scientists) may have a 'competitive' relationship.

Given these advantages, does the SE result in something that can provide insight into certain phenomena? The answer to this question lies in part with the ability of the researcher to understand and be wary of, the potential obstacles. According to Alvesson these obstacles consist of an understanding and an ability to deal with issues of 'closeness', 'language', and 'subjectivity' (of self and other). Issues of 'closeness' and 'subjectivity' have been previously explained. In addition, the ability to deal with the 'politics' of producing the 'right' account may in turn sway the 'self-ethnographic' account. What is meant by this is that the self-ethnographer is indeed a member of a certain cultural community. The account may not be flattering of that community. Therefore, the politics of community belonged-ness and the overarching need of the researcher to continue to be an integral part of the cultural community may impact the content of the self-ethnographic account.

There is no doubt that politics plays a part in the text of the account of the SE. Yet politics also weaves its way into scholarship in general. The basic issue is that not all scholarship is value-free, implying that 'interests' of 'self' and 'others' may cloud or distort data and observation as well as interpretations resulting from data and observation.

The self-ethnographer must be true to her/his self in connection with the research being done. Granted, the self-ethnographer is an employee in some capacity within the cultural setting. In my specific case, I was an employee within a major department of a major university. However, as soon as cognition switches to 'manager qua researcher' the emphasis shifts from managerialism to developing an informed account of value to others. In developing this account, the self-ethnographer draws upon his/her knowledge of the specific phenomena based upon the corpus of 'relevant' literature as well as prior experience. Since the research is based on a specific phenomenon (IT diffusion) there are certain biases that I may bring to the research. These biases are based on experience as related to IT and the user's role in the diffusion process, as well as knowledge of the IT, MIS and related literature.

These biases are key in SE because they contribute to the identification of 'revealing' episodes that emerge from the total flow of events surfacing from the 'home base' of the researcher. The type of data collection done by the self-ethnographer can be classified as 'emergent-spontaneous'. This implies that the researcher, by being in the work place, is in a 'scanning mode'. This is meta-phorically similar to having a form of built-in radar constantly turned on and activated. 'Blips' occur on the radar screen in a manner similar to events occurring in the 'home base'. The biases, interests, and theoretical knowledge of the researcher cause some of those 'blips' to be focused upon and paid attention to, because they relate to the research interest of the manager/research-er. These events as 'blips' are then incorporated into the ethnographic account. If done correctly, these events (blips) function as 'micro-anchors' of social reality and are then woven into the ethnographic account. Alvesson explains the process as follows:

> An emergent-spontaneous study is carried out when something revealing happens. In such a study the researcher waits for something interesting/generative to pop up. It may sound risky and not very ambitious. . ..There are, however, some advantages, the most significant one is that it increases the likelihood of coming up with interesting material. (Alvesson, 2003a, p.192)

In this manner the benefit or value of the research is in the text and analysis of the ethnographic account. Specifically, it resides in how they relate the 'micro-anchored' chunks of reality of the home base to the 'taken-for-granted' assump-tions of the organization as a whole. Further, the experience level of the self-ethnographer coupled with knowledge of applicable scholarly based theory permits a deeper analysis of the relationship between the 'micro-event' and the 'macro-assumptions' of the phenomena.

Experience and theory can also generate another vector of analysis to shed light on the assumptions of the home base, as compared to the assumptions underlying phenomena external to the organization or as presented in the rele-vant literature. This oscillation between 'micro and macro' internal to the home base and 'micro and macro' assumptions external to the home base has the potential to produce a compelling research account with a wide degree of scholarly interest (see also Chumer, 2002, for a broader discussion).

The value of weaving the experience of the researcher into the ethnographic account is to connect with the experience of the reader. The value to furthering scholarship is 'mixing' the right level of generalization with the right level of local variation. The main point to emphasize in concluding this chapter is that, in building knowledge about ICT diffusion in Library 1, and in the identification of emerging phenomena in Virtual 1, involvement and researcher immersion in the day-to-day affairs of the 'actors' yielded critical insights. Central to both projects was researcher closeness to the phenomena being investigated, and a reflexive mood. An approach based in the positivist (or even traditional ethnographic) tradition would not have been equipped to generate these types of insights, or to contribute to theoretical development in the same way and to the same extent.

REFERENCES

Adler, P. A., & Adler, P. (1987). *Membership roles in the field*. Sage, London.

Alvesson, M. (2003a). Methodology for close up studies: struggling with closure and closeness. *Higher Education, 46*(2), 167–193.

Alvesson, M. (2003b). Beyond Neo-Positivists Romantics and Localists – A Reflexive Approach to Interviews in Organization Research. *Academy of Management Review, 28*(1), 13–33.

Alvesson, M., & Karreman, D. (2000a). Varieties of discourse: On the study of organizations through discourse analysis. *Human Relations, 54*(9), 1125–1149.

Alvesson, M., & Karreman, D. (2000b). Taking the linguistic turn in organizational research: Challenges, responses, consequences. *Journal of Applied Behavioural Sciences, 36*(2), 136–158.

Audet, M., Landry, M., & Dery, R. (1986). Science and problem solving: Similarities, dissimilarities, and extensions in the field of administrative science. *Philosophy of the Social Sciences, 16*, 409–440.

Behling, O. (1980). The case for the natural science model for research in organizational behaviour and organization theory. *Academy of Management Review, 5*, 483–490.

Burrell, G., & Morgan, G. (1979). *Sociological paradigms and organizational analysis*. Heineman, London.

Chumer, M.J. (2002). Towards an understanding of user centeredness within information technology diffusion: A self ethnography. DAI-A-63/05_ ISBN 0-493-70233-4.

Chumer, M., Hull, R., & Prichard, C. (2000). Introduction: Situating discussions about knowledge. *Managing knowledge*. In Prichard, C., Hull, R., Chumer, M., & Willmott, H. (Eds.), Macmillan, London.

Clegg, S. (1994). *Frameworks of power*. Sage, London.

Dervin, B. (1983). An overview of sense-making research: Concepts, methods and results. *Paper presented at the annual meeting of the International Communication Association*, Dallas, TX.

Dervin, B. (1992). From the mind's eye of the user: The sense-making qualitative-quantitative methodology. *Qualitative research in information management*. In Glazier, J., & Powell, R. (Eds.), Libraries Unlimited, Englewood, CO, pp. 61–84.

Dervin, B. (1995). The Relationship of User-Centered Evaluation to Design: Addressing Issues of Productivity and Power. *Comments delivered at 37th Allerton Institute on How We Do User Centered Design and Evaluation of Digital Libraries: A Methodological Forum. Allerton Park and Conference Center*, University of Illinois: Monticello, IL.

Foucault, M. (1980). *Power/knowledge*. Pantheon, New York.

Geertz, C. (1973). *The interpretation of cultures*. Basic Books, New York.

Geertz, C. (1988). *Work and lifes: The anthropologist as author.* Polity Press, Oxford.

Geertz, C. (1997). *After the fact.* Harvard University Press, Cambridge, MA.

Gioia, D., & Pitre, E. (1990). Multiparadigm perspectives on theory building. *Academy of Management Review, 15*(4), 584–602.

Heidegger, M. (1962). *Being and time.* (J. Macquarrie & E. Robinson, Trans.) Harper and Row, New York.

Husserl, E. (1931). *Ideas: General introduction to pure phenomenology.* (W. R. Boyce Gibson, Trans.) George Allen and Unwin Ltd, London.

Husserl, E. (1969). *Formal and transcendental logic.* (D. Cairns, Trans.) Martinus Nijhoff, The Hague.

Husserl, E. (1990). *On the phenomenology of the consciousness of internal time (1893–1917) (Brough, J. B., Trans.).* Kluwer Academic Publishers, London.

Kirk, J., & Miller, M. (1986). *Reliability and validity in qualitative research.* Sage, London.

Krathwohl, D. (1993). *Methods of educational and social science research.* Longman Publishing Group, New York.

Lander, D. (2000). Re-pairing knowledge worker and service worker: A critical autobiography of stepping into the shoes of my other. *Managing knowledge.* In Prichard, C., Hull, R., Chumer, M., & Willmott, H. (Eds.), Macmillan, London.

Latour, B. (1993). *We have never been modern.* Harvard University Press, Cambridge, MA.

Mills, C. W. (1959). *The sociological imagination.* Oxford University Press, New York.

Miller, G. (1997). Building bridges: the possibilities of analytic dialogue between ethnography, conversation analysis and Foucault. *Qualitative research.* In Silverman, D. (Ed.), Sage, London.

Mingers, J. (2000). What is it to be critical? Teaching a critical approach to management under-graduates. *Management Learning, 31*(2). (Forthcoming; previously published in 1998 as Warwick Business School Business Paper No. 284.).

Rogers, E. (1995). *Diffusion of innovations,* (4th ed.). Free Press, New York.

Schultze, U. (2000). A confessional account of an ethnography about knowledge work. *MIS Quarterly, 24*(1), 3–41.

Schutz, A. (1982). *Life forms and meaning structure.* (H. Wagner, ed. and Trans.) Routledge, London.

Van Maanen, J. (1988). *Tales of the field on writing ethnography.* The University of Chicago Press, Chicago.

Van Maanen, J., (Ed.), (1995). *Representation in ethnography,* Sage, Thousand Oaks, CA.

Weick, K. (1988). Enacted sensemaking in crises situations. *Journal of Management Studies, 25,* 305–317.

Weick, K. (1993). The collapse of sensemaking in organizations: The Mann Gulch disaster. *Administrative Sciences Quarterly, 38,* 628–652.

Weick, K. (1995). *Sensemaking in organizations.* Sage, Thousand Oaks, CA.

Wolcott, H. (1995). Making a study more ethnographic. *Representation in ethnography.* In Van Maanen, J. (Ed.), Sage, Thousand Oaks, CA.

FURTHER READINGS

Lash, S. (1990). *The sociology of postmodernism.* Routledge, London.

Marcus, G., & Fischer, M. (1986). *Anthropology as cultural critique.* University of Chicago Press, Chicago.

Chapter 9

Information Systems and Power: A Foucauldian Perspective

Bill Doolin

9.1 INTRODUCTION

The implementation of information systems in organizations is typically discussed in relation to concepts of efficiency and rationality. However, a more critical analysis of information systems suggests that in practice they function in diverse ways related to the social and political processes that exist in the organization (e.g. Kling & Iacono, 1984; Kling & Scacchi, 1980; Markus, 1981, 1983). The visibility that information systems provide to particular aspects of organizational activity means that they become objects around which interests are negotiated and political processes enacted (Burchell, Clubb, Hopwood, Hughes, & Nahapiet, 1980). This analysis of the politics and power surrounding information systems in organizations has been extended by a number of authors who incorporate the ideas of various social theorists such as Michel Foucault (e. g. Bloomfield, Coombs, & Owen, 1994; Orlikowski, 1991), Anthony Giddens (e.g. Orlikowski & Robey, 1991; Walsham, 1993), Jurgen Habermas (e.g. Klein & Hirschheim, 1991; Myers & Young, 1997) and Bruno Latour (Bloomfield, Coombs, Cooper, & Rea, 1992; Doolin, 1999a).

This chapter adds to this body of work through a critical analysis of the implementation of the outcome of implementing a large information system within a newly corporatized New Zealand hospital. The information system crossed internal organizational boundaries and had the potential to significantly affect work practices within the hospital. The interpretation offered draws on an understanding of power influenced by the work of Foucault. It utilizes a view of information systems that focuses on the role of information systems in mediating and reinforcing the particular knowledges and meanings instituted in organizational practices (Bloomfield & Coombs, 1992).

This theoretical perspective was chosen because the author was interested in how the information system studied was involved in mobilizing a particular representation or understanding of organizational reality, given the new commercial environment in which the hospital operated after reform of the public health sector in New Zealand during the 1990s. These reforms were associated with the international rise of neo-liberal thinking about economic and social organization (Barry, Osborne, & Rose, 1993; King, 1987) and the emergence of a 'new public management' (Ferlie, Ashburner, Fitzgerald, & Pettigrew, 1996). New Zealand has not been the only country to undergo such public sector reforms in recent years. In particular, the similarity of the UK National Health Service reforms of the late 1980s and early 1990s to those in New Zealand provide a useful point of comparison. As a result, the attempted use of information systems as a management control mechanism has become of increasing importance in both UK and New Zealand hospitals. Thus, the underlying research question that informs this chapter is: How are information systems implicated in the exercise of power in organizations?

The focus of the case study discussed in this chapter is a hospital 'casemix' information system. Casemix information systems link detailed information on hospital patient treatment and clinical activity with associated costs, as a basis for contracting and for revealing the relative efficiency of clinical resource usage. In New Zealand, reform of the public health sector in the 1990s led to a managed market for health services and an increasing insistence on the adoption of private sector business discourses and practices. In this context, the deployment of casemix information systems was ostensibly concerned with improving operational efficiency and the allocation of limited economic resources in hospitals. The intention was to generate and disseminate information on medical activity and its cost among clinical staff and management. The problem of health care was translated into one of a lack of the appropriate information required to control costs and to enable a more efficient use of existing resources. This translation was accompanied by an implicit delegation to information technology that involved keeping track of resource usage (Bloomfield, 1995).

The next two sections of the chapter review the theoretical consideration of power and information systems. The case study used as a basis for the chapter is then introduced, followed by a narrative description of the history of the information system studied. This is followed by a discussion of the findings of the case study in light of the theoretical framework outlined earlier. The chapter ends with some conclusions about the contribution of this work and the utility of a Foucauldian perspective on power in information systems research.

9.2 FOUCAULT AND POWER

Conventional conceptions of power assume that power exists as a capacity that can be possessed and exercised over others in a mechanical or causal manner. Power is seen primarily as something that denies, represses or coerces. Such a 'zero sum' notion of power implies that shifts in organizational power are the result of corresponding changes in the organizational distribution of resources, such as information, which confer power on their possessors (Bloomfield & Coombs, 1992; Clegg, 1989; Lukes, 1974). Foucault seeks to overturn these conventional views of power. He proposes a discursive and relational notion of power, in which power is not possessed but is a capacity for action that resides in social relations. It exists only when it is exercised and when it is put into action (Foucault, 1980, 1982).

The disciplinary power that Foucault describes operates through the normalizing effect of discourse. Discourse is 'a set of ideas and practices which condition our ways of relating to, and acting upon, particular phenomena' (Knights & Morgan, 1991, p. 253). Individuals come to understand the world in the terms of the discourse and various social practices that reproduce this world-view as truth. Power achieves its effects through individuals' reproduction of these discursive practices – ways of thinking, speaking and acting that are instituted in organizational practices. Norms and values constitutive of dominant organizational discourses are embodied in these practices. As individuals reproduce these practices they internalize particular social and institutional norms, which constitute the truth of what is normal in organizational relations. This is a process of subjectification, from which individuals derive meaning and identity, and through which they orientate their day-to-day decisions and actions, in accordance with a certain understanding of organizational reality (Bloomfield & Coombs, 1992; Bloomfield et al., 1994; Knights & Murray, 1994; Knights & Willmott, 1989; Orlikowski, 1991).

Understood in this way, the exercise of power involves the normalization of individuals' judgements about legitimate and non-legitimate actions. In organizational activities, people are faced with a field of possible responses and reactions. Power becomes a question of structuring the field of possible actions of others (Foucault, 1982). That is, 'power is exercised over those who are in a position to choose, and it aims to influence what their choices will be' (Hindess, 1996, p. 100). Control is furthered through organizational members disciplining themselves, rather than as the object of some mechanistically derived managerial power. For example, managerial discourses such as being strategic, act upon the subjectivity of individuals, constituting the sense of what it is to be a manager, and constraining certain ways of thinking and acting, while opening up others (Knights & Murray, 1994). Similarly, to the extent that accountability for efficient resource use (however that may be defined) becomes an accepted norm in an organization, it may define what appropriate behaviour is for individuals in certain roles (Bloomfield, Coombs, Owen, & Taylor, 1997).

9.3 POWER AND INFORMATION SYSTEMS

Bloomfield (1991) suggests that information systems represent the organization, in that the collective understanding of the organization is mediated and redefined through the fabrication of the system. In the fabrication of information systems, the constitutive concepts of the dominant discourses and knowledges instituted in organizational practices have to be defined and organizational phenomena reconciled with them. The embedding of constitutive concepts of dominant organizational discourses in an information system helps the rules, values and assumptions they represent to become reified and taken for granted. This discursive nature of information systems suggests that they are implicated in mobilizing particular representations of organizational reality. They can underpin the framework of meaning within which organizational participants regulate their own behaviour in the exercise of disciplinary power (Bloomfield & Coombs, 1992; Bloomfield et al., 1994).

Various technologies of evaluation and calculation make visible the activities of individuals in organizations and calculate the extent to which they depart from a norm of performance (Foucault, 1977; Johnson, 1993; Miller, 1994). Examples include the comparative application of performance information, or other forms of surveillance (such as supervision, routinization, rationalization, formalization, mechanization) that seek to increase control of organizational members' behaviour (Clegg, 1989; Hardy & Clegg, 1996). Increasingly, information technology mediates this process. Calculative practices such as those facilitated by information systems render social phenomena visible in a particular way. This has two possible effects.

First, representational, inscriptional and computational techniques associated with information systems render individuals calculable, and thus governable. Some activities are given an existence and attention, while others remain unrecognized, enabling managerial knowledge to make stronger truth claims (Boland & Schultze, 1996). Second, the development of information systems to monitor and scrutinize particular organizational activities facilitates control by making individuals more calculating with respect to their own actions. Individuals learn to survey themselves and discipline themselves (Clegg, 1989; Coombs, Knights, & Willmott, 1992). Their actions are influenced through a mechanism of self-monitoring, rather than direct control and supervision. This invokes the notion of an electronic panopticon, in which organizational participants are enlisted in their own control through their belief that they are subject to constant surveillance (Bloomfield et al., 1994; Orlikowski, 1991).

However, information systems such as those described above, cannot be understood simply as management control pursued by electronic means, constituting organizational participants as passive victims of surveillance. Those over whom power is exercised are recognized and maintained as people who act and could do otherwise (Foucault, 1982; Knights & Morgan, 1991). There is a general tendency among those subject to power and control, to resist by means of challenging or diverting the systems and rules imposed on them (Clegg, 1989; Covaleski, Dirsmith, & Michelman, 1993). Disciplinary technologies such as comparative surveillance information systems are not exclusively constraining. In fact, the 'double-edged' nature of disciplinary power implies that such systems are also empowering in the sense that they provide a legitimate space for action (Bloomfield & Coombs, 1992).

9.4 THE CASE STUDY

The longitudinal case study analysed in this chapter focuses on the evolution of a casemix information system in a large New Zealand hospital between 1988 and 2001. The hospital is a regional health provider, which provides a comprehensive range of health services for a geographically dispersed population. A hospital is a complex organization with strong internal cultures, and within which organizational activity depends on a negotiated order and cooperation between diverse occupational and professional groups (Reed & Anthony, 1993). The analysis presented here is grounded in a belief that the outcome of information systems development in such an organization cannot simply be reduced to technical or managerial imperatives (Bloomfield & McLean, 1996; Knights & Murray, 1997).

The organizational terrain surrounding information systems implementation is intimately bound up in power relations, and any specific outcome is the result of a contested and negotiated process. A critical approach to interpretive information systems research is required to open up the 'black box' of information technology, and confront issues of power in technological and organizational change (Doolin, 1998; Knights & Murray, 1994). Accordingly, this chapter attempts to analyse the development of the information system studied as both a condition and a consequence of a broader set of social and political relations. It reflects the problematic and socially constructed nature of organizations by demonstrating how information systems are implicated in the definition of particular representations of organizational reality (Knights 1995).

The main source of data for the study came from extended informal interviews with a range of people from all levels of the organization. In 1996, forty people were interviewed for an average of one hour each. The hospital had just been reorganized into clinical units based on clinical specialties and headed by clinician managers. In a number of the new clinical units, interviews were conducted with the clinical unit director, operations manager, clinical consultants and charge nurses. Corporate and support managers, information systems personnel and administrative staff were also interviewed. Topics covered included the operation of clinical units after the recent organizational restructuring, the ongoing development of major information systems for contracting and patient management, and the use of computerized information by clinical unit staff. A wide range of additional topics also arose.

During 2001, a further six interviews were conducted with clinicians, managers and information systems personnel. These were used to ascertain in what ways the casemix information system had continued to be used and implicated in activities within the hospital. Where appropriate, excerpts from the interview transcripts are used to illustrate certain points in this chapter. Other data collection techniques were used to supplement the interviewing. These included the review of a range of internal documentation and management correspondence, annual reports, business plans, organizational charts, information systems strategic plans, management consultant reports and project documentation. Where possible, unit or project meetings, seminars, the use of information technology, and clinic and ward activity were directly observed.

9.5 THE CASEMIX INFORMATION SYSTEM

This section summarizes the historical development of the casemix system at the hospital studied. Table 9.1 provides a timeline of the key events in the history of the system.

TABLE 9.1 Key Events in the History of the Casemix Information System Studied

1987	Government contracts external consultants to cost activities in a number of hospitals, including the one studied in this chapter.
1988	'Transition' software is purchased by a consortium of pilot hospitals
Resource management system is developed at the hospital studied and monthly data summaries are produced
1991	Incoming government announces reform of the public health sector, including the corporatization of public hospitals
1993	New general management structure is introduced to the hospital
Hospital is incorporated as a 'Crown Health Enterprise'
Casemix system is reinvented as a tool for clinical budgeting
1994	Commencement of contracting for service provision with Regional Health Authority
Regional Health Authority requires casemix information for payment of contracts
1996	Hospital is restructured into clinical units, with clinical directors made clinically *and* financially accountable
Casemix system is used to track patient episodes through different units and to match them with appropriate contracts
Clinical casemix project team formed to disseminate clinical casemix information to clinical end-users
1999	Hospital reorganizes under a new CEO, clinical units being reconstituted into larger structures
2001	Hospital ceases to exist as a Crown Health Enterprise, and is instead administered as a District Health Board
Casemix system is still in existence, but largely relegated to a contract management role

9.5.1 Computerization and Costing

The casemix information system at the hospital studied has a relatively long history. The hospital was one of four pilot sites selected as part of a government-instigated initiative in the mid to late 1980s to develop a computerized resource management system capable of linking costs to clinical activities. Continually increasing public expectations and health expenditure were causing the government concern, and hospitals were coming under pressure to contain or cut costs. According to one information systems manager working in the hospital at the time, central government felt that it was not getting the information that it wanted from hospitals on the costs of procedures.

By 1988 a number of hospitals had collaborated in the sourcing of a computer software product called 'Transition'. Transition would collect various cost data and generate a range of reports concerned with cost management in the hospital. A consortium was formed which bought the license for Transition in New Zealand and implemented the software at the pilot hospitals, including those studied. Data on resources consumed during patient diagnosis and treatment were collected from the hospital's operational areas and transferred into the Transition system where they were linked with the appropriate patient episode. Patient episodes were then grouped into appropriate categories, and a range of reports was generated. The information generated could be used to build a budget for the hospital. It was possible to track individual patient treatments throughout the hospital on a cost and activity basis. Information could be produced at different levels of aggregation, including patient group, medical specialty or even individual clinician. In this sense, Transition fulfilled the criteria for a casemix system.

The casemix system was intended to be a fully integrated computerized information system for hospital cost accounting and product line management. It was promoted as a comprehensive management decision support system that would enhance decision-making, introduce accountability, improve resource use and ensure high quality patient care. In practice, its implementation was problematic. In general, computerization in the New Zealand health system has a poor track record. Previous large-scale and expensive centralized health information systems projects had produced little tangible clinical benefit. This engendered a degree of cynicism or even resistance towards computer systems in general by hospital staff. Experiences with similar initiatives in the United Kingdom health context suggested that casemix information systems needed to be presented to clinicians as non-threatening, and that incentives were required for clinicians to act on the information generated (Pollitt, Harrison, Hunter, & Marnoch, 1988). To use Latour's (1987) terminology, clinical staff at the hospital had to be 'enrolled' in the project. Their active participation was essential for the generation and collection of accurate and valid data that could be used in the system.

Instead, after years of development and data collection, after constant requests for input data without witnessing any tangible or usable output, clinical staff became disillusioned with the casemix project (Lawrence, Alam, & Lowe, 1994). Instead of the promised clinical system for clinical users, the casemix system was perceived as just another management tool and lost credibility with clinical staff. There was little incentive for clinical staff to cooperate in the data collection. Time spent on data collection was seen as a distraction from the primary clinical focus of patient care. Compliance with the casemix system was a duplication of established patient management procedures and an imposition on their professional expertise and practice, and the ability to compare one clinician with another meant that the system was seen as threatening:

> 'It was seen as a threat by the doctors because it ... compared one against the other. They never got the information, but the information was pouring out and going off to Department of Health and all other places. And they saw it as "Hey, you're checking to see if I'm doing my job properly and comparing me with my colleagues, and I don't like that".' (Interview with an operations analyst, August 1996)

A common explanation given of why end users (whether managerial or clinical) did not use the casemix information provided emphasized the lack of stimulus or incentive for its use and that the casemix system was 'before its time'. By 1993, that time had come.

9.5.2 Corporatization and Contracting

The 1991 incoming New Zealand government initiated a rapid and radical reform of the public health sector. By July 1993, public hospitals were incorporated as 'Crown Health Enterprises' – state-owned companies with a statutory objective to perform as efficient and successful businesses. General management structures were introduced to the new organizations, and generic managers were recruited from industries outside the health sector. The creation of four Regional Health Authorities separated the purchase of health care services from their provision. The reforms were intended to force hospitals to take a more commercial approach to health care provision, and to link funding with production in such a way as to make hospitals more accountable.

Accompanying the changes was a new emphasis on accounting and information systems, and large numbers of experts from these disciplines entered the hospitals. The importation of managers, accountants and information systems specialists from the private sector introduced new ways of thinking and speaking about medical and management practice. These experts from outside the health service had their own bodies of expert knowledge and professional allegiances (Bloomfield & Coombs, 1992; Lawrence, Alam, Northcott, & Lowe, 1997).

The new environment placed renewed emphasis on the casemix system at the hospital studied. Contracting with a Regional Health Authority required the setting of a price for treatment, which, in turn, required information on costs and volumes. The continued need for information to control costs was now complemented by a demand for information on patient throughputs as part of the contracting arrangements:

> 'It was becoming clear that contracting between purchasers and providers had to be a lot more sophisticated than it was, and was a lot more difficult and complex than it was initially imagined. At the same time people elsewhere were trying to think, "How do you control costs in the organisation and how do you actually manage revenues?"' (Interview with a corporate manager, May 1996)

Considerable effort was put into re-costing hospital activities, and the casemix system was used to produce detailed information on particular treatment costs and what those costs represented. Financial reports were produced which tracked patient utilization of clinical resources as the patient progressed through the hospital. The casemix system was refocused as a bottom-up budgeting tool in an attempt to overcome the previous lack of end-user interest, by making the information produced by the system more relevant in the new commercial environment. Profit figures were reported for various responsibility centres within the hospital, and a contribution report was imposed by senior management as a standard way of measuring financial and contractual performance within the organization. The increased visibility offered by the contribution reports focused management attention on profit- or loss- making areas. However, the emphasis was still heavily on producing financial information and there seemed little incentive for clinicians to become involved in collecting and using such information.

9.5.3 Clinical Casemix Information

The involvement of clinicians in casemix management at the hospital studied depended upon the implementation of a casemix information system that they perceived as having some clinical benefit. Clinician involvement was important in sustaining the legitimacy of the casemix system. The active cooperation was required of clinicians and other health professionals with the operation of accounting and control systems designed to monitor medical activity (Coombs, 1987). The historical financial focus of the casemix project meant that clinical utilization of casemix information had been neglected. However, by 1996 hospital management was making a serious attempt to enrol clinical staff into casemix management through the provision of clinical casemix information, as well as information on costs, volumes and revenues. Clinical casemix information included measures of length of stay, day surgery versus inpatient surgery, operating theatre time management, and off-hours laboratory usage (Doolin, 1999b).

By specifically targeting clinicians and the medical staff able to influence their decisions, and by focusing on patient care, management hoped to secure the cooperation of a large number of medical professionals in producing a reliable source of clinical activity information. Recourse was made to a quality discourse in an attempt to construct the interests of clinicians as congruent with those of management. This involved translating the notion of patient care in terms of effectiveness and efficiency:

> 'Effectiveness is basically the target that we're using for the clinician population because that is still their number one. You know, they want to provide quality patient care. But if you get into true effectiveness, meaning that your resources are being used appropriately . . . then you're going to come out with efficiency . . . You don't bring dollars up to them because that's a conflict of interest, big time . . . That's where best practice, clinical review, those sort of aspects will be of interest. And you're not hitting them over the head with costs that they see as a conflict of interest, and it's going to turn them off and make them very defensive. All that is is politics.' (Interview with an IS manager, August 1996)

Management's intention in producing and disseminating the clinical case-mix information was to interest clinicians in monitoring the resource consequences of their treatment decisions and involve clinicians in resource management. By costing to a clinical level and making that information available, it was hoped that clinicians would modify their clinical behaviour towards efficient practice:

> 'You suddenly realise what's left is to change clinical practice. In other words, if you're to reduce your costs and make a profit instead of a loss from how you're paid for every inpatient admission, you've got to change the way the doctors . . . what tests they're doing, how long they keep the person in hospital for, because then they flow on to your nursing costs and everything else.' (Interview with a unit director, March 1996)

It was an acknowledgement by management of their inability to manage clinicians directly. Instead, the casemix system would be used to produce information that would enable clinicians to see their performance contrasted with others (Edwards, 1992):

> 'There are difficulties overall with actually managing doctors. I believe the only way of managing doctors is to get information through information systems which provide them with the sort of reports in which peer pressure will bring some conformance to expenditure.' (Interview with a corporate manager, March 1996)

At the hospital, some attempts were made to use casemix information to encourage peer review among clinicians (Doolin, 1999b). Clinical casemix reports were presented to clinicians for internal benchmarking within units that management felt were cohesive in their operation. One unit director introduced the use of clinical casemix information for developing standard treatment protocols to the senior clinicians in the unit. Clinical audit was another common interest that managers could exploit in order to introduce the clinical casemix information to clinicians.

A number of clinicians were sceptical about the relevance of these approaches to using casemix information in the local context of the hospital. One senior clinician pointed out the difficulty in using clinical casemix information to compare individual clinicians with different sub-specializations at a local level, particularly given the size of New Zealand population centres and the number of specialists involved. Clinicians were also frequently able to provide alternative explanations for outlier patterns of treatment or for variations between individual clinicians. Some clinicians argued that the diagnostic categories used in the casemix system were not sufficiently detailed for clinical management purposes. Others would question the accuracy of the casemix information or the validity of the procedures used to construct it, placing enormous pressure on the managers at the hospital in presenting the information (Doolin, 1999b).

Nevertheless, casemix information became an accepted framework for discussion between clinicians and managers. It structured the debate over resource utilization in such a way that clinical efficiency had to be demonstrated in terms of the concepts and definitions associated with casemix management (e.g. diagnostic categories, standard costs, performance against contract, profit and loss). Some clinicians were prepared to accept that the casemix information might provide useful information. Several senior clinicians were exploring the possibilities presented by the casemix information system, in their new roles as clinician managers. Even sceptical clinicians could recognize the usefulness of the casemix information system in arguing for more resources:

> 'I won't say it's not useful, because [the unit director is] able to show that we're grossly under-funded. That's a very useful thing to be able to show ... [W]e are showing that there are more of certain things being done each year and that we need more money to cope with that. That's useful. I'll accept that.' (Interview with a consultant surgeon, September 1996)

In 1996, the casemix information system was an essential element in the reorganization of the hospital around clinical units, a new organizational form based on clinical specialities and headed by clinician managers (Doolin, 2001). Information from the casemix system offered a way to divide the hospital into visible and manageable parts built around identifiable revenue streams related to clinical specialities. The casemix information system was needed to coordinate the movement of patients between the new clinical units, and to match the associated resource utilization with the relevant purchaser–provider contracts. The casemix system was intended to facilitate decentralization of responsibility to clinical unit directors and to encourage flexible operations. At the same time, it provided a more centralized monitoring and scrutiny of the activities of the decentralized clinical units (Orlikowski, 1991).

9.6 CHANGE AGAIN

In 1998, after an apparent disagreement with the hospital's Board over (ironically) the purchase of another major information system, the CEO and two other senior officials resigned. Continued financial pressures led the incoming CEO to introduce a new round of restructuring in 1999. In this reorganization of the hospital, clinical units lost much of their business autonomy and were reconstituted into larger structures. The use of contribution reports generated from the casemix information system was never followed through, as management fell back on more familiar budgetary and financial management approaches based on the General Ledger (Interview with a corporate manager, December 2001). The role of clinician managers largely disappeared as the reorganized hospital separated clinical leadership from management, running clinical specialties through clinical directors supported by a range of business and operations managers.

With this restructuring, the role of the casemix information system became focused primarily on contract management, a tool for measuring performance against contracts with the funding authority, rather than a tool for the comparative evaluation and control of clinical performance (cf. Bloomfield et al., 1997). This shift in meaning, together with the discontinuation of the organizational forms with which the casemix system had become interrelated, relegated the casemix system to a relatively minor role.

In 2001, a change of government saw the hospital dis-established as a Crown Health Enterprise, and instead administered as a District Health Board. At this time, after many years of operation, the widespread use of information from the casemix system throughout the hospital had never materialized.

9.7 DISCUSSION

In the hospital studied, the introduction of private sector experts in accounting, management and information technology, and the extensive development of management information systems, promoted new discourses and ways of understanding organizational reality. Management and market-related discourses were of primary importance to managers and related experts in the hospital. Their sense of identity was grounded in the distinction between their perspective on the organization and the traditional professional, medical perspective. Accordingly, the hospital became a business, patients were customers, and administrators became managers (cf. Parker, 1997).

The new management information, economic language and decision-making criteria also permeated (to varying degrees) the everyday activities of other organizational participants in the hospital. The traditional meaning systems of health professionals were challenged and potentially reconstructed by managerial and economic notions of effectiveness, efficiency, performance and quality (cf. Coombs et al., 1992). The pervasiveness of these discourses in the hospital was reflected by the use of terms such as 'the business', 'business units' and 'internal customers' in the everyday conversation of even those clinicians who were critical of the health reforms. Resisting these discourses involved reproducing them to an extent.

The casemix information system played an important role in mobilizing the concepts and norms associated with the new economic and management discourses. It offered an apparently concrete (although partial) representation of organizational reality, which helped give meaning to the various transactions and organizational practices in which it was utilized. To the extent that organizational participants drew upon the information, rules and resources embodied in the casemix system in their daily activity, they reproduced and reaffirmed its importance, form and content. As Bloomfield (1995, p. 511) comments:

> 'Staff . . . become increasingly locked into a whole new ensemble of routinized everyday practices whose regularity is mediated and reinforced through the actions delegated to information systems.'

In the hospital studied, the casemix system was implicated in the daily work of many organizational participants, providing a technical vocabulary to mediate the meanings given to events and relationships such as those between clinical units or with the Regional Health Authority as a purchaser of health services (Orlikowski, 1991):

> 'Casemix has become a part of the way we work. Just a day-to-day thing we're utilising . . . I mean, one's using it all the time. Whenever we're doing presentations or developing stuff for business plans, volumes for buying capital items . . . We use it for contract stuff. I mean it's just there, it's just being used.'
> (Interview with a unit director, September 1996)

Resisting or reconstructing the concepts and practices associated with the casemix information meant challenging the whole information system. This was a difficult undertaking given its technical complexity and the organizational resources tied up with it (Knights & Murray, 1994). The casemix system was presented as necessary for securing reimbursement from the Regional Health Authority. In this way, the existence of the casemix information system was linked to the existence of the organization, making it correspondingly more difficult to argue against the system (Latour, 1987).

Underlying the introduction of the casemix information system in the hospital was a belief that much of the hospital's resource expenditure was due to the patient treatment decisions of clinicians:

> 'Clinicians are the largest consumer of the hospital's resources . . . In the way that the health care system is currently working in New Zealand, the clinician will always have the end decision . . . You know, it's the clinician sitting there, looking one-on-one with his patient and with the hospital bed behind him. He is the one that decides if that patient gets the bed or not. He is the one that decides what the patient's pharmaceuticals are going to be. He decides what the patient's tests are going to be.' (Interview with an IS manager, September 1996)

Such attitudes form the justification for management intervention in clinical activity, whether directly or indirectly. If costs are driven by the treatment decisions of clinicians, then controlling costs require the management of clinical activity through the allocation of clinical budgets and its surveillance. Scrutinizing clinical procedures and explicitly linking patient treatment decisions to standard costs make clinical activity visible. Management can influence decisions on admissions, treatment, length of stay and discharge:

> 'In the name of ensuring efficiency and financial viability, hospital administrators can, and have become, empowered to manage a hospital's case mix, to demand greater cost consciousness from clinicians, to experiment with new matrix structures in hospitals and to implant extensive computerized information systems.' (Chua & Degeling, 1993, p. 304)

At the hospital studied, direct control over resource use was attempted through monitoring and making visible the financial implications of clinical decisions. Using this information, managers could make stronger truth claims in their attempts to contain clinical resource usage. The definition of clinical specialities as semi-autonomous business units and the introduction of a standard contribution report for each unit were ways of measuring financial and contractual performance and of focusing management attention on profit- and loss-making areas. This encouraged an understanding of organizational reality grounded in economic notions of value and commodity. The visibility given to concepts incorporated in this information, such as profit or loss, average length of stay or performance against contract volume, introduced new practices of accounting for clinical performance.

While the inscriptions generated by the casemix information system facilitated the attempted direct control over the financial aspects of clinical practice, the casemix information was also intended to engender a degree of resource efficiency and self-discipline in clinicians' treatment decisions. Management's view was that objective information on resource usage would lead to rational decision-making by clinicians and to more efficient and responsible medical practice as less expensive treatment protocols were pursued. However, part of the ambiguity surrounding the implementation of the casemix information system at the hospital studied lay in the ability of clinicians to resist its application in various ways.

The surveillance process facilitated through the casemix system increased the visibility of the resources used for patient care, leading to a degree of defensiveness and concern on the part of clinicians. Some felt that the information would be used to justify management decisions on financial grounds, ignoring clinical issues. Many of the clinicians at the hospital remained unconvinced about the validity of the monitoring attempted through the casemix information system. In effect, many clinicians at the hospital were resisting their constitution as users and subjects of casemix information (Bloomfield & Vurdubakis, 1997; Bloomfield et al., 1997):

> 'I choose to ignore it most of the time . . . All casemix seems to have been so far, to me, is a way for the Regional Health Authority to describe what they're going to buy, and I guess I'm not prepared to have the case mix dictated in that fashion. If patients need treatment they need treatment . . . I'm not prepared to have my practice organised in that fashion.' (Interview with a consultant surgeon, September 1996)

To an extent, the position taken by this clinician and others was made possible through the actions of those senior clinicians who had taken on roles as clinician managers and who were, in effect, acting as 'change absorbers' (Jacobs, 1995), protecting their colleagues from more direct contact with management. In many cases, the new organizational form represented by clinical units was only loosely coupled with the internal processes within units. This relative decoupling of clinician behaviour from the formal requirements of the new structure was facilitated by a strong medical professional identity and autonomy (Doolin, 2001).

A critical perspective on the implementation and use of the casemix information system in the hospital studied would view the system as implicated in the attempted normalization of medical practice through the increased surveillance of clinicians and clinical activity. Scrutinizing clinical procedures and explicitly linking patient treatment decisions to standard costs make clinical activity visible and susceptible to intervention by management, which can influence decisions on admissions, treatment, length of stay and discharge. A casemix information system provides a view on clinical practice that highlights variances between the performance of individual clinicians or clinical specialities. From this perspective, a casemix information system is an attempt to influence clinicians' behaviour towards 'normal' work practices, through the comparative application of performance information (Chua & Degeling, 1993; Covaleski et al., 1993; Feinglass & Salmon, 1990).

By accepting the role and legitimacy of the casemix system and reproducing the practices based around it, the potential exists for clinicians to regulate their own behaviour so as to accommodate the new understanding of organizational reality and the criteria for decision-making provided through these discursive practices. However, it was difficult to discern much evidence that this self-disciplining phenomenon was occurring among most clinicians in the case study presented here.

If a discourse is not pervasive and its associated practices are not routinely performed, then disciplinary power is not exercised. The casemix information system and the various inscriptions it produced, did not become widely used by doctors in their everyday work and talk. The casemix system was largely dominated by financial and costing perspectives and had produced little information of perceived clinical relevance or benefit. With a few exceptions, doctors at the hospital had a poor opinion of the validity of the casemix information and expressed little interest in using it to inform their practice. There was a perception that the diagnostic coding performed in order to generate the casemix information was increasingly influenced by a financial need to maximize cost recovery rather than being based on clinical correctness.

Even the inclusion of clinical information that might be expected to interest doctors in using the casemix system was insufficient to encourage the widespread adoption of information produced. Six years after its introduction, clinical casemix information was used only sporadically by individual clinicians. As

the information systems manager responsible for the clinical casemix information commented:

> 'The information is there. I think it's something of a mindset that they [doctors]
> don't want to use it just at the moment. I think it will. I like to think that people will
> start using information and change the way they practise, but they haven't thought
> about it at the moment.' (Interview with an information systems manager,
> December 2001)

9.8 CONCLUSION

The purpose of this chapter was to explore how information systems might be
implicated in the exercise of power in organizations. To do this, a Foucauldian
perspective on power was used to interpret the casemix information system
studied as a disciplinary technology (Doolin, 1998). That is, an information
system capable of mobilizing a particular view or representation of the hospital
through its use in various discursive practices to do with costing, contract
management and clinical performance measurement and, thus, providing a
source of meaning with which hospital staff could make sense of their decisions
and actions.

From a critical perspective, the casemix information system was an attempt
to control clinicians by constituting them as subjects of a management discourse.
For example, clinicians were defined as capable of reviewing and managing
their own clinical practice using casemix information. For a time, the interde-
pendency of the casemix information system and the organizational units within
which it was used and which it helped to structure did help to promulgate the new
management and economic discourse and to produce more defined accountabil-
ities for clinicians.

However, despite the initial perceived centrality of the casemix information
system to the operation of the hospital in a contractual and corporatized environment, the system failed to achieve a critical mass in terms of its use, particularly with the clinicians by whom it was intended to be used. Its use was neither
enforced nor voluntarily embraced. It was generally perceived by clinicians as a
management tool rather than of clinical benefit and, crucially, clinicians were
able to challenge its validity and resist its application to their work.

Eventually, in yet another reorganization of the hospital, the casemix system
lost much of its significance, as clinical units and the idea of 'clinician managers' that had come to underpin the rationale for the casemix system disappeared. This meant that the casemix information lost its potential to become the
dominant view of organizational reality within the hospital. Without its pervasive use to structure, organize and manage daily activities in the hospital, the
power effects potentially exercised through it did not eventuate.

This case study offers two particular contributions to the growing body of
critical information systems research. First, it demonstrates the possibility of
resistance that is integral to the conception of power presented in this chapter.

The normalizing potential of Foucault's disciplinary power is often presented as monolithic and overwhelming. However, organizational participants are actors who can do otherwise when subjected to disciplinary technologies. In the case study, clinicians could and did resist the application of comparative casemix information, some even using the casemix system themselves to argue for more resources. The implication is that information systems associated with attempts to increase management control of organizational participants are also capable of empowering those over whom control is attempted, by making available a legitimate arena for action in the organization.

Second, it provides an empirical example of the application of a Foucauldian perspective on power to an understanding of the implementation of organizational information systems. Despite its use in related academic fields, such as critical management studies (Mitev, 2006), with a few important exceptions, the work of Foucault has been largely neglected by information systems researchers (Willcocks, 2004, 2006). This is unfortunate, as we need ways to critically theorize power and how information systems are implicated in its exercise in organizational and social relations. It is also given a degree of urgency by the increasing penetration of information and communication technologies into everyday lives in the 'information society' (Webster, 1995). As Willcocks (2006, p. 292) puts it in emphasizing the continuing relevance of Foucault's work for contemporary information systems research: 'How indeed can the growth of technological capabilities be disconnected from the intensification of power relations?'

REFERENCES

Barry, A., Osborne, T., & Rose, N. (1993). Liberalism, neo-liberalism and governmentality: Introduction. *Economy and Society, 22*(3), 265–266.

Bloomfield, B. P. (1991). The role of information systems in the UK National Health Service: Action at a distance and the fetish of calculation. *Social Studies of Science, 21*(4), 701–734.

Bloomfield, B. P. (1995). Power, machines and social relations: Delegating to information technology in the National Health Service. *Organization, 2*(3/4), 489–518.

Bloomfield, B. P., & Coombs, R. (1992). Information technology, control and power: The centralization and decentralization debate revisited. *Journal of Management Studies, 29*(4), 459–484.

Bloomfield, B. P., & McLean, C. (1996). Madness and organization: Informed management and empowerment. *Information technology and changes in organizational work.* In Orlikowski, W. J., Jones, M.R., & DeGross, J.I. (Eds.), Chapman and Hall, Boca Raton, FL, pp. 371–393.

Bloomfield, B. P., & Vurdubakis, T. (1997). Visions of organization and organizations of vision: The representational practices of information systems development. *Accounting, Organizations and Society, 22*(7), 639–668.

Bloomfield, B. P., Coombs, R., Cooper, D. J., & Rea, D. (1992). Machines and manoeuvres: Responsibility accounting and the construction of hospital information systems. *Accounting, Management and Information Technologies, 2*(4), 197–219.

Bloomfield, B. P., Coombs, R., & Owen, J. (1994). The social construction of information systems: The implications for management control. *The Management of information and communication technologies: Emerging patterns of control.* In Mansell, R. (Ed.), Aslib, London, pp. 143–157.

Bloomfield, B. P., Coombs, R., Owen, J., & Taylor, P. (1997). Doctors as managers: Constructing systems and users in the National Health Service. *Information technology and organizations: Strategies, networks and integration.* In Bloomfield, B.P., Coombs, R., Knights, D., & Littler, D. (Eds.), Oxford University Press, Oxford, pp. 112–134.

Boland, R. J., & Schultze, U. (1996). From work to activity: Technology and the narrative of progress. *Information technology and changes in organizational work.* In Orlikowski, W.J., Walsham, G., Jones, M.R., & DeGross, J.I. (Eds.), Chapman and Hall, Boca Raton, FL, pp. 308–324.

Burchell, S., Clubb, C., Hopwood, A., Hughes, J., & Nahapiet, J. (1980). The roles of accounting in organizations and society. *Accounting, Organizations and Society, 5*(1), 5–27.

Chua, W. F., & Degeling, P. (1993). Interrogating an accounting-based intervention on three axes: Instrumental, moral and aesthetic. *Accounting, Organizations and Society, 18*(4), 291–318.

Clegg, S. R. (1989). *Frameworks of power.* Sage, London.

Coombs, R. W. (1987). Accounting for the control of doctors: Management information systems in hospitals. *Accounting, Organizations and Society, 12*(4), 389–404.

Coombs, R., Knights, D., & Willmott, H. C. (1992). Culture, control and competition; towards a conceptual framework for the study of information technology in organizations. *Organization Studies, 13*(1), 51–72.

Covaleski, M. A., Dirsmith, M. W., & Michelman, J. E. (1993). An institutional theory perspective on the DRG framework, case-mix accounting systems and health-care organizations. *Accounting, Organizations and Society, 18*(1), 65–80.

Doolin, B. (1998). Information technology as disciplinary technology: Being critical in interpretive research on information systems. *Journal of Information Technology, 13*(4), 301–311.

Doolin, B. (1999a). Sociotechnical networks and information management in health care. *Accounting, Management and Information Technologies, 9*(2), 95–114.

Doolin, B. (1999b). Casemix management in a New Zealand hospital: Rationalisation and resistance. *Financial Accountability & Management, 15*(3–4), 397–417.

Doolin, B. (2001). Doctors as managers: New Public Management in a New Zealand hospital. *Public Management Review, 3*(2), 231–254.

Edwards, B. (1992). Controlling doctors. *Handbook of Public Services Management.* In Pollitt, C., & Harrison, S. (Eds.), Blackwell, London, pp. 107–117.

Feinglass, J., & Salmon, J. W. (1990). Corporatization of medicine: The use of medical management information systems to increase the clinical productivity of physicians. *International Journal of Health Services, 20*(2), 233–252.

Ferlie, E., Ashburner, L., Fitzgerald, L., & Pettigrew, A. (1996). *The new public management in action.* Oxford University Press, Oxford.

Foucault, M. (1977). *Discipline and punish: The birth of the prison.* Penguin, New York.

Foucault, M. (1980). *Power/knowledge: Selected interviews and other writings 1972–1977.* Pantheon, New York.

Foucault, M. (1982). The subject and power. *Beyond Structuralism and Hermeneutics.* In Foucault, M. (Ed.), Harvester Wheatsheaf, New York, pp. 208–226.

Hardy, C., & Clegg, S. R. (1996). Some dare call it power. *Handbook of Organization Studies.* In Clegg, S.R., Hardy, C., & Nord, W.R. (Eds.), Sage, London, pp. 622–641.

Hindess, B. (1996). *Discourses of power: From Hobbes to Foucault.* Blackwell, London.

Jacobs, K. (1995). Budgets: A medium of organizational transformation. *Management Accounting Research, 6*(1), 59–75.

Johnson, T. (1993). Expertise and the state. *Foucault's New Domains.* In Gane, M., & Johnson, T. (Eds.), Routledge, New York, pp. 139–152.

King, D. S. (1987). *The new right: Politics markets and citizenship.* Macmillan, New York.

Klein, H. K., & Hirschheim, R. (1991). Rationality concepts in information system development methodologies. *Accounting, Management and Information Technologies, 1*(2), 157–187.

Kling, R., & Iacono, S. (1984). The control of information systems developments after implementation. *Communications of the ACM, 27*(12), 1218–1226.

Kling, R., & Scacchi, W. (1980). Computing as social action: The social dynamics of computing in complex organizations. *Advances in Computers, 19,* 249–327.

Knights, D. (1995). Refocusing the case study: The politics of research and researching politics in IT management. *Technology Studies, 2*(2), 230–254.

Knights, D., & Morgan, G. (1991). Corporate strategy, organizations and subjectivity: A critique. *Organization Studies, 12*(2), 251–273.

Knights, D., & Murray, F. (1994). *Managers divided: Organisation politics and information technology management.* Wiley, New York.

Knights, D., & Murray, F. (1997). Markets, managers and messages: Managing information systems in financial services. *Information technology and organizations: Strategies, networks and integration.* In Bloomfield, B.P., Coombs, R., Knights, D., & Littler, D. (Eds.), Oxford University Press, Oxford, pp. 36–56.

Knights, D., & Willmott, H. (1989). Power and subjectivity at work: From degradation to subjugation in social relations. *Sociology, 23*(4), 535–558.

Latour, B. (1987). *Science in action: How to follow scientists and engineers through society.* Harvard University Press, Harvard.

Lawrence, S., Alam, M., & Lowe, T. (1994). The great experiment: Financial management reform in the NZ health sector. *Accounting, Auditing and Accountability Journal, 7*(3), 68–95.

Lawrence, S., Alam, M., Northcott, D., & Lowe, T. (1997). Accounting systems and systems of accountability in the New Zealand health sector. *Accounting, Auditing and Accountability Journal, 10*(5), 665–683.

Lukes, S. (1974). *Power: A radical view.* Macmillan, New York.

Markus, M. L. (1981). Implementation politics: Top management support and user involvement. *Systems, Objectives, Solutions, 1,* 203–215.

Markus, M. L. (1983). Power, politics and MIS implementation. *Communications of the ACM, 26*(6), 430–444.

Miller, P. (1994). Accounting and objectivity: The invention of calculating selves and calculable spaces. *Rethinking Objectivity.* In Megill, A. (Ed.), Duke University Press, Durham, NC, pp. 239–264.

Mitev, N. N. (2006). Postmodernism and criticality in information systems research: What critical management studies can contribute. *Social Science Computer Review, 24*(3), 310–325.

Myers, M. D., & Young, L. W. (1997). Hidden agendas, power and managerial assumptions in information systems development: An ethnographic study. *Information Technology and People, 10*(3), 224–240.

Orlikowski, W. J. (1991). Integrated information environment or matrix of control? The contradictory implications of information technology *Accounting, Management and Information Technologies, 1*(1), 9–42.

Orlikowski, W. J., & Robey, D. (1991). Information technology and the structuring of organizations. *Information Systems Research, 2*(2), 143–169.

Parker, M. (1997). Dividing organizations and multiplying identities. *Ideas of Difference.* In Hetherington, K., & Munro, R. (Eds.), Blackwell, London, pp. 112–136.

Pollitt, C., Harrison, S., Hunter, D., & Marnoch, G. (1988). The reluctant managers: Clinicians and budgets in the NHS. *Financial Accountability and Management, 4*(3), 213–233.

Reed, M., & Anthony, P. (1993). Between an ideological rock and an organizational hard place: NHS management in the 1980s and 1990s. *The political economy of privatization*. In Clarke, T., & Pitelis, C. (Eds.), Routledge, New York, pp. 185–202.

Walsham, G. (1993). *Interpreting information systems in organizations*. Wiley, New York.

Webster, F. (1995). *Theories of the information society*. Routledge, New York.

Willcocks, L. P. (2004). Foucault power/knowledge and information systems: Reconstructing the present. *Social theory and philosophy for information systems*. In Mingers, J., & Willcocks, L.P. (Eds.), Wiley, New York, pp. 238–296.

Willcocks, L. P. (2006). Michel Foucault in the social study of ICTs: Critique and reappraisal. *Social Science Computer Review, 24*(3), 274–295.

PART III

Review and Critique

Enamouring, Provoking and Imagining: Three Lenses of Critical Information Systems Research?

José-Rodrigo Córdoba and Carole Brooke

10.1 INTRODUCTION

Our journey in this book so far has led us to reflect on how critically oriented research can improve information systems (IS) practice. In this penultimate chapter, we want to reflect on the purposes and implications of doing this type of research and how we can develop it in the future. Whilst we have seen a variety of research approaches that adopt the label 'critical', we also think there is a need within the field of IS to take stock and reflect on what we have and do, and how we will continue contributing towards the development of IS research in general. In this chapter, we provide an introduction and a view of research as having three different (purposeful) lenses: '*enamouring the camel*' (enticing, alluring critical ideas); '*provoking the lion*' (reacting to and challenging non-critical approaches in IS practice); and '*imagining the child*' (establishing possibilities for dialogue and creativity with 'non-critical' perspectives). We reflect on existing contributions to research (including some of the chapters in this volume) using these three lenses, and we define possibilities for the future.

10.2 REFLECTIONS THROUGH A DIFFERENT LENS

The pervasiveness of information technologies in different spheres of life is still a key source of attention for researchers, and we continuously produce perspectives, ideas, methodologies and descriptions that help us to assess the implications of information systems and technologies in society. The use of critical theories in information systems has grown considerably, such that we now propose that we can distinguish a body of knowledge called 'critical IS'. As a body of knowledge, it becomes relevant to assess how critical IS research develops in relation to mainstream practice, and what contributions it can continue to make.

The meaning of critical IS research, though, is still a contested issue (Brooke, 2002a, 2002b; Klein & Huynh, 2004; Lyytinen, 1992), and lacks a single or common definition. The dynamism of this area has produced some common routes but many different avenues. An area of critical IS research that has become popular is the use of Habermas' theories (Cecez-Kecmanovic et al., 2002; Jackson, 1992; Klein & Huynh, 2004). As a result, this research emphasizes the analysis or achievements regarding principles, practices and methods to address issues of distorted communication, alienation and societal conditions. Information systems and technologies are, then, vehicles that could embed existing communications practices or that could challenge them.

In practice, we also find that to improve our research we need to be able to recognize power relations and emancipation at the local level (Brooke, 2002a; Córdoba, 2007; Doolin, this volume). With the development of more postmodern accounts (see also McAulay, this volume), we find that critical IS research is increasingly entangled in the 'new' and the 'old'; 'new' because novel (critical) ideas are used to define new avenues for research; 'old' because some of us have made our voices heard in the larger IS community. As a result, the label 'critical' has become, in many cases, part of the 'establishment' in academic conferences. Furthermore, some of what we normally consider 'mainstream research' (i.e. interpretive) is considered by its authors as critical (Avgerou, 2001; McGrath, 2005; Walsham, 1993). This complicates our picture of critical IS research, but we also believe that it offers new opportunities for reflection and development.

According to McGrath (2005), the use of critical theories to research IS needs to reflect more the variety of practical applications in this domain, something that Lyytinen (1992) already laid out to complement critiques of 'scientific' programmes in IS research. McGrath goes on to suggest that critical IS applications need to show how they use critically informed methodologies, and how empirical studies inform the definition of concepts and constructs (Klein & Huynh, 2004). Whilst one aim in critical IS research would be to produce a coherent, methodologically robust and theoretically aware body of knowledge which can stand up to mainstream IS research, other aims include pluralism as a strategy forward (Brooke, 2002a). A more accommodating goal would be to continue working on several fronts, and to try to make room for a variety of perspectives.

Interestingly, what could be seen as tensions and contradictions in the meaning of critical IS research, show us that in 'mainstream' IS research there is a need to account for the contradictions, unintended effects, multiple interpretations, conflicts and indeterminacy that information systems can bring to organizations (Robey & Boudreau, 1999). There is also a need to include the 'virtual' into the domain of IS practice and account for the implications that this dimension can bring to the design and implementation of IS (Poster, 2003). We find ourselves sharing concerns about the complexity of the phenomena of IS, and the need to be more inclusive, whilst continuing our quest to provide alternative ways to understand and manage such phenomena.

To address the above issues, this chapter explores the meaning of critical IS research by viewing it through three 'purposeful lenses'. Our inspiration for these three lenses comes from Estanislao Zuleta's appreciation of different stages in the process of reading as an intellectual activity (the camel, the lion and the child – Zuleta, 1982). In this chapter, we seek to extend Zuleta's ideas by combining them with our own three perspectives of 'enamouring', 'provoking' and 'imagining'.

10.3 THREE PURPOSEFUL LENSES

Before we move on to look in some depth at the ideas of Zuleta, we will briefly outline the main tenets of our three lenses, highlighting the advantages and limitations of each. By presenting these lenses, our intention is not to produce a grand narrative, nor is it to generate a meta-theory for critical IS research. Rather, it is to develop a framework to help critical researchers reflect on their own contributions to the analysis and development of ideas. We hope that this can lead to the opening up of new avenues for dialogue and study. We begin by summarizing the main features of enamouring, provoking and imagining before going on to introduce Zuleta's three intellectual states of reading (camel, lion and child). We then combine the two. In so doing, we attempt to draw out some possible readings and reflections on existing work in IS research (including some of the contributions in this book).

From an 'enamouring' perspective, we tend to see developments that provide theoretically sound and appealing arguments to develop alternative practices in IS research. As such, they have attracted audiences to produce innovative and challenging accounts of IS practices. Theory is often introduced to re-interpret IS phenomena and advance our understanding (Mingers & Willcocks, 2004). Researchers contribute enormously by showing how a (i.e. critically informed) theory can inform IS practice. However, by privileging theories or innovations, we think researchers could be at risk of isolating their practice (not subjecting it to review by others) and of failing to engage with mainstream IS research.

'Provoking' on the other hand can describe developments that challenge radically traditional (or non-critical) practices in IS research. A strong element of *denouncing* is found here, and a reference to critical theories is called upon to substantiate the actions of provocation and denouncing (Alvesson & Willmott, 1992). Often the denunciation contains a re-interpretation of critical ideals of IS phenomena (Cukier, this volume; Cecez-Kecmanovic and Janson, this volume; Hirschheim & Klein, 1994). As with enamouring, provoking can bring new perspectives and angles to bear on existing IS phenomena. However, a potential limitation is the lack of practical ways to engage with traditional or 'mainstream' research; in other words, it can emphasize the denouncing aspect at the expense of 'doing something about it'. The latter, in our view, should be undertaken with explicit ethical concerns in mind. This means that provoking needs further engagement, with a view to considering the wider impacts that IS have in the society (Klein & Huynh, 2004). A number of alternatives to make critical IS research more practical have been proposed, including using systems method-ologies in a critical and ethically informed way (Córdoba, 2007; Jackson, 1992; Ulrich, 2001).

A third view of 'imagining' can be a valuable way to look at approaches to IS research, by recognizing the value of traditional developments in the IS field and the tensions generated by critical perspectives. Imagining means to 'forget' about the present whilst we still live in it, with a view to developing the future (Foucault, 1984). Imagining, we believe, should be explicitly guided by ethical concerns (Stahl, 2004, this volume), and should encourage self-reflection in IS researchers, fostering their continuous engagement with the traditional (criti-cally and non-critically informed) IS research.

The aim of these three perspectives is to encourage critical IS researchers to reflect on their current practice and to inform constructive debate about the future. We propose that the reader can also use these ideas to address the tensions that emerge in mainstream IS practice and identify new creative possibilities. Importantly, we stress that the three views are not mutually exclusive and do not represent a particular discourse. Rather, they can be seen as complementary and research may fit into more than one characterization at the same time.

10.4 ZULETA AND ROLES OF THE PROCESS OF READING

The Colombian philosopher Estanislao Zuleta writes on the meaning of *reading* as an intellectual activity. He invites us to recognize this as a continuous cycle of production guided by the existence of a 'problem' in the mind of the reader (Zuleta, 1982). In this process, both the writer and the reader are connected. The former produces a code that the latter needs to decipher. This process, though, is not without conflict, and Zuleta (2005a) advocates conflict as a springboard to develop new ideas. Zuleta takes ideas from Nietzsche (1969) and suggests that in reading a text, one can assume three different roles: that of being a camel, a lion, or a child.

The camel-like role is about admiring, acknowledging ideas, ideals and their masters. The *camel* has a strong dedication to work, to 'suffer' and persevere in trying to understand. The camel reader is driven by a desire to join the writer and their passion embedded in the code that is being read. The camel reader waits patiently and with dedication for this moment. Zuleta (1982) acknowledges the value of reading as admiring; it requires dedication and flare, to open up oneself to ideas, to abandon what one understands about the modern condition. This type of reader is anxious, desperate, with a voracity to assimilate and to consume. They have illusions of understanding after reading. As an intellectual activity, reading requires being calm, patient, being willing to ruminate, to go back and to reflect.

However, reading as an intellectual activity does not end there; it necessitates conflict, and avoiding the idealization of what is being read so that the reader goes beyond the 'you must' given by a text (Zuleta, 1982, 2005a) and continues the journey. Reading needs to be driven by questions and not by ideologies. Furthermore, ideologies need to be continuously questioned. Therefore, reading requires exerting critical thinking, often opposing what has been read or written. In this case, the spirit of a reader transforms into that of a *lion*, a solitary creature that, in the desert, faces demons and dragons. Initially, this reader assumes the 'you must' pull of what is being deciphered as their own inner duty, but then later rebels. A lion-like reader comes to oppose anything that resembles imposition and hierarchy, and lives in continuous denial. Readers challenge pre-established orders and are able to embrace contradictions, paradoxes and 'unthinkable' descriptions in their writings. They also seek lion-like texts to echo their own discontents and inner conflicts. By doing so, they try to identify with in the writers and yet they have to endure the writers' own conflicts as their own. This becomes a source of conflict and rebellion, but also of creativity.

Finally, Zuleta suggests the reader can morph from lion into *child*. A child-like reader is characterized by innocence, acknowledgement, acceptance, forgiveness and a new beginning (an act of their own creation). This does not necessarily mean another rebellion against the establishment. It is a creative and playful flow in the aftermath of tensions, a flow that overcomes previous resentments and, in so doing, helps the reader to decipher the writer's own code, driving the reader to continue with (possibly new) questions. Harmony may then be achieved from reading, a state of community between reader and writer, where both interact creatively, although not necessarily in equal directions or with the same purposes. Reading becomes an internally-driven activity, motivated by the desire for a clearer quest, a sort of aesthetic perfection, a continuous posing of views and a creation of new ones.

In Figure 10.1 these three roles in reading are presented. The arrow indicates a continuous flow between them to suggest that reading, like life, is a continuous experience involving questioning, seeking and understanding.

For Zuleta (1982), reading begins with interpretation. Reading requires one to work actively in deciphering or producing a unique code, to find the value that

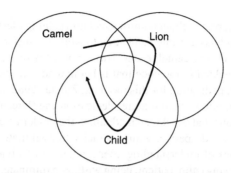

FIGURE 10.1   Three roles involved in reading as an intellectual activity.

the text assigns to each of its constituent elements. It requires continuously moving between these three roles if it is to enlighten thinking. Often, prevailing ideologies, preconceptions and even frustrations undermine creativity and re-flection in the activity of reading (and writing). Zuleta (1982, p. 3) argues that:

> ...Only if these three things (camel, lion, child) are combined, does the activity of philosophical thinking take place. When any of these dominates as the only activity, it is a frustration waiting to happen, a gloomy philosophy, dogmatism or an idealisation of any kind, a rebellious philosophy that is simply a rebellion.

If roles are not continuously combined (and if the beginning and end point in the above diagram are not different), then the result could be a passive admira-tion, a continuous or meaningless opposition, a failure to decipher the unique-ness of what is being read, a failure to produce something unique with its own true meaning, or a failure to follow one's own concerns. 'The trouble with reading...', Zuleta (1982, p. 6) argues, '...is that there is never a common code with what one reads if it is a well-written piece'. In personal terms, this also means that life without difficulties would be passive, full of conformism and unchallenging. A life without tests becomes a meaningless challenge in itself, a life that fails to embrace one's own questions and answers; a life without a journey (Zuleta, 2005a).

Reflecting further, Zuleta (2005a) emphasizes conflict (i.e. questioning our taken-for-granted assumptions or simply discomfort with having reached an end point) as an important engine for creativity and intellectual production in soci-ety. Zuleta is very much concerned with the potential stagnation that too much emphasis on, or adherence to, a single perspective (or ideology) can generate for individuals. This means that as a process, reading (or writing) should not only entail the production and consumption of particular (and static) perspectives, it should also embrace a continuous desire to understand, to narrate, to describe, to question and to create. Zuleta's (1982, 2005a) perspective does not pre-suppose an integration between these roles. Instead, it is an invitation to identify conflicts that could exist between them, a dialogue where creative tensions are retained with the purpose of constructing new possibilities.

In the Spanish-speaking world, Zuleta's ideas are becoming very influential. By continuously assuming an attitude of critical awareness (one of whose manifestations could be 'reading'), Zuleta lays out the possibility to educate ourselves and others by promoting the conflict of ideas as a way to generate dialogue (Melgarejo, 2003). In relation to critical IS research, Zuleta's ideas could lead us to consider approaches that favour complementarity between different perspectives (Brooke, 2002a). However, far from suggesting this, we would like to use the above ideas to encourage reflection on the nature of critical IS. We do this through combing our 'lenses' with Zuleta's roles of reading. Our intention is to foster creativity and imagination about 'a problem' – the problem here being the meaning of critical IS research – and to encourage researchers not to leave their own critical ideals underexposed. As Zuleta says, one cannot leave life unattended or resting in unquestionable premises (Zuleta, 2005a, 2005b).

10.4.1 Enamoured by the Camel

We now explore 'enamouring' approaches to do (read, write) critical IS research combined with the role of reading as a camel. In this lens, accounts of critical IS research are seen as innovative in their use of theories, approaches or methods. They engage readers with novel and unconventional accounts, providing alternative interpretations or insights. This chapter itself could, therefore, be seen to be enamouring in its attempt to bring a new perspective to critical IS research. Other chapters in this book that we see as enamouring in this way include, for example, McAulay's use of semiotics to explore 'unquestionable' meanings in the IS strategy of Sainsbury's PLC. The novelty of his approach can be used to unveil some hidden group interests. Similarly, Basden's chapter proposes using Dooyeweerd's philosophy to re-conceptualize IS practice.

As readers, having experienced some enamouring accounts, we may be left with a desire to try them out, to experience their use in practice, to ruminate on their ideas and, possibly, to make them our own. We feel we have gained insightful understandings about IS phenomena as a result of applying novel methods, theories or techniques. Within this lens we also situate recent developments that incorporate 'new' theories such as critical realism (Mingers, 2001 or Basden's (2002) incorporation of a Christian perspective). We can also find novelty in accounts which aim to make sense of IS practice as a whole (e.g. Checkland & Holwell, 1998; Wilson, 2002) or that facilitate an understanding of IS and its impacts on society. This enamouring lens can also apply to forms of systems thinking which embrace methodological pluralism (Jackson, 1999; Mingers, 1997; Mingers & Brocklesby, 1996). An enamouring lens can also show how particular principles and methodologies can be applied to different developments in IS practice (Clarke, 2007; Jackson, 1992).

Although this purposeful lens can provide us with a sense of admiration, rumination and insight, we think that a critical journey using only this approach (as reader or writer) is still incomplete. It might be that, even though these ideas are appealing, our own ethical concerns do not find resonance, or that their novelty requires further effort to integrate them into IS practice. It may even be that their sheer novelty requires us to think beyond traditional IS practice and to explore theories and concepts in isolation before we attempt to synthesize them with concrete applications.

An enamouring account could focus on reading and writing for an audience in much the same way as an audience reads a scholarly work (Davis, 1986). By just presenting itself as novel, the use of this lens can leave researchers feeling isolated, and the readers wondering about how to continue their journey. Excessive emphasis on enamouring could result in an inability to engage in dialogue, or to being bounded by the rationality of only one perspective. This is what Jackson (1985, 1999) calls 'isolationism' or 'imperialism' in science.

In response to this, we propose that a more provoking type of reading is also required. Inspired by Zuleta, we suggest, therefore, provoking the lion. In order to exercise critical thinking an enamouring perspective would make explicit its own ethics and limitations, and facilitate some conflict about itself. It would declare its own humbleness (something that perhaps we need to reconsider in critical IS research), and be more explicit about what it is reacting against. It would leave questions for its readers, and would provide ways of engaging in dialogue with individuals from other 'lenses'. It would also leave individuals (readers and writers) with an appetite for further reading or with practical insights into how to integrate what has been admired with more traditional (i. e. non-critical) IS research. In short, an enamouring lens could be usefully developed towards being a quest for challenge and self-critique.

10.4.2 Provoking the Lion

Through a provoking lion-like lens, critical IS research features as a reaction to the establishment (whatever it might be), or the purported neutrality of information systems and technologies (Alvesson & Willmott, 1996; Lyytinen, 1992). The provoking lens challenges existing ideas, practices or interpretations of IS phenomena – including critically informed ones. An emphasis on provoking is particularly evident in some of the chapters of this book. They include reviews of emancipatory principles in practice (see the chapters by Basden, and by Cecez-Kecmanovic and Janson), Habermasian re-interpretations of emancipatory principles for IS practice (see the chapters by Cecez-Kecmanovic and Janson, and Cukier), and alternative accounts of the understanding of power and information systems (see the chapter by Doolin).

In contrast to enamouring, the provoking lens offers a direct and value-laden confrontation with what has been commonly developed and assumed. The confrontation is explicit and a set of values is given that should be exhibited to counteract the dominant ones. Critical theories or critical analyses of IS phenomena are used to support challenges to incumbent sets of values. This provocation can be informed by developments in other areas, such as critical management studies (Alvesson & Willmott, 1996; Introna, 1997), and even theoretically opposing perspectives; for instance, Habermasian (Klein & Huynh, 2004) or Foucauldian (Bloomfield & Coombs, 1992; Doolin, 2004; Introna, 1997; Knights & Sturdy, 1990). In our view, Doolin's chapter in this book offers a provoking account of how IS simultaneously became an instrument of control and resistance within the dynamics of a hospital setting. Using a Foucauldian perspective, his account is a reaction to the apparent 'control' that IS helped to reinforce in employees. Doolin offers the values of resistance and relational power to counteract and complement existing interpretations of IS as control based, and stimulates possibilities for alternative representations, decision making and action. Cecez-Kecmanovic and Janson's chapter also offers a re-interpretation of emancipatory practice by showing how the 'ideals' of participation and communication in IS development take place, and how user training and the development of a co-operative culture around IS can foster these. Their account is a reaction to the 'grand' emancipatory ideal of workers' liberation through IS and to the achievement of consensus as a condition for rational dialogue.

Provoking research often privileges values such as participation, the need to have more democratic and dialogical communication, flexibility and incorporation of human needs (Cecez-Kecmanovic et al., 2002; Introna, 1997, 2003; Mumford, 1983). Also, works influenced by Foucault usually focus on strategic action based around power relations. With these or other values, a provoking lens can produce interpretations of IS phenomena with an explicit view; for instance, IS as a panopticon or surveillance mechanism (Ball & Wilson, 2000). A provoking lens which explicitly declares its own stance can also help practitioners to challenge the values which tend to define the boundaries of intervention analysis in IS practices such as planning or evaluation (Clarke & Lehaney, 2000; Córdoba & Midgley, 2006).

However, there is only so much that critical values and ideals being used to 'provoke' can achieve. Often the need to maintain a critical stance can lead IS researchers writing 'provoking' accounts to remain attentive and challenging, but also to continuously react to anything that does not look critical. As warned by Zuleta (1982), an overemphasis on denial can lead to isolation, continuous resentment and even de-personalization. As critical IS researchers, we could create our own possibilities for action in order to take the provoking to the imagining. We could go back and consider which core values we, as researchers, want to promote, and the purpose of our research. For Zuleta (1982), conflict should lead to creation, to definition of new possibilities, to self-knowledge and to a review of one's own taken-for-granted assumptions. In such cases, conflict should be continuous, not static or leading to intellectual stagnation.

An issue of concern that critical IS researchers should consider here, is the potential inability of a provoking lens to go beyond critique or re-interpretation (s), thereby, failing to provide practical opportunities for reflection, dialogue and engagement with established IS research. A lack of self-reflection in provoking critical IS accounts can be further reinforced if some of the basic assumptions of critical are taken for granted, or not adequately contextualized. An example of this is Ericsson's (2003) account of the construction of entrepreneurship in a bus company. He argued that technologies (like a Green book), in conjunction with other techniques, had a dominating power over individuals. Here, emphasis on the existence of such technologies as per Foucault (or à la panopticon) seems to have been excessive and there is an absence of alternative interpretations or challenges to Foucault's ideas.

As we see it, the expression of certain values or stances in reaction to what we consider the establishment could become the basis for researchers to reflect on their own ethics (Stahl, this volume; Córdoba, 2006), and, possibly, to establish a new set of values (their own). In order to move to a more imagining lens, those adopting a provoking lion-like lens would need to suggest ways of going beyond critique, into action. In summary, as critical IS researchers, we first need to offer practical ways of inviting reflection and dialogue with non-critical perspectives, then we need to suggest ways to act. We believe that this possibility is provided by several chapters in this book. Cecez-Kecmanovic and Janson, for instance, reflect on how critical ideals, principles and theories can be put into practice via self-reflection on wider issues (not only IS) in the workplace. McAulay's interpretations of strategy could also be taken forward to explore further dialogue and more practical guidelines for self-reflection in relation to dominant ways of defining strategy. Doolin's account could be further developed to suggest practical ways to guide decision making in relation to IS and power.

Employing a provoking lens, then, is not only about denouncing IS phenomena and denying the non-critical based on critical ideas. It should also be about recognizing the limitations of one's own perspectives in studying IS phenomena, using critical theories or approaches, and inviting others to undertake dialogue and reflective action in IS practice.

10.4.3 Imagining the Child

In order to establish grounds for dialogue and creativity in the field, we now come full circle to the imagining lens. This lens can offer features enamouring and provoking, but goes further to enable writers and readers to address their own questions, not only with the help of critical theories, but also with what can be called traditional IS research. Imagining, as we see it, is about defining the future while acting on the present, moving on constantly and seeking creative conflict by revealing different perspectives whilst overcoming the tendency towards resentment.

Within this lens, we locate developments that account for contradictory interpretations of the impacts of IS (Robey & Boudreau, 1999). We also situate here critical systems thinking research which aims to promote dialogue between different perspectives in the design and implementation of information systems

(Clarke, 2001; Córdoba & Midgley, 2006; Jackson, 1992). As Córdoba and Midgley (2006) show, it is possible that critical self-reflection can lead to new purposes for the design and implementation of information systems, and collective action by those involved. Dialogue between critical and non-critical camps should not result simply in a dominant set of values to be used in a particular context (Ulrich, 2003), but should encourage the development of new possibilities that take account of the strengths and weaknesses of existing ideas. Using an imagining lens, we argue that it is important to maintain dialogue between different perspectives and other lenses, and that action should be defined following self-reflection (individually or collectively) on ethical issues.

So, we might ask 'how can action be defined?' Seen through an imaging lens, critical IS research is guided by continuous ethical reflection, based on one's own values. These values should be declared after admiring and reacting to other people's values (in other words, after being enamoured or provoked by reading or writing the critical IS accounts of others). We believe that critical IS research is heading in this direction now and is beginning to make the ethical explicit. For instance, Stahl's chapter in this book urges that our research should be directed to make a difference in the lives of people who are investigated; see also Stahl, 2004.

However, imagining does not mean ignoring other values or other interpretations of IS phenomena, or leaving out the present because of the future (Foucault, 1984). We argue that imagining also means acknowledging the existence of different ethical concerns or values that guide critical IS research (including those associated with the enamouring and provoking lenses). If there are to be any ethical criteria that guide critical IS research (Stahl, this volume; Varey et al., 2002), then these should be subjected to critical self-reflection by those adopting them.

We suggest that the result of imagining in critical IS research is a more self-conscious understanding of the scope and limitations of both critically and non-critically informed accounts of IS phenomena, with clear and ethically justifiable actions for practice. This comes through a process of both admiring the values of other researchers (an enamouring lens) and challenging them at the same time (a provoking lens). By so doing, we believe we can better learn to recognize or define our own values as researchers. Those conducting critical IS research could use the lenses of enamouring and provoking as a way of promoting self-reflection in their own work. Self-reflection could then be a way to create new forms of ethics, to integrate critical and non-critical accounts, and to open up new possibilities for inquiry.

10.5 CAN WE PROPOSE FUTURE POSSIBILITIES?

How can we propose a future for critical IS research? The ideas of this chapter suggest that we cannot (and should not) stop being creative or attracting newcomers to our area. Neither can we afford to leave the 'present' unattended, as critical IS research needs to continue being aware of IS phenomena and practice. Perhaps we need to imagine the future by being in the present, and continuously (re)define ourselves in the light of this present (Foucault, 1984), resisting any particular goal to become a coherent, coagulate and single discipline. Maybe we need to continuously oscillate between the possibilities of enamouring, provoking and imagining?

We have attempted to make sense of what we see as critical IS research by presenting three different lenses through which to view it. These lenses do not constitute a meta-theory as such but only a framework to facilitate reflection and further insight into the meaning of critical IS research. We make this distinction to avoid being seen as either 'modern' or 'post-modern'.

Our hope is that this framework can assist researchers to undertake readings of their own and others' works, to consider where critical IS research has been (what we do and how we do it), and where we can be in the future. Perhaps those who, like us, regard themselves as on a research journey might see elements of their own style and values in all three of the lenses. Or, perhaps, each lens shows us elements of our past, present and future journeys.

It was in this spirit and in attempting to be self-reflective, that we 're-read' our contribution to this book and considered such issues.

We feel our own account of critical IS research is enamouring in that it brings a novel view that enables us to engage in dialogue with people doing critical IS research. At the same time, our account is provoking because it has enabled us to 'read' other researchers' perspectives. We propose a way to reflect about the emphasis (enamouring, provoking and accepting) of their research. Also we have been provoking by suggesting the need for researchers to search for their own ethical values and make them more explicit. However, our account could also be seen as imagining, because it has brought to the surface values concerned with the accommodation of different critical perspectives, and the importance of ethical self-reflection as a way to create new possibilities for research and action.

To summarize, we propose that future critical IS research should not aim only to provide a single theory or approach to enamour audiences about the usefulness of critical ideas. It should, rather, use provoking elements to denounce, and imagining features to self-reflect so that the contribution of so-called traditional approaches to information systems design can still be valued. Ethical self-reflection, dialogue and debate among and between perspectives and individuals can lead to creativity when an imagining lens is applied, leading to new possibilities for action. By recognizing one's own research emphasis and promoting the development of creative tensions with other researchers, we hope that our ideas can stimulate critical IS researchers to propose new ways of continuing their work.

Most importantly, we acknowledge the necessarily limited nature of our own reading of the wide variety of work represented in this book. We believe we have given a defensible interpretation of the chapters we selected to view through our lenses, yet, we stress that there is no definitive account to be had. The process of reading, as seen within our framework, is inherently an on-going one. We, therefore, invite the reader to go back to those chapters (and the ones we did not include) to see what new possibilities can be created.

REFERENCES

Alvesson, M., & Willmott, H. (1992). Critical theory and management studies: An introduction. *Critical management studies.* In Alvesson, M., & Willmott, H. (Eds.), Sage, London, pp. 1–20.

Alvesson, M., & Willmott, H. (1996). *Making sense of management: A critical introduction.* Sage, London.

Avgerou, C. (2001). The significance of context in information systems and organizational change. *Information Systems Journal, 11,* 43–63.

Ball, K., & Wilson, D. (2000). Power, control and computer-based performance monitoring: A subjectivist approach to repertoires and resistance. *Organization Studies, 21*(3), 539–565.

Basden, A. (2002). The critical theory of Herman Dooyeweerd? *Journal of Information Technology, 17*(4), 257–269.

Bloomfield, B., & Coombs, R. (1992). Information technology, control and power: The centralization and decentralization debate revisited. *Journal of Management Studies, 29*(4), 459–484.

Brooke, C. (2002a). Critical perspectives on information systems: An impression of the research landscape. *Journal of Information Technology, 17*(4), 271–283.

Brooke, C. (2002b). What does it mean to be 'critical' in IS research? *Journal of Information Technology, 17*(2), 49–57.

Cecez-Kecmanovic, D., Janson, M., & Brown, A. (2002). The rationality framework for a critical study of information systems. *Journal of Information Technology, 17*(4), 215–227.

Checkland, P., & Holwell, S. (1998). *Information, systems and information systems: Making sense of the field.* John Wiley and Sons, Chichester, UK.

Clarke, S. (2001). *Information systems strategic management: An integrated approach.* Routledge, London.

Clarke, S. (2007). *Information systems strategic management: An integrated approach,* (2nd ed.). Routledge, London.

Clarke, S., & Lehaney, B. (2000). Mixing methodologies for information systems development and strategy: A higher education case study. *Journal of the Operational Research Society, 51,* 542–566.

Córdoba, J. R. (2007). A critical systems view of power-ethics interactions in information systems evaluation. *Information Resources Management Journal, 20*(2), 74–89.

Córdoba, J. R. (2006). Using Foucault to analyse ethics in the practice of problem structuring methods. *Journal of the Operational Research Society, 57*(9), 1027–1034.

Córdoba, J. R., & Midgley, G. (2006). Broadening the boundaries: An application of critical systems thinking to IS planning in Colombia. *Journal of the Operational Research Society, 57*(9), 1064–1080.

Davis, S. M. (1986). That's classic—The phenomenology and rhetoric of successful social theories. *Philosophy of the Social Sciences, 16,* 285–301.

Doolin, B. (2004). Power and resistance in the implementation of a medical management information system. *Information Systems Journal, 14*(4), 343–362.

Ericsson, D. (2003). Technologies of the Entrepreneurial Self. *Paper presented at the 3rd Critical Management Studies Conference: Critique and inclusivity,* Lancaster.

Foucault, M. (1984). What is enlightenment? (C. Porter, Trans.) *The Foucault reader: An introduction to Foucault's thought*. In Rabinow, P. (Ed.), Penguin, London, pp. 32–50.

Hirschheim, R., & Klein, H. (1994). Realising emancipatory principles in information systems development: The case for ETHICS. *MIS Quarterly, 18*(1), 83–105.

Introna, L. D. (1997). *Management, information and power: A narrative of the involved manager*. Macmillan, Basingstoke, UK.

Introna, L. D. (2003). Disciplining information systems: Truth and its regimes. *European Journal of Information Systems, 12*, 235–240.

Jackson, M. C. (1985). Present positions and future prospects in management science. *Omega, 15*(6), 455–466.

Jackson, M. C. (1992). An integrated programme for critical thinking in information systems research. *Information Systems Journal, 2*, 83–95.

Jackson, M. C. (1999). Towards coherent pluralism in management science. *Journal of the Operational Research Society, 50*(1), 12–22.

Klein, H., & Huynh, M. Q. (2004). The critical social theory of Jurgen Habermas and its implications for IS research. *Social theory and philosophy for information systems*. In Mingers, J., & Willcocks, L. (Eds.), John Wiley and Sons, Chichester, UK, pp. 157–237.

Knights, D., & Sturdy, A. (1990). New technology and the self-disciplined worker in the insurance industry. *Deciphering science and technology*. In Varcoe, I., McNeil, M., & Yearley, S. (Eds.), Macmillan, London, pp. 126–154.

Lyytinen, K. (1992). Information systems and critical theory. *Critical management studies*. In Alvesson, M., & Willmott, H. (Eds.), Sage, London, pp. 159–180.

McGrath, K. (2005). Doing critical research in information systems: A case of theory and practice not informing each other. *Information Systems Journal, 15*(2), 85–101.

Melgarejo, M. (2003). La posibilidad del conflicto: Estanislao Zuleta, desafíos para pensar América Latina. Retrieved November, 2007, from http://lasa.international.pitt.edu/Lasa2003/Melgarejo-MariadelPilar.pdf.

Mingers, J. (1997). Multi-paradigm multimethodology. *Multimethodology: The theory and practice of combining management science methodologies*. In Mingers, J., & Gill, A. (Eds.), John Wiley and Sons, Chichester, UK, pp. 1–20.

Mingers, J. (2001). Combining IS research methods: Towards a pluralist methodology. *Information Systems Research, 12*(3), 240–259.

Mingers, J., & Brocklesby, J. (1996). Multimethodology: Towards a framework for critical pluralism. *Systemist, 18*, 101–131.

Mingers, J., & Willcocks, L., (Eds.), (2004). *Social theory and philosophy for information systems*, John Wiley and Sons, Chichester, UK.

Mumford, E. (1983). *Designing human systems for new technology: The ETHICS method*. Manchester Business School, Manchester.

Nietzsche, F. (1969). *Thus spoke Zarathustra: A book for everyone and no one*. (R. J. Hollingdale, Trans.) Penguin, Harmondsworth, UK.

Poster, M. (2003). The good, the bad and the virtual: Ethics in the age of information. *The ethical*. In Wyschogrod, E., & McKenny, G. (Eds.), Blackwell Publishing, Oxford, pp. 181–196.

Robey, D., & Boudreau, M. (1999). Accounting for the contradictory organizational consequences of information technology: Theoretical directions and methodological implications. *Information Systems Research, 10*(2), 167–185.

Stahl, B. (2004). The ethics of critical IS research. *Critical reflections on critical research in information systems: The second international CRIS workshop*. In Adam, A., Basden, A.,

Richardson, B. (Eds.), Information Systems, Organisation and Society Research Centre, University of Salford, Salford, UK, pp. 1–10.

Ulrich, W. (2001). Critically systemic discourse: A discursive approach to reflective practice in ISD (part 2). *Journal of Information Technology Theory and Application, 3*(3), 85–106.

Ulrich, W. (2003). Beyond methodology choice: Critical systems thinking as critically systemic discourse. *Journal of the Operational Research Society, 54*(4), 325–342.

Varey, R., Wood-Harper, A. T., & Wood, B. (2002). A theoretical review of management and information systems using a critical communications theory. *Journal of Information Technology, 17*(4), 229–239.

Walsham, G. (1993). *Interpreting information systems in organisations.* John Wiley and Sons, Chichester, UK.

Wilson, B. (2002). *Soft systems methodology: Conceptual model and its contribution.* John Wiley and Sons, Chichester, UK.

Zuleta, E. (1982). *Sobre la lectura.* Retrieved July 2006, from http://www.elabedul.net/Documentos/Zuleta_la_lectura.pdf.

Zuleta, E. (2005a). Elogio de la dificultad. *Elogio de la dificultad y otros ensayos.* In Zuleta, E. (Ed.), Hombre Nuevo Editores & Fundación Estanislao Zuleta, Medellín, Colombia, pp. 13–18.

Zuleta, E. (2005b). Tribulación y felicidad del pensamiento. *Elogio de la Dificultad y Otros Ensayos.* In Zuleta, E. (Ed.), Hombre Nuevo Editores & Fundación Estanislao Zuleta, Medellín, Colombia, pp. 19–37.

Chapter 11

Critical Social IS Research Today: A Reflection of Past Accomplishments and Current Challenges

Heinz Klein

Posthumously edited and extended by Carole Brooke and Bernd Carsten Stahl[1]

---

1. In this chapter, Heinz' own material appears in italics (not accounting for editorial changes). The remainder of the text was developed by Brooke and Stahl. We have tried to remain true to Heinz's views as expressed in the fragments we built upon and drawing upon some of his most recent draft papers elsewhere. We realize that our work represents an interpretation that may or may not be true to Heinz's original intentions. In the spirit of critical research we believe, however, that it is important to critically reflect on the text. Such reflection will always remain a collective enterprise that must be open to a multitude of voices.

11.1 INTRODUCTION

The 1984 Manchester Conference (Mumford et al., 1984) was probably the first academic venue that introduced at least two, paradigmatically contrasting critical research perspectives to the IS community. In the terminology of Burrell and Morgan (1979), *these two critical perspectives had affinity to the radical structuralist and radical humanist paradigms. The first critical perspective referred to itself as 'trade union approaches and action research'. It advocated a strong practical interventionist research programme applying a form of action research by co-operating with the Scandinavian trade unions. The second critical perspective had a strong commitment to social philosophy, in particular to* Habermas' (1984) *critical social theory in the version of his (now widely known) Theory of Communicative Action (TCA). Consequently, this perspective inherited a strong rationalist–analytic bias from Habermas' TCA, which was a fundamental revision of his earlier version of critical social theory as published in 'Knowledge and Human Interest'* (Habermas, 1968a). *These two paradigms or, maybe better, research philosophies (cf. Orlikowski and Baroudi, 1991) accounted for the theoretical basis of most of the early contributions that laid claim to be a type of Critical **Social IS** Research (CSISR) as it will be charac-terized later in this chapter[2]. Therefore, from the very beginning, critical research in the field (or emerging discipline) of IS was not only multi-paradigmatic, but it also immediately spawned diverse communities of research practices that interpreted the abstract principles of conflicting research paradigms in very different, and by no means compatible, ways. One immediate consequence of this was that these different communities of critical research practice did not communicate particularly well with each other.*

The first purpose of this chapter is to examine to what extent the contents of this book reflect the diversity of current CSISR, which Brooke's editorial introduction appears to emphasize. This will include a brief examination of the split into diverse critical research communities that marked the beginning of CSISR. We will consider if this is still clearly visible in the literature discussion today, to what extent it is reflected in this book and what its major fault lines might be. We will also reflect if we can see some coalescence around common concerns (e.g. a base of preferred theory and research meth-ods among critical researchers) or perhaps along the lines as suggested by Cordoba and Brooke (in this volume). In their chapter they seem to imply that

---

2. The phrase IS (information systems) should be given a wide interpretation to include what is now often called IT application and social software. We shall use IS and IT application as synonyms, but prefer the abbreviation IS for the sake of maintaining historical continuity. The fundamental ideas driving recent IT and semantic web applications (e.g. Feigenbaum et al., 2007) can be traced back to the very beginnings of computer science with Vannevar Bush's instant access to a world-wide library 'faster than you can think', Licklider's ideas on man-machine-communication, the exper-imentation with dialectical IS, AI work on semantic memories, and high quality natural language translation, etc.

by reading conflicting lines of critical social research (CSR) with different perspectives (which they call lenses), we could preserve diversity and fruitful tension, yet also enable a kind of critical IS research 'that establishes grounds for dialogue and creativity in the field'. In its ambitious form, this would include dialogue across the whole field of IS and across paradigmatic lines. Perhaps this is an idea that is very similar to what is introduced below as 'fundamental criticism', even though its philosophical inspiration comes from a rather different culture and history of thought.

*Regardless of which ideas are more appealing (or 'enamouring') to the reader, it is important to understand what the community structure (in which critical researchers are embedded) implies for the current state of critical IS research as it is reflected in the **topics, theoretical basis** and preferred **research methods** of the contributions to this volume. It also has implications for the status and recognition of critical research in the field at large. For example, do most established IS researchers accept that we have a critical research paradigm (or at least a visibly emerging critical research tradition) in addition to the positivist and interpretive paradigm communities, or is this still widely doubted?*

The second purpose of this chapter is to use the analysis of the current state of critical IS research as a basis to identify some of the challenges that critical IS researchers face as a group. This applies, regardless of whether they see themselves as heterogeneous groups, or as members of larger critical research communities for which shared perspectives and social bonds are stronger than the differences defining their diversity.

*The general approach taken here is to examine the contributions in this book from an historical-evolutionary perspective of critical **social** research in IS (CSISR). In order to address the first purpose, I will use the contributions in this book as examples illustrating some prominent, essential characteristics that could capture the meaning of CSISR (which will be used as the short form) as it has so far manifested itself in the existing body of **critical** IS publications. Given that all research tends to be critical in some sense of the word, it seems important to distinguish **social** critique from **other forms of critique in IS research**. For addressing the second purpose I plan to examine to what extent the contributions in this book simply reflect the current state of the art in CSISR, or whether some of them point to developments that break the past mould. If the latter is the case, this book would add to the diversity of the current state of the art in CSISR. Exploring this question in some detail could shed light not only on the current state, but also on the unresolved future challenges of CSISR.*

By casting a wide net to bring in insights from past and contemporary critical research, the intention is to relate the significance of the critical research contributions in this book to a larger meaning context. This context will be constructed from the general characteristics of critical research, which can be gleaned from the existing body of CSISR literature. This could also lead to the discovery of important commonalities and differences between the collection of articles in this volume, which may not be immediately apparent. These general characteristics of critical research can then be used as a basis for comparing the articles in this volume with the current status of CSISR in general.

Of course, the sample of the contributions in this book is much too small to make representative generalizations on the status of CSISR in IS in a statistical sense. It is, however, large enough to propose some hypothetical patterns, which can then be used as a basis for asking to what extent these patterns can be found elsewhere. In order to address the two purposes of this chapter, it may also be useful to identify which types of critical research found elsewhere might not be represented here. The converse is, of course, equally important: are there any types of critical reasoning or empirical methods represented in the book that are, in some sense, unique because they cannot easily be linked to kindred viewpoints in the extant body of critical work at large? Hopefully, this kind of analysis will reveal strengths, weaknesses and blind spots in current critical research, with an emphasis on those phenomena of particular interest for IS researchers.

The remainder of this chapter is organized into three sections. Section two begins by asking which characteristics have typically been associated with CSR? and which published works illustrate these? Under the heading of the nature of critical research, we shall first extract some criteria from the past to make it clearer what is meant by CSISR, without implying that these criteria should limit the evolving nature of CSISR. For example, we shall explore to what extent Lyytinen's (1992) classical analysis of the principal impacts of critical research in IS is still fruitful for describing the potential impact of current critical research contributions as reported in this book chapter. This section concludes with introducing the important distinction between meta-critical analysis and critical field studies. This helps to update Lyytinen's framework both from a substantive and methodological viewpoint.

Section three will characterize the most important aspects of each book chapter from the perspective of the criteria introduced in section 2. This will add details to better explain the general discussion of the chapters as presented. Of course, this is not the only way to interpret and compare the contributions.

Finally, section four engages in a reflective discussion of what the previous analysis implies about the current state and status of CSISR, with a view to presenting conclusions about unresolved challenges for the future of critical research in general, and CSISR in particular. In this context, it is also appropriate to raise the question of whether one or more paradigms of critical research currently exist or, perhaps, none at all. The recognition of CSISR will always heavily depend on the perceptions of the IS research community at large. A major challenge for critical researchers could be to solidify their community bonds and address issues of under-representation. This is a common concern regardless of intellectual commitments because it impacts upon the resource base for continuing CSISR of any kind. Specifically, this challenge concerns how CSR can be made more visible through premier journals and conferences to the IS research community as a whole.

11.2 THE CHARACTERISTICS AND DIVERSITY OF CRITICAL RESEARCH IN IS

What are the criteria or characteristics by which we can recognize CSR in general and, specifically, CSISR? The phrase 'critical social research in general' is to remind us that the critical research perspective has migrated from other disciplines into IS, in particular from social philosophy, sociology and management studies. Such a definitional exercise is necessary, because Burrell and Morgan's (1979) *text is the closest we have to a history of the critical research tradition, but* Ritzer (1975, p. 164) *had clearly recognized the likely prospects of a critical research paradigm with reference to* Jay (1973). *Therefore, what should or should not count as CSISR is a matter of debate, and the proposal of some criteria must not be interpreted as a misguided attempt at fixing once and for all the meaning of critical research ex cathedra.*

Clearly all research is by its nature critical to some extent, but not all research is necessarily **socially** *critical. For example, Einstein's relativity theories were highly critical of Newton's physics, but neither one of those two theories are what should be called* **socially** *critical; even though Galileo's heliocentric theory did also have socially liberating impacts for the freedom of inquiry. We must recognize that multiple forms of critique exist, all of which are important and which might also be observed in the discourses of IS research.*

In order to avoid terminological confusion, we should distinguish between at least three forms of critique in academia. The **first form of critique** *is known from the peer review process of academic publications. It serves to improve manuscript quality and to identify those submissions that are truly new to the research community as a whole. Kant's 'Critique of Pure Reason'* (Kant, 1781) *is usually credited with a* **second form of critique**. *It is concerned with the limits of human knowledge, including the conditions which constrain and enable human inquiry in science and other forms of knowledge creation. It includes the critique of the limits and biases of a dominant orthodoxy in research practices. Examples are the criticisms of scholasticism by the originators of the age of enlightenment or, more recently, the criticisms of the limits of positivism from Husserl's 'Crisis of the European Sciences'* (Husserl, 1970) *and from the works of Bernstein, Habermas and many others. Given the interdependence between research methods and substance, this type of critique can be an important feature of positivist, interpretive and CSR (as will be recognized below in category E of Table 11.2).*

However, even though the second type of critique is often found in the CSR literature, it is not unique to it and, therefore, not a defining characteristic. Rather, it is the typical domain of philosophers concerned with the nature of human knowledge and the advancement of knowledge through science or *other forms of inquiry. In contrast, the focus of the **third type of critique** is the functioning of society and its subunits, that is institutions, organizations, family and other groupings. It is the target of what I have called above **social critique**. This kind of critique is unique to CSR and is concerned with the analysis of prevailing social conditions that prevent the achievement of certain values. Although it is very controversial which values should be selected to guide social critique, we can note the typical values with which past critical social researchers have concerned themselves. That is, enlightenment, justice and freedom. Critique (in this sense):*

> *'denotes a reflection on a system of constraints which are humanly produced: distorting pressures to which individuals, or a group of individuals, or the human race as a whole, succumb in their process of self-formation'*
> (Connerton, 1976, p. 18).

*In light of this general analysis, I propose a tentative set of criteria (first presented in 2001) in Table 11.1, for identifying likely candidates for CSISR contributions[3]. They primarily apply to critical social **field** research, critical action research or methodical analyses aimed at improving such types of research. This table is only partially suited to analysing critical research that does not rely on field research. Therefore, the subsequent Table 11.2 introduces an additional set of criteria focusing on typical topics or impacts of CSISR that can be applied to all the types of critical research that have come to my attention.*

The first three criteria in Table 11.1 are identical to those proposed by Alvesson and Willmott (1992, p. 433–434, marked as AW). As these three have already been described well in a premier journal, I limit elaboration here to the last three criteria, noting that they reflect work in progress and have not yet withstood the fire of peer review. One criterion omitted in Table 11.1 stipulates that CSR should be guided by 'core concepts and ideas from one or more critical theorists' that have achieved a recognized status (cf. Klein & Myers, in press, for a modified set of seven criteria). The same point is argued in Stahl's contribution under the heading of 'critical theories' and, therefore, need not be repeated here. Also, all of the book chapters appear to meet this requirement.

The criterion formulated as HK4 recognizes that critical research tends to apply a broader range of approaches to evidence-giving than positivism or interpretivism, because it is not only concerned with 'what is', but also with 'what could be' and what 'what should be', that is what is ethically desirable. The theoretical basis for these modes of evidence-giving has been developed in informal logic, the results of which found their way into a general theory of

---

3. To avoid possible misconceptions, I emphasize that this table has been constructed from presentations at Manchester and Pretoria University going back to 2001 and is now introduced here *after* I was given the final set of chapters. I did not suggest these criteria to the book editors for selecting or rejecting submissions to this volume. In fact, the contributions of Stahl and of Cecez-Kecmanovic and Janson suggest somewhat different definitions for characteristics of CSISR and these are most welcome.

TABLE 11.1 Proposed Characteristics of Critical Social Research (CSR)

Tentative Critical Social Research (CSR) Characteristics	Principal Focus of chapter by...
AW1: It should be concerned with conditions of human existence which facilitate the realization of human needs and potentials and ...	Cecez-Kecmanovic and Janson; Cukier and Rodrigues; Basden
AW2: ... support a process of critical self-reflection and associated self-transformation and ...	Brooke (to an extent); Stahl; Cecez-Kecmanovic and Janson; Córdoba and Brooke; McAulay
AW3: ... be sensitive to a broader set of institutional issues relating particularly to social justice, due process and human freedom.	Stahl; Oliver and Romm; Cukier and Rodrigues; Doolin
HK4: In addition, CSR should incorporate explicit principles of evidence-giving (or an explicit truth theory) for the evaluation of claims made throughout the research process, e.g. by questioning the knowledge and beliefs legitimating social practices and...	Cukier and Rodrigues; Chumer; Oliver and Romm; McAulay
HK5: ... accept fallibilism or the ethics of agnosticism, i.e. embrace principles for self-correction and the rejection of claims to accepted knowledge without proper evidence supporting such claims and...	Stahl
HK6: ...suggest how the critique of social conditions or practices could be met to achieve long-term betterment of the conditions of human existence (as a safeguard against 'unrealistic' and destructive negativism).	Cecez-Kecmanovic and Janson; Basden; Doolin

differing forms of argumentation known as discourse theory. Based on the fundamental work of Toulmin (1958) *about the structure of arguments, discourse theory demonstrates that the Popperian methods of science admit an insufficient range of evidence-giving methods into 'The Logic of Scientific Discovery'* (Popper, 1959). *However, it also provides some safeguards against complete relativism, sometimes polemically characterized as 'everything goes' (cf. the summaries in* Habermas (1968b). *It builds upon and expands the Kantian heritage of critical reason, which requires researchers to remain sensitive to the limits of human reasoning as such (cf. Critique of Pure Reason) and liberate their research from authoritarian 'tutelage'* (Kant, 1781). *Discourse theory re-unites, under one conceptual roof, Kant's three-fold distinction between pure reason (epistemological evidence-giving of what humans can know), practical reason (ethical modes of reasoning on what humans should do) and aesthetic judgments (how to reason about questions of beauty and good taste). It deals not only with evidence-giving for factual claims (as, for instance, with Popper's logic of fallibilism), but it also*

TABLE 11.2 Categories for Examining the Impact of Critical Research on IS. (Those labelled A, B and C are quoted from Lyytinen, 1992, p. 168, but in a difference sequence.)

Amended Lyytinen (1992) Categories of Impact	Chapters Illustrating these Categories
A. Criticism of the underlying instrumental rationality bias in information systems design and use, and their un-reflected acceptance of a 'management ideology'	Cukier and Rodrigues; Oliver and Romm; Cecez- Kecmanovic and Janson; Basden
B. Classification and criticism of existing 'technology-driven' development models and the exploration of alternative approaches to develop and use information systems	Cecez-Kecmanovic and Janson; Klein (to some extent); Basden
C. Criticism of the dominating research canons and their imperfections of the 'scientistic programme'	Basden (implied)
D. Meta-critical analysis of the opportunities and short-comings of CSR	Brooke; Córdoba and Brooke; Klein
E. Introduction of new theoretical foundations or research methods and principles for doing critical research	McAulay; Chumer; Doolin; Basden; **Córdoba and Brooke**

addresses the logic of legal reasoning, moral arguments and aesthetic arguments as they apply to the evaluation of art. The formulation of HK4 also relates to Churchman's (1971) notion of a 'guarantor' of design which, in the words of Ulrich (1983, p. 261), is 'a source of guarantee presupposed in each design effort'. Such explicit principles of evidence-giving would also seem to apply to the design of any research projects, because they are basically designs for inquiry in the sense of Churchman (1971, pp. 22).

HK5 is influenced by the agnostic ethical postulate that if a person is logically not entitled to a belief, then she or he is not entitled to it morally either. This is the opposite of theological faith, in particular, if faith embraces the principle credo quia absurdum est ('I believe it because it is absurd'). HK6, the last principle, simply formulates what is widely espoused, namely that mere theorizing without any concern for practicality is not fruitful. However, the notion of 'practical relevance' has to be interpreted very broadly. Simply giving voice to suppressed minorities, or helping those in disadvantaged social positions to better understand their situations, should count as sufficient, otherwise very few research efforts (past and present) could pass this hurdle.

The 2005 Information Systems Journal debate between McGrath, Avgerou and Walsham surfaced criteria that overlap with the above six and help to further clarify the nature of critical research. This debate (cf. Cecez-Kecmanovic, Klein, & Brooke, 2008) suggested that critical research typically (1) is engaging 'with questions that are of an overtly political or moral nature'

(Avgerou, 2005, p. 106); (2) *is driven by the motivation 'to focus on what is wrong with the world rather than what is right'; (3) requires the choice of an appropriate theory; and (4) has the intent to influence others. Of these, (2) and (4) are adapted from* Walsham (2005, pp. 111–115) *recognizing that they are reported with the intent to communicate personal learning about the nature of CSR and not to propose a measurement checklist to legitimate some types of CSR at the exclusion of others.*

Before applying these criteria to the contributions in this book, it is necessary to deal with an important limitation of Table 11.1. *As already noted, it presumes a certain methodological genre of critical research, namely empirical field studies, action research or proposals for improving socially beneficial IS applications through prototypes. Thus, by itself,* Table 11.1 *is not suitable to classify all types of critical research. For example, it cannot deal with critical research of a methodological or self-reflective nature. To deal with this limitation,* Table 11.2 *supplements* Table 11.1 *with an impact characterization of critical research contributions. It expands on* Lyytinen's 1992 *analysis of the impacts that critical research has had on IS research in general, by applying ideas from Habermas' CST.* Lyytinen (1992) *is a good example for what, in* Table 11.2, *I call 'meta-critical' analysis, because it does not analyse a specific social situation in the real world, but examines the critical research literature itself. I define the term 'meta-critical' by analogy with Ritzer's definition of 'meta-theoretical'. Basically, meta-theory studies existing theories rather than the social or physical world directly:*

> *'To put it (too) strongly, a metatheorist is one who studies sociological theories of the social world, while a theorist is one who studies the social world more directly in order to create (or apply) sociological theory'.* (Ritzer 2001 p. 14[4])

Similarly, a critical theorist can study existing critical social theories. This is quite common and examples exist in this volume. In his meta-critical analysis, Lyytinen identified three categories (cf. Lyytinen, 1992 ibid. p. 168), *in which critical research has had – in his opinion – 'modest' impact. These categories provide a good starting point, as* Table 11.2 *illustrates. However, they do not cover his own meta-critical contributions to critical research, for example his own (1992) book chapter or the later articles by* Hirschheim, Klein, and Lyytinen (1996), Wilson (1997) *or* Stahl (2008), *all of which are of a meta-critical nature. Therefore, this category is added as point D. Another obvious impact category of critical research is contributions to broadening the conceptual base of CSR by introducing new critical theories; sometimes illustrated by an empirical field study. Examples of such work include the first introductions of*

---

4. With the caveat '...(too) strongly...' Ritzer warns that the two categories can overlap within the same publication. Most theorists also engage in some 'metatheorizing' and vice versa (c.f. p. 14); similarly, Ritzer, 1991 p. 2–3.

Habermas or Marxism into the discourse of the IS research community. The Manchester proceedings (Mumford et al., 1984) provided a good example of this with the explanation of the trade-union led approaches or the critical social theory perspective. More recent work in this theory-foundation category has introduced Giddens, Foucault and Bourdieu (amongst others) into the critical discourse. Both Basden and Doolin are examples in this volume and, thus, category E completes Table 11.2.

With the addition of categories D and E, Table 11.2 can account for all of the book chapters. It should be obvious that none of the categories in Table 11.2 are mutually exclusive, for example a contribution could begin with category A in Table 11.2 and then make a contribution to other categories. However, in practice, an article or book chapter will rarely emphasize more than two categories.

11.3 A CONCISE ANALYSIS OF THE CHAPTER CONTRIBUTIONS

The purpose of this section is to apply the previous characterization of the features and major accomplishments of CSISR to place the contributions within this book in a broader context. To some extent this overlaps with the two chapters authored or co-authored by Brooke. It is, therefore, important to first note a fundamental point of agreement before focusing on the differences in assessment.

*A principal common ground between Brooke's introductory editorial chapter and the analysis presented in this chapter is that, from the very start, both chapters alert the audience to the observation that, despite its relatively small size, CSISR is **not** an homogenous or monolithic community. Rather, it experiences important tensions. Using the Punch and Judy metaphor, Brooke adroitly makes the point that there is more than one way of theoretically grounding CSR. She does this by pointing to the differences between two recognized social theorists, Habermas and Foucault. This is a change from the 1984 bifurcation into Marxist and Habermas-inspired directions, as was noted in the introduction to this chapter. Brooke provides a type of meta-critical analysis that prepares us to look out for fundamental differences in the underlying intellectual tectonic of the chapters that follow. Both Brooke's introductory chapter and this one, agree that, in principle, diversity is a source of motivation and creativity. Both also see that there are potential risks associated with it. However, Brooke is relatively silent on the nature of the differences and why they might cause difficulty when seeking ways to maintain fruitful dialogue among different critical traditions, on the one hand, and, on the other, research philosophies or traditions in the field as a whole. If* diversity in CSISR exists and if it can create a positive stimulus for the development of our field, then it is important that we consider further the nature of these differences and how we can recognize them. *Without some common understanding of what the principal traditions are, along with their foundational points of intellectual contention, dialogue runs the risk of* *leading to more misunderstandings, creating more communication barriers, rather than shared understandings from which co-operation might grow.*

Indeed, a closer analysis of all the chapters in this book reveals that more than just two traditions fuel diversity and conflict in CSISR. Table 11.3 *lists each chapter in this book with the purpose of identifying its most important theoretical foundations along with other differences.*

Until recently two main strands of critical research have tended to be emphasized in the literature. The first developed from Marx to the early establishment of the Frankfurt School, and to Habermas and Apel, and focused on reformulating the enlightenment ideal. This can be referred to as the neo-humanist tradition, for short. The second strand can be traced from Nietzsche, to Heidegger and Foucault. This can be referred to as the post-modern strand of critical research (Cecez-Kecmanovic et al., 2008).

Elsewhere (Klein & Myers, in press) it has been argued that, mainly through an increased recognition of the influence of Bourdieu, these two strands of critical research can be reconceptualized to produce three strands. Very briefly, these three are characterized by:

i. having an emphasis on ethnographic fieldwork and giving emphasis to the unequal distribution of social resources leading to discrimination (Bourdieu, 1977, 1990),

ii. constituting genealogical/archival research that leads to increased awareness and self-emancipation (Foucault), and

iii. the application of conceptual tools to produce a systematic theory which can help emancipate others, leading to some sort of improvement of the conditions (Habermas).

However, following our analysis in Table 11.3, we can now propose that the field of CSISR displays more diversity than even these three types can express. Indeed, the analysis in Table 11.3 *reveals that the critical research contributions in this book alone, have drawn upon (at least) five theoretical perspectives of CSISR. (That is, as explicitly used in the critical field studies reported here* and according to our own interpretations of them.) These five perspectives can be grouped as follows:

1. Marx (at least one chapter)
2. Dooyeweerd (one chapter)
3. *Habermas – including TCA* along with related hard/soft systems (*at least three chapters*)
4. *Foucault* (at least two chapters)
5. Hermeneutics—for example Zuleta, Husserl, Heidegger, etc. (at least three chapters)

The purpose in making this list is two-fold: to enable more direct comparison with existing strands of critical research, and to demonstrate that the variety of approaches within CSISR already potentially extends beyond them. In creating

TABLE 11.3 The Diversity in Contemporary CSISR Manifested in this Book, (Legend: JH's TCA = Juergen Habermas Theory of Communicative Action)

Chapter no, first author and title keywords	Principal theoretical foundation	Impact (cf. Table 11.2) or critical intent (cf. Stahl, in this book)	Preferred research method/s
1. Brooke. The Punch and Judy of Critical IS Research	Foucault and Habermas contrasted	Challenging first impressions; to sensitize the field of critical inquiry in IS to deeper scrutiny and diversity	Introductory polemic for the book; meta-critique of influences
2. Stahl. Critical Research and Ethics	A selection of ideas dealing with power and ethics, excerpted from Marx, and Rawls (2001) with most emphasis on JH's theory of law and discourse ethics	Revealing the multiple ethical basis of critical research, which in current theorizing can be implicit and explicit, e.g. JH reliance on discourse theory	A meta-theoretical analysis of different critical positions with a philosophical literature analysis
3. Basden. Making the Critical Approach More Useful	Cosmonic philosophy cf. Dooyeweerd (1984), which seeks to explore the philosophical implications of the creation-fall-redemption vs. the modernistic nature-freedom ground motive	Broadening the conceptual basis of JH TCA to make it less abstract and, thereby, more practical by adopting the 15 aspects from Dooyeweerd's philosophy and demonstrating how they can be applied to concrete problems	Conceptual-philosophical analysis of alleged internal inconsistencies in the TCA having some affinity with the hard (HST) and soft systems thinking perspectives
4. Cecez-Kecmanovic. Participatory and Emancipatory ISD	Alvesson and Willmott's (1992) emancipatory framework and organizational communication aspects	Re-examining the meaning and challenges of a participatory and emancipatory IS development project through critical reflection on practice, considering pragmatic questions regarding the adoption of participatory and emancipatory ideas and ideals and practical usefulness, and the conditions for emancipatory IS development practices	Reflection of case records from a fourteen-year long study of the Colruyt Company, a Belgian retail company that engages in participatory and emancipatory IS development

5. Oliver. The Adoption of ERP Systems	JH's TCA with emphasis on rationality types to reveal drivers and influences	Exposing that ERP and technology justification processes of organization were driven more by trend-following than by instrumental rationality	*Critical Social Theory Analysis using grounded theory*
6. Cukier. Applying Habermas' Validity Claims to Technology Planning	*JH's TCA with emphasis on its concept of universal pragmatics*	Revealing distortions in public media discourse of IT applications in college level education by downplaying true IT costs and risk leading to unrealistic decisions	*Discourse analysis using text excerpts from publications in a variety of print media*
7. McAulay. Semiotics and Information Technology	Semiotics	Revealing the potential of elitist language use to privilege particular personal or group interests over others through the ways in which some interpretations are considered to be legitimate whilst others are stigmatized	*Text analysis from a structuralist, post-structuralist and post-modernist perspective*
8. Chumer. Self-Ethnography as a 'Critical' Research Approach	*Philosophical foundations of the hermeneutical tradition (Heidegger, 1962; Husserl, 1931, 1969, 1990; Heidegger, 1931; Husserl, 1931, 1969, 1990; Schutz, 1982) plus methods text on applying ethnography in the field*	Exploring the potential of a self-ethnographic 'approach' to enhance knowledge created through positivistic methodologies by using qualitative approaches especially ethnographies including the emerging self-ethnography	*Methodological reflection of experiences in building theory based on field notes; the researcher collected these during actual involvement with the research setting (the field) as a library manager*
9. Doolin. IS and Power in Organizations	Foucauldian perspective (emphasizing analyses of power and resistance)	Revealing impact of power plays by different stakeholders, especially doctors' and administrators' role in cancelling the anticipated benefits of the IS	*Case data from a large hospital administrative IS*

TABLE 11.3 (*Continued*)

Chapter no, first author and title keywords	Principal theoretical foundation	Impact (cf. Table 11.2) or critical intent (cf. Stahl, in this book)	Preferred research method/s
10. *Córdoba. Three Lenses of Critical IS Research*	Zuleta's work on the process of reading and learning; a development onwards from the hermeneutic circle	*Presenting a proposal of how to approach the diversity of the critical research literature from a reader's perspective to 'open avenues for dialogue' between conflicting critical traditions*	*A 'meta-critical' analysis of the implications of the proposed three lenses for doing and reflecting upon critical research*
11. *Klein. CSISR Today*	*Ritzer (1991) on 'metatheorizing': literature on prior meta-theoretical analysis of CSISR*	*Revealing the principal characteristics of CSISR and the intellectual origins of its diversity with a view to identifying the challenges which contemporary critical researchers face to become more visible and relevant in the future*	*Conceptual philosophical literature analysis to present a meta-theoretical perspective of the current state of critical research and its challenges*

Note: The discussion of the chapters at this point always was intended to be brief but, nevertheless, to be a cross-chapter comparison, along with personal comments from Heinz. We are not, therefore, in a position to write this section in more detail. For the sake of completeness, we have added a few pointers but, short of repeating much of what has already been said in the introduction to this book (and elsewhere in the volume) on the specific contribution of each chapter, we felt it was best to keep our modification of this section to a minimum.

such a list, then, we are suggesting that the two or three strands outlined earlier can be even further disaggregated in order to better take account of the increasing diversity and richness of the application of ideas within CSISR. *As was the case with* Table 11.2, *these 'categories' are not necessarily mutually exclusive; the purpose is to identify only their primary emphasis.* We can now highlight several characteristics of the chapters we have reviewed and, through a consideration of their choices of topics, theory, and method, extend our understanding of the increasing diversity in CSISR.

The first thing we note is that a number of the chapters (including this one) attempt some sort of meta-critique. Amongst the issues surfaced are the dangers of paradigmatic hegemony (at the level of theory choice), the implications of ossification in attitude (about what 'counts' as critical research and what does not), and the self-defeating tendency to remain inarticulate (or at least inexplicit) with regard to personal ethics.

Many of the authors in this volume promote diversity in theoretical tradition, even where such diversity presents immediate issues of potential incommensurability. *Stahl's chapter* (although linked closely elsewhere with the neo-humanist tradition – see Cecez-Kecmanovic et al., 2008) is a good example of the latter, given that he recognizes Marxism, the Frankfurt School, Foucault and critical realism as potential theoretical foundations. *Basden's contribution is noteworthy in that it brings to bear a perspective that other critical researchers have not yet adopted. The work of Dooyeweerd is relatively unknown within the field of CSISR, but it has some characteristics (Dooyeweerd calls them 'aspects') that have already been surfaced concerning the quality of work life and in the arena of socio-technical systems. The theorization of Dooyeweerd's 15 aspects usefully broadens out such value concerns.* It is also unique amongst existing works in CSISR because, rather than drawing its inspiration from the usual secular repertoire, it takes it from a spiritual (Christian) foundation.

Some of the chapters also display interesting variations in their combinations of theory and method. This is evident, for example, in relation to group 3 in our list above. The contribution from Cecez-Kecmanovic and Janson is based on familiar territory for contemporary CSISR, namely Habermas' critical social theory (CST) and his use of TCA. However, their research extends beyond the usual theoretical application in that it *addresses some misconceptions of an immanent dogmatism of Habermas' CST (with reference to Wilson's 1997 summary of these). It then goes further to apply TCA in order to present and critically reflect upon case data.* The longtitudinal case study, in itself, is novel given that it is a relatively unusual example of an organization deploying IS with explicitly articulated intentions towards employee participation and emancipation. Thus, the chapter extends our understanding in several different directions at once: with respect to departures in theory application as well as insights on method, through its presentation and analysis of the field data.

The research accounts by Oliver and Romm, and by Cukier and Rodrigues also draw upon Habermas' TCA and CST. In particular, the juxtaposition of

Habermas and grounded theory in the work of Oliver and Romm is unusual. The combination produces some surprising insights. For instance, far from demonstrating that 'rationality' was a key driver, the research suggested that peer pressure and trend-following were key influences on the technology justification process. In both these chapters we see ideas from Habermas taken as points of departure but each leads in different directions – one focusing on discourse analysis and the other on grounded theory.

An obvious example in this book of the use of Foucault's ideas is Doolin's application of Foucault's theory of power to an evaluation of a case study at a large hospital. His analysis of the relationships between health professionals, and other stakeholders, focuses on issues of power, influence and resistance. One of Doolin's primary concerns is to evaluate the attempts by management to intensify both managerial control and the penetration of technology into the workplace. In so doing, he is able to reveal ways in which individuals and groups can appropriate power in order to protect their own needs. He shows how a controlling technology can be harnessed, through social relations, to produce an empowering effect and to create a 'legitimate arena for action in the organization'. One of Doolin's main objectives in this piece is to demonstrate to other researchers that Foucault's ideas are worthy of further exploration and adoption by CSISR scholars. He suggests that its under-representation in the literature should now be challenged.

Although the work of Bourdieu is not explicitly applied in any of the chapters in this book, McAulay and Chumer's accounts both display a relationship with that lineage (as proposed in Klein & Myers, in press) and, more specifically, demonstrate point 4 in our list, a diversification of CSISR, branching out of hermeneutics. Insofar as Cordoba and Brooke's chapter also draws upon hermeneutics and a re-interpretation of Zuleta, it, too, can be included in this category. McAulay and Chumer share a common concern for text and its interpretation, and both display post-structuralist/post-modernist traits, although they approach their topics in different ways. McAulay's exploration focuses on the symbolic aspects, artefacts and actions involved in reading and interpretation, whereas Chumer's self-ethnography places a key emphasis on the individual - especially the actual researcher as they struggle with being 'the researched' and 'the researching' simultaneously. Chumer's chapter is, moreover, unusual in that it draws upon ideas from Heidegger, an author apparently not generally used as a critical theorist in CSISR (see Cecez-Kecmanovic et al., 2008)

It could be argued that there is less of an emphasis in this book on postmodernism (e.g. of Derrida, Lyotard and others according to Heinz Klein) than might be expected of the critical research field generally. However, it is reasonable to note that, although this approach is widely evident in publications in the topics of management and organization, it is still under-represented within the more specific field of CSISR. Whilst Heinz made a memo note to himself that the explicit use of Bourdieu, for example, is lacking here he, nevertheless, identified some links between chapters and the post-strucuturalist and post-modernist streams of inquiry; notably those drawing upon the symbolic aspects of text and communication.

Now that we have made some observations about the contributions in this volume and the extent to which they indicate the existence of diversification within CSISR, it is time to broaden our scope and consider the current state of CSISR as a whole. We conclude this chapter and this book, therefore, with a section of reflection and discussion.

11.4 REFLECTION AND DISCUSSION: THE CURRENT STATE OF CSISR: ACCOMPLISHMENTS, DISCONTENTS AND CHALLENGES

11.4.1 The diversity: Reason for pride and discontent

This book has shown that CSISR is a research field that is characterized by diversity. This diversity can be seen in preferred theories, approaches, methodologies, and research questions. The diversity is such that one can justifiably ask whether there is a common theme that unites all CSISR. Several chapters in the book have tried to give an answer to this question and outline what it is that makes research in IS critical. It remains to be seen whether the commonalities are sufficient for CSISR scholars to arrive at criteria that allow them to mutually respect and promote their work.

The diversity of the field renders it interesting and lively, which might be a source of pride. At the same time, it is also a main cause for discontent and disagreement. *In 1991, Orlikowski and Baroudi described only one critical research philosophy in their summary of multiple research perspectives in IS. While they were probably politically justified in simply omitting the Marxist view of critical research (as the Soviet Union had just collapsed), in light of the diversity revealed here, the single paradigm view of critical research can no longer be maintained. While there are some common social value concerns that most critical researchers appear to share, it is rather misleading to claim that all the contributions of this volume belong to the same research paradigm or research philosophy, as* Orlikowski and Baroudi (1991) *preferred to call it. This would apply even more to a broader sample of recent critical research publications.*

At the beginning of this chapter we noted that Burrell and Morgan's classification of research paradigms (Burrell & Morgan, 1979) included two that were named 'radical humanist' and 'radical structuralist'. These appear to have been collapsed into one under the umbrella term of 'critical IS'. Much has been written about paradigms and their commensurability, or lack thereof. Most of this has referred to positivism and interpretivism, but the debate concerning the commensurability or incommensurability of different streams of research in critical work is still in its infancy (Brooke, 2002). This situation is made all the more interesting given the proposition in this chapter of a proliferation of strands within CSISR beyond the usual two, or even three, previously suggested.

The debate between Habermas and Foucault that surfaced in several of the chapters in this volume may be an indicator of such underlying tensions.

It seems to be a widely shared goal of the community of critical IS scholars to overcome differences and reconcile contrasting approaches. The opposition to mainstream positivist research may be enough to unite different streams of critical research but whether this is, indeed, a prima facie case is not obvious and needs more evaluation. Some chapters in this book, meanwhile, appear to suggest that diversity in itself needs not only to be encouraged but also to be celebrated. This brings us to a related issue – ontological status.

11.4.2 Ontological focus of critical research: Appears to bridge Macro- and micro-analysis and, thereby, be ahead in the field.

CSISR can be more philosophically aware than competing research approaches. This may be caused by the fact that it has been, and currently remains, a fringe position that needs to invest more resources in questioning and establishing its fundamental positions. This includes the question of philosophical ontology, which mainstream IS research tends to ignore. Where the term 'ontology' is used at all by mainstream positivist IS scholars, it tends to refer to database-related ontologies; which, albeit based to some degree on the philosophical question of being, are rarely more than taxonomies of potential database entries. Interpretivist research is more ontologically aware and its proponents realize that ontological questions are at the heart of the interpretivist approach. Questions include: Is reality socially constructed and the result of social interactions? Does it exist independently? Does interpretation shape perceptions of an external reality? Interpretivism's roots in phenomenology force it to deal with these questions. In the area of IS, this has found its most interesting reflection in the question of the nature of technology. The issue of interpretive or interpretative (cf. Cadili & Whitley, 2005) flexibility of technology is still contested among interpretivists.

CSISR, however, poses the question of ontology even more directly. The critical aspect of such research requires researchers to question what used to be taken for granted, including the nature of 'being', of the research objects and research respondents, and the nature of social relations as affected by research. By refusing to be merely descriptive, critical scholars are open to questions such as how artefacts or social relationships are constituted and maintained, which factors can affect them and what the unspoken assumptions and consequences of artefacts or relationships may be. The wide range of theories that inform CSISR allow differing views on the ontology of phenomena and the conceptualization of vastly diverging issues. CSISR allows the simultaneous observation of macro-level influences, such as state intervention or international activities, and of micro-level issues, such as organizational particularities or technological affordances. This ontological sensitivity and the resulting ability to combine research foci that are traditionally separate (i.e. the micro and the macro level) are a strength that CSISR can build upon. It is part of the unique contribution that critical research can make to the IS field.

Elsewhere, Heinz Klein notes that both interpretative and critical research share the characteristic that they explicitly recognize the double hermeneutic relationship. That is, social research stands in a subject-subject relation to its sphere of inquiry. However, they are also different in that critical research can be argued to have a distinct epistemology and an explicit set of values, including articulation of the researchers' own code of ethics (Klein & Myers, in press). Undoubtedly, the contributors to this volume have, in different ways, made it clear that their research is based upon explicit criteria and certain ethical assumptions. However, it is useful to question whether all the authors represented in this volume have made explicit their own ethical stances within the context of their research as fully as they might have done (an issue raised by Stahl, this volume).

Heinz also suggests that the Kantian heritage of critical research gives it a 'quasi-etic' feel, drawing more heavily as it does upon 'a priori categories' external to the immediate research domain. We suggest that this presents an interesting situation for the field of CSISR and impacts upon the need for critical research to engage in suggestions for improvement. Put simply, CSISR displays an etic view (through its a priori theory foundations) but practices an emic perspective (in its application of theory, studying people from the 'inside'). This consideration leads us on to identify some potentially missed opportunities.

11.4.3 Missed Opportunity: The nature and potential role of fundamental criticism

One role that CSISR has so far failed to play but that, in principle, it is well equipped to do, is that of providing fundamental criticism of the IS field itself. Critical researchers tend to be somewhat interested in, and aware of, positions in the philosophy and sociology of sciences. As argued in this chapter, there are a number of such positions visible in the different contributions to this chapter. The familiarity with such figures of thought should enable critical scholars to provide alternative readings of the nature and activity of the IS discipline. While much CSISR does this to some degree, it is rarely acknowledged beyond critical discourses, even though such a fundamental criticism of the IS field would doubtlessly benefit the field as a whole, even from the more functional perspectives of mainstream IS research.

There are several possible explanations why this opportunity has been missed. The relatively small group of scholars engaged in critical research for the last two decades has, to a considerable degree, managed to gain recognition as well-established IS researchers. At the same time, the content of their critical work has been much less widely received than one could hope for. CSISR is still seen as a fringe activity that is theoretically complex and politically dangerous.

If CSISR wants to overcome this and contribute to the fundamental criticism of the IS discipline, with a view to furthering its aim of emancipation and empowerment, then CSISR will need to consider at least the following two challenges.

11.4.3.1 **Challenge 1**: Proposed stages of critical research and the intervention/ practical relevance deficit

Description or insight
archaeology,
genealogy,
intervention

CSISR may need to be more explicit about its aims and about the ways in which it is to be evaluated. While a mechanistic methodology (that involves following certain steps in order to guarantee a reliable outcome) is unlikely to emerge for CSISR, it may be possible to communicate more clearly what are the stages and objectives of a piece of research. If critical work aims to change the status quo, affect social reality, and be practical, then it will need to find ways of letting practical consequences influence the evaluation of research endeavour. This raises all sorts of theoretical and practical problems. How can we know whether an intervention was successful? Can we measure emancipation in any way? If not, is it even worth attempting to promote it? How can side effects of critical work be incorporated in its evaluation? How can one deal with research respondents whose view of emancipation differs from that of the researcher (problems of false consciousness)?

It is probably fair to argue that critical research aims to go beyond mere description and provide actual insight. Actual insight means that social realities are addressed at a deeper level than is superficially visible. In order to be transformative and practical, CSISR needs to be able to provide insights into the social structures that contribute to the development and reproduction of problematic power structures and instances of alienation. Foucauldian approaches, building on archaeology and genealogy, may be particularly suitable for such deeper insight. Certainly, depth of insight will be required if transformative intervention is to be successful. This leaves open the question of the criteria according to which such insight can be considered appropriate.

These and other related questions will need to be asked and the answers will have to convince not only critical scholars, but also the community of IS scholars in general.

11.4.3.2 **Challenge 2**: The missing paradigm perception and how to address the need for more visibility

A key problem that CSISR has faced from its inception is that it is not perceived as a viable independent research tradition. *This situation is made even more disturbing by the results of some recent literature searches. In spite of multiple research traditions*, Chen and Hirschheim (2004) *reached the conclusion that critical research contributions in IS journals as a whole are so sparse that this paradigm is 'invisible'. While this conclusion does not stand uncontested* (cf. Richardson & Robinson, 2007), *it appears to correspond to perceptions of the IS research community at large. While critical researchers may be justified to argue with Richardson and Robinson that numerical counts of publications in a selection of premier journals may not be the proper way to establish the existence of a paradigm, the political consequences of this state of affairs cannot be ignored without peril.*

The CSISR community will need to think about whether, and how, this problem is to be addressed. This will require not only increasing the numbers of critical research outputs, but also improving their depth of penetration. This necessitates engagement in activities which not all members of the community will welcome, such as engaging in 'mainstream' activities, the uphill struggle of publishing in non-critical journals and conferences, the writing of references for personnel and for funding decisions that are conducive to CSISR scholars. At the same time, though, critical scholars are likely to be sensitive to the political nature of all social interaction and should, therefore, be able to identify the crucial links between such functional activities and the overall transformative success of their critical work. There can be little doubt that such activities have been embraced by at least a relevant part of the community, as evidenced in a number of conference tracks, special journal issues, and, of course, this book. What remains to be seen, however, is whether such activities have the potential to improve the external perception and evaluation of CSISR.

It is important to remember that such attempts to raise the visibility of critical research not only contribute to the emancipation of the research respondents but also to the emancipation of the researchers themselves. Alienating working conditions, increasing threats of redundancy, and an over-emphasis on commercial considerations, characterize the working reality of many academics. Promoting critical views with the aim of a higher level of visibility and acceptance of critical research can, therefore, benefit critical researchers. It may allow them to develop alternative working structures and environments.

The need for professionals in learning and research development roles to retain and develop their own reflexive practice, and the nature of the environments within which they find themselves, may be in significant conflict with each other. (As this book goes to press, there have been some apparently notable examples of this.) How, then, do we contribute to the transformation of our own contexts? One interesting stimulus for debate is the launch in May 2007 of the Principles for Responsible Management Education (UN Global Compact, 2007). This initiative aims to make more explicit within education values such as inclusivity, sustainability, and social responsibility set against a global backdrop. A key role for critical researchers here could be, for instance, to engage in dialogue to evaluate whether such principles, when implemented, result in emancipation or incarceration of the diverse 'citizens' or stakeholders.

11.4.4 Concluding question: Fundamental values and ethics of critical research: are there alternatives to the enlightenment ideal?

The final question that this reflection returns to concerns the essence of CSISR and the implications that this definition carries. Despite its contested nature, CSISR will need to come to an agreement on what it stands for. The current volume suggests several views on what this might be. Drawing on this IS-oriented work, as well as the more established critical management studies literature, one can probably identify certain aspects such as sensitivity to injustice, non-functional interests, promotion of emancipation, issues of freedom, the importance of reflexivity, and so on (as presented in Table 11.1). It remains to be seen whether these aspects are sufficiently clear and concise yet, at the same time, broad enough to allow CSISR to develop. Either way, further discussion of the implications is needed. As we have already noted, one area of particular concern is the issue of values and ethics of critical research. Other related questions that deserve more deliberation are those of theory, impact, and methods (as indicated in Tables 11.2 and 11.3). Whether emancipation is possible and/or necessarily always desirable, and whether or not critical research can provide alternatives to the enlightenment hope (i.e. that a better understanding of the world can help to improve it – see Kant, 1781) is still unclear. A lively and critically reflected debate will be of as much, if not more, importance at this stage than the provision of authoritative answers. A highly reflective and philosophically aware research approach will, surely, enrich the entire IS research community. What does seem evident is that critical research can offer alternative readings and ways of understanding the world. It has numerous strengths, discussed in this chapter, and these may suffice in and of themselves as good reasons for a more general acceptance of the approach.

Hence, we are inclined to close on an upbeat note. These issues will continue to be the subject of much discussion by the community of IS scholars with an interest in critical research. In the interim, we hope that this chapter by Heinz Klein, together with the rest of this book, can provide a stimulus to the further development of what we perceive as an important and necessary aspect of scholarly debate.

REFERENCES[5]

Alvesson, M., & Willmott, H. (1992). On the idea of emancipation in management and organisation studies. *Academy of Management Review, 17*(3), 432–464.
Avgerou, C. (2005). Doing critical research in information systems: some further thoughts. *Information Systems Journal, 15,* 103–109.
Bourdieu, P. (1977). *Outline of a Theory of Practice.* Cambridge University Press, Cambridge, UK.
Bourdieu, P. (1990). *The Logic of Practice.* Stanford University Press, Stanford, CA.

5. This reference list may not reflect exactly the same editions that Heinz was intending to use.

Brooke, C. (2002). Critical perspectives on information systems: an impression of the research landscape. *Journal of Information Technology, 17*(4), 271–283.

Burrell, G., & Morgan, G. (1979). *Sociological Paradigms and Organizational Analysis.* Heinemann, London.

Cadili, S., & Whitley, E. A. (2005). On the interpretative flexibility of hosted ERP systems. *Journal of Strategic Information Systems, 14*(2), 167–195.

Cecez-Kecmanovic, D., Klein, H. K., & Brooke, C. (2008). Editorial: exploring the critical agenda in information systems research. *Information Systems Journal, 18*(2), 123–135.

Chen, W., & Hirschheim, R. (2004). A paradigmatic and methodological examination of information systems research from 1991 to 2001. *Information Systems Journal, 14,* 197–235.

Churchman, C. W. (1971). *The Design of Inquiring Systems: Basic Concepts of Systems and Organizations.* Basic Books, New York.

Connerton, P., (Ed.), (1976). *Critical Sociology.* Penguin, Harmondsworth, UK.

Dooyeweerd, H. (1984). *A New Critique of Theoretical Thought, Paideia Press, Ontario, Canada, Vols.1–4 (Original work published 1953-1958.).*

Feigenbaum, L., Herman, I., Hongsermeier, T., Neumann, E. and Stephens, S. (Dec 2007) *The Semantic Web in Action.* Scientific American. Accessed on 3 March 2008.

Habermas, J. (1968a). *Knowledge and Human Interests.* Heinemann, London.

Habermas, J. (1968b). *Moral Consciousness and Communicative Action,* (1995 edn.). The MIT Press, Cambridge, MA.

Habermas, J. (1984). *The Theory of Communicative Action – Reason and the Rationalisation of Society. (Vol 1), McCarthy, T. (trans.).* Beacon Press, Boston, M.A.

Heidegger, M. (1962). *Being and Time (Macquarrie J. and Robinson E., trans.).* Harper and Row, New York.

Hirschheim, R., Klein, H., & Lyytinen, K. (1996). Exploring the intellectual structures of information systems development: a social action theoretic analysis. *Accounting, Management and Information Technology, 6*(1/2), 1–64.

Husserl, E. (1970). *The Crisis of the European Sciences and Transcendental Phenomenology (Carr, D., trans.).* Northwestern University Press, Evanston, IL.

Husserl, E. (1931). *Ideas: General Introduction to Pure Phenomenology (Boyce Gibson, W.R., trans.).* George Allen and Unwin Ltd, London.

Husserl, E. (1969). *Formal and Transcendental Logic (Cairns, D., trans.).* Martinus Nijhoff, The Hague.

Husserl, E. (1990). *On the Phenomenology of the Consciousness of Internal Time (1893-1917) (Brough, J.B., trans.).* Kluwer Academic Publishers, London.

Jay, M. (1973). *The Dialectical Imagination.* Little Brown, Boston.

Kant, I. (1781). *Critique of Pure Reason,* (2003 edn.). Palgrave Macmillan, Hampshire, UK.

Klein, H.K. and Myers, M. (in press) A Set of Principles for Conducting and Evaluating Critical Field Studies in Information Systems.

Lyytinen, K. (1992). Informations systems and critical theory. *Critical Management Studies.* In Alvessson, M., & Willmott, H. (Eds.), Sage, London, pp. 159–180.

Mumford, E., Hirschheim, R., Fitzgerald, G., & Wood-Harper, T., (Eds.), (1984). *Proceedings of the IFIP Working Group 8.2 Conference.* Manchester, UK.

Orlikowski, W. J., & Baroudi, J. J. (1991). Studying Information Technology in Organizations: Research Approaches and Assumptions. *Information Systems Research, 2*(1), 1–28.

Popper, K. R. (1959). *The Logic of Scientific Discovery,* (1st edn 1934.). Basic Books, New York.

Rawls, J. (2001). *Justice as Fairness: A Restatement.* Belknap Press, Cambridge, Mass.

Richardson, H., & Robinson, B. (2007). The mysterious case of the missing paradigm: a review of critical information systems research 1991–2001. *Information Systems Journal, 17*(3), 251–270.

Ritzer, G. (1975). *Sociology: A Multiple Paradigm Science.* Allyn & Bacon, Boston.

Ritzer, G. (1991). *Metatheorizing in Sociology.* Lexington Books, Lexington, MA.

Ritzer, G. (2001). *Explorations in Social Theory.* Sage, London.

Schutz, A. (1982) Life Forms and Meaning Structure (Wagner, H., trans. and ed.) London: Routledge.

Stahl, B. C. (2008). The ethical nature of critical research in information systems. *Information Systems Journal, 18*(2), 137–163.

Toulmin, S. E. (1958). *The Uses of Argument.* Cambridge University Press, Cambridge, UK.

Ulrich, W. (1983). *Critical heuristics of social planning: a new approach to practical philosophy. Berne, Switzerland: Haupt. Reprint edition.* Wiley, Chichester, UK. 1994.

UN Global Compact. (2007) The Principles for Responsible Management Education. http://www.aacsb.edu/Resource_Centers/PRME_final.pdf: last accessed on 19 August 2008.

Walsham, G. (2005). Learning about being critical. *Information Systems Journal, 15,* 111–117.

Wilson, F. (1997). The truth is out there: the search for empancipatory principles in information systems design. *Information Technology and People, 10,* 187–204.

Index

For Product Safety Concerns and Information please contact our
EU representative GPSR@taylorandfrancis.com Taylor & Francis
Verlag GmbH, Kaufingerstraße 24, 80331 München, Germany